The Expos You Can't Afford to Miss!

Whitman Expos stand out as North America's foremost producer of coin and currency shows, hosting three annual industry-leading events in Baltimore.

Y0-ACC-989

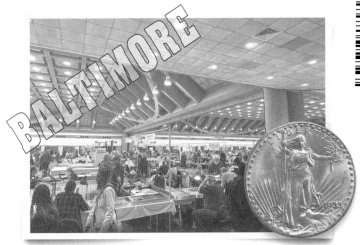

Held three times a year (Spring, Summer, and Fall) at the Baltimore Convention Center, the Expos enjoy a strategic location accessible to over 5 million people within a three-hour drive of downtown Baltimore, 30 minutes by car from the BWI national airport. In attendance are over 300 professional booth-holders from across the nation and worldwide. Stack's Bowers Galleries is the official auctioneer, holding marquee events and lot viewing as well. Convenient parking and accommodations of various levels are available within walking distance. For more details about attending or exhibiting at an upcoming Whitman Expo, visit www.whitman expos.com or reach out via email at info@whitmanexpo.com.

www.whitmanexpos.com

"Wisdom begins in wonder."

- Socrates

OFFICIAL BLUE BOOK OF UNITED STATES COINS™

The Official Blue Book®

HANDBOOK OF
UNITED STATES
COINS
2025

R. S. YEOMAN

JEFF GARRETT, SENIOR EDITOR

Q. David Bowers, Research Editor
Kenneth Bressett, Editor Emeritus
Dennis Tucker, Publisher

82nd EDITION

An Illustrated Catalog of Prices Generally Paid
by Dealers for All American Coins—1616 to Date

Containing Mint records and wholesale prices for U.S. and related coins from 1616
to the present time, including colonials, regular issues, commemoratives, ter-
ritorials, gold, bullion coins, Proof sets, and Mint sets. Information on collecting
coins—how coins are produced—mints and mintmarks—grading of coins—location
of mintmarks—preserving coins—starting a collection—history of mints—and
interesting descriptions of all U.S. copper, nickel, silver, and gold coins. Illustrated.

Handbook of United States Coins™
THE OFFICIAL BLUE BOOK OF UNITED STATES COINS™

THE OFFICIAL BLUE BOOK and OFFICIAL BLUE BOOK OF UNITED
STATES COINS are trademarks of Whitman Publishing.

Whitman Publishing
SINCE 1934

Printed in China

© 2024 Whitman Publishing
4001 Helton Drive • Florence, AL 35630

The precious-metal spot prices in use for this edition are as follows:	
Silver	$25
Gold	$2,000
Platinum	$1,000
Palladium	$1,200

CONTRIBUTORS TO THIS EDITION

Senior Editor: Jeff Garrett. Research Editor: Q. David Bowers.
Editor Emeritus: Kenneth Bressett. Publisher: Dennis Tucker.
Coordinating Editor: Diana Plattner. Graphics and Layout: Matthew Heller.

John Agre	Steve Ivy
John Albanese	Amandeep Jassal
Russell Augustin	Mike Joyce
Lee J. Bellisario	Donald H. Kagin
Mark Borckardt	Bradley S. Karoleff
Philip Bressett	Jim Koenings
William Bugert	John Kraljevich
H. Robert Campbell	Dwight N. Manley
Elizabeth Coggan	David McCarthy
Gary and Alan Cohen	Harry Miller
Stephen M. Cohen	Lee S. Minshull
Marc Crane	Michael Moline
Adam Crum	Keith Moon
Raymond Czahor	Robert M. Paul
John Dannreuther	Patrick Ian Perez
Charles Davis	Robert Rhue
Matt Draiss	Steve Roach
Steven Ellsworth	Greg Roberts
David Fanning	Greg Rohan
John Feigenbaum	P. Scott Rubin
Michael Fey	Ian Russell
Gerry Fortin	Mark Salzberg
Pierre Fricke	Matthew Savanich
John Frost	Gerald R. Scherer Jr.
Mike Fuljenz	Jeff Shevlin
Ben Garrett	Roger Siboni
Ronald J. Gillio	James Simek
Rusty Goe	Jon Sullivan
Bob Green	Barry Sunshine
Thomas Hallenbeck	Anthony Terranova
James Halperin	Troy Thoreson
Ash Harrison	Ben Todd
Stephen Hayden	Rick Tomaska
Brian Hendelson	Tom Uram
Brian Hodge	

The following organizations have contributed to this edition: The Barber Coin Collectors Society, the Liberty Seated Collectors Club, and the Rittenhouse Society.

Special credit is due to the following for service in past editions: Bill Fivaz, David W. Lange, Ed Metzger, Eric P. Newman, Neil Shafer, and Glenn Smedley.

Special photo credits are due to the following: Heritage Auctions, Numismatic Guaranty Company, PCGS, the Smithsonian Institution, Stack's Bowers Galleries, and the United States Mint.

Since 1942, annually revised editions of the *Official Blue Book of United States Coins*™ have aided thousands of people who have coins to sell or are actively engaged in collecting United States coins. The popular coin-folder method of collecting by date has created ever-changing premium values, based on the supply and demand of each date and mint. Through its panel of contributors, the Blue Book has, over the years, reported these changing values. It also serves as a source of general numismatic information to all levels of interest in the hobby.

The values shown are representative prices paid by dealers for various United States coins. These are averages of prices assembled from many widely separated sources. On some issues slight differences in price among dealers may result from proximity to the various mints or heavily populated centers. Other factors, such as local supply and demand or dealers' stock conditions, may also cause deviations from the prices listed. While many coins bring no premium in circulated grades, they usually bring premium prices in Mint State and Proof. Extremely rare and valuable coins are usually sold at public auction, and prices vary according to current demand.

THIS BOOK LISTS PRICES MANY COIN DEALERS WILL PAY.

Premium prices are the average amount dealers will pay for coins (according to condition) if required for their stock. This book is not a retail price list.

IF YOU HAVE COINS TO SELL

Whitman Publishing is not in the rare-coin business; however, chances are that the dealer from whom you purchased this book is engaged in the buying and selling of rare coins—contact them first. In the event that you purchased this book from a source other than a numismatic establishment, consult your local telephone directory for the names of coin dealers (they will be found sometimes under the heading of "Stamp and Coin Dealers"). If you live in a city or town that does not have any coin dealers, obtain a copy of one of the trade publications (such as *Coin World* [www.coinworld.com] or *Numismatic News* [www.numismaticnews.net]) or check the Internet in order to obtain the names and addresses of many of the country's leading dealers. Coin dealers who belong to the congressionally chartered American Numismatic Association (and who must abide by its code of ethics) are listed at www.money.org.

You will find current average *retail* valuations of American coins (the prices you can expect to pay a professional coin dealer) in the latest edition of *A Guide Book of United States Coins*™ by R.S. Yeoman, edited by Jeff Garrett. Coin collectors popularly call this the *Red Book*. Pricing in even greater detail is included in Mega Red—*A Guide Book of United States Coins, Deluxe Edition.*

HOW TO READ THE CHARTS

A dash in a price column indicates that coins in that grade exist even though there are no current sales or auction records for them. (The dash does *not* necessarily mean that such coins are exceedingly rare.) Italicized prices indicate unsettled or speculative values. A number of listings of rare coins do not have prices or dashes in certain grades. This indicates that they are not available or not believed to exist in those grades.

Mintages of Proof coins are listed in parentheses.

Italicized mintages are estimates.

Numismatics or coin collecting is one of the world's oldest hobbies, dating back several centuries. Coin collecting in America did not develop to any extent until about 1840, as our pioneer forefathers were too busy carving a country out of wilderness to afford the luxury of a hobby. The discontinuance of the large-sized cent in 1857 encouraged many people to attempt to accumulate a complete set of the pieces while they were still in circulation. One of the first groups of collectors to band together for the study of numismatics was the American Numismatic Society, founded in 1858 and still a dynamic part of the hobby (www.numismatics.org). Lack of an economical method to house a collection held the number of devotees of coin collecting to a few thousand until Whitman Publishing and other manufacturers placed low-priced coin boards and folders on the market in the 1930s. Since that time, the number of Americans collecting coins has increased many-fold.

THE PRODUCTION OF COINS

To collect coins intelligently it is necessary to have some knowledge of the manner in which they are produced. Coins are made in factories called "mints." The Mint of the United States was established at Philadelphia by a resolution of Congress dated April 2, 1792. The act also provided for the coinage of gold eagles ($10), half eagles, and quarter eagles; silver dollars, half dollars, quarter dollars, dimes (originally spelled "disme"), and half dismes or half dimes; and copper cents and half cents. The first coins struck were one-cent and half-cent pieces, in March of 1793 on a hand-operated press. Most numismatic authorities consider the half disme of 1792 the first United States coinage, quoting the words of George Washington as their authority. Washington, in his annual address, November 6, 1792, said, "There has been a small beginning in the coining of the half dimes, the want of small coins in circulation calling the first attention to them." Though the half disme is considered America's first coinage, it was not the first coinage produced by the Mint; these coins were produced off premises in July of 1792 before the mint was completed. In the new Philadelphia Mint are a number of implements from the original mint, and some coins discovered when the old building was wrecked. These coins included half dismes, and the placard identifying them states that Washington furnished the silver and gave some of the pieces to his friends as souvenirs.

Prior to the adoption of the Constitution, the Continental Congress arranged for the issuance of copper coins under private contract. These are known as the 1787 *Fugio coppers* from their design, which shows a sundial and the Latin word "fugio"—"I Fly" or, in connection with the sundial, "Time Flies." The ever-appropriate motto "Mind Your Business" is also on the coin.

In the manufacture of a coin, the first step is die preparation. Dies for early federal coinage were prepared by hand; generally, letters and numbers were added with punches, while portraits and other designs were engraved into the die. Eventually, eagles, Liberty heads, and the like were also added with hubs and punches. After about 1836, many dies were made from masters, which contained all elements except the date and, if applicable, the mintmark. The addition of an element to a master die ensured its consistent placement throughout the life of the die. Today, many design tasks are performed with three-dimensional computer graphics. Mint artists are either sculptor-engravers or medallic sculptors, and their work takes place mainly at the Philadelphia Mint. The dies are made of soft steel, which is hardened after the impression is received. The die is then dressed or finished to remove imperfections and make it suitable for coining. A typical die for production coinage can be used to strike hundreds of thousands of pieces. Dies for special issues such as Proofs are replaced more often.

The hand method of cutting dies accounts for the many die varieties of early United States coins. Where the amount of coinage of a given year was large enough to wear out many dies, each new die placed in the coining press created another die variety of that year. The dies being cut by hand, no two were exactly alike in every detail, even though some of the major elements such as the head or wreath, were sunk into the die by individual master punches. Of the cents dated 1794, more than sixty different die varieties have been discovered.

Thousands of dies are now used by the mints of the United States each year, but they are all made from one master die, which is produced in the following manner:

After the design is settled upon, the plaster of paris or wax model is prepared several times the actual size of the coin. When this model is finished an electrotype (an exact duplicate in metal) is made and prepared for the reducing lathe. The reducing lathe is a machine that works on the principle of the pantograph, only in this case the one point traces or follows the form of the model while another much smaller point in the form of a drill cuts away the steel and produces a reduced-size die of the model. The die is finished and details are sharpened or worked over by an engraver with chisel and graver. The master die is used to make duplicates in soft steel which are then hardened and ready for the coining press. To harden dies, they are placed in cast-iron boxes packed with carbon to exclude the air, and when heated to a bright red are cooled suddenly with water.

In the coinage operations the first step is to prepare the metal. Among the alloys that have been used are the following: silver coins, 90% silver and 10% copper; five-cent pieces, 75% copper and 25% nickel; one-cent pieces, 95% copper and 5% zinc. (The 1943 cent consists of steel coated with zinc; and the five-cent piece of 1942–1945 contains 35% silver, 56% copper, and 9% manganese.) Under the Coinage Act of 1965, the composition of dimes, quarters, and half dollars was changed to eliminate or reduce the silver content of these coins. The copper-nickel "clad" dimes, quarters, half dollars, and dollars are composed of an outer layer of copper-nickel (75% copper and 25% nickel) bonded to an inner core of pure copper. The silver clad half dollar and dollar have an outer layer of 80% silver bonded to an inner core of 21% silver, with a total content of 40% silver. Current cents are made from a core of 99.2% zinc, 0.8% copper, with a plating of pure copper. Dollars are composed of a pure copper core with outer layers of manganese-brass.

Alloys are melted in crucibles and poured into molds to form ingots. The ingots are in the form of thin bars and vary in size according to the denomination of the coin. The width is sufficient to allow three or more coins to be cut from the strips.

The ingots are next put through rolling mills to reduce the thickness to required limits. The strips are then fed into cutting presses which cut circular blanks of the approximate size of the finished coin. The blanks are run through annealing furnaces to soften them; next they move through tumbling barrels, rotating cylinders containing cleaning solutions which clean and burnish the metal; and finally into centrifugal drying machines.

The blanks are next fed into a milling machine which produces the raised or upset rim. The blank, now called a *planchet,* is now ready for the coining press.

The planchet is held firmly by a collar, as it is struck under heavy pressure varying from 40 tons for the one-cent pieces and dimes to 170 tons for silver dollars. Upper and lower dies impress the design on both sides of the coin. The pressure is sufficient to produce a raised surface level with that of the milled rim. The collar holding the blank for silver or clad coins is grooved. The pressure forces the metal into the grooves of the collar, producing the "reeding" on the edge of the finished coin.

HOW A PROOF COIN IS MADE

Selected dies are inspected for perfection and are highly polished and cleaned. They are again wiped clean or polished after every 15 to 25 impressions and are replaced frequently to avoid imperfections from wear. Coinage blanks are polished and cleaned to assure high quality in striking. They are then hand fed into the coinage press one at a time, each blank receiving two blows from the dies to bring up sharp, high-relief details. The coinage operation is done at slow speed. Finished Proofs are individually inspected and are handled by gloves or tongs. They also receive a final inspection by packers before being sonically sealed in special plastic cases.

Certain coins, including Lincoln cents, Buffalo nickels, quarter eagles, half eagles, eagles, and double eagles, between the years 1908 and 1916, were made with Matte Proof (nickel and silver) and Sand Blast and Satin Proof (gold) finishes. These later Proofs have a dull frosted surface which was either applied to the dies, or produced by special treatment after striking.

MINTS AND MINTMARKS

In addition to the Philadelphia Mint, the U.S. government has from time to time established branch mints in various parts of the country. At present, branch mints operate in Denver, West Point, and San Francisco. Starting in 1968, Proof sets as well as some of the regular coins were produced at the San Francisco Mint and Assay Office. The Denver Mint has operated since 1906. A mint was operated at New Orleans from 1838 to 1861 and again from 1879 to 1909. Mints were also in service at Carson City, Nevada, from 1870 to 1893; at Charlotte, North Carolina, from 1838 to 1861; at Dahlonega, Georgia, from 1838 to 1861; and at San Francisco since 1854. The U.S. government also supplied a mint in the Philippines (M mintmark) in the early 1900s.

Coins struck at Philadelphia before 1979 (except 1942 to 1945 five-cent pieces) do not bear a mintmark. Historically the mintmark was used only for branch mints. Modern exceptions include the 2017-P Lincoln cent and the Kennedy half dollar, which both use the P for Philadelphia. All circulating coins struck after 1967 have the mintmark on the obverse. The letters signifying the various mints are as follows:

    C—Charlotte, North Carolina (gold coins only; 1838–1861)
    CC—Carson City, Nevada (1870–1893)
    D—Dahlonega, Georgia (gold coins only; 1838–1861)
    D—Denver, Colorado (1906 to date)
    O—New Orleans, Louisiana (1838–1861; 1879–1909)
    P—Philadelphia, Pennsylvania (1793 to date; P not used in early years)
    S—San Francisco, California (1854 to date)
    W—West Point, New York (1984 to date)

The mintmark is of utmost importance to collectors because, historically, coinage of the branch mints has often been much smaller than quantities struck at Philadelphia. Many early coins of the branch mints are very scarce.

SLABBED VERSUS UNSLABBED COINS

In this handbook, values from under $1 up to several hundred dollars are for "raw" coins—that is, coins that have not been graded and encapsulated by a professional third-party grading service. Coins valued near or above $500 are assumed to be third-party graded. A high-value coin that has not been professionally certified as authentic, graded, and encapsulated by an independent firm is apt to be valued lower than the prices indicated.

The general effect of third-party grading and authentication has been to increase buyers' and sellers' comfort levels with the perceived quality of rare coins in the marketplace.

Coins in high grades that have been certified (professionally graded and guaranteed authentic) and encapsulated ("slabbed") may be valued significantly higher than similar coins that have not been so treated. In today's marketplace, "raw" or non-certified coins, are usually valued at less, except for modern U.S. Mint and bullion products.

DISTINGUISHING MARKS

The illustrations and explanations in this section will help the collector identify certain well-known varieties.

Half Cents of 1795–1796 Showing Location of Pole to Cap

The end of the pole lies parallel with the lines of the bust, which is pointed. On some coins, the pole is missing due either to engraver error (while cutting the die) or to an error in "relapping" (when the die is ground to remove wear, clash marks, etc.).

Pole to Cap   No Pole to Cap

Stemless Wreath Variety of Half Cents and Large Cents

For this variety, the difference is on the reverse side. Illustrations show both Stemless and Stems to Wreath types for comparison—stemless wreath found on the 1804, 1805, and 1806 half cents; and on the 1797, 1802, and 1803 large cents.

Stemless Wreath   Stems to Wreath

1864 Bronze Indian Head Cent With "L" on Ribbon

A small "L," the initial of the designer James B. Long-acre, was added to the Indian Head design late in 1864 and was continued through 1909. For coins in less than Fine condition, this small letter will often be worn away. The point of the bust is rounded on the 1864 variety without "L"; the bust is pointed on the variety with "L." The initial must be visible, however, for the 1864 variety to bring the higher premium. If the coin is turned slightly so that the portrait faces the observer, the highlighted details will usually appear to better advantage.

Designer Initials, Overstrikes, Die-Doublings, and Date Varieties

During 1909, initials appeared on the reverse of the Lincoln cent.
Starting in 1918, they appear below the shoulder.

Prior to 1990, mintmarks for all mints were usually applied directly to working dies at Philadelphia in a hand-punching operation. Occasionally, a die was accidentally marked with one letter on top of another.

Dies are produced by impressing the raised coin design of a hub into the end of a cylinder of steel. In early years the Mint made use of old dies by repunching the dates on their dies with new numbers. That practice was stopped prior to 1909. Since that time, all overdated coins have been the result of errors that occur when two different-dated hubs have been used in die preparation, and one is impressed over the other by accident.

1938-D, D Over S,
Buffalo Nickel

1918-S, 8 Over 7,
Standing Liberty Quarter
A variety of this kind is rarely found in coinage of the 20th century.

1942, 2 Over 1,
Mercury Dime

1955, Doubled-Die Obverse
Lincoln Cent

Large Date Cent
(1960)

Small Date Cent
(1960)

Large Date Cent
(1982)

Small Date Cent
(1982)

COUNTERFEIT COINS

Recognizing a spurious coin can be made easier through the use of common sense and an elementary knowledge of the techniques used by counterfeiters. It is well to keep in mind that the more popular a coin is among collectors and the public, the more likely it is that counterfeits and replicas will abound. Until recently, collector coins valued at under $100 were rarely replicated because of the high cost of making such items. The same was true of counterfeits made to deceive the public. Few counterfeit coins were made because it was more profitable for the fakers to print paper money. Today, however, counterfeiters in Asia and elsewhere create fakes of a surprising variety of coins, most notably silver dollar types, but also other denominations.

Coin dealers will rarely buy coins of exceptional rarity or value without being 100% certain of authenticity. Professional authentication of rare coins for a fee is offered by commercial grading services, and by some dealers.

Replicas

Reproductions of famous and historical coins have been distributed for decades by marketing firms and souvenir vendors. Most replicas are poorly made by the casting method, and are virtually worthless. They can sometimes be identified by a seam that runs around the edge of the piece where the two halves of the casting mold were joined together.

Counterfeits

For many centuries, counterfeiters have produced base-metal forgeries of gold and silver coins to deceive the public in the normal course of trade. These pieces are usually crudely made and easily detected on close examination. Crudely cast counterfeit copies of older coins are the most prevalent. These can usually be detected by the casting bubbles or pimples that can be seen with low-power magnification. Pieces struck from handmade dies are more deceptive, but the engravings do not match those of genuine Mint products.

Die-struck gold coin counterfeits have been mass produced overseas since 1950. Forgeries exist of most U.S. gold coins dated between 1870 and 1933, as well as all issues of the gold dollar and three-dollar gold piece. Most of these are very well made, as they were intended to pass the close scrutiny of collectors. Many gold coins of earlier dates have been counterfeited, and all coins dated before 1930 should be carefully examined.

Silver dollars dated 1804, Lafayette dollars, several of the low-mintage commemorative half dollars, and the 1795 half dimes have been forged in quantity. Minor-coin forgeries made in recent years are the 1909-S V.D.B.; 1914-D and 1955 doubled-die Lincoln cents; 1877 Indian Head cents; 1856 Flying Eagle cents; and, on a much smaller scale, a variety of dates of half cents and large cents. Nineteenth-century copies of colonial coins are also sometimes encountered.

Alterations

Coins are occasionally altered by the addition, removal, or change of a design feature (such as a mintmark or date digit) or by the polishing, sandblasting, acid etching, toning, or plating of the surface of a genuine piece. Among U.S. gold coins, only the 1927-D double eagle is commonly found with a spuriously added mintmark. On $2.50 and $5 gold coins, 1839 through 1856, New Orleans O mintmarks have been deceptively altered to C (for Charlotte, North Carolina) in a few instances.

Over a century ago, five-dollar gold pieces were imitated by gold plating 1883 Liberty Head five-cent coins without the word CENTS on the reverse. Other coins commonly created fraudulently through alteration include the 1799 large cent and the 1909-S; 1909-S V.D.B.; 1914-D; 1922, No D; and 1943, Copper, cents. The 1913 Liberty Head nickel has been extensively replicated by alteration of 1903 and 1912 nickels. Scarce, high-grade Denver and San Francisco Buffalo nickels of the 1920s; 1916-D and 1942, 42 Over 41, dimes; 1918-S, 8 Over 7, quarters; 1932-D and -S quarters; and 1804 silver dollars have all been made by the alteration of genuine coins of other dates or mints.

Detection

The best way to detect counterfeit coins is to compare suspected pieces with others of the same issue. Look at the photographs in this book for comparisons. Carefully check size, color, luster, weight, edge devices, and design details. Replicas generally have less detail than their genuine counterparts when studied under magnification. Modern struck counterfeits made to deceive collectors are an exception to this rule. Any questionable gold coin should be referred to an expert for verification.

Cast forgeries are usually poorly made and of incorrect weight. Base metal is often used in place of gold or silver, and the coins are lightweight and often incorrect in color and luster. Deceptive cast pieces have been made using real metal content and modern dental techniques, but these too usually vary in quality and color. Detection of alterations sometimes involves comparative examination of the suspected areas of a coin (usually mintmarks and date digits) at magnification ranging from 10x to 40x.

CONDITIONS OF COINS

Essential Elements of the Official ANA Grading System

Proof—A specially made coin distinguished by sharpness of detail and usually with a brilliant, mirrorlike surface. *Proof* refers to the method of manufacture and is not a condition, but normally the term implies nearly perfect condition unless otherwise noted.

Perfect Proof (PF-70)—The perfect coin, with strike and surface of the highest quality. No contact marks are visible under magnification. There are absolutely no hairlines, scuff marks, or defects.

Gem Proof (PF-65)—Brilliant surfaces with no noticeable blemishes or flaws. A few scattered, barely noticeable marks or hairlines.

Choice Proof (PF-63)—Reflective surfaces with only a few blemishes in secondary focal places. No major flaws.

Proof (PF-60)—Surface may have several contact marks, hairlines, or light rubs. Luster may be dull and eye appeal lacking.

Mint State—The terms *Mint State (MS)* and *Uncirculated (Unc.)* are used interchangeably to describe coins showing no trace of wear. Such coins may vary to some degree because of blemishes, toning, or slight imperfections, as described in the following subdivisions:

Perfect Uncirculated (MS-70)—Perfect new condition, showing no trace of wear. The finest quality possible, with no evidence of scratches, handling, or contact with other coins.

Gem Uncirculated (MS-65)—An above average Uncirculated coin that may be brilliant or lightly toned and that has very few contact marks on the surface or rim. MS-67 through MS-62 indicate slightly higher or lower grades of preservation.

Choice Uncirculated (MS-63)—Has some distracting contact marks or blemishes in prime focal areas. Luster may be impaired.

Uncirculated (MS-60)—Has no trace of wear but may show a number of contact marks, and surface may be spotted or lack some luster.

Choice About Uncirculated (AU-55)—Evidence of friction on high points of design. Most of the mint luster remains.

About Uncirculated (AU-50)—Traces of light wear on many of the high points. At least half of the mint luster is still present.

Choice Extremely Fine (EF-45)—Light overall wear on highest points. All design details are very sharp. Some of the mint luster is evident.

Extremely Fine (EF-40)—Light wear on design throughout, but all features sharp and well defined. Traces of luster may show.

Choice Very Fine (VF-30)—Light, even wear on the surface and highest parts of the design. All lettering and major features are sharp.

Very Fine (VF-20)—Moderate wear on high points. All major details are clear.

Fine (F-12)—Moderate to considerable even wear. Entire design is bold with overall pleasing appearance.

Very Good (VG-8)—Well worn with main features clear and bold, although rather flat.

Good (G-4)—Heavily worn, with design visible but faint in areas. Many details are flat.

About Good (AG-3)—Very heavily worn with portions of lettering, date, and legend worn smooth. The date may be barely readable.

A star (or similar notation) in the grade on a slab means "exceptional quality."

Important: Damaged coins, such as those that are bent, corroded, scratched, holed, nicked, stained, or mutilated, are worth less than those without defects. Flawless Uncirculated coins are generally worth more than values quoted in this book. Slightly worn coins ("sliders") that have been cleaned and conditioned ("buffed") to simulate Uncirculated luster are worth considerably less than perfect pieces.

Unlike damage inflicted after striking, manufacturing defects do not always lessen values. Examples include colonial coins with planchet flaws and weakly struck designs; early silver and gold with weight-adjustment "file marks" (parallel cuts made prior to striking); and coins with "lint marks" (surface marks due to the presence of dust or other foreign matter during striking).

Brief guides to grading are placed before each major coin type. Grading standards are not scientific and often vary among collectors, dealers, and certification services. For more on grading, consult the *Official ANA Grading Standards for United States Coins.*

PRESERVING AND CLEANING COINS

Most say, "Never clean a coin," and it is good advice! Cleaning coins almost always reduces their value. Collectors prefer coins in their original condition.

Some effort should be made to protect Uncirculated and Proof coins so they won't need cleaning. Tarnish on a coin is purely a chemical process caused by oxygen in the air acting on the metal, or by chemicals with which the coin comes in contact. One of the most common chemicals causing tarnish is sulphur; most paper, with the exception of specially manufactured "sulphur-free" kinds, contains sulphur due to the sulphuric acid that is used in paper manufacture; therefore do not wrap coins in ordinary paper. Also keep Uncirculated and Proof coins away from rubber bands (a rubber band placed on a silver coin for a few days will eventually produce a black stripe on the coin where the band touched). The utmost in protection is obtained by storing the coin in an airtight box, away from moisture and humidity, and by using holders made of inert materials.

Many coins become marred by careless handling. Always hold the coin by the edge. The accompanying illustration shows the right and wrong way to handle numismatic specimens. It is a breach of numismatic etiquette to handle another collector's coin except by the edge, even if it is not an Uncirculated or Proof piece.

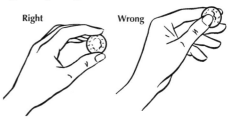

Right   **Wrong**

STARTING A COLLECTION

One may start a collection of United States coins with very little expense by systematically assembling the various dates and mintmarks of all the types and denominations that are now in general circulation, using Whitman's many different coin folders and albums, especially those for quarters and dollars with various designs.

With the exception of the price paid for the coin folder, collecting coins received in everyday business transactions entails no expense whatsoever; a Jefferson nickel taken out of circulation, for example, can always be spent for five cents if the occasion arises. Filling an album or two with coins found in circulation is probably the best method of determining whether coin collecting appeals to you. Not everyone can be a successful coin collector. It requires patience, intelligence of a high order, and a certain desire to know the meaning behind a lot of things that at first glance appear meaningless. You may not be cut out to be a collector but you'll never know until you look further into the subject, and if by the time an album or two of coins are collected you have no burning desire to acquire many more different coins, you will probably never be a collector. However, chances are that you will be, because if you have read this far in this book, it shows that you are interested in the subject.

High quality is the goal of every endeavor and coin collecting is no exception. After an album has been filled with circulated specimens, the next step will be to replace them with coins in Uncirculated condition, or perhaps to start collecting an obsolete series;

in either case, it will be necessary to purchase some coins from dealers or other collectors. The most logical way to keep abreast of the market, or obtain the addresses of the country's leading dealers, is to subscribe to one or more of the trade publications. These magazines carry advertisements of various dealers listing coins for sale. Moreover, through these sources the beginner may obtain price lists and catalogs from the dealers.

There are several good reference books available at reasonable prices which will be helpful to the collector who wishes to know more about U.S. coins and paper money. R.S. Yeoman's *A Guide Book of United States Coins™* (the "Red Book") lists retail values of all regular U.S. coins and also lists all coins of the U.S. colonial period and private and territorial gold coins, plus tokens, pattern pieces, errors, and other numismatic collectibles.

Most coin, book, and hobby dealers can supply the following titles:

> *The Official Red Book®: A Guide Book of United States Coins™*—R.S. Yeoman, edited by Jeff Garrett
>
> *The Official Red Book®: A Guide Book of United States Coins™, Deluxe Edition*—R.S. Yeoman, edited by Q. David Bowers
>
> *A Guide Book of Morgan Silver Dollars*—Q. David Bowers
>
> *The Expert's Guide to Collecting and Investing in Rare Coins*—Q. David Bowers
>
> *Coin Collecting: A Beginner's Guide to the World of Coins*—Kenneth Bressett
>
> *History of the United States Mint and Its Coinage*—David W. Lange
>
> *The Official ANA Grading Standards for United States Coins*—Kenneth Bressett, et al.
>
> *A Guide Book of United States Type Coins*—Q. David Bowers

Join a Coin Club

Beginners should join a coin club if they live in a city which has one. Associating with more experienced collectors will be of great benefit. Practically all larger cities have one or more clubs and they are being rapidly organized in smaller towns. Trade publications carry information about coin clubs and events such as coin shows and conventions.

The American Numismatic Association is a national organization that collectors can join. The ANA Web site (www.money.org) has a list of member coin clubs throughout the United States. Contact the ANA by mail at 818 North Cascade Avenue, Colorado Springs, CO 80903, or by phone at 800-367-9723.

SELLING YOUR COINS

Is it time to sell your coins? Perhaps you've inherited some of them; or maybe you've collected for years, and you want to explore a new pastime or you need to cash in on your investment. In any case, you have some decisions to make. Will you sell your collection privately, or at a public auction—or perhaps sell it yourself on the Internet? Will you sell locally or to dealers nationwide? What are the benefits of each path, and which will bring the greatest profits? To get started, ask yourself:

What Am I Selling?

Rolls of Modern Coins; Proof Sets; Modern Commemoratives; Bullion; Etc. This includes bulk investment coins, such as American Eagle bullion pieces, bags of common circulated coins, and so on. It also includes modern commemoratives and coin sets, not all of which have increased in value in the secondary market. Such accumulations are best sold privately to a coin dealer or to another collector. Auctioning them yourself, on the Internet, is another route. Consigning them to an auction house is not likely to be your best option; this venue is typically reserved for scarcer coins.

Coins With Sentimental—but Not Necessarily High-Dollar—Value. You might have inherited an accumulation (as opposed to a studiously compiled collection) of coins—for example, a coffee can full of Wheat cents. Your local coin dealer can make you an offer, either buying the entire lot or searching through them to "cherrypick" the better pieces. If you have the time, you might sell them yourself, through an Internet auction site. Also, you might donate them to a local Boy Scout troop or similar organization (this may be tax-deductible).

Rare and/or Significant Coins. For rare, valuable, and historically significant coins, public consigned auctions are often the best way to sell—dedicated collectors know they're good sources for scarce coins. A coin consigned to a well-established auction house with numismatic experience will be carefully studied, cataloged, and presented to a serious audience. You save the time and effort of searching for potential buyers. The auction firm makes money by collecting a commission on each sale.

Another option for selling your rare and significant coins is to approach a dealer nationally recognized as an expert in the field—for example, a specialist who focuses on colonial coins. You may also receive tax benefits from donating your coins to the American Numismatic Association (ANA), the American Numismatic Society, or a museum.

Selling to a Coin Shop

Your local coin shop has the advantage of the personal touch. Good coin-shop proprietors are happy to educate and advise their customers. An active coin dealer stays up to date on the hobby and the market, knows about tax and estate laws that might affect your sale, and can study your collection and make educated decisions. Many dealers have a wide audience for selling coins—which provides the leverage to offer you a good price.

A coin shop can be a venue for selling numismatic items of any value. The owner can often make you an offer and write you a check on the spot. Of course, very rare or specialized coins will likely fetch a higher price at public auction.

You should feel comfortable with the integrity of the shop's proprietor and staff. Talk to coin-collector friends, inquire at the local coin club, and check with the Better Business Bureau. Look at the shop's Web site, advertisements, and flyers or publications—do they project fairness and professionalism?

Coin shops can be found in a phone book or online business directory. Call to make sure the owner or a qualified assistant will be there to examine your coins. A busy dealer can schedule a convenient time to meet with you. Solicit at least two quotes before you decide to sell.

Selling Through the Mail

You can ship your coins to a dealer for their offer; again, trust is important. Does the dealer belong to the ANA or the Professional Numismatists Guild (www.pngdealers. com)? Does he advertise in hobby newspapers such as *Coin World* and *Numismatic News?* Search the dealer's name on the Internet: do you find satisfied customers, or complaints and concerns?

Inquire by mail, email, or phone before shipping any coins. The dealer might request a list beforehand, and should be able to give you a general idea of value without seeing the coins in person. Once you're comfortable and have decided to sell, ask the dealer for advice on shipping and insurance. Keep in mind that the dealer will need to examine your coins before making a firm offer.

Even if you live near a coin shop, you can broaden the playing field if you're open to selling your coins through the mail to established, respected dealers. This is a good option if you have the time. The entire transaction (finding dealers; packing and shipping; waiting for the check) will likely take longer than getting a local offer.

Selling to a Dealer at a Coin Show

Between the national coin shows and the hundreds of coin clubs that sponsor city and regional shows, chances are a show is held somewhere near you at least once a year. With dozens or even hundreds of dealers in one venue, you can shop your coins around before you sell; and, as at a coin shop, payment is immediate.

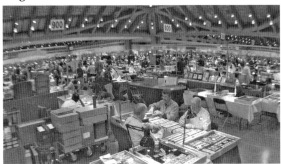

For best results, decide in advance which dealers would be best to appproach, especially if you'll have to travel a long way or you're interested in a narrow specialty.

Remember, a coin show is a public venue. Be alert; use common sense. Outside the show, do not publicize the fact that you're carrying valuable coins.

Most shows list participating dealers in their programs. Decide in advance the ones you want to approach (e.g., the silver-dollar specialists, if you have Morgan dollars to sell). Or simply stroll the aisles and introduce yourself to dealers who sell items similar to those in your collection. This is all part of the fun of a coin show.

Consigning at a Public Auction

Numismatic auction firms are often connected to larger retailers that also sell through the mail, online, etc. As always, reputation is important. Study a potential auction-eer's Web site; learn about their staff, past sales results, any media coverage they might receive. Look at their catalogs: are they professionally made? The effort and experience an auction firm brings to its work will affect how much your coins sell for.

Selling Online

Selling your coins yourself online can be fun, but it requires time and (usually) some skill with scanning or photography. Each auction site has its own rules, policies, and rates; read them carefully. Be security-conscious (e.g., rent a Post Office box instead of using your home address, and insist on full, guaranteed payment before you ship any coins). You can also use the Internet to sell your coins at a fixed price, through a bulletin-board posting or other announcement. Any online sale to the public requires you to take on responsibilities similar to those of a coin shop or auction firm. There is work involved, but the experience can be enjoyable and profitable.

Early American coins are rare in conditions better than those listed and consequently dealers pay much more for them.

BRITISH NEW WORLD ISSUES
Sommer Islands (Bermuda)

This coinage, issued around 1616, was the first struck for England's colonies in the New World. The coins were known as "Hogge Money" or "Hoggies."

The pieces were made of copper lightly silvered, in four denominations: shilling, sixpence, threepence, and twopence, indicated by Roman numerals. The hog is the main device and appears on the obverse side of each. SOMMER ISLANDS is inscribed within beaded circles. The reverse shows a full-rigged galleon with the flag of St. George on each of four masts.

Shilling

	AG	G	VG	F	VF	EF
Twopence	$2,250	$3,250	$5,500	$15,000	$25,000	$45,000
Threepence			25,000			
Sixpence	3,500	7,500	12,500	16,500	22,500	40,000
Shilling	2,500	4,000	6,250	20,000	35,000	55,000

Massachusetts
"New England" Coinage (1652)

In 1652 the General Court of Massachusetts ordered the first metallic currency to be struck in the British Americas, the New England silver threepence, sixpence, and shilling. These coins were made from silver bullion procured principally from the West Indies. Joseph Jenks made the punches for the first coins at his Iron Works in Saugus, Massachusetts, close to Boston where the mint was located. John Hull was appointed mintmaster; his assistant was Robert Sanderson.

NE Shilling (1652)

	G	VG	F	VF	EF
NE Threepence *(unique)*			—		
NE Sixpence *(8 known)*	$35,000	$55,000	$115,000	$185,000	$250,000
NE Shilling	30,000	45,000	65,000	85,000	115,000

Willow Tree Coinage (1653–1660)

The simplicity of the design on the N.E. coins invited counterfeiting and clipping of the edges. Therefore, they were soon replaced by the Willow Tree, Oak Tree, and Pine Tree series. The Willow Tree coins were struck from 1653 to 1660, the Oak Trees 1660 to 1667, and the Pine Trees 1667 to 1682. All of them (with the exception of the Oak Tree twopence) bore the date 1652. Many varieties of all of these coins exist. Values shown are for the most common types.

Sixpence

	Fair	G	VG	F	VF	EF
1652 Willow Tree Threepence *(3 known)*				—	—	—
1652 Willow Tree Sixpence *(14 known)*	$6,500	$15,000	$20,000	$40,000	$80,000	$125,000
1652 Willow Tree Shilling.	6,500	15,000	20,000	45,000	65,000	125,000

Oak Tree Coinage (1660–1667)

Twopence

Threepence

	G	VG	F	VF	EF	AU	Unc.
1662 Oak Tree Twopence	$300	$650	$1,250	$1,600	$3,000	$4,500	$7,500
1652 Oak Tree Threepence	450	700	2,000	3,500	7,500	12,500	22,500
1652 Oak Tree Sixpence	500	900	1,800	3,250	4,500	7,500	20,000
1652 Oak Tree Shilling.	500	900	1,800	3,500	4,500	6,500	17,500

Pine Tree Coinage (1667–1682)

The first Pine Tree coins were minted on the same size planchets as the Oak Tree pieces. Subsequent issues of the shilling were narrower and thicker, to conform to the size of English coins.

Shilling, Large Planchet (1667–1674)   Shilling, Small Planchet (1675–1682)

See next page for chart.

	G	VG	F	VF	EF	AU	Unc.
1652 Pine Tree Threepence	$600	$750	$1,250	$1,750	$3,200	$4,750	$11,000
1652 Pine Tree Sixpence	650	1,050	1,500	2,000	3,750	5,750	12,500
1652 Pine Tree Shilling, Large Planchet. . . .	650	1,250	2,000	3,000	4,750	6,500	16,000
1652 Pine Tree Shilling, Small Planchet. . . .	750	1,350	2,000	2,500	4,250	7,500	17,000

Maryland
Lord Baltimore Coinage

In 1659, Cecil Calvert, Lord Baltimore and Lord Proprietor of Maryland, had coinage struck in England for use in Maryland. There were four denominations: shilling, sixpence, fourpence (groat) in silver, and copper penny (denarium). The silver coins have the bust of Lord Baltimore on the obverse, and the Baltimore family arms with the denomination in Roman numerals on the reverse.

Fourpence (groat)   Lord Baltimore Shilling

	G	VG	F	VF	EF	AU
Penny copper *(9 known)*	$15,000	$30,000	$50,000	$85,000	$125,000	$165,000
Fourpence	2,000	3,500	7,000	10,000	17,500	35,000
Sixpence	1,500	2,500	4,500	5,500	8,000	12,500
Shilling	1,750	4,000	6,500	8,500	11,000	22,500

New Jersey
St. Patrick or Mark Newby Coinage

Mark Newby, who came to America from Dublin, Ireland, in November 1681, brought copper pieces believed by numismatists to have been struck in England circa 1663 to 1672. These are called St. Patrick coppers. The coin received wide circulation in the New Jersey Province, having been authorized to pass as legal tender by the General Assembly in May 1682. The smaller piece, known as a farthing, was never specifically authorized for circulation in the colonies.

St. Patrick Farthing

	G	VG	F	VF	EF	AU
St. Patrick "Farthing".	$135	$250	$550	$1,150	$2,500	$5,000
St. Patrick "Halfpenny"	350	650	1,000	1,500	3,650	15,000

COINAGE AUTHORIZED BY BRITISH ROYAL PATENT
American Plantations Tokens

These pieces struck in nearly pure tin were the first royally authorized coinage for the British colonies in America. They were made under a franchise granted in 1688 to Richard Holt. Restrikes were made circa 1828 from original dies.

	G	VG	F	VF	EF	AU	Unc.
(1688) James II Plantation Token Farthing . .							
1/24 Part Real	$150	$250	$450	$650	$1,250	$2,000	$3,750
1/24 Part Real, Restrike	50	75	150	225	300	500	1,150

Coinage of William Wood
Rosa Americana Coins

William Wood, an Englishman, obtained a patent from King George I to make coins for Ireland and the American colonies. The Rosa Americana pieces were issued in three denominations—halfpenny, penny, and twopence—and were intended for use in America.

Penny

	VG	F	VF	EF	AU	Unc.
(No date) Twopence, Motto in Ribbon	$125	$200	$425	$600	$1,250	$2,750
1722 Halfpenny, DEI GRATIA REX UTILE DULCI . . .	85	150	250	400	600	1,650
1722 Penny	85	150	250	400	650	1,650
1722 Twopence	135	200	275	525	800	2,000

Halfpenny

	F	VF	EF	AU	Unc.
1723 Halfpenny	$55	$115	$175	$350	$850

Entry continued on next page.

Twopence

	VG	F	VF	EF	AU	Unc.
1723 Penny............................	$55	$75	$150	$250	$450	$1,150
1723 Twopence *(illustrated)*................	85	110	175	450	700	1,500

Wood's Hibernia Coinage

The type intended for Ireland had a seated figure with a harp on the reverse side and the word HIBERNIA. Denominations struck were the halfpenny and the farthing with dates 1722, 1723, and 1724. Although these have no association with the Americas, because of the connection with William Wood many American collectors desire to obtain them.

1722, Hibernia   First Type   Second Type
Halfpenny

	G	VG	F	VF	EF	AU	Unc.
1722 Farthing, first type	$100	$225	$325	$850	$1,500	$3,500	$6,500
1722 Halfpenny (first or second type) ...	15	40	55	115	185	350	750

1723, Hibernia Farthing   1724, Hibernia Halfpenny

	G	VG	F	VF	EF	AU	Unc.
1723 Farthing.....................	$15	$25	$35	$75	$100	$250	$550
1723 Halfpenny....................	15	20	30	65	90	185	500
1724 Farthing.....................	25	40	95	250	450	750	1,750
1724 Halfpenny....................	15	35	65	170	325	500	1,000

Virginia Halfpennies

In 1773, coinage of a copper halfpenny was authorized for Virginia by the British Crown. The style is similar to the regular English coinage. These pieces did not arrive in Virginia until 1775, but after then they did circulate on a limited basis. Most examples known today are Uncirculated, by virtue of a hoard of several thousand pieces that came to light in the 19th century and was distributed in numismatic channels.

	G	VG	F	VF	EF	AU	Unc.
1773 Halfpenny...............	$25	$40	$75	$115	$225	$350	$800

EARLY AMERICAN AND RELATED TOKENS

Elephant Tokens

London Elephant Tokens

The London Elephant tokens were struck circa 1672 to 1694. Although they were undated, two examples are known to have been struck over 1672 British halfpennies. Most are struck in copper, but one is made of brass. The legend on this piece, GOD PRESERVE LONDON, is probably just a general plea for divine aid and not a specific reference to the outbreak of plague in 1665 or the great fire of 1666.

These pieces were not struck for the colonies, and probably did not circulate in America, although a few may have been carried there by colonists. They are associated with the 1694 Carolina and New England Elephant tokens, through a shared obverse die.

	VG	F	VF	EF	AU	Unc.
(1694) Halfpenny, GOD PRESERVE LONDON,						
Thick or Thin Planchet................	$250	$500	$850	$1,000	$1,650	$2,500

Carolina Elephant Tokens

Although no law is known authorizing coinage for Carolina, very interesting pieces known as Elephant tokens were made with the date 1694. These copper tokens were of halfpenny denomination. The reverse reads GOD PRESERVE CAROLINA AND THE LORDS PROPRIETERS 1694.

The Carolina pieces were probably struck in England and perhaps intended as advertising to heighten interest in the Carolina Plantation.

	VG	F	VF	EF	AU	Unc.
1694 CAROLINA.	$3,500	$6,500	$9,500	$15,000	$25,000	$35,000

New England Elephant Tokens

Like the Carolina Tokens, the New England Elephant tokens were believed to have been struck in England as promotional pieces to increase interest in the American colonies.

	F	VF	EF
1694 NEW ENGLAND.	$35,000	$55,000	$75,000

New Yorke in America Token

Little is known about the origin of this token. The design of a heraldic eagle on a regulated staff with oak leaf finials is identical to the crest found on the arms of William Lovelace, governor of New York, 1668 to 1673. It seems likely that this piece is a token farthing struck by Lovelace for use in New York.

	VG	F	VF	EF
(Undated) Brass or Copper.	$5,500	$11,500	$20,000	$35,000
(Undated) Pewter.	—	—		

Gloucester Tokens

This token appears to have been a private coinage by a merchant of Gloucester (county), Virginia. The only specimens known are struck in brass. The exact origin and use of these pieces are unknown.

	VF
1714 Shilling, brass *(2 known)*	$125,000

Higley or Granby Coppers

The Higley coppers were private issues. All the pieces were made of pure copper. There were seven obverse and four reverse dies. The first issue, in 1737, bore the legend THE VALUE OF THREEPENCE. After a time the quantity exceeded the local demand, and a protest arose against the stated value of the piece. The inscription was changed to VALUE ME AS YOU PLEASE.

	AG	G	VG	F
1737 THE VALVE OF THREE PENCE, CONNECTICVT, 3 Hammers..........	$7,000	$10,000	$20,000	$35,000
1737 THE VALVE OF THREE PENCE, I AM GOOD COPPER, 3 Hammers	8,000	15,000	32,500	50,000
1737 VALUE ME AS YOU PLEASE, I AM GOOD COPPER, 3 Hammers.......	7,500	10,500	20,000	35,000
(1737) VALUE ME AS YOU PLEASE, J CUT MY WAY THROUGH, Broad Axe...	7,500	11,500	20,000	35,000
1739 VALUE ME AS YOU PLEASE, J CUT MY WAY THROUGH, Broad Axe....	8,500	15,000	25,000	40,000

Hibernia–Voce Populi Coins

These coins, struck in the year 1760, were made in Dublin. Although these have no connection with America, they have been listed in numismatic publications in the United States for a long time and are collected by tradition.

Farthing (1760)

Halfpenny (1760)

	G	VG	F	VF	EF	AU	Unc.
1760 Farthing	$100	$160	$250	$650	$1,000	$1,750	$3,500
1760 Halfpenny................	45	75	115	175	275	600	750

Pitt Tokens

British politician William Pitt is the subject of these pieces, probably intended as commemorative medalets. He was a friend to the interests of America. The so-called halfpenny served as currency in England during a shortage of regular coinage.

	VG	F	VF	EF	AU	Unc.
1766 Farthing	$5,500	$12,500	$20,000			
1766 Halfpenny	350	600	1,150	$1,500	$2,000	

Rhode Island Ship Medals

Although this medal has a Dutch inscription, the spelling and design indicate an English or Anglo-American origin. It is believed that this token was struck in England circa 1779 for the Dutch market. Specimens are known in brass and pewter. As with many colonial issues, modern copies exist.

1778–1779, Rhode Island Ship Medal

Values shown are for brass pieces. Those struck in pewter are rare and valued higher.

	VF	EF	AU	Unc.
Rhode Island Ship Medal	$700	$1,250	$2,000	$3,500

John Chalmers Issues

John Chalmers, a silversmith, struck a series of silver tokens at Annapolis in 1783. Certain of the dies were by Thomas Sparrow, who also engraved bank-note plates. As most examples show wear today, these pieces seem to have served well in commerce.

	VG	F	VF	EF	AU
1783 Threepence	$1,350	$2,250	$4,500	$8,500	$12,500

	VG	F	VF	EF	AU
1783 Sixpence	$2,500	$4,500	$8,500	$15,000	$20,000
1783 Shilling	750	1,500	3,500	6,750	11,000

FRENCH NEW WORLD ISSUES

None of the coins of the French regime is strictly American. They were all general issues for the French colonies of the New World. The copper of 1717 to 1722 was authorized by edicts of 1716 and 1721 for use in New France, Louisiana, and the French West Indies.

Copper Sou or Nine Deniers

	VG	F	VF	EF
1721-B (Rouen)	$275	$550	$1,800	$4,000
1721-H (La Rochelle)	60	125	450	1,350
1722-H	60	125	450	1,350

French Colonies in General

Coined for use in the French colonies, these circulated only unofficially in Louisiana, along with other foreign coins and tokens. Most were counterstamped RF (République Française) for use in the West Indies. The mintmark A signifies the Paris Mint.

	VG	VF	EF	AU
1767 French Colonies, Sou	$55	$125	$375	$1,000
1767 French Colonies, Sou, counterstamped RF	50	100	165	350

CONTINENTAL CURRENCY PIECES

The Continental Currency pieces may have been experimental coins or patterns, possibly proposed as a paper-money substitute, or even commemorative medals. The exact nature of their monetary role, if any, is uncertain. They may have been struck in

Philadelphia from dies engraved by Elisha Gallaudet, or even made in Europe many years after 1776. As with many early pieces, numerous replicas exist.

	G	F	VF	EF	AU	Unc.
1776, CURENCY, pewter *(2 varieties)*	$7,500	$15,000	$20,000	$27,500	$32,500	$60,000
1776, CURENCY, silver *(2 known)*		500,000				
1776, CURRENCY, pewter	10,000	15,000	20,000	27,500	32,500	60,000
1776, CURRENCY, EG FECIT, pewter	10,000	16,500	22,500	32,500	38,500	70,000

SPECULATIVE ISSUES, TOKENS, AND PATTERNS

Nova Constellatio Coppers

The Nova Constellatio pieces were struck supposedly by order of Gouverneur Morris. Evidence indicates that they were all struck in Birmingham, England, and imported for American circulation as a private business venture.

1783, CONSTELLATIO,
Pointed Rays

1783, CONSTELLATIO,
Blunt Rays

1785, CONSTELLATIO,
Blunt Rays

1785, CONSTELLATIO,
Pointed Rays

POST-COLONIAL ISSUES

	VG	F	VF	EF	AU	Unc.
1783, CONSTELLATIO, Pointed Rays	$75	$125	$225	$550	$850	$1,750
1783, CONSTELATIO, Blunt Rays	75	125	250	800	1,750	3,250
1785, CONSTELLATIO, Pointed Rays	75	125	225	550	850	1,650
1785, CONSTELATIO, Blunt Rays	75	135	265	850	2,000	3,750

Immune Columbia Pieces

Nearly all of these are very rare. Many if not most seem to be unofficial, including pieces produced at the private Machin's Mills mint in Newburgh, New York.

**1785, Copper,
Star Reverse**

**1785, George III
Obverse**

	G	VG	F	VF	EF	AU
1785 Copper, Star Reverse			$12,500	$17,500	$25,000	
1785, George III Obverse	$2,500	$5,000	6,000	10,000		

1787, IMMUNIS COLUMBIA, Eagle Reverse

	G	VG	F	VF	EF	AU
1785, VERMON AUCTORI Obverse, IMMUNE COLUMBIA ..	$3,200	$5,500	$7,500	$22,500		
1787, IMMUNIS COLUMBIA, Eagle Reverse	200	500	1,000	2,000	$3,500	$7,500

Confederatio Coppers

The Confederatio and associated coppers have patriotic motifs and were made in small quantities for circulation. The die with the CONFEDERATIO legend was also combined with other designs such as a bust of George Washington, Libertas et Justitia of 1785, Immunis Columbia of 1786, the New York "Excelsiors," Inimica Tyrannis Americana, and others. In all there were 12 dies struck in 13 combinations. There are two types of the Confederatio reverse. In one instance the stars are contained in a small circle; in the other, larger stars are in a larger circle.

Typical Obverse

Small Circle Reverse

Large Circle Reverse

	VF
1785, Stars in Small Circle, various obverses	$45,000
1785, Stars in Large Circle, various obverses	50,000

Speculative Patterns

1786, IMMUNIS COLUMBIA

Eagle Reverse

Shield Reverse

	VF	EF
1786, IMMUNIS COLUMBIA, Eagle Reverse	$35,000	$50,000
1786, IMMUNIS COLUMBIA, Shield Reverse	27,500	35,000
(No date) (1786) Washington Obverse, Shield Reverse	60,000	
1786, Eagle Obverse, Shield Reverse	40,000	
1786, Washington Obverse, Eagle Reverse *(2 known)*	—	

COINAGE OF THE STATES AND VERMONT
Vermont

Reuben Harmon Jr. was granted permission to coin copper pieces for the Republic of Vermont beginning July 1, 1785. (Vermont would not become a state until 1791.) The franchise was extended for eight years in 1786, but in 1787 production was shifted to Machin's Mills, Newburgh, New York, in which Harmon had a proprietary interest. Although the Vermont coins were legally issued there, most other products of Machin's Mills were counterfeits, some dies for which were combined with Vermont pieces, creating several illogical pieces below, including the 1785 Immune Columbia and the 1788 Georgivs III Rex.

1785, IMMUNE COLUMBIA   **1785–1786, Plow Type**

POST-COLONIAL ISSUES

1786, Baby Head

	AG	G	VG	F	VF	EF
1785, IMMUNE COLUMBIA.	$2,000	$3,500	$5,500	$9,500	$18,500	$35,000
1785, Plow Type, VERMONTS.	90	150	300	425	1,500	3,000
1786, Plow Type, VERMONTENSIUM	75	125	220	325	850	2,000
1786, Baby Head.	115	170	325	750	2,250	5,500

1786–1787, Bust Left　　　　**1787, BRITANNIA**

1787, Bust Right

	AG	G	VG	F	VF	EF
1786, Bust Left	$40	$75	$180	$400	$1,200	$2,250
1787, Bust Left	2,000	3,750	6,500	12,500	25,000	—
1787, BRITANNIA.	35	65	85	115	225	850
1787, Bust Right *(several varieties)*	35	75	135	245	600	1,350

1788, Bust Right　　　　**1788, GEORGIVS III REX**

See next page for chart.

	AG	G	VG	F	VF	EF
1788, Bust Right *(several varieties)*	$35	$65	$125	$225	$550	$1,150
1788, GEORGIVS III REX	275	350	550	1,250	2,500	7,500

Note: This piece should not be confused with the common British halfpence with similar design and reverse legend BRITANNIA.

New Hampshire

New Hampshire was the first of the states to consider the subject of coinage following the Declaration of Independence.

William Moulton was empowered to make a limited quantity of coins of pure copper, authorized by the State House of Representatives in 1776.

	VG
1776 New Hampshire Copper	$100,000

Massachusetts

The coinage of Massachusetts copper cents and half cents in 1787 and 1788 was under the direction of Joshua Witherle. These were the first coins bearing the denomination *cent* as later established by Congress. Many varieties exist, the most valuable being the cent with arrows in the eagle's right talon (on the left side of the coin).

1787 Half Cent   **1787 Cent**

1788 Half Cent   **1788 Cent**

	G	F	VF	EF	AU	Unc.
1787 Half Cent	$65	$150	$270	$450	$750	$1,650
1787 Cent, Arrows in Right Talon	4,500	12,500	27,500			
1787 Cent, Arrows in Left Talon *(illustrated)*	65	150	350	750	1,350	3,000
1788 Half Cent	65	150	350	550	1,000	2,000
1788 Cent	65	150	375	600	1,000	2,500

Connecticut

Authority for establishing a mint near New Haven was granted by the state to Samuel Bishop, Joseph Hopkins, James Hillhouse, and John Goodrich in 1785. Today, well over 300 different die varieties are known of Connecticut coppers dated from 1785 to 1788. These pieces circulated widely and effectively; most are seen with significant evidence of circulation.

1785, Bust
Facing Right

1705, Bust
Facing Left

1786–1787, Mailed
Bust Facing Right

1786–1787, Mailed
Bust Facing Left

1787, Draped
Bust Facing Left

1788, Mailed
Bust Facing Right

1788, Mailed
Bust Facing Left

1788, Draped
Bust Facing Left

See next page for chart.

	AG	G	VG	F	VF	EF	AU
1785, Bust Facing Left...........	$35	$85	$150	$350	$1,000	$2,000	$4,000
1785, Bust Facing Right	20	40	55	80	275	750	2,000
1786, Mailed Bust Facing Right....	25	50	60	100	275	750	1,750
1786, Mailed Bust Facing Left.....	20	35	50	90	200	650	1,650
1787, Mailed Bust Facing Right....	25	45	75	200	500	950	2,000
1787, Mailed Bust Facing Left.....	20	30	45	75	200	550	1,650
1787, Draped Bust Facing Left	20	30	45	85	200	550	1,450
1788, Mailed Bust Facing Right....	20	30	55	125	325	750	1,650
1788, Mailed Bust Facing Left.....	20	30	35	100	225	600	1,750
1788, Draped Bust Facing Left	20	30	45	125	275	650	2,150

New York and Related Issues

Brasher Doubloons

Perhaps the most famous pieces coined before the establishment of the U.S. Mint at Philadelphia were those produced by a well-known goldsmith and jeweler, Ephraim Brasher of New York.

Brasher produced a gold piece weighing about 408 grains, approximately equal in value to a Spanish doubloon (about $15.00 in New York currency).

The punch-mark EB appears in either of two positions as illustrated. This mark is found on some foreign gold coins as well, and probably was so used by Brasher as evidence of his testing of their value. Many modern forgeries exist.

	EF
1787 New York gold doubloon, EB on Breast...	$4,000,000
1787 New York gold doubloon, EB on Wing...	4,000,000

New York Copper Coinage

No coinage was authorized by the State of New York following the Revolutionary War, although several propositions were considered. The only coinage laws passed were those regulating coins already in use. Private mints struck several unauthorized coppers.

	G	VG	F	VF	EF
1786, NON VI VIRTUTE VICI	$3,650	$5,500	$12,500	$22,500	$40,000

	G	VG	F	VF	EF
1787 EXCELSIOR Copper, Eagle on Globe Facing Right	$1,500	$3,500	$7,500	$17,500	$37,500
1787 EXCELSIOR Copper, Eagle on Globe Facing Left	1,500	2,500	6,500	13,500	27,500

1787, George Clinton and
New York Arms

1787, Indian and
New York Arms

1787, Indian and Eagle on Globe

	G	VG	F	VF	EF
1787, George Clinton and New York Arms	$6,500	$15,000	$50,000	$75,000	$165,000
1787, Indian and New York Arms	6,000	12,500	20,000	40,000	85,000
1787, Indian and Eagle on Globe	6,000	12,500	20,000	40,000	80,000

Georgivs/Britannia
"Machin's Mills" Copper Halfpennies Made in America

During the era of American state coinage, James F. Atlee and other coiners minted unauthorized, lightweight, imitation British halfpence. These American-made false coins have the same devices, legends, and, in some cases, dates as genuine regal halfpence, but contain less copper. Overall quality of these pieces is similar to that of British-made imitations, but details are more often poorly rendered or missing. Identification of American-made imitations has been confirmed by identifying punch marks and matching them to those of known engravers.

Dates used on these pieces were often evasive, and are as follows: 1771, 1772, and 1774 through 1776 for the first group; 1747 and 1787 for the second group; and 1776, 1778, 1787, and 1788 for the third group. Pieces generally attributed to Atlee can be identified by a single outline in the crosses (British Union) of Britannia's shield and large triangular dentils along the coin circumference. The more-valuable American-made pieces are not to be confused with the similar English-made George III counterfeits (some of which have identical dates), or with genuine British half-pence dated 1770 to 1775.

35

Group I coins dated 1771, 1772, and 1774 through 1776 have distinctive bold designs but lack the fine details of the original coins. Planchets are generally of high quality. Group II coins dated 1747 and 1787 are generally poorly made. The 1 in the date is not J-shaped, and the dentils are of various sizes. There are no outlines to the stripes in the shield. Group III coins dated 1776, 1778, 1787, and 1788, struck at Machin's Mills in Newberg, New York, are similar to coins of Group II, with their triangular-shaped dentils. Most have wide dates and berries in the wreath.

	AG	G	VG	F	VF	EF	AU
1747, GEORGIVS II. Group II	$85	$135	$250	$500	$2,250	$4,500	—
1771, GEORGIVS III. Group I	35	55	125	215	850	2,500	$3,500
1772, GEORGIVS III. Group I	40	80	165	325	950	2,500	5,000
1772, GEORGIUS III. Group I	45	115	200	450	1,650	3,500	—
1774, GEORGIVS III. Group I	30	45	85	165	500	1,250	3,000
1774, GEORGIUS III. Group I	40	85	150	275	1,150	2,750	—
1775, GEORGIVS III. Group I	30	45	85	165	450	1,150	3,000
1776, GEORGIVS III. Group III	95	165	265	550	1,500	4,000	—
1776, GEORCIVS III, Small Date	650	1,250	3,000	5,500	12,500	—	—
1778, GEORGIVS III. Group III	30	65	100	205	500	1,500	2,500
1784, GEORGIVS III	105	215	600	1,000	2,500	3,000	5,000
1787, GEORGIVS III. Group II	30	50	85	135	550	850	2,250
1787, GEORGIVS III. Group III	30	50	85	135	550	850	2,250
1788, GEORGIVS III. Group III	30	50	100	165	550	1,000	2,250

Note: Values shown are what coin dealers pay for the most common varieties in each category. Rare pieces can be worth significantly more. Also see related George III combinations under Connecticut, Vermont, and New York.

Nova Eborac Coinage for New York

1787, NOVA EBORAC Reverse,
Seated Figure Facing Right

1787, NOVA EBORAC Reverse,
Seated Figure Facing Left

	AG	G	F	VF	EF	AU
1787, NOVA EBORAC, Seated Figure Facing Right . . .	$35	$65	$165	$450	$1,000	$2,500
1787, NOVA EBORAC, Seated Figure Facing Left	30	50	135	350	750	1,650

New Jersey

On June 1, 1786, the New Jersey General Assembly granted to Thomas Goadsby, Albion Cox, and Walter Mould authority to coin some three million coppers no later than June 1788, on condition that they delivered to the treasurer of the state "one-tenth part of the full sum they shall strike and coin," in quarterly installments. These coppers were to pass current at 15 to the shilling. Produced in significant quantities, these coins are often seen in the market today and are widely collectible, although certain varieties can be rare and especially valuable.

Narrow Shield   Wide Shield

	AG	G	F	VF	EF	AU
1786, Narrow Shield	$20	$35	$100	$215	$550	$1,150
1786, Wide Shield	25	45	135	325	1,150	2,500

Small Planchet

	AG	G	F	VF	EF	AU
1787, Horse's Head Facing Right............	$20	$25	$85	$215	$400	$1,000

Fox Before Legend

	AG	G	F	VF	EF	AU
1788, Horse's Head Facing Right............	$20	$30	$105	$300	$500	$1,000
1788, Similar, Fox in Legend	50	85	285	950	2,250	6,500
1788, Horse's Head Facing Left.............	115	215	850	2,350	6,500	—

PRIVATE TOKENS AFTER CONFEDERATION
North American Tokens

This piece was struck in Dublin, Ireland. The obverse shows the seated figure of Hibernia facing left. Although dated 1781, it is believed to have been struck early in the next century.

	VG	F	VF	EF
1781, Copper or brass.	$35	$65	$115	$350

Bar Coppers

The Bar copper is undated and of uncertain origin. It has 13 parallel and unconnected bars on one side. On the other side is the large roman-letter USA monogram. The design was supposedly copied from a Continental Army uniform button.

	VG	F	VF	EF	AU
(Undated) (Circa 1785) Bar Copper	$1,500	$2,500	$5,500	$6,500	$8,500

Auctori Plebis Tokens

This token is sometimes included with the coins of Connecticut as it greatly resembles issues of that state. It was struck in England by an unknown maker.

	G	VG	F	VF	EF	AU	Unc.
1787, AUCTORI PLEBIS	$55	$85	$125	$300	$550	$1,250	$5,000

Mott Store Cards

This 19th century store card has long been considered an early token because of its date (1789). Most scholars believe it was most likely produced circa 1830 as a commemorative of the founding of the Mott Company, and probably served as a business card.

	VG	F	VF	EF	AU	Unc.
"1789," Mott Token	$50	$100	$200	$300	$350	$750

Standish Barry Threepence

Standish Barry, a Baltimore silversmith, circulated a silver threepence in 1790. The tokens were believed to have been an advertising venture at a time when small change was scarce.

	VG	F	VF	EF
1790 Threepence	$6,500	$12,500	$20,000	$35,000

Kentucky Tokens

These tokens were struck in England about 1795. Each star in the triangle represents a state, identified by its initial letter. These pieces are usually called *Kentucky cents* because the letter K (for Kentucky) happens to be at the top. In the 19th century these were often called *triangle tokens,* from the arrangement of the stars. Values are for the normal issue with plain edge; lettered-edge varieties exist and are scarcer.

	VG	VF	EF	AU	Unc.
(1792–1794) Copper, Plain Edge	$55	$100	$150	$300	$600

Franklin Press Tokens

This piece is an English tradesman's token, but, being associated with Benjamin Franklin, has accordingly been included in American collections.

	VG	VF	EF	AU	Unc.
1794, Franklin Press Token	$65	$100	$165	$350	$650

Talbot, Allum & Lee Cents

Talbot, Allum & Lee, engaged in the India trade and located in New York, placed a large quantity of English-made coppers in circulation during 1794 and 1795. ONE CENT appears on the 1794 issue and on the edge of the 1795 issue.

1794 Cent,
With NEW YORK

1795 Cent

	G	VG	VF	EF	AU	Unc.
1794 Cent, With NEW YORK.	$35	$40	$125	$175	$300	$850
1794 Cent, Without NEW YORK	225	300	1,300	2,500	3,500	8,000
1795 Cent	45	55	125	155	275	550

WASHINGTON PORTRAIT PIECES

An interesting series of coins and tokens dated from 1783 to 1795 bear the portrait of George Washington. The likenesses in most instances were faithfully reproduced and were designed to honor Washington. Many of these pieces were of English origin and made later than the dates indicate.

1783,
Military Bust

1783,
Draped Bust

	F	VF	EF	AU	Unc.
1783, Military Bust	$55	$100	$200	$450	$1,100
1783, Draped Bust	65	115	225	500	1,350

1783, UNITY STATES

	VG	F	VF	EF	AU	Unc.
1783, UNITY STATES	$35	$75	$125	$250	$350	$1,000

Undated Double-Head Cent

	VG	F	VF	EF	AU	Unc.
(Undated) Double-Head Cent	$45	$65	$125	$250	$500	$1,500

Obverse   **Large Eagle Reverse**   **Small Eagle Reverse**

	F	VF	EF	AU	Unc.
1791 Cent, Large Eagle (Date on Obverse)	$225	$275	$375	$650	$1,500
1791 Cent, Small Eagle (Date on Reverse).............	250	325	450	850	1,750

	F	VF	EF	AU
1791 Liverpool Halfpenny, Lettered Edge.......................	$750	$1,000	$1,750	$2,850

1792, Eagle With Stars, copper		—
1792, Eagle With Stars, silver		—
1792, Eagle With Stars, gold *(unique)*		—

**(1792) Undated Cent,
WASHINGTON BORN VIRGINIA**

**1792 Cent,
WASHINGTON PRESIDENT**

	VG	F	VF
(1792) Undated Cent, WASHINGTON BORN VIRGINIA, copper	$650	$1,100	$2,750
1792 Cent, WASHINGTON PRESIDENT, Plain Edge	1,750	4,500	8,750

1792 Getz Pattern　　　　**1793 Ship Halfpenny**　　　　**1795 Halfpenny, Grate Token**

	VG	F	VF	EF	AU	Unc.
1792, Getz Pattern, copper	$5,000	$10,000	$20,000	$35,000		
1793 Ship Halfpenny, Lettered Edge	50	115	200	300	$450	$2,250
1795, Grate Token, Lettered Edge	55	100	150	360	750	1,500
1795, Grate Token, Reeded Edge.	35	55	85	165	225	400

	F	VF	EF	AU	Unc.
1795, LIBERTY AND SECURITY Halfpenny, Plain Edge	$85	$150	$300	$600	$1,650
1795, LIBERTY AND SECURITY Halfpenny, Lettered Edge . . .	75	135	275	550	1,650
(1795) Undated, LIBERTY AND SECURITY Penny.	165	250	400	850	1,650

	G	F	VF	EF	AU
(1795) NORTH WALES Halfpenny	$55	$105	$250	$750	$1,600

	F	VF	EF	AU	Unc.
SUCCESS Medal, Large, Plain or Reeded Edge.	$135	$275	$500	$850	$1,750
SUCCESS Medal, Small, Plain or Reeded Edge.	115	225	450	800	1,700

FUGIO CENTS

The first coins issued by authority of the United States were the 1787 "Fugio" coppers. The legends have been credited to Benjamin Franklin by many, and the coins, as a consequence, have been referred to as *Franklin cents.*

1787, With
Pointed Rays

1787, With
Club Rays

	G	VG	F	VF	EF	AU	Unc.
Pointed Rays, STATES UNITED at Side of Circle							
(illustrated)	$175	$300	$500	$900	$1,350	$1,650	$3,000
Pointed Rays, UNITED STATES at Side of Circle	225	350	500	950	1,350	1,850	3,500
Club Rays, Rounded Ends	325	550	750	1,750	2,500	5,500	—

HALF CENTS

The half cent was authorized to be coined April 2, 1792. Originally the weight was to have been 132 grains, but this was changed to 104 grains by the Act of January 14, 1793, before coinage commenced. The weight was again changed to 84 grains January 26, 1796, by presidential proclamation in conformity with the Act of March 3, 1795. Coinage was discontinued by the Act of February 21, 1857. All were coined at the Philadelphia Mint.

LIBERTY CAP (1793–1797)

AG-3 About Good: Clear enough to identify.
G-4 Good: Outline of bust of Liberty clear, no details. Date readable. Reverse lettering incomplete.
VG-8 Very Good: Some hair details. Reverse lettering complete.
F-12 Fine: Most of hair detail visible. Leaves worn, but all visible.
VF-20 Very Fine: Hair near ear and forehead worn, other areas distinct. Some details in leaves visible.
EF-40 Extremely Fine: Light wear on highest parts of head and wreath.
AU-50 About Uncirculated: Only a trace of wear on Liberty's face.

Head Facing Left (1793)

	Mintage	AG-3	G-4	VG-8	F-12	VF-20	EF-40	AU-50
1793	35,334	$2,000	$2,850	$3,750	$6,500	$9,000	$15,000	$23,500

Head Facing Right (1794–1797)

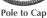

| Pole to Cap | Punctuated Date | No Pole to Cap |

	Mintage	AG-3	G-4	VG-8	F-12	VF-20	EF-40	AU-50
1794	81,600	$275	$425	$750	$1,200	$1,650	$4,500	$8,500
1795, All kinds	139,690							
1795, Lettered Edge, With Pole		275	375	675	1,050	1,850	3,650	6,000
1795, Lettered Edge, Punctuated Date		325	475	700	1,100	1,700	4,850	8,500
1795, Plain Edge, Punctuated Date		275	450	650	800	1,650	3,250	7,500
1795, Plain Edge, No Pole		225	350	650	825	1,350	3,000	5,250
1796, With Pole	1,390	11,500	13,500	21,500	32,500	40,000	55,000	85,000
1796, No Pole	5,090	26,500	38,500	50,000	100,000	125,000	185,000	250,000

* Included in number above.

1797, 1 Above 1, Plain Edge   **1797, Plain Edge**

	Mintage	AG-3	G-4	VG-8	F-12	VF-20	EF-40	AU-50
1797, All kinds.	127,840							
1797, 1 Above 1, Plain Edge		$250	$325	$600	$800	$1,350	$3,000	$5,500
1797, Plain Edge		275	350	650	1,050	1,450	3,500	7,000
1797, Lettered Edge		1,000	1,650	2,850	5,250	8,500	21,500	
1797, Gripped Edge.		55,000	85,000	120,000				

DRAPED BUST (1800–1808)

AG-3 About Good: Clear enough to identify.
G-4 Good: Outline of bust of Liberty clear, few details, date readable. Reverse lettering worn and incomplete.
VG-8 Very Good: Some drapery visible. Date and legends complete.
F-12 Fine: Shoulder drapery and hair over brow worn smooth.
VF-20 Very Fine: Only slight wear in previously mentioned areas. Slight wear on reverse.
EF-40 Extremely Fine: Light wear on highest parts of head and wreath.
AU-50 About Uncirculated: Wear slight on hair above forehead.

1st Reverse   **2nd Reverse**

	Mintage	AG-3	G-4	VG-8	F-12	VF-20	EF-40	AU-50
1800	202,908	$50	$75	$90	$125	$225	$525	$750
1802, 2 Over 0	20,266	500	850	1,350	2,750	6,500	15,000	
1803	92,000	45	70	90	140	250	650	1,250

Plain 4   **Crosslet 4**   **Stems to Wreath**   **Stemless Wreath**

	Mintage	AG-3	G-4	VG-8	F-12	VF-20	EF-40	AU-50
1804, All kinds.	1,055,312							
1804, Plain 4, Stems to Wreath		$75	$125	$200	$325	$450	$1,100	$2,500
1804, Plain 4, Stemless Wreath.		35	60	80	115	135	300	475
1804, Crosslet 4, Stemless Wreath . . .		50	75	90	120	175	325	550
1804, Crosslet 4, Stems to Wreath . . .		35	60	80	115	135	300	475

1804, "Spiked Chin"	Small 5	Large 5

	Mintage	AG-3	G-4	VG-8	F-12	VF-20	EF-40	AU-50
1804, "Spiked Chin" . . . .*		$35	$60	$95	$135	$195	$375	$700
1805, All kinds. 814,464								
1805, Medium 5, Stemless Wreath . . .		35	60	75	100	150	300	500
1805, Small 5, Stems to Wreath		400	650	1,250	2,500	7,500	16,500	30,000
1805, Large 5, Stems to Wreath		35	60	75	105	175	300	500

* Included in "1804, All kinds" mintage (previous page).

Small 6	Large 6	1808, 8 Over 7	Normal Date

	Mintage	AG-3	G-4	VG-8	F-12	VF-20	EF-40	AU-50
1806, All kinds. 356,000								
1806, Small 6, Stems to Wreath		$75	$150	$300	$525	$775	$2,250	$2,750
1806, Small 6, Stemless Wreath		35	65	80	100	140	275	450
1806, Large 6, Stems to Wreath		35	65	80	100	140	275	450
1807 476,000		35	65	80	100	140	300	575
1808, Normal Date 400,000		55	85	100	140	200	500	1,350
1808, 8 Over 7 . . . .*		100	150	250	450	1,500	3,000	8,500

* Included in number below.

CLASSIC HEAD (1809–1836)

G-4 Good: LIBERTY only partly visible on hair band. Lettering, date, and stars worn but visible.
VG-8 Very Good: LIBERTY entirely visible on hair band. Lower curls worn.
F-12 Fine: Only partial wear on LIBERTY, and hair at top worn in spots.
VF-20 Very Fine: Lettering clear-cut. Hair only slightly worn.
EF-40 Extremely Fine: Light wear on highest points of hair and leaves.
AU-50 About Uncirculated: Sharp hair detail with only a trace of wear on higher points.
MS-60 Uncirculated: Typical brown to red surface. No trace of wear.
MS-63 Choice Uncirculated: Well-defined color, brown to red. No traces of wear.

1828, 13 Stars	1828, 12 Stars

Dealers often pay more than the prices shown for brilliant or red Uncirculated coins, and less for spotted, cleaned, or discolored pieces.

	Mintage	AG-3	G-4	VG-8	F-12	VF-20	EF-40	AU-50	MS-60	MS-63
1809 1,154,572		$35	$55	$60	$65	$70	$120	$250	$600	$1,350
1810 215,000		40	55	60	100	200	500	650	1,500	2,500
1811 63,140		165	275	500	900	1,250	3,000	7,500	27,500	75,000

Chart continued on next page.

	Mintage	G-4	VG-8	F-12	VF-20	EF-40	AU-50	MS-60	MS-63	PF-63
1825	63,000	$55	$60	$65	$75	$150	$275	$575	$1,500	
1826	234,000	55	60	65	75	80	150	325	750	
1828, 13 Stars	606,000	55	60	65	75	80	125	190	500	
1828, 12 Stars	*	55	60	65	75	140	250	650	1,500	
1829	487,000	55	60	65	75	80	150	300	500	
1831	2,200									—
1832	51,000	55	60	65	75	80	125	200	450	$10,000
1833	103,000	55	60	65	75	80	125	200	450	5,500
1834	141,000	55	60	65	75	80	125	200	450	5,000
1835	398,000	55	60	65	75	80	125	200	450	5,000
1836										7,500

* Included in number above.

BRAIDED HAIR (1840–1857)

VG-8 Very Good: Beads in hair uniformly distinct. Hair lines visible in spots.
F-12 Fine: Hair lines above ear worn. Beads sharp.
VF-20 Very Fine: Lowest curl worn; hair otherwise distinct.
EF-40 Extremely Fine: Light wear on highest points of hair and on leaves.
AU-50 About Uncirculated: Very slight trace of wear on hair above Liberty's ear.
MS-60 Uncirculated: No trace of wear. Clear luster.
MS-63 Choice Uncirculated: No trace of wear.
PF-63 Choice Proof: Nearly perfect; only light blemishes.

Dealers often pay more than the prices shown for brilliant or red Uncirculated coins, and less for spotted, cleaned, or discolored pieces.

	PF-63			PF-63
1840, Original	$6,500	1845, Original		$12,500
1840, Restrike	6,000	1845, Restrike		5,000
1841, Original	6,000	1846, Original		7,500
1841, Restrike	6,000	1846, Restrike		6,500
1842, Original	7,500	1847, Original		6,000
1842, Restrike	5,000	1847, Restrike		5,000
1843, Original	7,000	1848, Original		8,500
1843, Restrike	6,000	1848, Restrike		4,500
1844, Original	1,000	1849, Original, Small Date		10,000
1844, Restrike	5,500	1849, Restrike, Small Date		5,000

Small Date

Large Date

	Mintage	G-4	VG-8	F-12	VF-20	EF-40	AU-50	MS-60	MS-63	PF-63
1849, Large Date	39,864	$55	$60	$70	$90	$125	$200	$375	$650	—
1850	39,812	70	105	145	225	350	550	850	1,750	$6,500
1851	147,672	55	60	65	70	75	125	160	350	3,500
1852										4,500
1853	129,694	55	60	65	70	75	80	150	350	
1854	55,358	55	60	65	70	75	85	150	350	6,500
1855	56,500	55	60	65	70	75	85	150	350	4,000
1856	40,430	55	60	65	70	75	90	165	450	4,000
1857	35,180	60	65	75	90	120	180	275	500	4,000

Cents and half cents were the first coins struck at the United States Mint. Coinage began in 1793 with laws stating that the cent should weigh exactly twice as much as the half cent. Large cents are dated every year from 1793 to 1857 with the exception of 1815, when a lack of copper prevented production. All were coined at the Philadelphia Mint. Varieties listed are those most significant to collectors. Numerous other die varieties may be found, as each of the early dies was individually made.

FLOWING HAIR (1793)

AG-3 About Good: Date and devices clear enough to identify.
G-4 Good: Lettering worn but readable. No detail on bust.
VG-8 Very Good: Date and lettering distinct, some details of head visible.
F-12 Fine: About half of hair and other details visible.
VF-20 Very Fine: Ear visible, most details visible.
EF-40 Extremely Fine: Wear evident on highest points of hair and back of temple.

Chain Reverse (1793)

AMERI. Reverse · AMERICA Reverse

	Mintage	AG-3	G-4	VG-8	F-12	VF-20	EF-40
1793, Chain, All kinds 36,103							
1793, AMERI. in Legend		$4,000	$6,500	$11,000	$18,000	$28,500	$75,000
1793, AMERICA		4,000	6,000	10,000	16,000	25,000	60,000

Wreath Reverse (1793)

Strawberry Leaf Variety

	Mintage	AG-3	G-4	VG-8	F-12	VF-20	EF-40
1793, Wreath, All kinds 63,353							
1793, Vine and Bars Edge		$1,500	$2,250	$3,250	$5,500	$10,000	$22,500
1793, Lettered Edge		1,500	2,250	3,250	5,500	10,000	22,500
1793, Strawberry Leaf. . . . . *(4 known)*		—	—	—			

LIBERTY CAP (1793–1796)

 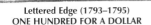

1793, Vine and Bars Edge
Chain and Wreath types only.

Lettered Edge (1793–1795)
ONE HUNDRED FOR A DOLLAR

Entry continued on next page.

Beaded Border (1793)

Head of 1793 (1793–1794)
Head in high, rounded relief.

Head of 1794 (1794)
*Well-defined hair;
hook on lowest curl.*

Head of 1795 (1794–1796)
*Head in low relief;
no hook on lowest curl.*

	Mintage	AG-3	G-4	VG-8	F-12	VF-20	EF-40
1793, Liberty Cap	11,056	$6,000	$8,500	$11,500	$17,500	$30,000	$85,000
1794, All kinds.	918,521						
1794, "Head of 1793"		1,000	1,250	2,500	6,500	15,000	40,000
1794, "Head of 1794"		200	300	450	1,000	1,750	3,500
1794, "Head of 1795"		200	300	450	1,000	1,650	3,750
1795, Lettered Edge	37,000	200	350	450	1,000	1,650	3,850
1795, Plain Edge	501,500	200	350	450	1,000	1,650	3,000
1796, Liberty Cap	109,825	225	350	600	1,250	2,000	5,250

DRAPED BUST (1796–1807)

AG-3 About Good: Clear enough to identify.
G-4 Good: Lettering worn, but clear; date clear. Bust lacking in detail.
VG-8 Very Good: Drapery on Liberty partly visible. Less wear in date and lettering.
F-12 Fine: Hair over brow smooth; some detail showing in other parts of hair.
VF-20 Very Fine: Hair lines slightly worn. Hair over brow better defined.
EF-40 Extremely Fine: Hair above forehead and left of eye outlined and detailed. Only slight wear on olive leaves.

LIHERTY Error

	Mintage	AG-3	G-4	VG-8	F-12	VF-20	EF-40
1796, Draped Bust	363,375	$115	$200	$350	$800	$1,100	$4,500
1796, LIHERTY Error	*	700	1,250	2,350	3,500	6,000	13,500

* Included in number above.

LARGE CENTS

Gripped Edge		With Stems		Stemless	

	Mintage	AG-3	G-4	VG-8	F-12	VF-20	EF-40
1797, All kinds. 897,510							
1797, Gripped Edge, 1795-Style Reverse . . .		$140	$250	$325	$750	$1,500	$3,750
1797, Plain Edge, 1795-Style Reverse.		225	325	1,050	2,000	3,750	6,500
1797, 1797 Reverse, With Stems.		90	160	275	550	1,000	2,250
1797, 1797 Reverse, Stemless		135	225	600	675	1,500	5,750

1798, 8 Over 7	1799, 9 Over 8	1800 Over 1798	1800, 80 Over 79

	Mintage	AG-3	G-4	VG-8	F-12	VF-20	EF-40
1798, All kinds. 1,841,745							
1798, 8 Over 7		$175	$325	$550	$750	$1,500	$3,500
1798		65	95	225	400	650	1,250
1799, 9 Over 8 . . . . *		3,000	5,500	10,000	20,000	35,000	165,000
1799, Normal Date . . . . *		2,750	3,750	8,500	12,500	25,000	115,000
1800, All kinds. 2,822,175							
1800, 1800 Over 1798		50	70	120	250	600	3,500
1800, 80 Over 79		50	65	135	225	500	2,500
1800, Normal Date		50	70	120	275	500	2,250

* Included in "1798, All kinds," mintage.

Fraction 1/000	Corrected Fraction	1801 Reverse, 3 Errors

	Mintage	AG-3	G-4	VG-8	F-12	VF-20	EF-40
1801, All kinds. 1,362,837							
1801, Normal Reverse.		$50	$70	$125	$275	$400	$1,550
1801, 3 Errors: 1/000, One Stem, and IINITED		100	250	550	1,150	2,750	7,500
1801, Fraction 1/000.		70	105	250	425	1,000	3,750
1801, 1/100 Over 1/000		70	120	250	475	1,150	4,500
1802, All kinds. 3,435,100							
1802, Normal Reverse.		60	90	115	200	350	1,100
1802, Fraction 1/000.		55	90	135	350	475	1,750
1802, Stemless Wreath		55	90	135	275	550	1,150

1803, Small Date, Blunt 1	1803, Large Date, Pointed 1	Small Fraction	Large Fraction

See next page for chart.

	Mintage	AG-3	G-4	VG-8	F-12	VF-20	EF-40
1803, All kinds.	3,131,691						
1803, Small Date, Small Fraction.		$50	$65	$105	$225	$390	$1,000
1803, Small Date, Large Fraction		50	65	105	225	390	1,000
1803, Large Date, Small Fraction		5,000	7,000	11,500	13,500	25,000	
1803, Large Date, Large Fraction		135	225	360	800	2,000	7,500
1803, 1/100 Over 1/000		60	115	180	360	750	1,600
1803, Stemless Wreath		55	90	135	250	375	1,000

Broken Dies

All genuine 1804 cents have crosslet 4 in date and a large fraction.
The 0 in date is in line with O in OF on reverse.

	Mintage	AG-3	G-4	VG-8	F-12	VF-20	EF-40
1804 **(a)**	*96,500*	$1,500	$2,250	$3,250	$4,500	$7,500	$17,500
1805	941,116	50	65	90	180	360	850
1806	348,000	50	65	110	260	425	1,500

a. Values shown are for coins with normal or broken dies.

Small 1807, 7 Over 6
(Blunt 1)

Large 1807, 7 Over 6
(Pointed 1)

	Mintage	AG-3	G-4	VG-8	F-12	VF-20	EF-40
1807, All kinds.	829,221						
1807, Small 7 Over 6, Blunt 1		$1,350	$2,000	$4,500	$16,500	$20,000	
1807, Large 7 Over 6		65	130	190	340	650	$1,000
1807, Small Fraction		60	90	160	260	1,250	7,000
1807, Large Fraction		50	75	100	200	450	1,000

CLASSIC HEAD (1808–1814)

AG-3 About Good: Details clear enough to identify.

G-4 Good: Legends, stars, and date worn, but plain.

VG-8 Very Good: LIBERTY all readable. Liberty's ear visible. Details worn but plain.

F-12 Fine: Hair on forehead and before ear nearly smooth. Ear and hair under ear sharp.

VF-20 Very Fine: Some detail in all hair lines. Slight wear on leaves on reverse.

EF-40 Extremely Fine: All hair lines sharp. Very slight wear on high points.

	Mintage	AG-3	G-4	VG-8	F-12	VF-20	EF-40
1808 1,007,000		$65	$110	$180	$375	$750	$1,750
1809 222,867		120	250	475	1,000	1,500	3,500

1810, 10 Over 09	1810, Normal Date	1811, Last 1 Over 0	1811, Normal Date

	Mintage	AG-3	G-4	VG-8	F-12	VF-20	EF-40
1810, All kinds. 1,458,500							
1810, 10 Over 09		$80	$125	$200	$450	$800	$2,250
1810, Normal Date		75	120	190	400	750	1,750
1811, All kinds. 218,025							
1811, Last 1 Over 0.		140	240	400	800	1,300	7,000
1811, Normal Date		90	150	260	500	1,250	3,000
1812 1,075,500		65	110	200	375	650	1,750
1813 418,000		65	110	200	375	650	1,750
1814 357,830		65	110	200	375	650	1,750

MODIFIED LIBERTY HEAD (1816–1857)

G-4 Good: Details on Liberty's head partly visible. Even wear in date and legends.
VG-8 Very Good: LIBERTY, date, stars, and legends clear. Part of hair cord visible.
F-12 Fine: All hair lines visible. Hair cords uniformly visible.
VF-20 Very Fine: Hair cords only slightly worn. Hair lines only partly worn, all well defined.
EF-40 Extremely Fine: Both hair cords stand out sharply. All hair lines sharp.
AU-50 About Uncirculated: Only traces of wear on hair and highest points on leaves and bow.
MS-60 Uncirculated: Typical brown surface. No trace of wear.
MS-63 Choice Uncirculated: Some distracting contact marks or blemishes in prime focal areas. Impaired luster possible.

Matron Head (1816–1835)

1817, 13 Stars   1817, 15 Stars

Dealers often pay more than the prices shown for brilliant or red Uncirculated coins, and less for spotted, cleaned, or discolored pieces.

	Mintage	G-4	VG-8	F-12	VF-20	EF-40	AU-50	MS-60	MS-63
1816 2,820,982		$20	$25	$35	$70	$205	$300	$550	$800
1817, 13 Stars. 3,948,400		22	25	35	70	150	250	450	800
1817, 15 Stars. . . . . *		28	34	55	130	550	900	2,000	4,500
1818 3,167,000		16	22	29	50	130	200	350	750

* Included in number above.

1819, 9 Over 8

1820, 20 Over 19

	Mintage	G-4	VG-8	F-12	VF-20	EF-40	AU-50	MS-60	MS-63
1819	2,671,000	$16	$21	$30	$50	$135	$260	$525	$1,000
1819, 9 Over 8	*	16	21	30	65	225	450	950	1,500
1820	4,407,550	20	25	30	40	125	225	300	650
1820, 20 Over 19	*	20	25	35	65	300	525	1,000	1,850
1821 **(a)**	389,000	35	50	135	300	950	1,500	7,500	18,000
1822	2,072,339	20	30	50	110	260	500	1,000	1,800

* Included in number above. **a.** Wide and closely spaced AMER varieties are valued the same.

1823, 3 Over 2

1824, 4 Over 2

1826, 6 Over 5

	Mintage	G-4	VG-8	F-12	VF-20	EF-40	AU-50	MS-60	MS-63
1823, 3 Over 2	*	$90	$200	$400	$750	$2,000	$5,500	$17,500	—
1823, Normal Date	*	110	175	400	675	2,150	5,250	16,500	—
1824, 4 Over 2	*	90	110	160	310	675	2,500	10,000	$20,000
1824, Normal Date .	1,262,000	45	90	130	225	400	625	2,250	3,750
1825	1,461,100	35	50	75	110	275	575	1,450	3,000
1826, 6 Over 5	1,517,425	90	110	180	300	750	1,350	7,500	15,000
1826, Normal Date	**	35	55	85	110	210	425	850	1,750
1827	2,357,732	45	65	90	125	165	275	850	2,250

* Included in number below. ** Included in number above.

Date Size, Through 1828

Date Size, 1828 and Later

	Mintage	G-4	VG-8	F-12	VF-20	EF-40	AU-50	MS-60	MS-63
1828, Large Narrow Date	2,260,624	$25	$40	$50	$70	$240	$350	$1,000	$2,000
1828, Small Wide Date	*	75	110	160	225	350	550	1,850	3,000
1829	1,414,500	45	65	90	110	225	400	1,000	2,000
1830	1,711,500	25	35	50	65	160	260	700	2,000
1831	3,359,260	25	35	45	65	120	210	450	750
1832	2,362,000	25	35	45	65	110	200	500	1,250
1833	2,739,000	25	35	45	70	115	210	400	1,000
1834	1,855,100	25	35	45	65	135	325	550	850
1835	3,878,400	25	35	50	60	120	200	750	1,150

* Included in number above.

Matron Head Modified (1835–1839) and Braided Hair (1837–1857)

G-4 Good: Considerably worn. LIBERTY readable.

VG-8 Very Good: Hairlines smooth but visible; outline of ear clearly defined.

F-12 Fine: Hairlines at top of head and behind ear worn but visible. Braid over brow plain; ear clear.

VF-20 Very Fine: All details sharper than for F-12. Only slight wear on hair over brow.

EF-40 Extremely Fine: Hair above ear detailed, but slightly worn.

AU-50 About Uncirculated: Trace of wear on high points of hair above ear and eye and on highest points on leaves and bow.

MS-60 Uncirculated: Typical brown surface. No trace of wear.

MS-63 Choice Uncirculated: Some distracting contact marks or blemishes in prime focal areas. Impaired luster possible.

1839, 1839 Over 1836

Dealers often pay more than the prices shown for brilliant or red Uncirculated coins, and less for spotted, cleaned, or discolored pieces.

	Mintage	G-4	VG-8	F-12	VF-20	EF-40	AU-50	MS-60	MS-63
1836	2,111,000	$22	$35	$50	$65	$110	$300	$475	$750
1837	5,558,300	20	23	30	50	100	160	375	650
1838	6,370,200	20	23	30	50	100	150	275	475
1839	3,128,661	20	25	35	55	165	210	400	600
1839, 1839 Over 1836, Plain Cords . . . . . .*	340	550	1,150	3,500	7,500	15,000	—	—
1840	2,462,700	20	25	30	40	75	185	400	750
1841	1,597,367	20	40	60	95	120	175	650	1,000
1842	2,383,390	20	25	30	40	75	200	500	1,000

* Included in number above.

Small Letters

Large Letters

"Head of 1840" Petite Head (1839–1843)	"Head of 1844" Mature Head (1843–1857)

	Mintage	G-4	VG-8	F-12	VF-20	EF-40	AU-50	MS-60	MS-63
1843, Petite, Small Letters	2,425,342	$20	$25	$30	$35	$65	$160	$450	$850
1843, Petite, Large Letters . . . .*	22	28	35	55	180	290	450	750
1843, Mature, Large Letters . . . .*	25	30	40	60	315	400	525	1,450
1844, Normal Date	2,398,752	20	25	30	35	70	175	450	1,150
1844, 44 Over 81 . . . .*	65	90	110	180	360	675	1,350	2,750
1845	3,894,804	20	25	30	35	40	100	215	375
1846	4,120,800	20	25	30	35	50	125	250	475
1847	6,183,669	20	25	30	35	65	125	275	375
1847, 7 Over "Small 7" . . . .*	45	65	90	110	250	350	1,000	1,850

* Included in number above.

Mintage	G-4	VG-8	F-12	VF-20	EF-40	AU-50	MS-60	MS-63
1848 6,415,799	$20	$25	$30	$40	$65	$135	$250	$450
1849 4,178,500	20	25	30	40	65	175	400	550
1850 4,426,844	20	25	30	35	45	115	150	225

1844, 44 Over 81

1851, 51 Over 81

1847, 7 Over "Small" 7

Dealers often pay more than the prices shown for brilliant or red Uncirculated coins, and less for spotted, cleaned, or discolored pieces.

Mintage	G-4	VG-8	F-12	VF-20	EF-40	AU-50	MS-60	MS-63
1851, Normal Date . . 9,889,707	$20	$25	$30	$40	$45	$100	$150	$250
1851, 51 Over 81 . . . . *	45	65	90	110	160	325	475	1,000
1852 5,063,094	20	25	30	35	45	100	150	250
1853 6,641,131	20	25	30	35	45	100	150	250
1854 4,236,156	20	25	30	35	45	100	150	250

* Included in number above.

1855, Upright 5's

1855, Slanting 5's

1855, Knob on Ear

Mintage	G-4	VG-8	F-12	VF-20	EF-40	AU-50	MS-60	MS-63
1855, All kinds. 1,574,829								
1855, Upright 5's.	$20	$25	$30	$35	$45	$95	$150	$250
1855, Slanting 5's	20	25	30	35	45	125	155	250
1855, Slanting 5's, Knob on Ear.	35	45	65	90	110	200	350	675
1856, Upright 5 2,690,463	20	25	30	35	45	125	150	250
1856, Slanting 5 . . . . *	20	25	30	35	45	125	150	250

* Included in number above.

1857, Large Date

1857, Small Date

Mintage	G-4	VG-8	F-12	VF-20	EF-40	AU-50	MS-60	MS-63
1857, Large Date. . . . 333,546	$45	$85	$115	$150	$200	$300	$500	$1,000
1857, Small Date. . . . . *	45	90	120	150	200	300	500	1,000

* Included in number above.

FLYING EAGLE (1856–1858)

The Act of February 21, 1857, provided for the coinage of the new copper-nickel small cent. The 1856 Flying Eagle cent was not an authorized Mint issue, as the law governing the new-size coin was enacted after the date of issue. It is believed that nearly 1,000 original strikings and 1,500 or more restrikes were made of the 1856. They are properly referred to as *patterns*.

G-4 Good: All details worn, but readable.
VG-8 Very Good: Details in eagle's feathers and eye evident, but worn.
F-12 Fine: Eagle-head details and feather tips sharp.
VF-20 Very Fine: Considerable detail visible in feathers in right wing and tail.
EF-40 Extremely Fine: Slight wear, all details sharp.
AU-50 About Uncirculated: Slight wear on eagle's left wing and breast.
MS-60 Uncirculated: No trace of wear. Light blemishes.
MS-63 Choice Uncirculated: Some distracting contact marks or blemishes in prime focal areas. Some impairment of luster possible.
PF-63 Choice Proof: Nearly perfect.

1858, 8 Over 7

1856–1858, Large Letters

1858, Small Letters

Dealers often pay more than the prices shown for brilliant Uncirculated and Proof coins, and less for spotted, cleaned, or discolored pieces.

	Mintage	G-4	VG-8	F-12	VF-20	EF-40	AU-50	MS-60	MS-63	PF-63
1856	*(1,000–1,500)* **(a)**	$5,500	$6,000	$7,500	$9,000	$9,500	$11,750	$13,000	$18,000	$15,000
1857	17,450,000	16	25	32	50	110	225	475	750	
. . . .	*(100)*									5,500
1858, Large Letters . .	24,600,000	16	25	32	50	110	225	475	750	
. . . .	*(100)*									5,500
1858, 8 Over 7 . . . .*		65	90	115	260	500	850	3,000	6,000	
1858, Small Letters . . . .*		16	25	32	50	110	225	475	800	
. . . .	*(200)*									5,500

* Included in mintage for 1858, Large Letters. **a.** Most of those seen are Proofs; a small number have been designated circulation strikes.

INDIAN HEAD (1859–1909)

The small cent was redesigned in 1859, and a representation of Miss Liberty wearing a Native American war bonnet was adopted as the obverse device. The 1859 reverse was also changed to represent a laurel wreath. In 1860 the reverse was modified to display an oak wreath with a small shield at the top. From 1859 into 1864, cents were struck in copper-nickel. In 1864 the composition was changed to bronze, although copper-nickel cents were also struck during that year.

G-4 Good: No LIBERTY visible.
VG-8 Very Good: At least some letters of LIBERTY readable on head band.
F-12 Fine: LIBERTY mostly visible.
VF-20 Very Fine: Slight but even wear on LIBERTY.
EF-40 Extremely Fine: LIBERTY sharp. All other details sharp. Only slight wear on ribbon end.
AU-50 About Uncirculated: Very slight trace of wear above the ear and the lowest curl of hair.
MS-60 Uncirculated: No trace of wear. Light blemishes.
MS-63 Choice Uncirculated: Some distracting contact marks or blemishes in prime focal areas. Impaired luster possible.
PF-63 Choice Proof: Nearly perfect.

Without Shield at Top of Wreath (1859 Only)

With Shield on Reverse (1860–1909)

Variety 1 – Copper-Nickel, Laurel Wreath Reverse (1859)

Dealers often pay more than the prices shown for brilliant Uncirculated coins, and less for spotted, cleaned, or discolored pieces.

	Mintage	G-4	VG-8	F-12	VF-20	EF-40	AU-50	MS-60	MS-63	PF-63
1859 . . . . . . (800) . . .	36,400,000	$9	$11	$15	$30	$90	$150	$275	$575	$1,350

Variety 2 – Copper-Nickel, Oak Wreath With Shield (1860–1864)

	Mintage	G-4	VG-8	F-12	VF-20	EF-40	AU-50	MS-60	MS-63	PF-63
1860 . . . . . . (1,000) . .	20,566,000	$8	$11	$14	$30	$45	$70	$145	$340	$600
1861 . . . . . . (1,000) . .	10,100,000	18	20	30	45	70	100	145	340	1,000
1862 (1,500–2,000) . .	28,075,000	7	8	10	20	40	60	120	300	600
1863 . . (800–1,000) . .	49,840,000	7	8	10	20	40	60	120	300	600
1864 . . (800–1,000) . .	13,740,000	17	20	25	30	60	90	125	325	600

Variety 3 – Bronze (1864–1909)

1864, Indian Head Cent With "L"

	Mintage	G-4	VG-8	F-12	VF-20	EF-40	AU-50	MS-60	MS-63	PF-63
1864, All kinds.	39,233,714									
1864, No L (150).		$10	$15	$20	$35	$45	$55	$80	$95	$450
1864, With L (20).		35	60	100	130	175	210	300	375	—
1865 . . (750–1,000) . .	35,429,286	10	13	20	25	35	50	85	125	250
1866 . . (725–1,000) . .	9,826,500	40	50	65	90	135	180	260	375	175
1867 . . (850–1,100) . .	9,821,000	40	55	70	90	135	180	240	320	175
1868 . . (750–1,000) . .	10,266,500	40	50	70	90	135	180	225	300	225
1869 . . (850–1,100) . .	6,420,000	60	90	160	200	300	390	525	625	550
1870 . . . . . . (1,000) . .	5,275,000	45	95	125	175	220	300	450	500	450
1871 . . . . (960) . .	3,929,500	60	85	125	165	325	400	500	590	225
1872 . . (850–1,100) . .	4,042,000	75	105	160	260	350	450	550	650	200
1873 (1,500–2,000) . .	11,676,500	16	32	50	60	125	160	220	325	250
1874 (1,000–1,200) . .	14,187,500	16	26	45	50	75	105	135	180	250
1875 (1,000–1,250) . .	13,528,000	16	26	45	50	90	120	165	210	300
1876 (1,500–2,000) . . .	7,944,000	25	35	60	100	140	190	225	250	175
1877 (1,250–1,500)	852,500	350	500	700	1,000	1,650	2,250	3,350	4,500	2,750

Dealers often pay more than the prices shown for brilliant or red Uncirculated coins, and less for spotted, cleaned, or discolored pieces.

	Mintage	G-4	VG-8	F-12	VF-20	EF-40	AU-50	MS-60	MS-63	PF-63
1878 . . . . (2,350). . . 5,797,500		$22.00	$28.00	$50.00	$110.00	$165.00	$200	$240	$260	$165
1879 . . . . (3,200). . 16,228,000		5.00	7.00	13.00	26.00	45.00	50	60	115	165
1880 . . . . (3,955). . 38,961,000		2.00	2.50	5.00	8.50	20.00	33	45	60	165
1881 . . . . (3,575). . 39,208,000		2.00	2.50	5.00	6.00	18.00	33	38	60	165
1882 . . . . (3,100). . 38,578,000		2.00	2.50	5.00	6.00	18.00	25	38	70	165
1883 . . . . (6,609). . 45,591,500		2.00	2.50	5.00	6.00	18.00	26	38	80	165
1884 . . . . (3,942). . 23,257,800		3.50	5.00	5.50	11.00	22.00	35	46	75	165
1885 . . . . (3,790). . 11,761,594		7.50	8.00	10.00	22.00	48.00	60	90	125	165
1886 . . . . (4,290). . 17,650,000		4.50	8.00	14.00	46.00	115.00	130	150	195	200
1887 . . . . (2,960). . 45,223,523		1.50	2.00	3.00	4.00	14.00	22	35	75	165
1888 . . . . (4,582). . 37,489,832		2.50	2.75	3.00	5.50	16.00	18	48	105	165
1889 . . . . (3,336). . 48,866,025		0.85	1.50	2.00	3.00	8.00	18	38	55	165
1890 . . . . (2,740). . 57,180,114		0.85	1.50	2.00	2.75	7.00	18	38	55	165
1891 . . . . (2,350). . 47,070,000		0.85	1.50	2.00	2.75	8.00	18	38	60	165
1892 . . . . (2,745). . 37,647,087		1.50	1.75	2.50	3.50	9.00	18	38	78	165
1893 . . . . (2,195). . 46,640,000		1.25	1.50	2.00	3.00	7.00	18	38	75	165
1894 . . . . (2,632). . 16,749,500		4.00	5.00	10.00	14.00	33.00	45	65	105	165
1895 . . . . (2,062). . 38,341,574		0.85	1.10	1.50	2.00	4.50	20	32	70	165
1896 . . . . (1,862). . 39,055,431		0.85	1.10	1.50	2.00	4.50	18	32	65	165
1897 . . . . (1,938). . 50,464,392		0.85	1.10	1.50	2.00	4.50	18	32	60	165
1898 . . . . (1,795). . 49,821,284		0.85	1.10	1.50	2.00	4.50	15	28	60	165
1899 . . . . (2,031). . 53,598,000		0.85	1.10	1.50	2.00	4.50	15	28	55	165
1900 . . . . (2,262). . 66,831,502		0.80	1.00	1.40	2.00	4.50	15	28	55	165
1901 . . . . (1,985). . 79,609,158		0.80	1.00	1.40	2.00	4.50	15	28	55	165
1902 . . . . (2,018). . 87,374,704		0.80	1.00	1.40	2.00	4.50	15	28	55	165
1903 . . . . (1,790). . 85,092,703		0.80	1.00	1.40	2.00	4.50	15	28	55	165
1904 . . . . (1,817). . 61,326,198		0.80	1.00	1.40	2.00	4.50	15	28	55	165
1905 . . . . (2,152). . 80,717,011		0.80	1.00	1.40	2.00	4.50	15	28	55	165
1906 . . . . (1,725). . 96,020,530		0.80	1.00	1.40	2.00	4.50	15	28	55	165
1907 . . . . (1,475). 108,137,143		0.80	1.00	1.40	2.00	4.50	15	28	55	165

Location of Mintmark S on Reverse of
Indian Head Cent (1908 and 1909 Only)

	Mintage	G-4	VG-8	F-12	VF-20	EF-40	AU-50	MS-60	MS-63	PF-63
1908 . . . . (1,620). . . 32,326,367		$0.80	$1.00	$1.40	$2	$4.50	$15	$28	$55	$165
1908S 1,115,000		65.00	75.00	90.00	100	150.00	165	220	375	
1909 . . . . (2,175). . . 14,368,470		3.50	5.50	6.25	8	13.00	20	30	60	165
1909S 309,000		225.00	250.00	300.00	400	450.00	550	775	1,150	

LINCOLN, WHEAT EARS REVERSE (1909–1958)

Victor D. Brenner designed this cent, which was issued to commemorate the 100th anniversary of Abraham Lincoln's birth. The designer's initials (V.D.B.) appear on the reverse of a limited quantity of cents of 1909. Later in the year they were removed from the dies but restored in 1918 as very small incuse letters beneath the shoulder. The Lincoln type was the first cent to have the motto IN GOD WE TRUST.

G-4 Good: Date worn but apparent. Lines in wheat heads missing. Full rims.
VG-8 Very Good: Half of lines visible in upper wheat heads.
F-12 Fine: Wheat lines worn but visible.
VF-20 Very Fine: Lincoln's cheekbone and jawbone worn but separated. No worn spots on wheat heads.
EF-40 Extremely Fine: Slight wear. All details sharp.
AU-50 About Uncirculated: Slight wear on cheek and jaw and on wheat stalks.
MS-60 Uncirculated: No trace of wear. Light blemishes. Brown or red-brown color.
MS-63 Choice Uncirculated: No trace of wear. Slight blemishes. Red-brown color.
MS-65 Gem Uncirculated: No trace of wear. Barely noticeable blemishes. Nearly full red color.
PF-63 Choice Proof: Reflective surfaces with only a few blemishes in secondary focal places. No major flaws.

Location of mintmark S or D on obverse of Lincoln cent.

Designer's Initials V.D.B. (1909 Only)

No V.D.B. on Reverse (1909–1958)

Dealers often pay more than the prices shown for brilliant Uncirculated coins, and less for spotted, cleaned, or discolored pieces.

	Mintage	G-4	VG-8	F-12	VF-20	EF-40	AU-50	MS-60	MS-63	MATTE PF-63
1909, V.D.B.										
. . . (1,194). . .27,995,000		$3.00	$4.00	$5.00	$7.00	$9.00	$10.00	$15.00	$20.00	$8,500
1909S, V.D.B. 484,000		550.00	625.00	750.00	850.00	1,100.00	1,200.00	1,450.00	1,750.00	
1909 . . . (2,618). . .72,702,618		1.10	1.35	1.75	2.20	4.50	7.50	9.00	15.00	450
1909S 1,825,000		55.00	60.00	75.00	100.00	110.00	150.00	250.00	275.00	
1910 . . . (4,083). .146,801,218		0.20	0.25	0.30	0.40	2.75	6.50	12.00	16.00	375
1910S 6,045,000		9.00	11.00	14.00	18.00	35.00	52.50	70.00	80.00	
1911 . . . (1,725). .101,177,787		0.20	0.25	0.80	1.25	5.00	7.50	12.00	25.00	375
1911D 12,672,000		3.75	4.75	7.50	18.00	40.00	50.00	60.00	95.00	
1911S 4,026,000		20.00	25.00	30.00	35.00	50.00	70.00	125.00	210.00	
1912 . . . (2,172). . .68,153,060		0.80	1.25	1.75	4.00	9.00	18.00	22.00	30.00	375
1912D 10,411,000		5.00	7.00	8.00	22.00	50.00	77.50	120.00	200.00	
1912S 4,431,000		11.00	13.00	15.00	26.00	47.50	75.00	125.00	180.00	
1913 . . . (2,983). . .76,532,352		0.25	0.40	1.25	2.50	14.00	20.00	24.00	40.00	375
1913D 15,804,000		1.50	1.75	2.20	5.50	35.00	45.00	70.00	145.00	
1913S 6,101,000		5.50	8.00	10.50	18.00	37.50	75.00	140.00	200.00	
1914 . . . (1,365). . .75,238,432		0.35	0.60	1.25	4.00	13.50	28.00	38.00	50.00	375
1914D **(a)** 1,193,000		115.00	165.00	200.00	250.00	600.00	1,000.00	1,850.00	2,750.00	
1914S 4,137,000		11.00	14.00	16.00	20.00	60.00	95.00	220.00	325.00	
1915 . . . (1,150). . .29,092,120		1.10	2.00	2.75	7.50	30.00	35.00	50.00	70.00	375
1915D 22,050,000		1.10	2.10	4.50	7.50	22.00	32.50	50.00	70.00	
1915S 4,833,000		10.00	12.00	17.00	22.00	52.50	70.00	200.00	400.00	
1916 . . . (1,050). .131,833,677		0.15	0.20	0.40	1.50	5.50	10.00	12.50	17.50	1,250
1916D 35,956,000		0.35	0.65	1.75	2.50	9.00	20.00	60.00	75.00	
1916S 22,510,000		0.60	1.25	2.20	9.00	19.00	34.00	75.00	125.00	
1917 196,429,785		0.10	0.15	0.20	0.75	3.00	8.00	11.00	20.00	
1917D 55,120,000		0.35	0.75	2.00	3.00	25.00	32.00	50.00	100.00	
1917S 32,620,000		0.30	0.40	0.80	1.75	7.50	17.50	50.00	115.00	

a. Beware of altered date or mintmark. No V.D.B. on shoulder of genuine 1914-D cent.

SMALL CENTS

Designer's initials placed on Lincoln's shoulder next to rim, starting in 1918.

For brilliant Unc. coins before 1934, dealers usually pay more than the prices shown. They pay less for spotted, cleaned, or discolored pieces.

Mintage	G-4	VG-8	F-12	VF-20	EF-40	AU-50	MS-60	MS-63
1918 288,104,634	$0.10	$0.15	$0.20	$0.35	$2.75	$5.00	$8.00	$13.00
1918D 47,830,000	0.35	0.60	0.80	2.50	10.00	22.00	52.00	100.00
1918S 34,680,000	0.15	0.50	0.80	2.00	7.50	20.00	50.00	125.00
1919 392,021,000	0.10	0.15	0.20	0.25	0.80	3.25	5.00	13.00
1919D 57,154,000	0.35	0.80	1.10	2.50	7.00	18.00	42.50	75.00
1919S 139,760,000	0.10	0.20	0.60	1.75	4.00	11.00	32.50	80.00
1920 310,165,000	0.08	0.10	0.25	0.60	1.75	4.75	10.00	15.00
1920D 49,280,000	0.25	0.35	0.80	1.75	8.00	24.00	50.00	80.00
1920S 46,220,000	0.25	0.35	0.80	1.75	8.00	24.00	75.00	125.00
1921 39,157,000	0.20	0.30	0.45	1.75	7.50	14.00	30.00	42.50
1921S 15,274,000	0.90	1.25	2.50	4.25	25.00	47.50	75.00	165.00
1922D 7,160,000	11.00	13.50	15.00	18.50	28.50	47.50	75.00	165.00
1922, No D **(b)** . . . . . . *	375.00	500.00	600.00	725.00	1,350.00	2,750.00	7,500.00	15,000.00
1923 74,723,000	0.08	0.10	0.15	0.50	3.00	6.50	8.00	14.00
1923S 8,700,000	4.00	5.00	6.00	7.50	32.50	60.00	170.00	400.00
1924 75,178,000	0.05	0.08	0.12	0.25	2.50	5.00	12.00	25.00
1924D 2,520,000	19.00	23.00	30.00	35.00	75.00	95.00	200.00	400.00
1924S 11,696,000	0.75	0.85	1.50	3.25	22.00	55.00	80.00	250.00
1925 139,949,000	0.05	0.08	0.12	0.25	1.75	3.25	6.00	10.00
1925D 22,580,000	0.35	0.45	1.20	1.60	9.00	20.00	42.50	85.00
1925S 26,380,000	0.35	0.45	1.20	1.60	7.00	19.00	70.00	165.00
1926 157,088,000	0.05	0.08	0.12	0.25	0.85	3.25	5.00	8.00
1926D 28,020,000	0.75	0.90	2.00	4.00	10.00	22.00	75.00	120.00
1926S 4,550,000	6.50	8.00	9.00	11.00	25.00	50.00	175.00	375.00
1927 144,440,000	0.05	0.08	0.12	0.25	0.85	3.25	5.00	9.00
1927D 27,170,000	0.35	0.60	0.85	1.75	5.00	17.50	40.00	60.00
1927S 14,276,000	0.35	0.60	0.85	1.75	10.00	27.50	65.00	145.00
1928 134,116,000	0.05	0.08	0.12	0.20	0.65	2.50	5.00	10.00
1928D 31,170,000	0.25	0.45	0.80	1.50	4.00	12.50	30.00	55.00
1928S 17,266,000	0.30	0.45	0.80	1.60	6.00	22.00	65.00	80.00
1929 185,262,000	0.05	0.08	0.12	0.20	1.00	3.25	4.25	6.00
1929D 41,730,000	0.20	0.45	0.75	1.75	4.00	9.00	16.00	35.00
1929S 50,148,000	0.20	0.45	1.20	1.75	4.25	10.00	12.50	20.00
1930 157,415,000	0.05	0.08	0.10	0.20	0.60	1.75	2.50	3.50
1930D 40,100,000	0.06	0.10	0.15	0.30	1.20	3.25	6.50	10.00
1930S 24,286,000	0.06	0.10	0.20	0.65	0.85	4.25	6.00	7.00
1931 19,396,000	0.35	0.40	0.50	1.10	2.50	7.00	12.50	15.00
1931D 4,480,000	3.25	3.75	4.25	5.00	8.50	22.50	35.00	55.00
1931S 866,000	45.00	50.00	60.00	70.00	75.00	90.00	100.00	135.00
1932 9,062,000	0.90	1.10	1.75	2.25	4.00	8.50	11.50	15.00
1932D 10,500,000	0.90	1.00	1.25	1.75	2.50	8.00	11.50	19.00
1933 14,360,000	0.90	1.00	1.50	1.75	4.00	8.00	11.00	15.00
1933D 6,200,000	2.50	2.75	3.50	5.00	8.00	12.50	16.50	20.00

* Included in number above. **b.** 1922 cents with a weak or missing mintmark were made from extremely worn dies that originally struck normal 1922-D cents. Three different die pairs were involved; two of them produced "Weak D" coins. One die pair (no. 2, identified by a "strong reverse") is acknowledged as striking "No D" coins. Weak D cents are worth considerably less. Beware of removed mintmark.

Chart continued on next page.

	Mintage	G-4	VG-8	F-12	VF-20	EF-40	AU-50	MS-60	MS-63	PF-63
1934	219,080,000	$0.03	$0.03	$0.03	$0.03	$0.10	$1.00	$3.00	$4.50	
1934D	28,446,000	0.04	0.06	0.08	0.15	0.50	2.00	9.00	15.00	
1935	245,388,000	0.03	0.03	0.03	0.04	0.06	0.20	2.00	3.00	
1935D	47,000,000	0.03	0.03	0.03	0.04	0.20	0.50	3.00	4.00	
1935S	38,702,000	0.03	0.04	0.04	0.04	0.12	1.25	4.00	6.00	
1936 . . . . (5,569) . .	309,632,000	0.03	0.03	0.03	0.04	0.06	0.25	1.00	3.00	$300
1936D	40,620,000	0.03	0.03	0.03	0.04	0.08	0.20	1.00	3.00	
1936S	29,130,000	0.03	0.03	0.03	0.04	0.10	0.20	1.00	3.00	
1937 . . . . (9,320) . .	309,170,000	0.02	0.03	0.03	0.03	0.05	0.20	0.50	3.00	50
1937D	50,430,000	0.02	0.03	0.03	0.03	0.06	0.30	0.80	4.00	
1937S	34,500,000	0.03	0.03	0.03	0.04	0.06	0.30	0.80	4.00	
1938 . . . (14,734) . .	156,682,000	0.02	0.03	0.03	0.03	0.05	0.30	0.75	2.00	40
1938D	20,010,000	0.02	0.03	0.05	0.06	0.15	0.50	1.00	5.00	
1938S	15,180,000	0.06	0.08	0.10	0.12	0.15	0.30	1.00	4.00	
1939 . . . (13,520) . .	316,466,000	0.02	0.03	0.03	0.03	0.03	0.20	0.30	2.50	40
1939D	15,160,000	0.06	0.08	0.10	0.12	0.15	0.35	1.00	4.00	
1939S	52,070,000	0.03	0.03	0.05	0.08	0.10	0.30	1.00	4.00	
1940 . . . (15,872) . .	586,810,000	0.02	0.03	0.03	0.03	0.03	0.20	0.30	2.00	30
1940D	81,390,000	0.02	0.03	0.03	0.03	0.03	0.20	0.40	2.00	
1940S	112,940,000	0.02	0.03	0.03	0.03	0.04	0.20	0.40	2.75	
1941 . . . (21,100) . .	887,018,000	0.02	0.03	0.03	0.03	0.03	0.20	0.30	2.00	30
1941D	128,700,000	0.02	0.03	0.03	0.03	0.03	0.40	0.80	3.00	
1941S	92,360,000	0.02	0.03	0.03	0.03	0.04	0.35	1.00	4.00	
1942 . . . (32,600) . .	657,796,000	0.02	0.03	0.03	0.03	0.03	0.10	0.15	1.00	30
1942D	206,698,000	0.02	0.03	0.03	0.03	0.03	0.10	0.25	1.50	
1942S	85,590,000	0.02	0.03	0.03	0.03	0.10	1.00	2.25	6.00	

Variety 2 – Zinc-Coated Steel (1943)

	Mintage	F-12	VF-20	EF-40	MS-60	MS-63	MS-65
1943	684,628,670	$0.05	$0.10	$0.15	$0.70	$1.25	$3.25
1943D	217,660,000	0.05	0.10	0.15	0.90	2.00	4.50
1943S	191,550,000	0.06	0.12	0.20	1.20	2.75	9.00

Variety 1 (Bronze) Resumed (1944–1958)

1944-D, D Over S

1955, Doubled-Die Obverse

	Mintage	VF-20	EF-40	MS-63	MS-65	PF-65
1944	1,435,400,000	$0.03	$0.03	$0.25	$1.60	
1944D	430,578,000	0.03	0.03	0.20	1.50	
1944D, D Over S . . . . *		65.00	85.00	225.00	450.00	
1944S	282,760,000	0.03	0.03	0.20	1.50	

* Included in number above.

SMALL CENTS

	Mintage	VF-20	EF-40	MS-63	MS-65	PF-65
1945	1,040,515,000	$0.03	$0.03	$0.20	$0.50	
1945D	266,268,000	0.03	0.03	0.15	0.50	
1945S	181,770,000	0.03	0.03	0.10	1.00	
1946	991,655,000	0.03	0.03	0.10	0.50	
1946D	315,690,000	0.03	0.03	0.15	1.00	
1946S	198,100,000	0.03	0.03	0.15	1.25	
1947	190,555,000	0.03	0.03	0.25	0.75	
1947D	194,750,000	0.03	0.03	0.12	0.50	
1947S	99,000,000	0.03	0.03	0.15	1.50	
1948	317,570,000	0.03	0.03	0.15	0.50	
1948D	172,637,500	0.03	0.03	0.12	0.60	
1948S	81,735,000	0.03	0.03	0.20	1.50	
1949	217,775,000	0.03	0.03	0.30	0.75	
1949D	153,132,500	0.03	0.03	0.20	0.75	
1949S	64,290,000	0.04	0.05	0.50	2.00	
1950 (51,386)	272,635,000	0.03	0.03	0.25	0.50	$45
1950D	334,950,000	0.03	0.03	0.10	0.50	
1950S	118,505,000	0.03	0.03	0.25	0.80	
1951 (57,500)	284,576,000	0.03	0.03	0.25	0.80	40
1951D	625,355,000	0.03	0.03	0.10	0.50	
1951S	136,010,000	0.03	0.03	0.25	0.60	
1952 (81,980)	186,775,000	0.03	0.03	0.15	0.60	20
1952D	746,130,000	0.03	0.03	0.15	0.60	
1952S	137,800,004	0.03	0.03	0.50	1.50	
1953 (128,800)	256,755,000	0.03	0.03	0.10	0.50	15
1953D	700,515,000	0.03	0.03	0.10	0.50	
1953S	181,835,000	0.03	0.04	0.12	0.75	
1954 (233,300)	71,640,050	0.03	0.06	0.15	0.85	10
1954D	251,552,500	0.03	0.03	0.05	0.30	
1954S	96,190,000	0.03	0.03	0.05	0.30	
1955 (378,200)	330,958,200	0.03	0.03	0.06	0.30	5
1955, Doubled-Die Obverse	*	1,000.00	1,100.00 (a)	1,350.00	3,500.00	
1955D	563,257,500	0.03	0.03	0.05	0.25	
1955S	44,610,000	0.10	0.15	0.15	0.50	
1956 (669,384)	420,745,000	0.03	0.03	0.05	0.25	3
1956D	1,098,201,100	0.03	0.03	0.05	0.30	
1957 (1,247,952)	282,540,000	0.03	0.03	0.05	0.30	3
1957D	1,051,342,000	0.03	0.03	0.05	0.30	
1958 (875,652)	252,525,000	0.03	0.03	0.05	0.30	3
1958D	800,953,300	0.03	0.03	0.05	0.30	

* Included in number above. **a.** For MS-60 Uncirculated coins, dealers usually pay $1,200.

LINCOLN, MEMORIAL REVERSE (1959–2008)

Small Date   Large Date

	Mintage	MS-63	MS-65	PF-65
1959 (1,149,291)	609,715,000	$0.02	$0.10	$1.50

1969-S, Doubled-Die Obverse	Small Date, Numbers Aligned at Top	Large Date, Low 7 in Date	Enlarged Detail of 1972 Doubled-Die Obverse

	Mintage	MS-63	MS-65	PF-63
1959D 1,279,760,000		$0.02	$0.10	
1960, Lg Dt . . 586,405,000		0.02	0.10	
. . . . (1,691,602)				$0.75
1960, Sm Dt . . . . *		1.00	2.70	
. . . . *				9.50
1960D,				
Lg Dt . . 1,580,884,000		0.02	0.10	
1960D, Sm Dt . . . . *		0.02	0.10	
1961 753,345,000		0.02	0.10	
. . . . (3,028,244)				0.50
1961D 1,753,266,700		0.02	0.10	
1962 606,045,000		0.02	0.10	
. . . . (3,218,019)				0.50
1962D 1,793,148,140		0.02	0.10	
1963 754,110,000		0.02	0.10	
. . . . (3,075,645)				0.50
1963D 1,774,020,400		0.02	0.10	
1964 2,648,575,000		0.02	0.10	
. . . . (3,950,762)				0.50
1964D 3,799,071,500		0.02	0.10	
1965 1,497,224,900		0.03	0.12	
1966 2,188,147,783		0.04	0.12	
1967 3,048,667,100		0.03	0.12	
1968 1,707,880,970		0.03	0.12	
1968D 2,886,269,600		0.02	0.12	
1968S 258,270,001		0.02	0.15	
. . . . (3,041,506)				0.35
1969 1,136,910,000		0.05	0.20	
1969D 4,002,832,200		0.03	0.15	
1969S 544,375,000		0.03	0.15	
. . . . (2,934,631)				0.35
1969S, DDO . . . . *		20,000.00	—	
1970 1,898,315,000		0.05	0.20	
1970D 2,891,438,900		0.02	0.10	
1970S, Sm Dt				
(High 7) . . . . (a)		20.00	30.00	
. . . . (b)				20.00
1970S, Lg Dt				
(Low 7) . 690,560,004		0.03	0.20	
. . . . (2,632,810)				0.25
1971 1,919,490,000		$0.05	$0.20	
1971D 2,911,045,600		0.03	0.20	
1971S 525,133,459		0.03	0.20	
. . . . (3,220,733)				$0.25
1972, DDO . . . . **		250.00	325.00	
1972 2,933,255,000		0.02	0.10	
1972D 2,665,071,400		0.02	0.10	
1972S 376,939,108		0.02	0.10	
. . . . (3,260,996)				0.25
1973 3,728,245,000		0.02	0.10	
1973D 3,549,576,588		0.02	0.10	
1973S 317,177,295		0.02	0.15	
. . . . (2,760,339)				0.25
1974 4,232,140,523		0.02	0.10	
1974D 4,235,098,000		0.02	0.10	
1974S 409,426,660		0.03	0.20	
. . . . (2,612,568)				0.25
1975 5,451,476,142		0.02	0.10	
1975D 4,505,275,300		0.02	0.10	
1975S . . . . (2,845,450)				1.60
1976 4,674,292,426		0.02	0.10	
1976D 4,221,592,455		0.02	0.10	
1976S . . . . (4,149,730)				1.25
1977 4,469,930,000		0.02	0.10	
1977D 4,194,062,300		0.02	0.10	
1977S . . . . (3,251,152)				1.00
1978 5,558,605,000		0.02	0.10	
1978D 4,280,233,400		0.02	0.10	
1978S . . . . (3,127,781)				1.00
1979 6,018,515,000		0.02	0.10	
1979D 4,139,357,254		0.02	0.10	
1979S, Type 1 . . (3,677,175)				1.75
1979S, Type 2 . . . . *				2.00
1980 7,414,705,000		0.02	0.10	
1980D 5,140,098,660		0.02	0.10	
1980S . . . . (3,554,806)				1.00
1981 7,491,750,000		0.02	0.10	
1981D 5,373,235,677		0.02	0.10	
1981S, Type 1 . . (4,063,083)				1.50
1981S, Type 2 . . . . *				14.00

* Included in number above. ** Included in number below. **a.** Included in circulation-strike mintage for 1970-S, Large Date (Low 7). **b.** Included in Proof mintage for 1970-S, Large Date (Low 7).

	Large Date					Small Date		

	Mintage	MS-63	MS-65	PF-63
1982, Lg Dt . .10,712,525,000	$0.02	$0.10	
1982, Sm Dt . . . .*	0.03	0.12	

	Mintage	MS-63	MS-65	PF-63
1982D, Lg Dt. .6,012,979,368	$0.02	$0.10	
1982S, Sm Dt . . (3,857,479)			$1.60

* Included in number above.

Copper-Plated Zinc (1982–2008)

	Close AM		Wide AM	

1995, Doubled Die showing strong doubling on word LIBERTY.

	Mintage	MS-63	MS-65	PF-63
1982, Lg Dt . . . .*	$0.02	$0.25	
1982, Sm Dt . . . .*	0.02	0.30	
1982D, Lg Dt. . . . .*	0.05	0.20	
1982D, Sm Dt . . . .*	0.01	0.10	
1983 7,752,355,000	0.01	0.10	
1983D 6,467,199,428	0.01	0.10	
1983S . . . . (3,279,126)	0.01	0.05	$1.10
1984 8,151,079,000	0.01	0.05	
1984, Dbl Ear . . . .**	50.00	100.00	
1984D 5,569,238,906	0.01	0.10	
1984S . . . . (3,065,110)			1.10
1985 5,648,489,887	0.01	0.05	
1985D 5,287,339,926	0.01	0.05	
1985S . . . . (3,362,821)			1.25
1986 4,491,395,493	0.01	0.06	
1986D 4,442,866,698	0.01	0.05	
1986S . . . . (3,010,497)			2.00
1987 4,682,466,931	0.01	0.05	
1987D 4,879,389,514	0.01	0.05	
1987S . . . . (4,227,728)			1.10
1988 6,092,810,000	0.01	0.05	
1988D 5,253,740,443	0.01	0.05	
1988S . . . . (3,262,948)			2.00
1989 7,261,535,000	0.01	0.05	
1989D 5,345,467,111	0.01	0.05	
1989S . . . . (3,220,194)			2.00
1990 6,851,765,000	0.01	0.05	
1990D 4,922,894,533	0.01	0.05	
1990S . . . . (3,299,559)			2.00
1990, Pf, No S . . . .**		—	
1991 5,165,940,000	0.01	0.05	

	Mintage	MS-63	MS-65	PF-63
1991D 4,158,446,076	$0.01	$0.05	
1991S . . . . (2,867,787)			$6.75
1992 4,648,905,000	0.01	0.05	
1992, Close AM **(a)** . . . . . .**	—	—	
1992D 4,448,673,300	0.01	0.05	
1992D, Close AM **(a)** . . . . .**	—	—	
1992S . . . . (4,176,560)			1.10
1993 5,684,705,000	0.01	0.05	
1993D 6,426,650,571	0.01	0.05	
1993S . . . . (3,394,792)			3.00
1994 6,500,850,000	0.01	0.05	
1994D 7,131,765,000	0.01	0.05	
1994S . . . . (3,269,923)			3.00
1995 6,411,440,000	0.01	0.05	
1995, DblDie Obv . . . .**	20.00	26.00	
1995D 7,128,560,000	0.01	0.05	
1995S . . . . (2,797,481)			3.00
1996 6,612,465,000	0.01	0.05	
1996D 6,510,795,000	0.01	0.05	
1996S . . . . (2,525,265)			1.25
1997 4,622,800,000	0.01	0.05	
1997D 4,576,555,000	0.01	0.05	
1997S . . . . (2,796,678)			4.00
1998 5,032,155,000	0.01	0.05	
1998, Wide AM **(b)**. . . . . . .**	2.00	10.00	
1998D 5,225,353,500	0.01	0.05	
1998S . . . . (2,086,507)			3.00
1998S, Close AM **(a)** . . . . .**			150.00
1999 5,237,600,000	0.01	0.05	
1999, Wide AM **(b)**. . . . . . .**		—	
1999D 6,360,065,000	0.01	0.05	

* Included in previous section's mintages. ** Included in number above. **a.** The circulation-strike hub adopted in 1993, with AM almost touching, was accidentally used on these cents. **b.** Varieties were made using Proof dies that have a wide space between AM in AMERICA. The letters nearly touch on other Uncirculated cents.

Chart continued on next page.

	Mintage	MS-63	MS-65	PF-63
1999S . . . . (3,347,966)				$2.00
1999S, Close AM (a) . . . . .**				30.00
2000 5,503,200,000	$0.01	$0.05		
2000, Wide AM (b). . . . . . .**	2.00	5.00		
2000D 8,774,220,000	0.01	0.05		
2000S . . . . (4,047,993)				1.20
2001 4,959,600,000	0.01	0.05		
2001D 5,374,990,000	0.01	0.05		
2001S . . . . (3,184,606)				1.20
2002 3,260,800,000	0.01	0.05		
2002D 4,028,055,000	0.01	0.05		
2002S . . . . (3,211,995)				1.20
2003 3,300,000,000	0.01	0.05		
2003D 3,548,000,000	0.01	0.05		
2003S . . . . (3,298,439)				1.20

	Mintage	MS-63	MS-65	PF-63
2004 3,379,600,000	$0.01	$0.05		
2004D 3,456,400,000	0.01	0.05		
2004S . . . . (2,965,422)				$1.20
2005 3,935,600,000	0.01	0.05		
2005D 3,764,450,500	0.01	0.05		
2005S . . . . (3,344,679)				1.20
2006 4,290,000,000	0.01	0.05		
2006D 3,944,000,000	0.01	0.05		
2006S . . . . (3,054,436)				1.20
2007 3,762,400,000	0.01	0.05		
2007D 3,638,800,000	0.01	0.05		
2007S . . . . (2,577,166)				1.20
2008 2,558,800,000	0.01	0.05		
2008D 2,849,600,000	0.01	0.05		
2008S . . . . (2,169,561)				1.20

** Included in number above. **a.** The circulation-strike hub adopted in 1993, with AM almost touching, was accidentally used on these cents. **b.** Varieties were made using Proof dies that have a wide space between AM in AMERICA. The letters nearly touch on other Uncirculated cents.

LINCOLN, BICENTENNIAL (2009)

One-cent coins issued during 2009 are a unique tribute to President Abraham Lincoln, recognizing the bicentennial of his birth and the 100th anniversary of the first issuance of the Lincoln cent. These coins use four different design themes on the reverse to represent the four major aspects of President Lincoln's life. The obverse of each of these coins carries the traditional portrait of Lincoln that has been in use since 1909.

The special reverse designs, released as quarterly issues throughout 2009, are described as: Birth and Early Childhood in Kentucky (designer, Richard Masters; sculptor, Jim Licaretz); Formative Years in Indiana (designer and sculptor, Charles Vickers); Professional Life in Illinois (designer, Joel Iskowitz; sculptor, Don Everhart); and Presidency in Washington (designer, Susan Gamble; sculptor, Joseph Menna). Those issued for commercial circulation are made of the exact same copper-plated composition used since 1982. Special versions included in collector sets are made of the same metallic composition as was used for the original 1909 cents (95% copper, 5% tin and zinc).

2009 Lincoln cent reverse designs

	Mintage	MS-63	MS-65	PF-65
2009, Birth and Early Childhood.	284,400,000	$0.05	$0.10	
2009, Birth and Early Childhood, copper, Satin finish.	784,614		4.00	
2009D, Birth and Early Childhood	350,400,000	0.05	0.10	
2009D, Birth and Early Childhood, copper, Satin finish.	784,614		4.00	
2009S, Birth and Early Childhood . . . . (2,995,615)				$2
2009, Formative Years.	376,000,000	0.05	0.10	
2009, Formative Years, copper, Satin finish	784,614		4.00	
2009D, Formative Years.	363,600,000	0.05	0.10	

	Mintage	MS-63	MS-65	PF-65
2009D, Formative Years, copper, Satin finish	784,614		$4.00	
2009S, Formative Years	(2,995,615)			$2
2009, Professional Life	316,000,000	$0.05	0.10	
2009, Professional Life, copper, Satin finish	784,614		4.00	
2009D, Professional Life	336,000,000	0.05	0.10	
2009D, Professional Life, copper, Satin finish	784,614		4.00	
2009S, Professional Life	(2,995,615)			2
2009, Presidency	129,600,000	0.05	0.10	
2009, Presidency, copper, Satin finish	784,614		4.00	
2009D, Presidency	198,000,000	0.05	0.10	
2009D, Presidency, copper, Satin finish	784,614		4.00	
2009S, Presidency	(2,995,615)			2

LINCOLN, SHIELD REVERSE (2010 TO DATE)

Since the conclusion of the 2009 Bicentennial One-Cent Program, one-cent coins feature a reverse that has "an image emblematic of President Lincoln's preservation of the United States of America as a single and united country." The Union Shield design is by Lyndall Bass, sculpted by Joseph Menna.

	Mintage	MS-65	PF-63
2010	1,963,630,000	$0.01	
2010D	2,047,200,000	0.01	
2010S	(1,689,216)		$2
2011	2,402,400,000	0.01	
2011D	2,536,140,000	0.01	
2011S	(1,673,010)		2
2012	3,132,000,000	0.01	
2012D	2,883,200,000	0.01	
2012S	(1,239,148)		2
2013	3,750,400,000	0.01	
2013D	3,319,600,000	0.01	
2013S	(1,274,505)		2
2014	3,990,800,000	0.01	
2014D	4,155,600,000	0.01	
2014S	(1,193,699)		2
2015	4,691,300,000	0.01	
2015D	4,674,000,000	0.01	
2015S	(1,099,182)		2
2016	4,698,000,000	0.01	
2016D	4,420,400,000	0.01	
2016S	(1,011,624)		2
2017P	4,361,220,000	0.01	
2017D	4,272,800,000	0.01	
2017S	(979,475)		2

	Mintage	MS-65	PF-63
2018	4,066,800,000	$0.01	
2018D	3,736,400,000	0.01	
2018S	(901,072)		$2
2019	3,542,800,000	0.01	
2019D	3,497,600,000	0.01	
2019S	(1,062,662)		2
2019W	346,117		5
2019W, Proof	(601,327)	0.01	
2019W, Reverse Proof	(412,708)	0.01	
2020	3,560,800,000	0.01	
2020D	4,035,600,000	0.01	
2020S	(823,909)		2
2021	3,925,820,000	0.01	
2021D	3,982,800,000	0.01	
2021S	(814,340)		2
2022	3,129,200,000	0.01	
2022D	3,230,400,000	0.01	
2022S	(646,177)		2
2023		0.01	
2023D		0.01	
2023S			2
2024		0.01	
2024D		0.01	
2024S			2

TWO-CENT PIECES (1864–1873)

The Act of April 22, 1864, which changed the copper-nickel cent to a lighter-weight bronze composition, included a provision for a new coin, the two-cent piece. Its weight was specified as 96 grains, and its bronze alloy the same as for the cent. The two-cent piece was the nation's first circulating coin to bear the motto IN GOD WE TRUST.

There are two varieties for 1864, the first year of issue: the scarcer Small Motto, and the Large Motto. The differences are illustrated in the close-ups below. On the Small Motto variety, the stem to the cluster of leaves below TRUST is plainly visible, the D in GOD is wide, the first T in TRUST is close to the ribbon crease, and the U in TRUST is squat. On the Large Motto variety there is no stem, the D is narrow, the first T is farther from the crease, and the U is tall and narrow.

1864, Small Motto

1864, Large Motto

G-4 Good: At least part of IN GOD visible.
VG-8 Very Good: WE weakly visible.
F-12 Fine: Complete motto visible. The word WE weak.
VF-20 Very Fine: WE is clear, but not strong.
EF-40 Extremely Fine: The word WE bold.
AU-50 About Uncirculated: Traces of wear visible on leaf tips, arrow points, and the word WE.
MS-60 Uncirculated: No trace of wear. Light blemishes.
MS-63 Choice Uncirculated: Some distracting contact marks or blemishes in prime focal areas. Some impairment of luster possible.
PF-63 Choice Proof: Reflective surfaces with only a few blemishes in secondary focal places. No major flaws.

Dealers often pay more than the prices shown for brilliant red choice Uncirculated and Proof coins, and less for cleaned or discolored pieces.

	Mintage	G-4	VG-8	F-12	VF-20	EF-40	AU-50	MS-60	MS-63	PF-63
1864, Small Motto.............. *		$125	$175	$275	$375	$525	$750	$1,000	$1,250	$20,000
1864, Large Motto *(100+)*.. 19,822,500		13	15	18	25	35	55	75	145	500
1865 ....*(500+)*.. 13,640,000		13	15	18	25	35	55	75	145	400
1866 ....*(725+)*... 3,177,000		13	15	18	25	35	55	95	145	400
1867 ....*(625+)*... 2,938,750		13	15	18	25	35	55	95	145	400
1868 ....*(600+)*... 2,803,750		13	15	18	30	40	60	125	175	400
1869 ....*(600+)*... 1,546,500		20	32	35	40	55	75	135	185	400
1870 ....*(1,000+)*.....861,250		20	35	40	45	75	125	175	275	400
1871 ....*(960+)*.....721,250		25	40	45	55	85	135	185	325	500
1872 ....*(950+)*......65,000		250	300	400	500	700	1,100	2,000	2,500	800
1873 ....*(600)*............										2,400

* Included in number below.

SILVER THREE-CENT PIECES (TRIMES) (1851–1873)

This smallest of United States silver coins was authorized by Congress March 3, 1851. The first three-cent silver pieces had no lines bordering the six-pointed star. From 1854 through 1858 there were two lines, while issues of the last 15 years show only one line. Issues from 1854 through 1873 have an olive sprig over the III and a bundle of three arrows beneath.

G-4 Good: Star worn smooth. Legend and date readable.
VG-8 Very Good: Outline of shield defined. Legend and date clear.
F-12 Fine: Only star points worn smooth.
VF-20 Very Fine: Only partial wear on star ridges.
EF-40 Extremely Fine: Ridges on star points visible.
AU-50 About Uncirculated: Trace of wear visible at each star point. Center of shield possibly weak.
MS-60 Uncirculated: No trace of wear. Light blemishes.
MS-63 Choice Uncirculated: Some distracting contact marks or blemishes in prime focal areas. Some impairment of luster possible.
PF-63 Choice Proof: Reflective surfaces with only a few blemishes in secondary focal places. No major flaws.

Mintmark location.

| **No Outline Around Star** (1851–1853) | **Three Outlines to Star,** **Large Date** (1854–1858) | **Two Outlines to Star,** **Small Date** (1859–1873) | **1862,** **2 Over 1** |

Dealers usually pay higher prices for well-struck examples.

	Mintage	G-4	VG-8	F-12	VF-20	EF-40	AU-50	MS-60	MS-63	PF-63
1851	5,447,400	$30	$35	$40	$45	$65	$115	$135	$225	—
1851O	720,000	45	50	65	85	165	300	650	900	
1852	18,663,500	30	35	40	45	65	115	135	225	—
1853	11,400,000	30	35	40	45	65	115	135	225	
1854	671,000	35	40	45	55	80	125	250	550	$6,500
1855	139,000	50	55	65	80	135	165	500	1,150	2,650
1856	1,458,000	35	40	45	55	85	155	225	500	1,850
1857	1,042,000	35	40	45	55	85	155	250	500	1,850
1858 *(210)*	1,603,700	35	40	45	55	85	155	250	450	1,350
1859 *(800)*	364,200	35	40	45	55	75	115	150	275	600
1860 *(1,000)*	286,000	35	40	45	55	75	115	150	275	775
1861 *(1,000)*	497,000	35	40	45	55	75	115	150	275	600
1862, 2/1	*	35	40	45	55	85	135	300	400	
1862 *(550)*	343,000	35	40	45	55	75	115	150	275	600
1863 *(460)*	21,000				475	550	650	850	1,500	600
1864 *(470)*	12,000				475	550	650	950	1,250	600

	Mintage	VF-20	EF-40	AU-50	MS-60	MS-63	PF-63
1865	(500)....8,000	$500	$550	$675	$1,000	$1,500	$675
1866	(725)...22,000	550	650	750	775	1,250	675
1867	(625)....4,000	475	550	750	1,000	1,600	675
1868	(600)....3,500	1,050	1,400	1,550	3,500	5,500	675
1869	(600)....4,500	450	500	650	850	1,650	675
1870	(1,000)....3,000	500	550	650	800	1,050	675
1871	(960)....3,400	450	500	625	650	850	675
1872	(950)....1,000	1,150	1,250	1,750	2,500	3,500	675
1873, Close 3, Proof only	(600)........						1,250

* Included in number below.

NICKEL THREE-CENT PIECES (1865–1889)

Three-cent pieces struck in a nickel alloy were intended to replace the earlier silver three-cent coins, which were hoarded by the public during the Civil War. The Mint struck more than 11 million three-cent coins of the new composition (75% copper and 25% nickel) in 1865, their first year of issue, compared to only 8,000 silver pieces. The nickel coins were all made at the Philadelphia Mint. They have a plain (non-reeded) edge.

G-4 Good: Date and legends complete though worn. III smooth.
VG-8 Very Good: III half worn. Rims complete.
VF-20 Very Fine: Three-quarters of hair details visible.
EF-40 Extremely Fine: Slight, even wear.
AU-50 About Uncirculated: Slight wear on hair curls, above forehead, and on wreath and numeral III.
MS-60 Uncirculated: No trace of wear. Light blemishes.
MS-63 Choice Uncirculated: Some distracting contact marks or blemishes in prime focal areas. Some impairment of luster possible.
PF-63 Choice Proof: Reflective surfaces with only a few blemishes in secondary focal places. No major flaws.

Dealers often pay more than the prices shown for brilliant choice Unc. and Proof coins, and less for spotted, cleaned, or discolored pieces.

	Mintage	G-4	VG-8	F-12	VF-20	EF-40	AU-50	MS-60	MS-63	PF-63
1865 . . . . *(500+)* . .11,382,000		$12	$14	$15	$20	$35	$45	$95	$150	$1,150
1866 . . . . *(725+)* . . 4,801,000		11	13	14	17	35	45	95	150	250
1867 . . . . *(625+)* . . 3,915,000		11	13	16	17	35	45	95	150	250
1868 . . . . *(600+)* . . 3,252,000		11	13	14	17	35	45	95	150	250
1869 . . . . *(600+)* . . 1,604,000		11	13	14	18	35	45	95	150	250
1870 . . . . . *(1,000+)* . . 1,335,000		11	13	14	17	35	45	95	165	250
1871 . . . . *(960+)* 604,000		11	13	16	17	35	65	115	185	250
1872 . . . . *(950+)* 862,000		11	13	16	20	35	65	125	250	250
1873 . . . . . . *(1,100+)* 390,000		15	18	20	25	45	65	115	225	250
1874 . . . . *(700+)* 790,000		15	18	20	25	45	65	125	165	250
1875 . . . . *(700+)* 228,000		11	13	20	25	35	45	120	165	250
1876 . . . . . *(1,150+)* 162,000		20	25	30	35	40	65	165	195	265
1877, Pf only . . *(900)*					800	1,000				1,600
1878, Pf only *(2,350)*					425	550				650
1879 . . . . . . *(3,200)* 38,000		45	60	85	95	110	150	225	300	250
1880 . . . . . . *(3,955)* 21,000		75	95	115	125	150	175	265	375	250
1881 . . . . . . *(3,575)* . . 1,077,000		11	13	15	17	30	45	100	165	225
1882 . . . . . . *(3,100)* 22,200		75	100	135	165	200	250	275	475	225
1883 . . . . . . *(6,609)* 4,000		225	275	350	375	500	650	1,150	2,500	235
1884 . . . . . . *(3,942)* 1,700		600	750	950	1,200	1,500	2,750	3,500	6,000	325
1885 . . . . . . *(3,790)* 1,000		700	850	1,100	1,350	1,800	2,400	3,000	5,000	275
1886, Pf only *(4,290)*					200	225				250
1887 . . . . . . *(2,960)* 5,001		200	250	275	350	450	500	650	700	250
1887, 7/6 . . . . *					225	250				350
1888 . . . . . . *(4,582)* 36,501		35	45	55	65	80	115	210	250	250
1889 . . . . . . *(3,436)* 18,125		65	85	125	145	150	185	210	300	250

* Included in number above.

SHIELD (1866–1883)

The Shield type nickel was made possible by the Act of May 16, 1866. Its weight was set at 77-16/100 grains with the same composition as the nickel three-cent piece.

G-4 Good: All letters in motto readable.
VG-8 Very Good: Motto clear and stands out. Rims slightly worn but even. Part of shield lines visible.
F-12 Fine: Half of each olive leaf worn smooth.
EF-40 Extremely Fine: Slight wear to leaf tips and cross over shield.
AU-50 About Uncirculated: Traces of light wear on only the high design points. Half of mint luster present.
MS-60 Uncirculated: No trace of wear. Light blemishes.
MS-63 Choice Uncirculated: Some distracting blemishes in prime focal areas. Impaired luster possible.
PF-63 Choice Proof: Reflective surfaces. Only a few blemishes in secondary focal areas. No major flaws.

With Rays (1866–1867) Without Rays (1867–1883)

1873, Close 3 1873, Open 3 Typical Example of
1883, 3 Over 2
Other varieties exist.

Dealers often pay more than the prices shown for brilliant choice Unc. and Proof coins, and less for spotted, cleaned, or discolored pieces.

	Mintage	G-4	VG-8	F-12	VF-20	EF-40	AU-50	MS-60	MS-63	PF-63
1866, Rays . . . . . . *(600+)* . .14,742,500		$22	$25	$45	$65	$100	$145	$200	$350	$1,200
1867, Rays . . . . *(25+)* . .2,019,000		25	30	50	75	115	165	250	400	22,500
1867, Without										
Rays . . . . *(600+)* . .28,890,500		22	25	28	35	50	65	100	160	325
1868 . . . . *(600+)* . .28,817,000		22	25	28	35	50	65	100	160	325
1869 . . . . *(600+)* . .16,395,000		22	25	28	35	50	65	100	160	325
1870 . . . .*(1,000+)* . . .4,806,000		22	25	32	55	65	95	150	250	325
1871 . . . . *(960+)* . . . 561,000		55	75	105	150	200	265	325	625	325
1872 . . . . *(950+)* . .6,036,000		22	25	28	55	65	105	175	200	325
1873, Close 3 . . .*(1,100+)* 436,050		28	35	45	65	100	150	275	500	325
1873, Open 3 4,113,950		24	25	35	45	60	135	250		
1874 . . . . *(700+)* . .3,538,000		22	25	35	55	85	100	175	250	325
1875 . . . . *(700+)* . .2,097,000		30	35	45	75	115	135	185	275	325
1876 . . . .*(1,150+)* . .2,530,000		22	30	40	75	115	135	175	250	325
1877, Pf only . . . (900).			1,250	1,500	1,650					2,250
1878, Pf only . . . (2,350).			600	750	850					1,050
1879 . . . . (3,200). 25,900		400	550	600	700	1,150	1,400	2,000	2,500	325
1880 . . . . (3,955). 16,000		1,750	2,100	2,500	3,200	5,000	7,000	11,000	20,000	350
1881 . . . . (3,575). 68,800		200	275	325	350	425	550	850	1,000	325
1882 . . . . (3,100). . . .11,472,900		22	25	28	35	50	65	100	165	325
1883 . . . . (5,419). 1,451,500		22	25	28	35	50	65	100	165	325
1883, 3 Over 2 . . . . *		185	250	400	550	700	750	1,350		

* Included in number above.

LIBERTY HEAD (1883–1913)

In 1883 the design was changed to the "Liberty head." This type first appeared without the word CENTS on the coin, merely a large letter V. These "CENTS-less" coins were goldplated by fraudsters and passed as $5 pieces. Later in that year the word CENTS was added.

G-4 Good: No details in head. LIBERTY obliterated.
VG-8 Very Good: Some letters in LIBERTY legible.
F-12 Fine: All letters in LIBERTY legible.
VF-20 Very Fine: LIBERTY bold, including letter L.
EF-40 Extremely Fine: LIBERTY sharp. Corn grains at bottom of wreath visible on reverse.
AU-50 About Uncirculated: Traces of light wear on only high points of design. Half of mint luster present.
MS-60 Uncirculated: No trace of wear. Contact marks possible. Surface may be spotted, or luster faded.
MS-63 Choice Uncirculated: No trace of wear. Light blemishes.
PF-63 Choice Proof: Reflective surfaces. Only a few blemishes in secondary focal areas. No major flaws.

Variety 1, Without CENTS (1883 Only)   Variety 2, With CENTS (1883–1913)   Mintmark Location

Dealers often pay more than the prices shown for brilliant choice Unc. and Proof coins, and less for spotted, cleaned, or discolored pieces.

	Mintage	G-4	VG-8	F-12	VF-20	EF-40	AU-50	MS-60	MS-63	PF-63
1883, Without CENTS	(5,219) . . . 5,474,300	$4	$5.00	$6.00	$7	$10	$12	$35	$60	$250
1883, CENTS	(6,783) . . 16,026,200	12	20.00	25.00	40	60	85	115	150	225
1884	(3,942) . . 11,270,000	13	22.00	25.00	40	60	95	125	215	225
1885	(3,790) . . . 1,472,700	235	425.00	550.00	825	950	1,150	1,650	3,000	850
1886	(4,290) . . . 3,326,000	125	175.00	240.00	325	450	550	1,000	1,600	450
1887	(2,960) . . 15,260,692	8	12.00	20.00	25	55	70	105	185	225
1888	(4,582) . . 10,167,901	18	25.00	40.00	75	115	165	215	275	225
1889	(3,336) . . 15,878,025	8	10.00	20.00	35	55	95	115	155	225
1890	(2,740) . . 16,256,532	4	10.00	18.00	25	40	85	115	165	225
1891	(2,350) . . 16,832,000	4	5.00	14.00	25	40	85	115	155	225
1892	(2,745) . . 11,696,897	4	5.00	14.00	25	45	85	115	180	225
1893	(2,195) . . 13,368,000	4	5.00	14.00	25	40	60	115	155	225
1894	(2,632) . . . 5,410,500	10	20.00	65.00	115	175	225	300	400	225
1895	(2,062) . . . 9,977,822	3	5.00	10.00	25	40	75	115	185	225
1896	(1,862) . . . 8,841,058	4	10.00	25.00	40	80	115	150	250	225
1897	(1,938) . . 20,426,797	2	3.00	5.00	12	25	50	75	135	225
1898	(1,795) . . 12,530,292	2	3.00	5.00	12	30	55	100	160	225
1899	(2,031) . . 26,027,000	1	1.50	2.50	6	20	40	75	115	225
1900	(2,262) . . 27,253,733	1	1.50	2.50	6	20	40	65	100	225
1901	(1,985) . . 26,478,228	1	1.50	2.50	6	20	40	65	100	225
1902	(2,018) . . 31,480,579	1	1.50	2.50	6	20	40	65	100	225
1903	(1,790) . . 28,004,935	1	1.50	2.50	6	20	40	65	100	225
1904	(1,817) . . 21,403,167	1	1.50	2.50	6	20	40	65	100	225
1905	(2,152) . . 29,825,124	1	1.50	2.50	6	20	40	65	100	225
1906	(1,725) . . 38,612,000	1	1.50	2.50	6	20	40	65	100	225
1907	(1,475) . . 39,213,325	1	1.50	2.50	6	20	40	65	100	225
1908	(1,620) . . 22,684,557	1	1.50	2.50	6	20	40	65	100	225

	Mintage	G-4	VG-8	F-12	VF-20	EF-40	AU-50	MS-60	MS-63	PF-63
1909 . . . . (4,763). . . 11,585,763		$1	$1.50	$2.50	$7.50	$20	$40	$65	$100	$225
1910 . . . . (2,405). . . 30,166,948		1	1.50	2.25	5.00	20	40	65	100	225
1911 . . . . (1,733). . . 39,557,639		1	1.50	2.25	5.00	20	40	65	100	225
1912 . . . . (2,145). . . 26,234,569		1	1.50	2.25	5.00	20	40	65	100	225
1912D 8,474,000		2	3.00	8.00	25.00	55	150	200	250	
1912S 238,000		80	100.00	135.00	325.00	750	1,100	1,350	1,500	
1913 Liberty Head *(5 known)*. . . .							3,000,000			

INDIAN HEAD OR BUFFALO (1913–1938)

The Buffalo nickel was designed by James E. Fraser, whose initial F is below the date. He modeled the bison after Black Diamond in the New York Central Park Zoo.

G-4 Good: Legends and date readable. Buffalo's horn does not show.
VG-8 Very Good: Horn worn nearly flat.
F-12 Fine: Horn and tail smooth but partially visible. Obverse rim intact.
VF-20 Very Fine: Much of horn visible. Indian's cheekbone worn.
EF-40 Extremely Fine: Horn lightly worn. Slight wear on Indian's hair ribbon.
AU-50 About Uncirculated: Traces of light wear on high points of design. Half of mint luster present.
MS-60 Uncirculated: No trace of wear. May have several blemishes.
MS-63 Choice Uncirculated: No trace of wear. Light blemishes.
Matte PF-63 Choice Proof: Crisp surfaces. Only a few blemishes in secondary focal areas. No major flaws.

Variety 1 – FIVE CENTS on Raised Ground (1913)

Dealers often pay more than the prices shown for brilliant choice Unc. coins, and less for spotted, cleaned, weakly struck, or discolored pieces.

	Mintage	G-4	VG-8	F-12	VF-20	EF-40	AU-50	MS-60	MS-63	MATTE PF-63
1913, Variety 1 . . (1,520) . . 30,992,000		$6	$8	$10	$12	$16	$18	$25	$45	$1,000
1913D, Variety 1 5,337,000		10	13	15	20	25	35	40	55	
1913S, Variety 1 2,105,000		30	35	40	45	50	65	95	165	

Variety 2 – FIVE CENTS in Recess (1913–1938)

Mintmark Below FIVE CENTS   1916, Doubled-Die Obverse   1918-D, 8 Over 7

	Mintage	G-4	VG-8	F-12	VF-20	EF-40	AU-50	MS-60	MS-63	MATTE PF-63
1913, Variety 2 29,857,186		$6	$8	$10	$12	$14	$16	$25	$40	
. . . .(1,514)										$750
1913D, Variety 2 4,156,000		85	110	115	125	150	170	225	325	
1913S, Variety 2 1,209,000		150	200	250	300	375	450	650	850	
1914 20,664,463		10	13	14	15	20	25	35	75	
. . . .(1,275)										750

Chart continued on next page.   73

Dealers often pay more than the prices shown for brilliant choice Unc. coins, and less for spotted, cleaned, weakly struck, or discolored pieces.

	Mintage	G-4	VG-8	F-12	VF-20	EF-40	AU-50	MS-60	MS-63	MATTE PF-63
1914D	3,912,000	$65.00	$75.00	$90.00	$115	$165	$225	$300	$400	
1914S	3,470,000	17.00	25.00	30.00	40	55	115	155	300	
1915	20,986,220	2.50	3.00	4.00	7	12	25	35	60	
. . . .	(1,050)									$800
1915D	7,569,000	12.00	20.00	27.00	35	80	100	185	250	
1915S	1,505,000	25.00	40.00	60.00	125	275	400	650	1,150	
1916	63,497,466	2.00	3.00	4.00	5	8	15	35	65	
. . . .	(600)									1,000
1916, DblDie Obv	* 4,000.00	5,500.00	7,250.00	9,000	15,000	20,000	45,000	100,000	
1916D	13,333,000	10.00	15.00	20.00	25	55	65	125	225	
1916S	11,860,000	7.00	10.00	14.00	25	55	85	150	275	
1917	51,424,019	3.00	3.50	4.00	5	8	16	45	150	
1917D	9,910,000	12.00	20.00	30.00	50	100	200	350	600	
1917S	4,193,000	15.00	25.00	60.00	80	145	250	750	1,250	
1918	32,086,314	2.00	3.00	3.50	6	16	25	125	250	

* Included in number above.

	Mintage	G-4	VG-8	F-12	VF-20	EF-40	AU-50	MS-60	MS-63
1918D, 8 Over 7 . . . . . . **	$550.00	$850.00	$1,750.00	$2,500.00	$6,500.00	$8,500	$25,000	$35,000
1918D	8,362,000	15.00	25.00	40.00	80.00	165.00	250	450	800
1918S	4,882,000	9.00	15.00	35.00	65.00	145.00	275	650	1,650
1919	60,868,000	1.00	1.50	2.00	3.00	8.00	20	40	115
1919D (a)	8,006,000	11.00	20.00	45.00	75.00	175.00	275	650	1,250
1919S (a)	7,521,000	5.00	12.00	35.00	75.00	175.00	300	650	1,300
1920	63,093,000	0.50	0.75	1.25	2.50	8.00	20	50	100
1920D (a)	9,418,000	5.00	12.00	22.00	75.00	185.00	285	525	1,150
1920S	9,689,000	2.50	6.00	12.00	55.00	140.00	200	500	1,100
1921	10,663,000	1.00	3.00	4.00	10.00	25.00	55	85	250
1921S	1,557,000	40.00	65.00	100.00	225.00	575.00	900	1,500	2,750
1923	35,715,000	1.00	1.50	2.00	5.00	7.50	20	45	125
1923S (a)	6,142,000	4.00	6.00	15.00	65.00	165.00	250	450	800
1924	21,620,000	0.50	0.60	1.00	4.00	12.00	30	65	165
1924D	5,258,000	5.00	7.00	20.00	55.00	155.00	275	350	850
1924S	1,437,000	11.00	27.00	55.00	225.00	575.00	1,200	2,000	3,250
1925	35,565,100	1.00	1.50	3.00	4.00	10.00	18	30	85
1925D (a)	4,450,000	6.00	13.00	25.00	55.00	125.00	250	400	700
1925S	6,256,000	2.50	5.00	12.00	50.00	135.00	215	550	1,250
1926	44,693,000	0.35	0.45	1.00	3.00	4.00	12	22	50
1926D (a)	5,638,000	7.00	12.00	20.00	55.00	115.00	215	275	450
1926S	970,000	15.00	35.00	55.00	125.00	650.00	1,550	4,000	7,000
1927	37,981,000	0.50	0.55	0.75	1.50	6.00	10	30	55
1927D	5,730,000	1.00	4.00	5.00	20.00	55.00	95	135	300
1927S	3,430,000	1.00	1.50	4.00	22.00	75.00	175	700	1,750
1928	23,411,000	0.45	0.55	0.75	2.00	5.00	10	25	60
1928D	6,436,000	0.45	0.85	1.75	8.00	25.00	35	45	85
1928S	6,936,000	0.60	0.75	1.25	5.00	15.00	65	215	500
1929	36,446,000	0.35	0.40	0.60	2.00	5.00	10	20	45
1929D	8,370,000	0.45	0.60	0.80	3.00	15.00	25	40	85
1929S	7,754,000	0.45	0.60	0.75	0.90	5.50	18	25	75

** Included in number below. **a.** Dealers pay considerably more for Uncirculated pieces with full, sharp details.

1937-D, "3-Legged" Variety

1938-D, D Over S

Dealers often pay more than the prices shown for brilliant choice Unc. coins, and less for spotted, cleaned, weakly struck, or discolored pieces.

	Mintage	G-4	VG-8	F-12	VF-20	EF-40	AU-50	MS-60	MS-63	PF-63
1930	22,849,000	$0.45	$0.50	$0.70	$0.80	$5.00	$11.00	$16	$40	
1930S	5,435,000	0.45	0.50	0.70	0.80	6.00	15.00	65	100	
1931S	1,200,000	8.00	10.00	11.00	12.00	20.00	30.00	45	75	
1934	20,213,003	0.35	0.45	0.55	0.75	3.00	9.00	16	40	
1934D	7,480,000	0.50	0.75	1.25	3.00	9.00	25.00	55	85	
1935	58,264,000	0.35	0.45	0.55	0.75	1.25	5.00	10	25	
1935D	12,092,000	0.35	0.50	1.00	3.00	6.00	20.00	45	55	
1935S	10,300,000	0.35	0.45	0.55	0.75	2.00	7.50	30	45	
1936 . . . . (4,420) . .	118,997,000	0.35	0.45	0.55	0.75	1.25	4.00	10	25	$750
1936D	24,814,000	0.45	0.60	0.75	0.95	1.75	4.50	15	20	
1936S	14,930,000	0.35	0.45	0.55	0.75	1.25	4.50	10	15	
1937 . . . . (5,769) . .	79,480,000	0.35	0.45	0.55	0.75	1.25	3.00	10	20	750
1937D	17,826,000	0.35	0.45	0.55	0.75	1.25	4.00	10	15	
1937D, 3-Legged . . . .*	350.00	400.00	450.00	525.00	675.00	850.00	2,000	4,750	
1937S	5,635,000	0.35	0.45	0.55	0.75	1.25	4.00	11	25	
1938D	7,020,000	1.00	1.10	1.50	1.75	2.00	4.00	11	15	
1938D, D Over S . . . .*	2.00	5.00	6.00	7.00	8.00	15.00	35	40	

* Included in number above.

JEFFERSON (1938–2003)

This nickel was originally designed by Felix Schlag. He won an award of $1,000 in a competition with some 390 artists. It established the definite public approval of portrait and pictorial rather than symbolic devices on our coinage. On October 8, 1942, the wartime five-cent piece composed of copper (56%), silver (35%), and manganese (9%) was introduced to eliminate nickel, a critical war material. A larger mintmark was placed above the dome. The letter P (Philadelphia) was used for the first time, indicating the change of alloy. The designer's initials FS were added below the bust starting in 1966. The mintmark position was moved to the obverse starting in 1968.

VG-8 Very Good: Second porch pillar from right nearly gone, other three still visible but weak.

F-12 Fine: Jefferson's cheekbone worn flat. Hair lines and eyebrow faint. Second pillar weak, especially at bottom.

VF-20 Very Fine: Second pillar plain and complete on both sides.

EF-40 Extremely Fine: Cheekbone, hair lines, eyebrow slightly worn but well defined. Base of triangle above pillars visible but weak.

MS-63 Select Uncirculated: No trace of wear. Slight blemishes.

MS-65 Choice Uncirculated: No trace of wear. Barely noticeable blemishes.

PF-65 Gem Proof: Brilliant surfaces. No noticeable blemishes or flaws. May have a few barely noticeable marks or hairlines.

Mintmark located at right of building.

Mintmark, starting in 1968.

See next page for chart.

Coin dealers usually pay more than the Mint State prices shown for Uncirculated Jefferson nickels with fully struck steps visible in Monticello.

	Mintage	VG-8	F-12	VF-20	EF-40	MS-63	MS-65	PF-65
1938 . . . . . (19,365). . . 19,496,000		$0.10	$0.12	$0.20	$0.25	$4.00	$10	$55
1938D 5,376,000		0.25	0.35	0.75	1.00	4.00	8	
1938S 4,105,000		0.40	0.60	0.85	1.50	6.00	10	
1939 . . . . . (12,535). . 120,615,000		0.08	0.10	0.12	0.25	4.00	5	55
1939D 3,514,000		1.20	1.60	3.00	5.00	35.00	50	
1939S 6,630,000		0.25	0.30	0.50	1.50	25.00	40	
1940 . . . . . (14,158). . 176,485,000		0.05	0.05	0.05	0.10	1.00	4	55
1940D 43,540,000		0.05	0.05	0.05	0.10	1.25	4	
1940S 39,690,000		0.05	0.05	0.05	0.10	1.25	8	
1941 . . . . . (18,720). . 203,265,000		0.05	0.05	0.05	0.10	0.50	5	45
1941D 53,432,000		0.05	0.05	0.05	0.10	1.25	5	
1941S 43,445,000		0.05	0.05	0.05	0.10	1.50	8	
1942 . . . . . (29,600). . . 49,789,000		0.05	0.05	0.05	0.10	1.25	8	45
1942D 13,938,000		0.10	0.15	0.25	2.00	20.00	30	

Wartime Silver Alloy (1942–1945)

Mintmark Location   **1943-P, 3 Over 2**

	Mintage	VG-8	F-12	VF-20	EF-40	MS-63	MS-65	PF-65
1942P . . . . (27,600). . . 57,873,000		$1	$1.10	$1.20	$1.40	$4	$10	$85
1942S 32,900,000		1	1.10	1.20	1.40	4	10	
1943P, 3 Over 2 . . . . *			15.00	20.00	50.00	300	450	
1943P 271,165,000		1	1.10	1.20	1.40	3	10	
1943D 15,294,000		1	1.10	1.20	1.40	5	10	
1943S 104,060,000		1	1.10	1.20	1.40	3	10	
1944P 119,150,000		1	1.10	1.20	1.40	5	15	
1944D 32,309,000		1	1.10	1.20	1.40	5	10	
1944S 21,640,000		1	1.10	1.20	1.40	4	10	
1945P 119,408,100		1	1.10	1.20	1.40	3	10	
1945D 37,158,000		1	1.10	1.20	1.40	3	12	
1945S 58,939,000		1	1.10	1.20	1.40	3	10	

* Included in number below.

Prewar Composition, Mintmark Style Resumed (1946–1965)

1954-S, S Over D   **1955-D, D Over S**

	Mintage	VF-20	EF-40	MS-63	MS-65	PF-65
1946 161,116,000		$0.05	$0.05	$0.60	$5	
1946D 45,292,200		0.05	0.05	0.60	4	
1946S 13,560,000		0.05	0.06	0.35	4	

NICKEL FIVE-CENT PIECES

	Mintage	VF-20	EF-40	MS-63	MS-65	PF-65
1947	95,000,000	$0.05	$0.05	$0.35	$4.00	
1947D	37,822,000	0.05	0.05	0.35	4.00	
1947S	24,720,000	0.05	0.06	0.35	5.00	
1948	89,348,000	0.05	0.05	0.35	3.00	
1948D	44,734,000	0.05	0.06	0.75	2.00	
1948S	11,300,000	0.05	0.06	0.50	2.00	
1949	60,652,000	0.05	0.10	2.00	5.00	
1949D	36,498,000	0.05	0.05	0.75	3.00	
1949D, D Over S	*	18.00	30.00	125.00	225.00	
1949S	9,716,000	0.05	0.10	0.50	3.00	
1950	(51,386) 9,796,000	0.05	0.10	0.50	2.50	$30.00
1950D	2,630,030	3.00	3.50	10.00	17.00	
1951	(57,500) 28,552,000	0.05	0.06	1.25	5.00	25.00
1951D	20,460,000	0.05	0.06	1.50	4.00	
1951S	7,776,000	0.05	0.10	1.50	4.00	
1952	(81,980) 63,988,000	0.05	0.05	0.35	3.00	18.00
1952D	30,638,000	0.05	0.05	2.00	5.00	
1952S	20,572,000	0.05	0.05	0.55	4.00	
1953	(128,800) 46,644,000	0.05	0.05	0.25	2.50	18.00
1953D	59,878,600	0.05	0.05	0.25	2.75	
1953S	19,210,900	0.05	0.05	0.30	3.00	
1954	(233,300) 47,684,050	0.05	0.05	0.50	4.00	9.00
1954D	117,183,060	0.05	0.05	0.40	10.00	
1954S	29,384,000	0.05	0.05	0.50	5.00	
1954S, S Over D	*	2.50	5.00	18.00	35.00	
1955	(378,200) 7,888,000	0.06	0.08	0.40	5.00	6.00
1955D	74,464,100	0.05	0.05	0.25	7.00	
1955D, D Over S **(a)**	*	3.00	5.00	35.00	100.00	
1956	(669,384) 35,216,000	0.05	0.05	0.25	7.00	1.00
1956D	67,222,940	0.05	0.05	0.25	7.00	
1957	(1,247,952) 38,408,000	0.05	0.05	0.25	5.00	1.00
1957D	136,828,900	0.05	0.05	0.25	5.00	
1958	(875,652) 17,088,000	0.05	0.05	0.20	4.00	1.50
1958D	168,249,120	0.05	0.05	0.15	4.00	
1959	(1,149,291) 27,248,000	0.05	0.05	0.15	3.00	0.85
1959D	160,738,240	0.05	0.05	0.15	2.50	
1960	(1,691,602) 55,416,000	0.05	0.05	0.15	2.50	0.85
1960D	192,582,180	0.05	0.05	0.15	3.00	
1961	(3,028,144) 73,640,100	0.05	0.05	0.15	4.00	0.85
1961D	229,342,760	0.05	0.05	0.15	4.00	
1962	(3,218,019) 97,384,000	0.05	0.05	0.15	3.00	0.85
1962D	280,195,720	0.05	0.05	0.15	7.00	
1963	(3,075,645) 175,776,000	0.05	0.05	0.15	3.00	0.85
1963D	276,829,460	0.05	0.05	0.15	8.00	
1964	(3,950,762) 1,024,672,000	0.05	0.05	0.15	2.50	0.85
1964D	1,787,297,160	0.05	0.05	0.15	1.00	
1965	136,131,380	0.05	0.05	0.15	1.00	

* Included in number above. **a.** Varieties exist. Values are for the variety illustrated on previous page.

1966 Through 2003

	Mintage	MS-63	MS-65	PF-65		Mintage	MS-63	MS-65	PF-65
1966	156,208,283	$0.10	$1		1968D	91,227,880	$0.10	$1	
1967	107,325,800	0.10	1		1968S	100,396,004	0.10	1	

Chart continued on next page.

	Mintage	MS-63	MS-65	PF-65
1968S, Proof	(3,041,506)			$0.75
1969D	202,807,500	$0.10	$1.00	
1969S	120,165,000	0.10	0.80	
	(2,934,631)			0.75
1970D	515,485,380	0.10	3.00	
1970S	238,832,004	0.10	2.00	
	(2,632,810)			0.75
1971	106,884,000	0.25	0.80	
1971D	316,144,800	0.10	0.80	
1971S	(3,220,733)			0.75

	Mintage	MS-63	MS-65	PF-65
1972	202,036,000	$0.10	$0.80	
1972D	351,694,600	0.10	0.80	
1972S	(3,260,996)			$1.00
1973	384,396,000	0.10	0.80	
1973D	261,405,000	0.10	0.80	
1973S	(2,760,339)			0.75
1974	601,752,000	0.10	0.80	
1974D	277,373,000	0.10	0.80	
1974S	(2,612,568)			1.00

	Mintage	MS-65	PF-65
1975	181,772,000	$0.75	
1975D	401,875,300	0.75	
1975S	(2,845,450)		$0.85
1976	367,124,000	0.75	
1976D	563,964,147	0.75	
1976S	(4,149,730)		0.85
1977	585,376,000	0.75	
1977D	297,313,422	0.75	
1977S	(3,251,152)		0.75
1978	391,308,000	0.75	
1978D	313,092,780	0.75	
1978S	(3,127,781)		0.75
1979	463,188,000	0.75	
1979D	325,867,672	1.00	
1979S, Type 1	(3,677,175)		0.75
1979S, Type 2	*		1.00
1980P	593,004,000	0.50	
1980D	502,323,448	0.50	
1980S	(3,554,806)		0.75
1981P	657,504,000	0.50	
1981D	364,801,843	0.50	
1981S, Type 1	(4,063,083)		1.00
1981S, Type 2	*		2.00
1982P	292,355,000	3.00	
1982D	373,726,544	2.00	
1982S	(3,857,479)		1.00
1983P	561,615,000	3.00	
1983D	536,726,276	1.50	
1983S	(3,279,126)		1.00
1984P	746,769,000	1.25	
1984D	517,675,146	0.75	
1984S	(3,065,110)		1.50
1985P	647,114,962	0.50	
1985D	459,747,446	0.50	
1985S	(3,362,821)		1.25
1986P	536,883,483	0.50	
1986D	361,819,140	0.50	
1986S	(3,010,497)		2.75
1987P	371,499,481	0.70	
1987D	410,590,604	0.75	

	Mintage	MS-65	PF-65
1987S	(4,227,728)		$1.00
1988P	771,360,000	$0.60	
1988D	663,771,652	0.60	
1988S	(3,262,948)		2.00
1989P	898,812,000	0.50	
1989D	570,842,474	0.50	
1989S	(3,220,194)		1.75
1990P	661,636,000	0.50	
1990D	663,938,503	0.50	
1990S	(3,299,559)		1.75
1991P	614,104,000	0.50	
1991D	436,496,678	0.50	
1991S	(2,867,787)		2.00
1992P	399,552,000	0.75	
1992D	450,565,113	0.50	
1992S	(4,176,560)		1.25
1993P	412,076,000	0.30	
1993D	406,084,135	0.30	
1993S	(3,394,792)		1.50
1994P	722,160,000	0.50	
1994D	715,762,110	0.30	
1994S	(3,269,923)		1.25
1995P	774,156,000	0.30	
1995D	888,112,000	0.30	
1995S	(2,797,481)		2.00
1996P	829,332,000	0.30	
1996D	817,736,000	0.30	
1996S	(2,525,265)		1.00
1997P	470,972,000	0.30	
1997D	466,640,000	0.50	
1997S	(2,796,678)		1.75
1998P	688,272,000	0.30	
1998D	635,360,000	0.30	
1998S	(2,086,507)		1.75
1999P	1,212,000,000	0.30	
1999D	1,066,720,000	0.30	
1999S	(3,347,966)		2.00
2000P	846,240,000	0.30	
2000D	1,509,520,000	0.30	
2000S	(4,047,993)		1.75

* Included in number above.

	Mintage	MS-65	PF-65
2001P	675,704,000	$0.20	
2001D	627,680,000	0.20	
2001S	(3,184,606)		$1.75
2002P	539,280,000	0.20	
2002D	691,200,000	0.20	

	Mintage	MS-65	PF-65
2002S	(3,211,995)		$1.50
2003P	441,840,000	$0.20	
2003D	383,040,000	0.20	
2003S	(3,298,439)		1.50

WESTWARD JOURNEY (2004–2005)

The Westward Journey Nickel Series™ commemorates the bicentennial of the Louisiana Purchase and the journey of Meriwether Lewis and William Clark to explore that vast territory. **2004**—*Obverse:* traditional portrait of Jefferson. *Reverses:* Louisiana Purchase / Peace Medal reverse, by Mint sculptor Norman E. Nemeth. Keelboat reverse, by Mint sculptor Al Maletsky. **2005**—*Obverse:* new portrait of Jefferson, designed by Joe Fitzgerald after a 1789 marble bust by Jean-Antoine Houdon, and rendered by Mint sculptor Don Everhart. *Reverses:* American Bison reverse, designed by Jamie Franki and produced by Norman E. Nemeth. "Ocean in View" reverse, designed by Joe Fitzgerald and produced by Mint sculptor Donna Weaver.

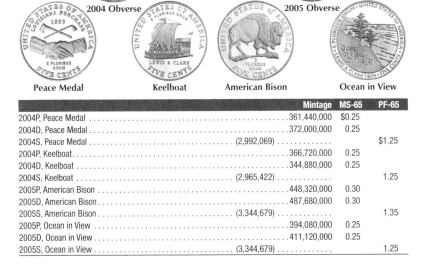

2004 Obverse   2005 Obverse

Peace Medal   Keelboat   American Bison   Ocean in View

	Mintage	MS-65	PF-65
2004P, Peace Medal	361,440,000	$0.25	
2004D, Peace Medal	372,000,000	0.25	
2004S, Peace Medal	(2,992,069)		$1.25
2004P, Keelboat	366,720,000	0.25	
2004D, Keelboat	344,880,000	0.25	
2004S, Keelboat	(2,965,422)		1.25
2005P, American Bison	448,320,000	0.30	
2005D, American Bison	487,680,000	0.30	
2005S, American Bison	(3,344,679)		1.35
2005P, Ocean in View	394,080,000	0.25	
2005D, Ocean in View	411,120,000	0.25	
2005S, Ocean in View	(3,344,679)		1.25

JEFFERSON MODIFIED (2006 TO DATE)

In 2006 the Monticello design of 1938 to 2003 was returned to the reverse of the nickel five-cent coin. A new obverse motif featured a facing portrait of Thomas Jefferson, designed by Jamie Franki and sculpted by Donna Weaver. These designs have continued in use to date.

Felix Schlag's initials moved to reverse

	Mintage	MS-65	PF-63		Mintage	MS-65	PF-63
2006P	693,120,000	$0.25		2016P	786,960,000	0.20	
2006D	809,280,000	0.25		2016D	759,600,000	0.20	
2006S	(3,054,436)		$1.25	2016S	(1,011,624)		1.10
2007P	571,680,000	0.20		2017P	710,160,000	0.20	
2007D	626,160,000	0.20		2017D	663,120,000	0.20	
2007S	(2,577,166)		1.10	2017S	(979,475)		1.10
2008P	279,840,000	0.20		2018P	629,520,000	0.20	
2008D	345,600,000	0.20		2018D	626,880,000	0.20	
2008S	(2,169,561)		1.10	2018S	(901,072)		1.10
2009P	39,840,000	0.50		2019P	567,854,400	0.20	
2009D	46,800,000	0.50		2019D	527,040,000	0.20	
2009S	(2,179,867)		1.10	2019S	(1,062,662)		1.10
2010P	260,640,000	0.20		2020P	785,500,000	0.20	
2010D	229,920,000	0.20		2020D	837,600,000	0.20	
2010S	(1,689,216)		1.10	2020S	(823,909)		1.10
2011P	450,000,000	0.20		2020W	(464,658)		5.00
2011D	540,240,000	0.20		2020W, Reverse Proof	(313,183)		7.50
2011S	(1,673,010)		1.10	2021P	772,780,000	0.20	
2012P	464,640,000	0.20		2021D	798,000,000	0.20	
2012D	558,960,000	0.20		2021S	(814,340)		1.10
2012S	(1,239,148)		1.10	2022P	769,920,000	0.20	
2013P	607,440,000	0.20		2022D	777,600,000	0.20	
2013D	615,600,000	0.20		2022S	(646,177)		1.10
2013S	(1,274,505)		1.10	2023P		0.20	
2014P	635,520,000	0.20		2023D		0.20	
2014D	570,720,000	0.20		2023S			1.10
2014S	(1,193,699)		1.10	2024P		0.20	
2015P	752,880,000	0.20		2024D		0.20	
2015D	846,720,000	0.20		2024S			1.10
2015S	(1,099,182)		1.10				

HALF DIMES

The half dime types present the same general characteristics as larger United States silver coins. Authorized by the Act of April 2, 1792, they were not coined until February 1795, although dated 1794. At first the weight was 20.8 grains, and fineness .8924. By the Act of January 18, 1837, the weight was slightly reduced to 20-5/8 grains and the fineness changed to .900. Finally, the weight was reduced to 19.2 grains by the Act of February 21, 1853.

FLOWING HAIR (1794–1795)

AG-3 About Good: Details clear enough to identify.
G-4 Good: Eagle, wreath, bust outlined but lack details.
VG-8 Very Good: Some details on face. All lettering legible.
F-12 Fine: Hair ends visible. Hair at top smooth.
VF-20 Very Fine: Hair lines at top visible. Hair about ear defined.
EF-40 Extremely Fine: Hair above forehead and at neck well defined but shows some wear.

AU-50 About Uncirculated: Slight wear on high waves of hair, near ear and face, and on head and tips of eagle's wings.
MS-60 Uncirculated: No trace of wear. Light blemishes.
MS-63 Choice Uncirculated: Some distracting marks or blemishes in prime focal areas. Some impairment of luster possible.

For Uncirculated examples, coin dealers usually pay less than the prices shown for pieces that are weakly struck.

	Mintage	AG-3	G-4	VG-8	F-12	VF-20	EF-40	AU-50	MS-60	MS-63
1792 . . . .*		$27,500	$40,000	$52,500	$65,000	$85,000	$115,000	$125,000	$175,000	$300,000
1794 . . . .*		700	1,450	2,000	2,650	3,250	6,500	9,000	15,000	25,000
1795 86,416		650	1,200	1,450	1,850	2,650	4,500	5,250	8,000	10,000

* Included in number below.

DRAPED BUST (1796–1805)

AG-3 About Good: Details clear enough to identify.
G-4 Good: Date, stars, LIBERTY readable. Bust of Liberty outlined, but no details.
VG-8 Very Good: Some details visible.
F-12 Fine: Hair and drapery lines worn, but visible.
VF-20 Very Fine: Only left side of drapery indistinct.
EF-40 Extremely Fine: Details visible in all hair lines.
AU-50 About Uncirculated: Slight wear on bust, shoulder, and hair; wear on eagle's head and top of wings.
MS-60 Uncirculated: No trace of wear. Light blemishes.
MS-63 Choice Uncirculated: Some distracting marks or blemishes in prime focal areas. Impaired luster possible.

Small Eagle Reverse (1796–1797)

	Mintage	AG-3	G-4	VG-8	F-12	VF-20	EF-40	AU-50	MS-60	MS-63
1796, 6 Over 5 10,230		$850	$1,800	$2,250	$3,000	$4,250	$7,000	$11,000	$20,000	$27,500
1796, LIKERTY. . . . .*		650	1,200	1,500	2,750	3,500	6,250	7,500	16,000	22,500
1797, 15 Stars. 44,527		650	1,200	1,500	2,500	3,500	5,000	7,000	12,500	17,500
1797, 16 Stars. . . . .*		65	1,200	1,500	2,500	3,500	5,000	7,500	12,500	17,500
1797, 13 Stars. . . . .*		900	1,850	2,500	4,000	4,750	9,000	18,500	35,000	55,000

* Included in number above.

Heraldic Eagle Reverse (1800–1805)

1800 LIBEKTY

	Mintage	AG-3	G-4	VG-8	F-12	VF-20	EF-40	AU-50	MS-60	MS-63
1800	24,000	$450	$1,200	$1,350	$1,800	$2,500	$4,500	$6,500	$10,000	$15,000
1800, LIBEKTY	16,000	450	1,250	1,550	2,000	2,750	4,750	7,000	12,000	17,500
1801	27,760	450	1,250	1,600	1,800	2,500	4,500	6,500	14,500	20,000
1802	3,060	47,500	85,000	115,000	130,000	150,000	195,000	250,000	—	—
1803	37,850	500	1,250	1,450	1,650	2,500	4,500	6,500	10,000	27,500
1805	15,600	500	1,400	1,850	2,250	3,250	8,500	18,500	—	—

CAPPED BUST (1829–1837)

G-4 Good: Bust of Liberty outlined, no detail. Date and legend legible.
VG-8 Very Good: Complete legend and date plain. At least three letters
of LIBERTY on edge of cap show clearly.
F-12 Fine: All letters in LIBERTY visible.
VF-20 Very Fine: Full rims. Ear and shoulder clasp show plainly.
EF-40 Extremely Fine: Ear very distinct; eyebrow and hair well defined.
AU-50 About Uncirculated: Traces of light wear on many of the high points. At least half of mint luster
still present.
MS-60 Uncirculated: No trace of wear. Light blemishes.
MS-63 Choice Uncirculated: No trace of wear. Light blemishes. Attractive mint luster.

	Mintage	G-4	VG-8	F-12	VF-20	EF-40	AU-50	MS-60	MS-63
1829	1,230,000	$50	$65	$80	$105	$150	$205	$375	$750
1830	1,240,000	50	65	80	105	150	205	375	750
1831	1,242,700	50	65	80	105	150	205	375	750
1832	965,000	50	65	80	105	150	205	375	750
1833	1,370,000	50	65	80	105	150	205	375	750
1834	1,480,000	50	65	80	105	150	205	375	750
1835	2,760,000	50	65	80	105	150	205	375	750
1836	1,900,000	50	65	80	105	150	205	375	750
1837, Small 5 C.	871,000	80	110	115	155	265	550	1,350	2,000
1837, Large 5 C.	*	50	65	85	125	150	205	375	750

* Included in number above.

LIBERTY SEATED (1837–1873)

G-4 Good: LIBERTY on shield smooth. Date and letters legible.
VG-8 Very Good: At least three letters in LIBERTY visible.
F-12 Fine: Entire LIBERTY visible, weak spots.
VF-20 Very Fine: Entire LIBERTY strong and even.
EF-40 Extremely Fine: LIBERTY and scroll edges distinct.
AU-50 About Uncirculated: Traces of light wear on many of the high points. At least half of mint luster
still present.
MS-60 Uncirculated: No trace of wear. Light blemishes.
MS-63 Choice Uncirculated: No trace of wear. Light blemishes. Attractive mint luster.

Variety 1 – No Stars on Obverse (1837–1838)

	Mintage	G-4	VG-8	F-12	VF-20	EF-40	AU-50	MS-60	MS-63
1837	1,405,000	$30	$45	$75	125	$215	$350	$550	$900
1838O, No Stars	70,000	135	200	425	750	2,000	3,250	5,000	9,500

Variety 2 – Stars on Obverse (1838–1853)

From 1838 through 1859 the mintmark was located above the bow on the reverse. Large, medium, or small mintmark varieties occur for several dates.

	Mintage	G-4	VG-8	F-12	VF-20	EF-40	AU-50	MS-60	MS-63
1838	2,255,000	$25	$30	$35	$50	$75	$150	$250	$450
1839	1,069,150	25	30	32	40	75	150	275	450
1839O	1,100,000	25	30	35	55	115	300	750	1,500
1840	1,344,085	25	30	35	40	75	150	250	450
1840O	935,000	85	115	175	250	475	550	1,500	4,500
1841	1,150,000	25	30	32	35	45	100	140	300
1841O	815,000	60	85	125	175	250	325	1,000	2,000
1842	815,000	25	30	32	35	55	100	200	300
1842O	350,000	60	100	165	350	500	800	1,100	1,750
1843	815,000	25	28	30	35	50	100	150	300
1844	430,000	25	28	30	35	75	150	225	350
1844O	220,000	100	175	265	550	1,100	2,000	5,750	8,500
1845	1,564,000	25	28	30	35	50	105	150	300
1846	27,000	600	1,000	1,500	2,250	3,500	6,500	16,500	32,500
1847	1,274,000	25	28	30	35	50	100	145	250
1848	668,000	25	28	30	35	50	100	250	400
1848O	600,000	25	30	35	65	165	300	450	800
1849, 9 Over 6 . . . . *		30	40	65	85	125	200	500	750
1849, 9 Over Widely Placed 6 . . . . *		30	40	65	85	125	200	375	750
1849, Normal Date . . .	1,309,000	30	35	40	50	55	100	165	350
1849O	140,000	65	115	185	275	400	850	1,750	3,000
1850	955,000	25	28	30	35	45	100	145	250
1850O	690,000	25	28	30	50	100	200	550	1,200
1851	781,000	25	28	30	35	45	100	165	275
1851O	860,000	25	28	30	35	100	200	350	700
1852	1,000,500	25	28	30	35	50	105	135	250
1852O	260,000	30	40	85	125	225	400	850	2,250
1853, No Arrows	135,000	35	60	75	150	225	425	600	800
1853O, No Arrows	160,000	250	450	650	1,150	2,250	3,000	9,000	12,500

* Included in number below.

Variety 3 – Arrows at Date (1853–1855)

As on the dimes, quarters, and halves, arrows were placed at the sides of the date for a short period starting in 1853 to denote the reduction of weight.

	Mintage	G-4	VG-8	F-12	VF-20	EF-40	AU-50	MS-60	MS-63	PF-63
1853	13,210,020	$25	$28	$30	$35	$50	$105	$150	$250	—
1853O	2,200,000	25	28	30	35	85	110	350	850	
1854	5,740,000	25	28	30	35	50	105	150	250	$6,500

Chart continued on next page.

	Mintage	G-4	VG-8	F-12	VF-20	EF-40	AU-50	MS-60	MS-63	PF-63
1854O	1,560,000	$25	$28	$30	$40	$55	$125	$225	$675	
1855	1,750,000	25	28	30	35	50	100	140	250	$6,000
1855O	600,000	25	30	35	50	100	150	450	700	

Variety 2 Resumed, with Weight Standard of 1853 (1856–1859)

1858 Over Inverted Date

	Mintage	G-4	VG-8	F-12	VF-20	EF-40	AU-50	MS-60	MS-63	PF-63
1856	4,880,000	$22	$25	$30	$35	$50	$100	$135	$225	$3,500
1856O	1,100,000	22	25	30	35	75	185	375	1,000	
1857	7,280,000	22	25	30	35	50	100	135	225	1,750
1857O	1,380,000	25	27	30	35	50	120	250	500	
1858 . . . . . . (300)	3,500,000	22	25	30	35	50	100	120	225	650
1858, Over Inverted Date . . . .*		50	65	75	100	200	275	650	1,150	
1858O	1,660,000	22	25	30	35	50	100	150	300	
1859 . . . . . . (800)	340,000	22	25	30	35	50	100	150	250	650
1859O	560,000	22	25	30	65	85	145	250	400	

* Included in number above.

Variety 4 – Legend on Obverse (1860–1873)

	Mintage	G-4	VG-8	F-12	VF-20	EF-40	AU-50	MS-60	MS-63	PF-63
1860 . . . . . . (1,000)	798,000	$25	$30	$32	$35	$40	$60	$145	$225	$425
1860O	1,060,000	22	25	28	30	45	85	175	300	
1861 . . . . . . (1,000) . .	3,360,000	22	25	28	30	45	60	145	225	425
1862 . . . . . . (550) . .	1,492,000	20	25	28	30	40	60	145	225	425
1863 . . . . (460)	18,000	150	200	275	325	425	500	600	700	425
1863S	100,000	30	50	95	115	185	325	600	850	
1864 . . . . (470)	48,000	250	425	650	750	900	1,000	1,050	1,150	425
1864S	90,000	75	100	155	225	375	550	750	1,150	
1865 . . . . (500)	13,000	225	350	550	625	700	800	900	1,000	425
1865S	120,000	35	60	85	125	225	500	900	2,000	
1866 . . . . (725)	10,000	225	350	500	600	650	675	700	875	425
1866S	120,000	25	35	50	80	150	275	450	875	
1867 . . . . (625)	8,000	350	425	650	675	725	850	950	1,250	425
1867S	120,000	35	55	85	115	150	215	450	850	
1868 . . . . (600)	88,600	35	65	100	145	225	325	450	700	425
1868S	280,000	20	25	28	32	50	100	275	425	
1869 . . . . (600)	208,000	20	25	28	32	65	85	165	225	425
1869S	230,000	20	25	28	40	60	100	250	650	
1870 . . . . . . (1,000) . .	535,000	20	25	28	32	40	55	150	225	425
1870S (unique)									2,500,000	
1871 . . . . (960) . .	1,873,000	20	25	28	32	40	55	135	225	425
1871S	161,000	22	27	30	45	60	125	165	250	
1872 . . . . . . (950) . .	2,947,000	20	25	28	32	40	55	135	225	425
1872S	837,000	20	25	28	32	40	55	135	225	
1873 . . . . (600) . .	7,126,000	20	25	28	32	40	55	135	225	425
1873S	324,000	20	24	28	32	35	55	135	225	

The designs of the dimes, first coined in 1796, follow closely those of the half dimes up through the Liberty Seated type. The dimes in each instance weigh twice as much as the half dimes.

DRAPED BUST (1796–1807)
Small Eagle Reverse (1796–1797)

AG-3 About Good: Details clear enough to identify.
G-4 Good: Date legible. Bust outlined, but no detail.
VG-8 Very Good: All but deepest drapery folds worn smooth. Hair lines nearly gone and curls lacking in detail.
F-12 Fine: All drapery lines visible. Hair partly worn.
VF-20 Very Fine: Only left side of drapery indistinct.
EF-40 Extremely Fine: Hair well outlined with details visible.
AU-50 About Uncirculated: Traces of light wear on many of the high points. At least half of mint luster still present.
MS-60 Uncirculated: No trace of wear. Light blemishes.
MS-63 Choice Uncirculated: Some distracting marks or blemishes in prime focal areas. Impaired luster possible.

| | 1797, 16 Stars | | | | 1797, 13 Stars | | | |

	Mintage	AG-3	G-4	VG-8	F-12	VF-20	EF-40	AU-50	MS-60	MS-63
1796	22,135	$1,350	$2,500	$3,250	$3,750	$4,750	$7,500	$11,500	$16,500	$35,000
1797, All kinds	25,261									
1797, 16 Stars		1,350	2,500	3,250	3,750	5,000	7,500	11,500	25,000	40,000
1797, 13 Stars		1,400	2,750	3,500	5,000	6,500	12,000	17,500	45,000	75,000

Heraldic Eagle Reverse (1798–1807)

	Mintage	AG-3	G-4	VG-8	F-12	VF-20	EF-40	AU-50	MS-60	MS-63
1798, All kinds	27,550									
1798, 8 Over 7, 16 Stars on Reverse		$350	$850	$1,250	$1,600	$2,000	$3,000	$4,000	$6,500	$15,000
1798, 8 Over 7, 13 Stars on Reverse		1,500	3,500	5,500	7,500	9,500	14,500	23,500	35,000	
1798		300	900	1,100	2,000	2,250	3,500	4,500	8,500	12,500
1800	21,760	300	750	1,000	1,450	1,850	3,000	6,000	13,500	30,000
1801	34,640	350	750	1,350	1,750	2,850	4,500	9,000	35,000	45,000
1802	10,975	550	1,200	1,850	2,500	3,000	5,500	12,500	27,500	85,000
1803	33,040	350	850	1,200	1,500	2,000	3,850	5,500	45,000	85,000
1804	8,265	1,650	3,850	5,000	8,500	14,500	25,000	50,000	250,000	
1805	120,780	250	500	800	1,000	1,350	2,500	3,500	5,500	8,000
1807	165,000	250	500	750	850	1,350	2,250	3,000	5,000	7,750

CAPPED BUST (1809–1837)

G-4 Good: Date, letters, and stars discernible. Bust outlined, no details.
VG-8 Very Good: Legends and date plain. Some letters in LIBERTY visible.
F-12 Fine: Clear LIBERTY. Ear and shoulder clasp visible. Part of rim visible on both sides.
VF-20 Very Fine: LIBERTY distinct. Full rim. Ear and clasp plain and distinct.
EF-40 Extremely Fine: LIBERTY sharp. Ear distinct. Hair above eye well defined.
AU-50 About Uncirculated: Traces of light wear on only the high points of the design. Half of mint luster present.
MS-60 Uncirculated: No trace of wear. Light blemishes.
MS-63 Choice Uncirculated: Some distracting marks or blemishes in prime focal areas. Impaired luster possible.

Variety 1 – Wide Border (1809–1828)

| 1823, 3 Over 2 | 1824, 4 Over 2 | 1828, Large Date | 1828, Small Date |

	Mintage	G-4	VG-8	F-12	VF-20	EF-40	AU-50	MS-60	MS-63
1809	51,065	$500	$800	$1,250	$2,000	$3,000	$4,000	$5,000	$8,500
1811, 11 Over 09	65,180	165	275	700	1,000	1,500	2,000	2,850	6,000
1814	421,500	55	100	125	175	500	550	1,500	3,000
1820	942,587	55	85	125	185	425	650	1,500	2,000
1821	1,186,512	55	80	125	185	400	600	1,200	2,000
1822	100,000	1,500	2,500	4,000	6,000	8,000	10,000	17,500	25,000
1823, 3 Over 2, All kinds	440,000								
1823, 3 Over 2, Small E's		70	100	175	300	600	650	1,200	2,000
1823, 3 Over 2, Large E's		70	115	175	250	550	600	1,500	3,000
1824, 4 Over 2	510,000	75	115	225	425	750	1,100	1,350	2,500
1825	*	50	85	125	185	450	550	1,000	2,000
1827	1,215,000	50	85	125	200	450	550	1,000	2,000
1828, Large Date, Curl Base 2	125,000	85	100	125	450	900	1,500	4,000	8,500

* Included in number above.

Variety 2 – Modified Design (1828–1837)

| 1829, Small 10 C. | 1829, Large 10 C. | 1830, 30 Over 29 |

	Mintage	G-4	VG-8	F-12	VF-20	EF-40	AU-50	MS-60	MS-63
1828, Small Date, Square Base 2	*	$50	$60	$100	$150	$350	$550	$850	$2,000
1829, Small 10 C.	770,000	25	40	55	85	225	375	650	1,500
1829, Medium 10 C.	*	25	40	55	125	225	375	650	1,500
1829, Large 10 C.	*	25	40	55	150	350	500	650	2,500
1830, 30 Over 29	510,000	25	40	60	100	275	400	675	1,750

* Included in number above.

	Mintage	G-4	VG-8	F-12	VF-20	EF-40	AU-50	MS-60	MS-63
1830, Large 10 C. . . . *		$25	$40	$55	$85	$225	$375	$675	$1,500
1830, Small 10 C. . . . *		25	40	55	85	225	375	625	1,350
1831 771,350		25	40	55	85	225	375	625	1,350
1832 522,500		25	40	55	85	225	375	625	1,350
1833 485,000		25	40	55	85	225	375	625	1,350
1834 635,000		25	40	55	85	225	375	625	1,350
1835 1,410,000		25	40	55	85	225	375	625	1,350
1836 1,190,000		25	40	55	85	225	375	625	1,350
1837 359,500		25	40	55	85	225	375	625	1,350

* Included in mintage for 1830, 30 Over 29 (previous page).

LIBERTY SEATED (1837–1891)
Variety 1 – No Stars on Obverse (1837–1838)

G-4 Good: LIBERTY on shield not readable. Date and letters legible.
F-12 Fine: LIBERTY visible, weak spots.
VF-20 Very Fine: LIBERTY strong and even.
EF-40 Extremely Fine: LIBERTY and scroll edges distinct.
AU-50 About Uncirculated: Wear on Liberty's shoulder and hair high points.
MS-60 Uncirculated: No trace of wear. Light blemishes.
MS-63 Choice Uncirculated: Some distracting marks or blemishes in focal areas. Impaired luster possible.

No Drapery From Elbow
No Stars on Obverse

Mintmarks on Liberty Seated dimes on reverse, within or below the wreath. Size of mintmark varies on many dates.

	Mintage	G-4	F-12	VF-20	EF-40	AU-50	MS-60	MS-63
1837 682,500		$45	$115	$200	$400	$550	$850	$1,500
1838O 406,034		65	125	300	600	750	2,750	4,500

Variety 2 – Stars on Obverse (1838–1853)

No Drapery From Elbow, Tilted Shield
(1838–1840)

1838, Small Stars   **1838, Large Stars**

Drapery From Elbow, Upright Shield
(1840–1891)

	Mintage	G-4	F-12	VF-20	EF-40	AU-50	MS-60	MS-63
1838, All kinds. 1,992,500								
1838, Small Stars		$20	$45	$55	$250	$225	$500	$1,000
1838, Large Stars		12	25	50	125	175	325	600
1838, Partial Drapery		14	25	50	150	250	450	1,200
1839 1,053,115		12	25	50	115	200	300	650
1839O 1,288,000		20	60	100	200	250	500	1,500
1840, No Drapery 981,500		12	20	50	115	200	325	700
1840O, No Drapery 1,175,000		45	100	115	400	650	5,000	10,000
1840, Drapery 377,500		65	125	200	550	1,000	2,500	8,500

Chart continued on next page.

	Mintage	G-4	F-12	VF-20	EF-40	AU-50	MS-60	MS-63
1841 1,622,500		$12	$15	$25	$45	$100	$275	$550
1841O 2,007,500		20	35	55	125	200	650	1,100
1842 1,887,500		12	15	22	50	100	250	400
1842O 2,020,000		35	65	155	400	750	2,250	3,250
1843 1,370,000		12	15	22	50	100	250	600
1843O 150,000		135	450	1,000	2,250	7,500	50,000	100,000
1844 72,500		135	250	350	750	1,250	3,500	7,500
1845 1,755,000		12	15	20	50	125	250	500
1845O 230,000		55	200	450	1,000	2,500	10,000	25,000
1846 31,300		350	650	1,500	2,000	5,500	20,000	40,000
1847 245,000		25	30	65	125	300	1,000	2,500
1848 451,500		15	30	55	65	150	550	800
1849 839,000		15	30	30	55	150	375	625
1849O 300,000		25	55	125	300	550	2,000	3,750
1850 1,931,500		12	20	30	50	150	250	450
1850O 510,000		30	65	100	250	625	1,750	3,750
1851 1,026,500		12	15	30	45	150	325	550
1851O 400,000		20	55	100	250	850	2,000	2,850
1852 1,535,500		12	15	25	35	125	225	375
1852O 430,000		20	85	165	300	500	1,500	2,500
1853, No Arrows 95,000		150	300	400	650	850	1,000	1,500

Variety 3 – Arrows at Date (1853–1855)

	Mintage	G-4	F-12	VF-20	EF-40	AU-50	MS-60	MS-63	PF-63
1853, With Arrows . . 12,173,000		$12	$15	$25	$50	$125	$250	$500	$13,000
1853O 1,100,000		15	55	85	225	500	1,750	3,750	
1854 4,470,000		12	15	25	50	125	250	500	4,750
1854O 1,770,000		25	55	100	100	175	350	650	
1855 2,075,000		12	15	25	50	125	250	500	4,750

Variety 2 Resumed, With Weight Standard of Variety 3 (1856–1860)

Small Date, Arrows Removed (1856–1860)

	Mintage	G-4	F-12	VF-20	EF-40	AU-50	MS-60	MS-63	PF-63
1856, All kinds. 5,780,000									
1856, Large Date		$20	$65	$80	$150	$200	$500	$1,500	
1856, Small Date.		10	12	20	35	100	200	375	$2,150
1856O 1,180,000		20	50	80	125	300	600	1,000	
1856S 70,000		250	550	1,000	1,500	2,000	6,000	10,000	

	Mintage	G-4	F-12	VF-20	EF-40	AU-50	MS-60	MS-63	PF-63
1857	5,580,000	$10	$12	$18	$45	$100	$225	$375	$2,000
1857O	1,540,000	15	20	30	45	125	275	450	
1858 . . . . . . *(300+)*. . .	1,540,000	10	12	18	35	100	200	375	1,000
1858O	200,000	20	45	100	125	275	650	1,650	
1858S	60,000	225	350	750	1,350	1,750	6,500	12,500	
1859 . . . . . . *(800+)*. . . .	429,200	10	12	25	35	125	225	375	750
1859O	480,000	12	25	45	75	150	275	425	
1859S	60,000	200	400	850	2,400	425	15,000	25,000	
1860S	140,000	75	185	250	500	800	1,750	6,500	

Variety 4 – Legend on Obverse (1860–1873)

	Mintage	G-4	F-12	VF-20	EF-40	AU-50	MS-60	MS-63	PF-63
1860 . . . . . .*(1,000)*.	606,000	$8	$12	$15	$35	$65	$175	$225	$600
1860O	40,000	700	1,500	1,850	4,500	8,500	16,500	35,000	
1861 . . . . . .*(1,000)*. . .	1,883,000	8	12	15	25	50	125	225	600
1861S	172,500	150	325	500	700	1,000	3,750	13,500	
1862 . . . . *(550)*.	847,000	10	12	20	25	50	125	250	600
1862S	180,750	125	250	450	800	1,850	3,500	7,500	
1863 . . . . *(460)*.	14,000	650	1,000	1,350	1,750	2,000	2,500	3,000	600
1863S	157,500	115	250	400	750	1,000	2,750	6,500	
1864 . . . . *(470)*.	11,000	400	850	1,100	1,500	1,650	2,250	3,000	625
1864S	230,000	100	200	350	650	800	1,250	1,650	
1865 . . . . *(500)*.	10,000	650	1,000	1,250	1,750	2,000	2,500	3,000	625
1865S	175,000	100	300	550	850	2,250	5,500	12,500	
1866 . . . . *(725)*.	8,000	600	1,000	1,250	1,500	1,800	2,250	2,500	625
1866S	135,000	100	200	350	550	1,100	2,750	6,000	
1867 . . . . *(625)*.	6,000	750	1,200	1,350	1,500	1,650	2,500	3,000	575
1867S	140,000	100	200	325	600	1,100	2,500	3,500	
1868 . . . . *(600)*. . . .	464,000	15	20	30	50	100	200	500	500
1868S	260,000	50	115	200	400	500	1,150	2,000	
1869 . . . . *(600)*. . . .	256,000	20	30	65	155	165	450	650	450
1869S	450,000	25	50	100	200	250	550	750	
1870 . . . . . .*(1,000)*. . . .	470,500	12	20	25	70	100	200	350	450
1870S	50,000	250	500	600	800	900	1,500	2,500	
1871 . . . . *(960)*. . .	906,750	12	15	20	40	100	275	375	450
1871CC	20,100	2,750	5,500	7,000	13,500	20,000	35,000	—	
1871S	320,000	25	85	125	300	500	1,100	3,000	
1872 . . . . *(950)*. .	2,395,500	12	15	20	25	55	105	200	450
1872CC	35,480	1,250	2,500	3,250	9,000	20,000	75,000	—	
1872S	190,000	40	100	100	250	350	1,500	2,750	
1873, Close 3 *(600)*. . . *1,507,400*		12	20	25	40	65	200	300	450
1873, Open 3 . . . . *60,000*		12	35	45	85	150	600	850	
1873CC *(unique)* *12,400*								—	

Variety 5 – Arrows at Date (1873–1874)

In 1873, the dime was increased in weight from 2.49 grams to 2.50 grams. Arrows at the date in 1873 and 1874 indicate this change.

	Mintage	G-4	F-12	VF-20	EF-40	AU-50	MS-60	MS-63	PF-63
1873 . . . . (500). . .	2,377,700	$12	$20	$40	$115	$250	$300	$600	$800
1873CC	18,791	2,500	4,000	6,500	17,500	40,000	75,000	—	
1873S	455,000	12	25	50	135	400	700	1,250	
1874 . . . . (700). . .	2,940,000	12	20	40	125	225	325	600	800
1874CC	10,817	8,500	15,000	18,500	30,000	45,000	85,000	—	
1874S	240,000	40	85	125	275	550	850	1,650	

Variety 4 Resumed, With Weight Standard of Variety 5 (1875–1891)

	Mintage	G-4	F-12	VF-20	EF-40	AU-50	MS-60	MS-63	PF-63
1875 . . . . (700). .	10,350,000	$10	$12	$15	$25	$55	$125	$200	$425
1875CC	4,645,000	20	30	45	75	150	300	600	
1875S	9,070,000	10	12	15	25	50	125	200	
1876 . . . .(1,250)..	11,460,000	10	12	15	25	50	125	200	425
1876CC	8,270,000	15	30	45	75	150	300	500	
1876S	10,420,000	10	12	15	25	50	125	250	
1877 . . . . (510). . .	7,310,000	10	12	15	25	50	125	200	425
1877CC	7,700,000	15	30	45	75	150	250	600	
1877S	2,340,000	10	12	15	25	75	125	200	
1878 . . . . (800). . .	1,677,200	10	12	15	25	50	125	200	425
1878CC	200,000	165	250	275	350	750	1,250	2,000	
1879 . . . . . .(1,100).	14,000	125	200	285	425	450	500	550	425
1880 . . . . . .(1,355).	36,000	100	185	250	300	350	400	500	425
1881 . . . . (975).	24,000	125	200	250	300	350	550	850	425
1882 . . . . . .(1,100). . .	3,910,000	10	12	15	25	50	125	200	425
1883 . . . . . .(1,039). . .	7,674,673	10	12	15	25	50	125	200	425
1884 . . . . (875). . .	3,365,505	10	12	15	25	50	125	200	425
1884S	564,969	15	30	45	85	250	500	750	
1885 . . . . (930). .	2,532,497	10	12	15	25	50	125	200	425
1885S	43,690	600	900	1,250	2,000	3,250	5,000	6,500	
1886 . . . . (886). .	6,376,684	10	12	15	25	55	125	200	425
1886S	206,524	25	55	75	100	165	400	750	
1887 . . . . (710). .	11,283,229	10	12	15	25	50	125	200	425
1887S	4,454,450	10	12	15	25	65	125	200	
1888 . . . . (832). . .	5,495,655	10	12	15	25	50	125	200	425
1888S	1,720,000	10	12	15	30	50	250	500	
1889 . . . . (711). . .	7,380,000	10	12	15	25	50	125	200	425
1889S	972,678	15	20	30	45	115	250	600	
1890 . . . . (590). .	9,910,951	10	12	15	25	50	125	200	425
1890S	1,423,076	10	15	25	50	100	200	450	
1891 . . . . (600). .	15,310,000	10	12	15	25	50	125	200	425
18910	4,540,000	12	20	25	30	65	150	200	
1891S	3,196,116	10	12	15	25	50	125	200	

BARBER (1892–1916)

This type was designed by Charles E. Barber, chief engraver of the Mint. His initial B is at the truncation of the neck. He also designed the quarters and half dollars of the same period.

G-4 Good: Date and letters plain. LIBERTY obliterated.
VG-8 Very Good: Some letters visible in LIBERTY.
F-12 Fine: Letters in LIBERTY visible, though some weak.
VF-20 Very Fine: Letters of LIBERTY evenly plain.
EF-40 Extremely Fine: All letters in LIBERTY sharp, distinct. Headband edges distinct.
AU-50 About Uncirculated: Slight traces of wear on hair cheekbone and on leaf tips in wreath.
MS-60 Uncirculated: No trace of wear. Light blemishes.
MS-63 Choice Uncirculated: Some distracting blemishes in prime focal areas. Impaired luster possible.

Mintmark location is on reverse, below wreath.

	Mintage	G-4	VG-8	F-12	VF-20	EF-40	AU-50	MS-60	MS-63	PF-63
1892 .... (1,245)...	12,120,000	$3	$5.00	$10	$15	$25	$50	$100	$150	$350
1892O	3,841,700	7	12.00	25	45	55	65	135	300	
1892S	990,710	50	100.00	175	200	250	275	400	650	
1893, 3/2 ....*		100	150.00	200	250	400	550	1,200	1,650	—
1893 ..... (792)...	3,339,940	4	6.00	15	20	25	50	115	165	350
1893O	1,760,000	20	30.00	75	100	115	185	250	450	
1893S **(a)**	2,491,401	8	15.00	25	40	50	100	245	600	
1894 ..... (970)...	1,330,000	15	25.00	100	125	150	165	200	350	350
1894O	720,000	40	55.00	150	200	300	550	1,650	3,500	
1894S	24 **(b)**						2,000,000			
1895 ..... (880).....	690,000	65	100.00	250	350	400	475	600	700	350
1895O	440,000	400	450.00	800	1,150	2,000	2,750	4,500	10,000	
1895S	1,120,000	30	35.00	100	150	175	250	400	850	
1896 ..... (762)....	2,000,000	6	12.00	35	50	65	75	110	300	350
1896O	610,000	60	100.00	225	275	325	650	1,100	2,250	
1896S	576,056	75	150.00	225	250	350	450	750	1,250	
1897 ..... (731)....	10,868,533	3	3.50	4	10	20	45	100	150	350
1897O	666,000	45	85.00	225	275	325	450	850	1,000	
1897S	1,342,844	15	25.00	75	100	125	200	350	650	
1898 ..... (735)...	16,320,000	3	3.50	4	7	25	45	100	145	350
1898O	2,130,000	7	20.00	65	100	135	200	350	800	
1898S	1,702,507	4	10.00	25	30	75	100	400	1,150	
1899 ..... (846)...	19,580,000	3	3.50	4	8	15	45	100	145	350
1899O	2,650,000	5	20.00	50	85	125	175	300	750	
1899S	1,867,493	4	8.00	20	25	40	75	250	500	
1900 ..... (912)...	17,600,000	3	3.50	4	10	20	50	100	145	350

* Included in number below. **a.** Boldly doubled mintmark is valued slightly higher. **b.** Five of these were reserved for assay.

Chart continued on next page.

	Mintage	G-4	VG-8	F-12	VF-20	EF-40	AU-50	MS-60	MS-63	PF-63
1900O 2,010,000		$12	$30.00	$85	$125	$165	$200	$450	$850	
1900S 5,168,270		3	3.50	10	15	20	45	125	300	
1901 . . . . . . (813) . . . 18,859,665		3	3.50	4	8	20	45	100	145	$350
1901O 5,620,000		3	5.00	15	25	40	125	550	750	
1901S 593,022		60	135.00	300	350	450	600	1,250	1,850	
1902 . . . . . . (777) . . . 21,380,000		3	3.50	4	8	20	45	100	165	350
1902O 4,500,000		4	5.00	10	15	50	115	300	550	
1902S 2,070,000		7	15.00	40	65	100	135	300	650	
1903 . . . . . . (755) . . . 19,500,000		3	3.50	4	8	20	50	100	150	350
1903O 8,180,000		4	5.00	10	25	50	60	165	350	
1903S 613,300		50	95.00	275	375	550	750	1,000	1,350	
1904 . . . . . . (670) . . . 14,600,357		3	3.50	4	10	20	45	100	145	350
1904S 800,000		30	55.00	125	155	250	350	650	1,250	
1905 . . . . . . (727) . . . 14,551,623		3	3.50	4	8	20	50	100	145	350
1905O 3,400,000		4	10.00	25	35	85	100	225	325	
1905S 6,855,199		3	3.50	8	15	25	55	135	175	
1906 . . . . . . (675) . . . 19,957,731		3	3.50	4	8	20	50	100	145	350
1906D 4,060,000		3	3.50	4	8	25	55	100	225	
1906O 2,610,000		5	15.00	35	45	85	100	150	300	
1906S 3,136,640		3	3.50	10	15	40	100	200	250	
1907 . . . . . . (575) . . . 22,220,000		3	3.50	4	8	20	45	100	145	350
1907D 4,080,000		3	4.00	6	10	20	75	200	550	
1907O 5,058,000		4	8.00	25	30	40	75	125	250	
1907S 3,178,470		4	5.00	15	20	40	100	250	500	
1908 . . . . . . (545) . . . 10,600,000		3	3.50	4	8	20	45	100	145	350
1908D 7,490,000		3	3.50	4	8	20	45	100	165	
1908O 1,789,000		4	5.00	30	35	55	125	300	500	
1908S 3,220,000		3	3.50	10	15	25	100	250	500	
1909 . . . . . . (650) . . . 10,240,000		3	3.50	4	8	20	45	100	145	350
1909D 954,000		3	15.00	50	75	100	165	375	650	
1909O 2,287,000		3	5.00	8	15	35	115	225	500	
1909S 1,000,000		8	20.00	65	85	125	225	350	850	
1910 . . . . . . (551) . . . 11,520,000		3	3.50	4	8	20	50	100	145	350
1910D 3,490,000		3	3.50	4	15	30	55	150	300	
1910S 1,240,000		3	3.50	35	50	85	135	300	450	
1911 . . . . . . (543) . . . 18,870,000		3	3.50	4	8	20	50	100	145	350
1911D 11,209,000		3	3.50	4	8	20	50	100	145	
1911S 3,520,000		3	3.50	4	12	20	75	125	225	
1912 . . . . . . (700) . . . 19,349,300		3	3.50	4	8	20	50	100	145	350
1912D 11,760,000		3	3.50	4	8	20	45	100	145	
1912S 3,420,000		3	3.50	4	8	25	55	115	200	
1913 . . . . . . (622) . . . 19,760,000		3	3.50	4	8	20	45	100	145	350
1913S 510,000		25	35.00	100	135	225	300	600	1,150	
1914 . . . . . . (425) . . . 17,360,230		3	3.50	4	8	20	45	100	145	350
1914D 11,908,000		3	3.50	4	8	20	45	100	150	
1914S 2,100,000		3	3.50	5	15	25	45	125	225	
1915 . . . . . . (450) . . . 5,620,000		3	3.50	4	8	20	45	100	145	350
1915S 960,000		5	8.00	15	35	55	100	165	300	
1916 18,490,000		3	3.50	4	8	20	45	100	145	
1916S 5,820,000		3	3.50	4	8	20	45	100	145	

WINGED LIBERTY HEAD
OR "MERCURY" (1916–1945)

Although this coin is commonly called the *Mercury* dime, the main device is in fact a representation of Liberty. The wings crowning her cap are intended to symbolize liberty of thought. Designer Adolph Weinman's monogram, AW, is at the right of the neck. A centennial gold issue was struck in 2016.

G-4 Good: Letters and date clear. Lines and bands in fasces obliterated.
VG-8 Very Good: Half of sticks discernible in fasces.
F-12 Fine: All sticks in fasces defined. Diagonal bands worn nearly flat.
VF-20 Very Fine: Diagonal bands definitely visible.
EF-40 Extremely Fine: Only slight wear on diagonal bands. Braids and hair before ear clearly visible.
AU-50 About Uncirculated: Slight trace of wear. Most mint luster present.
MS-63 Choice Uncirculated: No trace of wear. Light blemishes. Attractive mint luster.
MS-65 Gem Uncirculated: Only light, scattered, non-distracting marks. Strong luster, good eye appeal.

Mintmark location is on reverse, left of fasces.

The Mint State prices shown are what coin dealers pay for average Uncirculated pieces with minimum blemishes. For coins with sharp strikes and split horizontal bands on the reverse, they usually pay much more.

	Mintage	G-4	VG-8	F-12	VF-20	EF-40	MS-60	MS-63	MS-65
1916	22,180,080	$2.50	$3.00	$4	$5.00	$6	$35	$65	$115
1916D	264,000	900.00	1,500.00	2,500.00	3,500.00	5,500	10,000	14,000	22,500
1916S	10,450,000	2.50	3.00	5.00	10.00	15	30	75	200
1917	55,230,000	2.00	2.05	2.10	2.50	4	15	40	125
1917D	9,402,000	2.50	3.00	8.00	12.00	40	85	175	600
1917S	27,330,000	2.00	2.05	2.10	3.00	10	75	150	275
1918	26,680,000	2.00	2.05	3.00	5.00	25	55	100	300
1918D	22,674,800	2.00	2.05	3.00	8.00	25	125	250	550
1918S	19,300,000	2.00	2.05	2.10	4.00	20	100	250	650
1919	35,740,000	2.00	2.05	2.10	2.50	8	35	115	300
1919D	9,939,000	2.00	2.05	5.00	15.00	40	250	500	1,200
1919S	8,850,000	2.00	2.05	6.00	15.00	30	250	650	1,500
1920	59,030,000	2.00	2.05	2.10	2.50	5	25	55	175
1920D	19,171,000	2.00	2.05	2.10	3.00	15	150	350	500
1920S	13,820,000	2.00	2.05	4.00	5.00	25	250	400	1,100
1921	1,230,000	35.00	55.00	85.00	185.00	400	1,200	2,000	2,850
1921D	1,080,000	40.00	85.00	135.00	235.00	500	1,500	2,000	2,650
1923	50,130,000	2.00	2.05	2.10	2.50	3	20	35	115
1923S	6,440,000	2.00	2.05	4.00	15.00	65	250	450	1,000
1924	24,010,000	2.00	2.05	2.10	2.50	10	20	50	150
1924D	6,810,000	2.00	2.05	3.00	15.00	45	225	350	850
1924S	7,120,000	2.00	2.05	2.10	10.00	55	250	400	1,350
1925	25,610,000	2.00	2.05	2.10	2.50	5	25	75	225
1925D	5,117,000	3.00	3.50	8.00	40.00	110	350	650	1,200
1925S	5,850,000	2.00	2.05	8.00	20.00	55	250	550	1,000
1926	32,160,000	2.00	2.05	2.10	2.50	4	25	55	200
1926D	6,828,000	2.00	2.05	2.10	10.00	25	135	225	500
1926S	1,520,000	6.00	10.00	20.00	55.00	250	1,350	2,000	3,000
1927	28,080,000	2.00	2.05	2.10	2.50	4	25	50	100
1927D	4,812,000	2.00	2.05	5.00	25.00	65	300	500	1,250

Chart continued on next page.

	Mintage	G-4	VG-8	F-12	VF-20	EF-40	MS-60	MS-63	MS-65
1927S	4,770,000	$2.00	$2.05	$3.00	$5.00	$20	$350	$550	$1,100
1928	19,480,000	2.00	2.05	2.10	2.50	4	20	50	100
1928D	4,161,000	2.00	2.05	8	20.00	55	150	350	750
1928S	7,400,000	2.00	2.05	3.00	5.00	15	115	225	350
1929	25,970,000	2.00	2.05	2.10	2.50	5	20	25	50
1929D	5,034,000	2.00	2.05	2.10	3.00	5	20	25	85
1929S	4,730,000	2.00	2.05	2.10	2.50	4	25	35	150
1930	6,770,000	2.00	2.05	2.10	2.50	4	15	25	75
1930S	1,843,000	2.00	2.05	3	5.00	12	45	100	225
1931	3,150,000	2.00	2.05	2.10	2.50	20	25	40	125
1931D	1,260,000	4.00	5.00	10	15.00	20	75	125	300
1931S	1,800,000	3.00	4.00	5	10.00	12	100	150	300

	Mintage	VG-8	F-12	VF-20	EF-40	MS-60	MS-63	MS-65	PF-63
1934	24,080,000	$2.00	$2.05	$2.10	$2.50	$15.00	$25	$30	
1934D	6,772,000	2.00	2.05	2.10	2.50	40.00	45	65	
1935	58,830,000	2.00	2.05	2.10	2.50	5.00	10	25	
1935D	10,477,000	2.00	2.05	2.10	2.50	16.00	35	50	
1935S	15,840,000	2.00	2.05	2.10	2.50	10.00	20	25	
1936 (4,130)	87,500,000	2.00	2.05	2.10	2.50	5.00	10	20	$550
1936D	16,132,000	2.00	2.05	2.10	2.50	25.00	20	30	
1936S	9,210,000	2.00	2.05	2.10	2.50	12.00	20	20	
1937 (5,756)	56,860,000	2.00	2.05	2.10	2.50	4.00	7	15	275
1937D	14,146,000	2.00	2.05	2.10	2.50	12.00	16	25	
1937S	9,740,000	2.00	2.05	2.10	2.50	12.00	16	25	
1938 (8,728)	22,190,000	2.00	2.05	2.10	2.50	12.00	15	20	125
1938D	5,537,000	2.00	2.05	2.10	2.50	9.00	10	16	
1938S	8,090,000	2.00	2.05	2.10	2.50	8.00	9	20	
1939 (9,321)	67,740,000	2.00	2.05	2.10	2.50	4.00	6	15	125
1939D	24,394,000	2.00	2.05	2.10	2.50	12.00	15	20	
1939S	10,540,000	2.00	2.05	2.10	2.50	12.00	15	20	
1940 (11,827)	65,350,000	2.00	2.05	2.10	2.50	4.00	6	15	100
1940D	21,198,000	2.00	2.05	2.10	2.50	4.00	6	16	
1940S	21,560,000	2.00	2.05	2.10	2.50	4.00	6	16	
1941 (16,557)	175,090,000	2.00	2.05	2.10	2.50	4.00	6	15	100
1941D	45,634,000	2.00	2.05	2.10	2.50	4.00	6	16	
1941S	43,090,000	2.00	2.05	2.10	2.50	4.00	6	16	
1942, 42 Over 41	*	280.00	300.00	350.00	425.00	2,400.00	4,250	10,000	
1942 (22,329)	205,410,000	2.00	2.05	2.10	2.50	4.00	6	15	100
1942D, 42 Over 41	*	250.00	300.00	350.00	375.00	2,400.00	4,500	13,500	
1942D	60,740,000	2.00	2.05	2.10	2.50	5.00	7	16	
1942S	49,300,000	2.00	2.05	2.10	2.50	6.00	7	16	
1943	191,710,000	2.00	2.05	2.10	2.50	4.00	6	15	
1943D	71,949,000	2.00	2.05	2.10	2.50	5.00	7	16	
1943S	60,400,000	2.00	2.05	2.10	2.50	5.00	7	15	
1944	231,410,000	2.00	2.05	2.10	2.50	4.00	6	15	
1944D	62,224,000	2.00	2.05	2.10	2.50	5.00	7	15	
1944S	49,490,000	2.00	2.05	2.10	2.50	5.00	7	16	
1945	159,130,000	2.00	2.05	2.10	2.50	4.00	6	15	
1945D	40,245,000	2.00	2.05	2.10	2.50	4.00	6	16	
1945S	41,920,000	2.00	2.05	2.10	2.50	5.00	7	16	
1945S, Micro S	*	3.00	3.25	4.00	5.00	20	18	45	

* Included in number above.

ROOSEVELT (1946 TO DATE)

John R. Sinnock (whose initials, JS, are at the truncation of the neck) designed this dime showing a portrait of Franklin D. Roosevelt. The design has heavier lettering and a more modernistic character than preceding types.

VF-20 Very Fine: Moderate wear on high points of design. All major details are clear.
EF-40 Extremely Fine: All lines of torch, flame, and hair very plain.
MS-63 Choice Uncirculated: Some distracting contact marks or blemishes in prime focal areas. Impaired luster possible.
MS-65 Gem Uncirculated: Only light, non-distracting scattered marks. Strong luster, good eye appeal.
PF-65 Gem Proof: Nearly perfect.

Mintmark on reverse,
1946–1964.

Silver Coinage (1946–1964)

	Mintage	VF-20	EF-40	MS-63	MS-65	PF-65
1946	255,250,000	$1.75	$1.75	$2.50	$6.00	
1946D	61,043,500	1.75	1.75	2.50	7.00	
1946S	27,900,000	1.75	1.75	4.00	10.00	
1947	121,520,000	1.75	1.75	2.50	6.00	
1947D	46,835,000	1.75	1.75	2.50	6.00	
1947S	34,840,000	1.75	1.75	2.50	6.00	
1948	74,950,000	1.75	1.75	2.50	6.00	
1948D	52,841,000	1.75	1.75	2.50	6.00	
1948S	35,520,000	1.75	1.75	2.50	6.00	
1949	30,940,000	1.75	1.75	14.00	20.00	
1949D	26,034,000	1.75	1.75	5.00	9.00	
1949S	13,510,000	1.75	1.75	25.00	40.00	
1950	(51,386) 50,130,114	1.75	1.75	6.50	8.00	$25
1950D	46,803,000	1.75	1.75	2.50	6.00	
1950S	20,440,000	1.75	1.75	20.00	35.00	
1951	(57,500) 103,880,102	1.75	1.75	2.00	5.00	25
1951D	56,529,000	1.75	1.75	2.00	5.00	
1951S	31,630,000	1.75	1.75	7.50	15.00	
1952	(81,980) 99,040,093	1.75	1.75	2.00	5.00	18
1952D	122,100,000	1.75	1.75	2.00	4.00	
1952S	44,419,500	1.75	1.75	3.75	6.25	
1953	(128,800) 53,490,120	1.75	1.75	2.50	4.50	20
1953D	136,433,000	1.75	1.75	2.50	4.50	
1953S	39,180,000	1.75	1.75	2.50	4.50	
1954	(233,300) 114,010,203	1.75	1.75	2.00	4.00	10
1954D	106,397,000	1.75	1.75	2.00	4.00	
1954S	22,860,000	1.75	1.75	2.00	4.00	

Chart continued on next page.

	Mintage	VF-20	EF-40	MS-63	MS-65	PF-65
1955 . . . .(378,200) 12,450,181		$1.75	$1.75	$2	$5.00	$8
1955D 13,959,000		1.75	1.75	2	4.00	
1955S 18,510,000		1.75	1.75	2	4.00	
1956 . . . .(669,384) 108,640,000		1.75	1.75	2	4.00	4
1956D 108,015,100		1.75	1.75	2	3.50	
1957 . . . .(1,247,952) 160,160,000		1.75	1.75	2	3.50	3
1957D 113,354,330		1.75	1.75	2	3.25	
1958 . . . .(875,652) 31,910,000		1.75	1.75	2	4.00	3
1958D 136,564,600		1.75	1.75	2	4.00	
1959 . . . .(1,149,291) 85,780,000		1.75	1.75	2	3.50	3
1959D 164,919,790		1.75	1.75	2	3.50	
1960 . . . .(1,691,602) 70,390,000		1.75	1.75	2	3.50	3
1960D 200,160,400		1.75	1.75	2		
1961 . . . .(3,028,244) 93,730,000		1.75	1.75	2	3.00	3
1961D 209,146,550		1.75	1.75	2	3.00	
1962 . . . .(3,218,019) 72,450,000		1.75	1.75	2	3.00	3
1962D 334,948,380		1.75	1.75	2	3.00	
1963 . . . .(3,075,645) 123,650,000		1.75	1.75	2	3.00	3
1963D 421,476,530		1.75	1.75	2	3.00	
1964 . . . .(3,950,762) 929,360,000		1.75	1.75	2	3.00	3
1964D 1,357,517,180		1.75	1.75	2	3.00	

Clad Coinage and Silver Proofs (1965 to Date)

*Mintmark on obverse,
starting in 1968.*

	Mintage	MS-63	MS-65	PF-65		Mintage	MS-63	MS-65	PF-65
1965	1,652,140,570	$0.15	$1.00		1973S	(2,760,339)			$0.80
1966	1,382,734,540	0.15	0.90		1974	470,248,000	$0.15	$0.50	
1967	2,244,007,320	0.15	0.80		1974D	571,083,000	0.15	0.50	
1968	424,470,400	0.15	0.80		1974S	(2,612,568)			0.80
1968D	480,748,280	0.15	0.80		1975	585,673,900	0.15	0.50	
1968S	(3,041,506)			$0.80	1975D	313,705,300	0.15	0.50	
1969	145,790,000	0.25	1.00		1975S	(2,845,450)			1.00
1969D	563,323,870	0.15	0.75		1976	568,760,000	0.15	0.50	
1969S	(2,394,631)			0.80	1976D	695,222,774	0.15	0.50	
1970	345,570,000	0.15	0.50		1976S	(4,149,730)			1.00
1970D	754,942,100	0.15	0.50		1977	796,930,000	0.15	0.50	
1970S	(2,632,810)			0.80	1977D	376,607,228	0.15	0.50	
1971	162,690,000	0.18	0.75		1977S	(3,251,152)			0.80
1971D	377,914,240	0.16	0.65		1978	663,980,000	0.15	0.50	
1971S	(3,220,733)			0.80	1978D	282,847,540	0.15	0.50	
1972	431,540,000	0.15	0.50		1978S	(3,127,781)			0.80
1972D	330,290,000	0.15	0.50		1979	315,440,000	0.15	0.50	
1972S	(3,260,996)			0.80	1979D	390,921,184	0.15	0.50	
1973	315,670,000	0.15	0.50		1979S, Type 1 . .	(3,677,175)			2.75
1973D	455,032,426	0.15	0.50		1979S, Type 2 . . . .*				4.00

* Included in number above.

Mintage	MS-63	MS-65	PF-65
1980P 735,170,000	$0.15	$0.50	
1980D 719,354,321	0.15	0.50	
1980S . . . . (3,554,806)			$0.80
1981P 676,650,000	0.15	0.50	
1981D 712,284,143	0.15	0.50	
1981S, Type 1 . . (4,063,083)			2.75
1981S, Type 2 . . . .*			14.00
1982, No Mmk.	30.00	50.00	
1982P 519,475,000	1.50	2.75	
1982D 542,713,584	0.60	1.50	
1982S . . . . (3,857,479)			1.50
1983P 647,025,000	1.25	2.75	
1983D 730,129,224	0.50	1.75	
1983S . . . . (3,279,126)			1.00
1984P 856,669,000	0.15	0.60	
1984D 704,803,976	0.20	0.75	
1984S . . . . (3,065,110)			1.00
1985P 705,200,962	0.15	0.60	
1985D 587,979,970	0.15	0.60	
1985S . . . . (3,362,821)			1.00
1986P 682,649,693	0.25	0.75	
1986D 473,326,970	0.25	0.75	
1986S . . . . (3,010,497)			1.75
1987P 762,709,481	0.15	0.60	
1987D 653,203,402	0.15	0.60	
1987S . . . . (4,227,728)			1.25
1988P 1,030,550,000	0.12	0.50	
1988D 962,385,489	0.12	0.50	
1988S . . . . (3,262,948)			1.75
1989P 1,298,400,000	0.10	0.50	
1989D 896,535,597	0.10	0.50	
1989S . . . . (3,220,194)			1.75
1990P 1,034,340,000	0.10	0.50	
1990D 839,995,824	0.10	0.50	
1990S . . . . (3,299,559)			1.00
1991P 927,220,000	0.10	0.50	
1991D 601,241,114	0.12	0.50	
1991S . . . . (2,867,787)			1.70
1992P 593,500,000	0.10	0.50	
1992D 616,273,932	0.10	0.50	
1992S . . . . (2,858,981)			1.50
1992S, Silver . . . (1,317,579)			3.00
1993P 766,180,000	0.10	0.50	
1993D 750,110,166	0.10	0.50	
1993S . . . . (2,633,439)			2.25
1993S, Silver . . . . (761,353)			3.50
1994P 1,189,000,000	0.10	0.50	
1994D 1,303,268,110	0.10	0.50	
1994S . . . . (2,484,594)			2.25
1994S, Silver . . . . (785,329)			3.75

Mintage	MS-63	MS-65	PF-65
1995P 1,125,500,000	$0.10	$0.50	
1995D 1,274,890,000	0.15	0.50	
1995S . . . . (2,117,496)			$5.50
1995S, Silver . . . . . (679,985)			7.50
1996P 1,421,163,000	0.10	0.50	
1996D 1,400,300,000	0.10	0.50	
1996W 1,457,000	6.00	11.00	
1996S . . . . (1,750,244)			1.25
1996S, Silver . . . . . (775,021)			3.50
1997P 991,640,000	0.10	0.50	
1997D 979,810,000	0.10	0.50	
1997S . . . . (2,055,000)			3.50
1997S, Silver . . . . (741,678)			7.00
1998P 1,163,000,000	0.10	0.50	
1998D 1,172,250,000	0.10	0.50	
1998S . . . . (2,086,507)			1.75
1998S, Silver . . . . . (878,792)			3.00
1999P 2,164,000,000	0.10	0.50	
1999D 1,397,750,000	0.10	0.50	
1999S . . . . (2,543,401)			1.75
1999S, Silver . . . . . (804,565)			3.50
2000P 1,842,500,000	0.10	0.50	
2000D 1,818,700,000	0.10	0.50	
2000S . . . . (3,082,572)			1.00
2000S, Silver . . . . . (965,421)			3.00
2001P 1,369,590,000	0.10	0.50	
2001D 1,412,800,000	0.10	0.50	
2001S . . . . (2,294,909)			0.75
2001S, Silver . . . . . (889,697)			3.00
2002P 1,187,500,000	0.10	0.50	
2002D 1,379,500,000	0.10	0.50	
2002S . . . . (2,319,766)			0.75
2002S, Silver . . . . . (892,229)			3.00
2003P 1,085,500,000	0.10	0.50	
2003D 986,500,000	0.10	0.50	
2003S . . . . (2,172,684)			0.75
2003S, Silver . . . (1,125,755)			3.00
2004P 1,328,000,000	0.10	0.50	
2004D 1,159,500,000	0.10	0.50	
2004S . . . . (1,789,488)			0.75
2004S, Silver . . . (1,175,934)			3.00
2005P 1,412,000,000	0.10	0.50	
2005D 1,423,500,000	0.10	0.50	
2005S . . . . (2,275,000)			0.75
2005S, Silver . . . (1,069,679)			3.00
2006P 1,381,000,000	0.10	0.50	
2006D 1,447,000,000	0.10	0.50	
2006S . . . . (2,000,428)			0.75
2006S, Silver . . . (1,054,008)			3.00
2007P 1,047,500,000	0.10	0.50	

* Included in number above.

Chart continued on next page.

	Mintage	MS-63	MS-65	PF-65
2007D 1,042,000,000	$0.10	$0.50	
2007S . . . . (1,702,116)			$0.75
2007S, Silver . . . . . (875,050)			3.00
2008P 391,000,000	0.10	0.50	
2008D 624,500,000	0.10	0.50	
2008S . . . . (1,405,674)			0.75
2008S, Silver . . . . . (763,887)			3.00
2009P 96,500,000	0.20	0.50	
2009D 49,500,000	0.20	0.50	
2009S . . . . (1,482,502)			0.75
2009S, Silver . . . . . (697,365)			3.00
2010P 557,000,000	0.10	0.50	
2010D 562,000,000	0.10	0.50	
2010S . . . . (1,103,815)			0.75
2010S, Silver . . . . . (585,401)			3.00
2011P 748,000,000	0.10	0.50	
2011D 754,000,000	0.10	0.50	
2011S . . . . (1,098,835)			0.75
2011S, Silver . . . . . (574,175)			3.00
2012P 808,000,000	0.10	0.50	
2012D 868,000,000	0.10	0.50	

	Mintage	MS-63	MS-65	PF-65
2012S . . . . (843,705)			$0.75
2012S, Silver . . . . . (445,612)			12.00
2013P 1,086,500,000	$0.10	$0.50	
2013D 1,025,500,000	0.10	0.50	
2013S . . . . (856,953)			0.75
2013S, Silver . . . . . (467,691)			3.00
2014P 1,125,500,000	0.10	0.50	
2014D 1,177,000,000	0.10	0.50	
2014S . . . . (783,256)			0.75
2014S, Silver . . . . . (472,107)			3.00
2015P 1,497,510,000	0.10	0.50	
2015P, Rev Pf,	0.10	0.50	
Silver (a) . . . .(74,430)			
2015D 1,543,500,000			20.00
2015S . . . . (711,872)			0.75
2015S, Silver . . . . . (387,310)			3.00
2015W, Silver (a). . .(74,430)			5.00
2016P 1,517,000,000	0.10	0.50	
2016D 1,437,000,000	0.10	0.50	
2016S . . . . (641,775)			0.75
2016S, Silver . . . . . (419,496)			3.00

a. Included in March of Dimes commemorative Proof set.

	Mintage	SP-69	SP-70
2016W, Gold (a) . . . . (124,885)	$200	$225

a. In 2016 the Mint issued a centennial version of the Winged Liberty Head ("Mercury") dime in gold.

	Mintage	MS-63	MS-65	PF-65
2017P 1,437,500,000	$0.10	$0.50	
2017D 1,290,500,000	0.10	0.50	
2017S . . . . (621,390)			$0.75
2017S, Silver . . . . . (406,986)			3.00
2018P 1,193,000,000	0.10	0.50	
2018D 1,006,000,000	0.10	0.50	
2018S . . . . (568,804)			0.75
2018S, Silver . . . . . (381,748)			3.00
2019P 1,147,500,000	0.10	0.50	
2019D 1,001,500,000	0.10	0.50	
2019S . . . . (649,954)			0.75
2019S, Silver . . . . . (461,125)			3.00
2020P 1,333,500,000	0.10	0.50	
2020D 1,445,000,000	0.10	0.50	
2020S . . . . (510,726)			0.75
2020S, Silver . . . . . (363,244)			3.00

	Mintage	MS-63	MS-65	PF-65
2021P 1,349,250,000	$0.10	$0.50	
2021D 1,481,000,000	0.10	0.50	
2021S . . . . (512,729)			$0.75
2021S, Silver . . . . . (350,323)			3.00
2022P 1,551,000,000	0.10	0.50	
2022D 1,583,000,000	0.10	0.50	
2022S . . . . (400,007)			0.75
2022S, Silver . . . . . (295,153)			3.00
2023P	0.10	0.50	
2023D	0.10	0.50	
2023S			0.75
2023S, Silver			3.00
2024P	0.10	0.50	
2024D	0.10	0.50	
2024S			0.75
2024S, Silver			3.00

LIBERTY SEATED (1875–1878)

The twenty-cent piece was a short-lived coin authorized by the Act of March 3, 1875. The edge of the coin is plain. Most of the 1876-CC coins were melted at the Mint and never released. The mintmark is on the reverse below the eagle.

G-4 Good: LIBERTY on shield obliterated. Letters and date legible.
VG-8 Very Good: One or two letters in LIBERTY barely visible. Other details bold.
F-12 Fine: Some letters of LIBERTY possibly visible.
VF-20 Very Fine: LIBERTY readable, but partly weak.
EF-40 Extremely Fine: LIBERTY mostly sharp. Only slight wear on high points of coin.
AU-50 About Uncirculated: Slight trace of wear on breast, head, and knees.
MS-60 Uncirculated: No trace of wear. Light blemishes.
MS-63 Choice Uncirculated: Some distracting blemishes in prime focal areas. Some impairment of luster possible.
PF-63 Choice Proof: Reflective surfaces with only a few blemishes in secondary focal places. No major flaws.

	Mintage	G-4	VG-8	F-12	VF-20	EF-40	AU-50	MS-60	MS-63	PF-63
1875 . . . . (1,200) 38,500		$155	$175	$215	$225	$300	$450	$700	$1,200	$2,250
1875CC 133,290		185	225	325	375	600	800	1,650	2,500	
1875S 1,155,000		100	110	150	165	200	250	650	850	
1876 . . . . (1,150) 14,750		185	250	300	375	450	500	850	1,250	2,250
1876CC 10,000							150,000	200,000	300,000	
1877 . . . . . . (510)					2,500	3,500				6,000
1878 . . . . . . (600)					1,750	2,000				3,250

Authorized in 1792, this denomination was not issued until four years later. The first type weighed 104 grains, the standard until modified to 103-1/8 grains by the Act of January 18, 1837. As with the dime and half dime, the weight was reduced and arrows placed at the date in 1853. Rays were placed in the field of the reverse during that year only.

DRAPED BUST (1796–1807)

AG-3 About Good: Details clear enough to identify.
G-4 Good: Date readable. Bust outlined, but no detail.
VG-8 Very Good: All but deepest drapery folds worn smooth. Hairlines nearly gone and curls lacking in detail.
F-12 Fine: All drapery lines visible. Hair partly worn.
VF-20 Very Fine: Only left side of drapery indistinct.
EF-40 Extremely Fine: Hair well outlined and detailed.
AU-50 About Uncirculated: Slight trace of wear on shoulder and highest waves of hair.
MS-60 Uncirculated: No trace of wear. Light blemishes.
MS-63 Choice Uncirculated: Some distracting marks or blemishes in focal areas. Impaired luster possible.

Small Eagle Reverse (1796)

	Mintage	AG-3	G-4	VG-8	F-12	VF-20	EF-40	AU-50	MS-60	MS-63
1796	6,146	$5,000	$9,500	$16,000	$25,000	$35,000	$50,000	$55,000	$80,000	$145,000

Heraldic Eagle Reverse (1804–1807)

	Mintage	AG-3	G-4	VG-8	F-12	VF-20	EF-40	AU-50	MS-60	MS-63
1804	6,738	$1,350	$2,750	$4,500	$6,500	$9,000	$25,000	$42,500	$80,000	$145,000
1805	121,394	135	275	375	600	1,200	2,500	4,000	8,500	15,000
1806, 6 Over 5	*	150	350	550	800	1,350	3,000	5,500	10,000	20,000
1806	206,124	135	265	400	550	1,000	2,300	3,500	7,500	15,000
1807	220,643	135	265	400	550	1,200	2,350	3,750	7,500	15,000

* Included in number below.

CAPPED BUST (1815–1838)
Variety 1 – Large Diameter (1815–1828)

AG-3 About Good: Details clear enough to identify.
G-4 Good: Date, letters, stars legible. Hair under Liberty's headband smooth. Cap lines worn smooth.
VG-8 Very Good: Rim well defined. Main details visible. Full LIBERTY on cap. Hair above eye nearly smooth.
F-12 Fine: All hair lines visible, but only partial detail visible in drapery. Shoulder clasp distinct.
VF-20 Very Fine: All details visible, but some wear evident. Clasp and ear sharp.
EF-40 Extremely Fine: All details distinct. Hair well outlined.
AU-50 About Uncirculated: Slight trace of wear on tips of curls and above the eye, and on the wing and claw tips.
MS-60 Uncirculated: No trace of wear. Light blemishes.
MS-63 Choice Uncirculated: Some distracting marks or blemishes in focal areas. Impaired luster possible.

Mintage	AG-3	G-4	VG-8	F-12	VF-20	EF-40	AU-50	MS-60	MS-63
1815 89,235	$95	$175	$300	$400	$550	$1,750	$2,000	$3,500	$5,500
1818, 8 Over 5 . . . .*	55	100	135	225	400	1,000	1,450	2,750	5,500
1818 361,174	55	100	125	225	375	1,000	1,450	2,750	5,500
1819 144,000	55	100	125	225	375	1,000	1,500	3,000	6,500
1820 127,444	55	100	125	225	375	1,000	1,500	2,850	5,000
1821 216,851	55	100	125	225	375	1,000	1,450	2,750	5,000
1822 64,080	95	160	250	350	750	1,250	2,000	2,750	6,500
1822, 25 Over 50 C. . . . .*	2,500	4,500	6,500	15,000	20,000	30,000	37,500	45,000	
1823, 3 Over 2 17,800	18,000	35,000	45,000	55,000	65,000	75,000	100,000	—	
1824, 4 Over 2 . . . .**	250	450	700	1,200	1,400	3,250	5,000	17,500	
1825 168,000	65	125	200	325	500	1,000	1,750	3,500	5,000
1827, Original (Curl									
Base 2 in 25 C.) (a). . . 4,000									175,000
1827, Restrike (Square									
Base 2 in 25 C.) (a). . . . . . .*									45,000
1828 102,000	45	90	125	190	325	800	1,650	2,750	4,500
1828, 25 Over 50 C. . . . .*	400	850	1,250	2,000	2,500	5,500	8,500	12,500	65,000

* Included in regular mintage. ** Included in 1825 mintage. **a.** The 7 is punched over a 3, which is punched over an earlier 2.

Variety 2 – Reduced Diameter (1831–1838), Motto Removed

G-4 Good: Bust of Liberty well defined. Hair under headband smooth. Date, letters, stars legible. Scant rims.
VG-8 Very Good: Details apparent but worn on high spots. Rims strong. Full LIBERTY.
F-12 Fine: All hair lines visible. Drapery partly worn. Shoulder clasp distinct.
VF-20 Very Fine: Only top spots worn. Clasp sharp. Ear distinct.
EF-40 Extremely Fine: Hair details and clasp bold and clear.

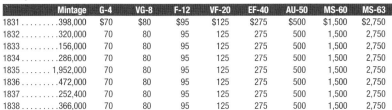

AU-50 About Uncirculated: Slight trace of wear on hair around forehead, on cheek, and at top and bottom tips of eagle's wings and left claw.
MS-60 Uncirculated: No trace of wear. Light blemishes.
MS-63 Choice Uncirculated: Some distracting contact marks or blemishes in prime focal areas. Impaired luster possible.

Mintage	G-4	VG-8	F-12	VF-20	EF-40	AU-50	MS-60	MS-63
1831 398,000	$70	$80	$95	$125	$275	$500	$1,500	$2,750
1832 320,000	70	80	95	125	275	500	1,500	2,750
1833 156,000	70	80	95	125	275	500	1,500	2,750
1834 286,000	70	80	95	125	275	500	1,500	2,750
1835 1,952,000	70	80	95	125	275	500	1,500	2,750
1836 472,000	70	80	95	125	275	500	1,500	2,750
1837 252,400	70	80	95	125	275	500	1,500	2,750
1838 366,000	70	80	95	125	275	500	1,500	2,750

LIBERTY SEATED (1838–1891)

G-4 Good: Scant rim. LIBERTY on shield worn off. Date and letters legible.
VG-8 Very Good: Rim fairly defined, at least three letters in LIBERTY evident.
F-12 Fine: LIBERTY complete, but partly weak.
VF-20 Very Fine: LIBERTY strong.
EF-40 Extremely Fine: Complete LIBERTY and edges of scroll. Shoulder clasp clear on Liberty's gown.
AU-50 About Uncirculated: Slight wear on Liberty's knees and breast and on eagle's neck, wing tips, and claws.
MS-60 Uncirculated: No trace of wear. Light blemishes.
MS-63 Choice Uncirculated: Some distracting marks or blemishes in focal areas. Impaired luster possible.

Variety 1 – No Motto Above Eagle (1838–1853)

Small Date

Mintmark location is on reverse, below eagle.

Large Date

	Mintage	G-4	VG-8	F-12	VF-20	EF-40	AU-50	MS-60	MS-63
1838	466,000	$25	$30	$45	$185	$375	$800	$1,350	$3,500
1839	491,146	25	30	45	185	375	800	1,350	3,500
1840	188,127	35	45	65	165	250	450	1,350	3,500
1840O	425,200	35	45	55	110	260	500	1,000	3,500
1841	120,000	40	65	90	185	350	550	1,000	1,500
1841O	452,000	35	45	50	85	225	280	650	1,250
1842, Small Date (Proof only)									45,000
1842, Large Date	88,000	45	60	95	180	300	550	1,250	3,250
1842O, Small Date	*	450	900	1,200	2,250	5,500	10,000	30,000	
1842O, Large Date	769,000	35	40	48	85	200	400	1,200	3,250
1843	645,600	35	40	45	50	150	180	500	1,000
1843O	968,000	32	50	110	250	650	1,000	2,000	4,500
1844	421,200	35	40	45	50	60	120	500	1,250
1844O	740,000	35	45	50	85	185	300	1,000	1,250
1845	922,000	25	30	40	50	100	150	450	800
1846	510,000	32	50	75	85	200	350	750	1,500
1847	734,000	35	40	50	65	75	200	500	1,350
1847O	368,000	75	110	250	400	650	1,250	5,500	10,000
1848	146,000	32	50	85	115	250	350	1,000	3,500
1849	340,000	35	40	50	55	80	225	750	1,000
1849O	(a)	1,050	1,500	2,250	2,650	5,500	6,000	14,500	17,500
1850	190,800	24	35	65	85	180	450	1,250	2,250
1850O	412,000	45	80	135	175	450	650	1,500	3,750
1851	160,000	65	125	225	300	450	700	1,000	1,750
1851O	88,000	350	500	775	1,000	2,250	3,000	8,000	
1852	177,060	45	65	95	200	350	550	900	1,350
1852O	96,000	250	375	550	1,200	1,600	5,000	8,000	22,500
1853, Recut Date, No Arrows or Rays	44,200	1,000	1,350	2,000	2,500	3,250	4,350	5,000	5,500

* Included in number below. **a.** Mintage for 1849-O included with 1850-O.

Variety 2 – Arrows at Date, Rays Around Eagle (1853)

1853, 3 Over 4

	Mintage	G-4	VG-8	F-12	VF-20	EF-40	AU-50	MS-60	MS-63
1853	15,210,020	$20	$25	$30	$55	$150	$300	$800	$1,250
1853, 3 Over 4	*	42	65	125	250	450	650	1,500	3,000
1853O	1,332,000	32	45	65	110	300	750	3,250	7,500

* Included in number above.

Variety 3 – Arrows at Date, No Rays (1854–1855)

	Mintage	G-4	VG-8	F-12	VF-20	EF-40	AU-50	MS-60	MS-63
1854	12,380,000	$20	$25	$27	$35	$75	$185	$500	$900
1854O	1,484,000	35	40	45	60	85	225	725	1,250
1855	2,857,000	20	25	27	35	75	225	450	850
1855O	176,000	100	150	250	550	1,250	2,250	4,500	12,500
1855S	396,400	125	200	300	450	850	1,250	2,750	7,500

Variety 1 Resumed, With Weight Standard of Variety 2 (1856–1865)

	Mintage	G-4	VG-8	F-12	VF-20	EF-40	AU-50	MS-60	MS-63	PF-63
1856	7,264,000	$20	$22	$30	$35	$75	$150	$250	$450	$3,500
1856O	968,000	35	40	55	100	185	400	900	1,500	
1856S	286,000	275	400	550	650	1,500	2,750	6,000	10,000	
1857	9,644,000	20	25	30	35	75	150	250	450	2,250
1857O	1,180,000	35	45	65	115	200	375	1,000	2,000	
1857S	82,000	225	350	450	600	850	1,500	3,500	6,500	
1858 . . . . . . *(300+)*. . .	7,368,000	20	25	30	35	75	150	300	450	1,250
1858O	520,000	34	40	55	90	200	450	3,250	7,500	
1858S	121,000	200	300	450	750	2,000	3,750	17,500	—	
1859 . . . . . . (800)	1,343,200	20	25	30	35	75	150	325	700	850
1859O	260,000	40	55	75	120	225	800	2,000	5,500	
1859S	80,000	325	450	700	1,000	3,250	8,000	—	—	
1860 . . . . (1,000)	804,400	20	25	30	35	85	165	400	750	850
1860O	388,000	34	40	55	75	185	325	850	1,500	
1860S	56,000	750	1,250	2,500	4,000	6,500	11,500	35,000	—	
1861 . . . (1,000)	4,853,600	20	25	26	35	85	165	260	500	850
1861S	96,000	500	700	1,000	1,800	3,500	7,500		—	
1862 . . . . . . (550)	932,000	20	25	35	45	100	165	400	550	850
1862S	67,000	145	250	325	450	1,000	1,800	3,250	6,000	
1863 . . . . . . (460)	191,600	25	35	45	85	350	500	850	1,250	850
1864 . . . . . . (470)	93,600	150	200	250	350	500	650	1,250	2,250	850
1864S	20,000	800	975	1,100	1,600	4,000	5,500	11,500	15,000	
1865 . . . . . . (500)	58,800	65	100	175	300	375	600	1,000	1,500	850
1865S	41,000	200	275	400	550	850	1,250	4,250	7,500	

Variety 4 – Motto Above Eagle (1866–1873)

	Mintage	G-4	VG-8	F-12	VF-20	EF-40	AU-50	MS-60	MS-63	PF-63
1866 . . . . . . (725)	16,800	$550	$850	$900	$1,050	$1,200	$1,400	$1,850	$2,250	$600
1866S	28,000	400	700	1,150	1,250	1,850	2,250	4,750	11,500	

Chart continued on next page.   **103**

	Mintage	G-4	VG-8	F-12	VF-20	EF-40	AU-50	MS-60	MS-63	PF-63
1867 . . . .(625) 20,000		$300	$475	$600	$800	$1,200	$1,450	$1,800	$3,000	$600
1867S 48,000		450	750	900	1,250	2,250	6,500	8,500	12,500	
1868 . . . .(600) 29,400		200	250	325	350	600	800	1,350	2,750	600
1868S 96,000		90	135	250	550	650	1,350	3,750	6,750	
1869 . . . .(600) 16,000		375	500	650	750	825	1,150	1,750	3,750	600
1869S 76,000		125	225	350	550	950	1,500	4,000	5,250	
1870 . . . . (1,000) 86,400		45	75	110	200	300	500	750	1,850	600
1870CC 8,340		7,000	11,500	16,500	20,000	45,000	115,000	—		
1871 . . . .(960) . . .118,200		35	50	100	110	225	350	550	1,200	600
1871CC 10,890		8,000	12,500	16,500	27,500	45,000	60,000	100,000	—	
1871S 30,900		650	1,000	1,500	2,000	3,000	3,750	5,750	8,500	
1872 . . . .(950) . . .182,000		45	65	120	175	300	425	1,150	1,850	600
1872CC 22,850		1,700	2,000	3,750	8,500	12,500	16,500	57,500		
1872S 83,000		1,850	2,000	2,500	3,500	5,000	7,500	12,500	25,000	
1873 . . . .(600) . . .212,000		65	90	135	200	280	400	900	1,750	600
1873CC 4,000				—	65,000	—	—			

Variety 5 – Arrows at Date (1873–1874)

	Mintage	G-4	VG-8	F-12	VF-20	EF-40	AU-50	MS-60	MS-63	PF-63
1873 . . . .(500) . . 1,271,200		$20	$22	$32	$65	$150	$300	$650	$850	$1,250
1873CC 12,462		5,000	7,500	10,000	15,000	22,500	50,000	85,000	135,000	
1873S 156,000		65	90	125	185	300	500	1,350	3,250	
1874 . . . .(700) 471,200		20	25	30	65	150	350	625	1,000	1,250
1874S 392,000		22	25	38	70	185	350	625	1,000	

Variety 4 Resumed, With Weight Standard of Variety 5 (1875–1891)

1877-S, S Over Horizontal S

	Mintage	G-4	VG-8	F-12	VF-20	EF-40	AU-50	MS-60	MS-63	PF-63
1875 . . . . . .(700) 4,292,800		$20	$22	$25	$30	$50	$110	$210	$375	$600
1875CC 140,000		185	275	425	700	1,150	1,750	4,250	6,750	
1875S 680,000		22	30	45	85	135	200	475	600	
1876 . . . (1,150) . . 17,816,000		20	22	25	30	50	110	210	375	600
1876CC 4,944,000		40	60	85	100	145	225	500	875	
1876S 8,596,000		20	22	26	30	50	110	210	375	
1877 . . . . . .(510) . . . 10,911,200		20	22	25	30	50	110	210	375	600
1877CC 4,192,000		40	60	80	100	135	250	400	1,000	
1877S 8,996,000		20	22	25	30	50	110	210	375	

	Mintage	G-4	VG-8	F-12	VF-20	EF-40	AU-50	MS-60	MS-63	PF-63
1877S, S Over Horizontal S . . . . .*		$22	$32	$55	$140	$200	$400	$550	$1,200	
1878 . . . . (800). . 2,260,000		20	22	25	30	50	110	200	375	$600
1878CC 996,000		40	50	60	90	225	300	650	1,050	
1878S 140,000		300	450	550	800	1,350	2,250	3,500	5,000	
1879 . . . . . . (1,100). 13,600		115	150	210	280	375	400	500	650	600
1880 . . . . . . (1,355). 13,600		115	150	210	280	400	425	525	650	600
1881 . . . . (975). 12,000		115	150	210	275	400	450	600	750	600
1882 . . . . . . (1,100). 15,200		115	150	210	275	375	400	525	625	600
1883 . . . . . . (1,039). 14,400		115	150	210	275	375	400	525	625	600
1884 . . . . (875). 8,000		160	200	250	275	375	400	525	625	600
1885 . . . . (930). 13,600		115	150	185	275	375	400	525	625	600
1886 . . . . (886). 5,000		250	300	400	450	550	750	1,000	1,300	600
1887 . . . . (710). 10,000		150	175	225	300	425	500	750	900	600
1888 . . . . (832). 10,001		135	200	210	275	375	500	550	900	600
1888S 1,216,000		20	22	25	30	50	145	275	550	
1889 . . . . . . (711). 12,000		115	150	210	250	300	350	550	850	600
1890 . . . . (590). 80,000		100	125	135	200	210	250	300	575	600
1891 . . . . (600). . 3,920,000		20	22	25	30	50	125	200	375	600
1891O 68,000		275	500	850	1,250	2,000	2,750	6,000	10,000	
1891S 2,216,000		20	22	25	30	50	125	250	375	

* Included in 1877-S regular mintage (previous page).

BARBER (1892–1916)

Like other silver coins of this type, the quarter dollars minted from 1892 to 1916 were designed by U.S. Mint chief engraver Charles E. Barber. His initial B is found at the truncation of the neck of Miss Liberty.

G-4 Good: Date and legends legible. LIBERTY worn off headband.
VG-8 Very Good: Some letters in LIBERTY legible.
F-12 Fine: LIBERTY completely legible but not sharp.
VF-20 Very Fine: All letters in LIBERTY evenly plain.
EF-40 Extremely Fine: LIBERTY bold, its ribbon distinct.
AU-50 About Uncirculated: Slight trace of wear above forehead, on cheek, and on eagle's head, wings, and tail.
MS-60 Uncirculated: No trace of wear. Light blemishes.
MS-63 Choice Uncirculated: Some distracting marks or blemishes in focal areas. Impaired luster possible.

PF-63 Choice Proof: Reflective surfaces with only a few blemishes in secondary focal places. No major flaws.

	Mintage	G-4	VG-8	F-12	VF-20	EF-40	AU-50	MS-60	MS-63	PF-63
1892 . . . . . . (1,245). . 8,236,000		$8.00	$9	$13	$20	$40	$100	$200	$250	$500
1892O 2,460,000		10.00	15	25	45	75	135	250	350	
1892S 964,079		25.00	45	65	100	175	350	500	800	
1893 . . . . (792). . 5,444,023		8.00	9	12	20	40	100	200	350	500
1893O 3,396,000		8.00	12	25	45	75	135	225	375	
1893S 1,454,535		15.00	25	50	85	125	250	350	850	
1894 . . . . (972). . 3,432,000		8.00	10	20	35	65	115	200	350	500
1894O 2,852,000		8.00	15	50	75	135	200	300	550	
1894S 2,648,821		8.00	10	25	45	115	150	225	450	
1895 . . . . (880). . 4,440,000		8.00	10	20	25	50	100	200	325	500
1895O 2,816,000		10.00	15	30	50	100	150	300	750	
1895S 1,764,681		15.00	25	50	85	125	200	300	750	
1896 . . . . (762). . 3,874,000		8.00	9	15	20	40	100	185	250	500
1896O 1,484,000		45.00	70	150	225	450	750	850	1,500	

Chart continued on next page.

QUARTER DOLLARS

	Mintage	G-4	VG-8	F-12	VF-20	EF-40	AU-50	MS-60	MS-63	PF-63
1896S 188,039		$500.00	$1,000.00	$1,500	$2,750	$4,000	$5,500	$12,000	$16,500	
1897 . . . . .(731) . .8,140,000		8.00	9.00	12	20	40	100	185	250	$500
1897O 1,414,800		25.00	50.00	150	250	450	650	1,200	1,850	
1897S 542,229		85.00	115.00	225	450	600	850	1,250	2,250	
1898 . . . . .(735) 11,100,000		8.00	9.00	12	20	40	100	185	250	500
1898O 1,868,000		10.00	25.00	65	125	250	350	650	1,000	
1898S 1,020,592		15.00	20.00	35	75	150	350	850	2,000	
1899 . . . . .(846) 12,624,000		8.00	9.00	15	20	40	100	185	250	500
1899O 2,644,000		7.00	8.00	25	50	85	150	375	550	
1899S 708,000		20.00	30.00	75	125	135	275	850	1,500	
1900 . . . . .(912) 10,016,000		8.00	9.00	12	20	40	100	185	250	500
1900O 3,416,000		10.00	20.00	55	85	125	300	550	700	
1900S 1,858,585		8.00	9.00	20	35	85	200	500	1,000	
1901 . . . . .(813) . .8,892,000		8.00	9.00	15	20	40	100	200	275	500
1901O 1,612,000		45.00	65.00	165	300	650	1,000	1,500	2,000	
1901S 72,664	3,500.00		8,000.00	12,500	16,500	25,000	27,500	40,000	50,000	
1902 . . . . .(777) 12,196,967		8.00	9.00	12	20	40	100	185	275	500
1902O 4,748,000		8.00	9.00	25	50	100	200	400	750	
1902S 1,524,612		10.00	15.00	25	55	115	200	450	700	
1903 . . . . .(755) . .9,759,309		8.00	9.00	12	20	40	100	200	350	500
1903O 3,500,000		8.00	9.00	20	45	85	150	350	725	
1903S 1,036,000		10.00	15.00	30	65	100	200	450	850	
1904 . . . . .(670) . .9,588,143		8.00	9.00	12	20	40	100	200	300	500
1904O 2,456,000		20.00	35.00	85	125	200	350	750	850	
1905 . . . . .(727) . .4,967,523		12.00	15.00	35	45	50	100	185	300	500
1905O 1,230,000		35.00	45.00	85	155	185	250	750	1,100	
1905S 1,884,000		15.00	25.00	55	75	100	150	450	1,000	
1906 . . . . .(675) . .3,655,760		8.00	9.00	11	20	40	100	175	250	500
1906D 3,280,000		8.00	9.00	11	20	40	85	175	285	
1906O 2,056,000		8.00	9.00	25	45	80	105	175	350	
1907 . . . . .(575) . .7,132,000		8.00	9.00	12	20	40	125	150	250	500
1907D 2,484,000		8.00	9.00	15	35	50	100	275	500	
1907O 4,560,000		7.00	8.00	12	25	55	125	185	350	
1907S 1,360,000		7.00	15.00	35	75	225	275	550	1,200	
1908 . . . . .(545) . .4,232,000		7.00	8.00	10	20	50	100	185	250	500
1908D 5,788,000		7.00	8.00	10	20	50	85	185	250	
1908O 6,244,000		7.00	7.00	10	20	50	85	185	250	
1908S 784,000		35.00	50.00	115	150	350	450	1,000	1,250	
1909 . . . . .(650) . .9,268,000		7.00	8.00	10	20	50	85	185	250	500
1909D 5,114,000		7.00	8.00	10	20	50	100	185	250	
1909O 712,000		50.00	150.00	400	750	2,250	3,000	4,000	4,500	
1909S 1,348,000		7.00	10.00	20	35	85	150	275	600	
1910 . . . . .(551) . .2,244,000		7.00	8.00	15	20	50	85	185	250	500
1910D 1,500,000		7.00	8.00	25	40	125	185	300	550	
1911 . . . . .(543) . .3,720,000		7.00	8.00	10	20	50	85	185	250	500
1911D 933,600		15.00	35.00	125	225	400	450	650	850	
1911S 988,000		7.00	8.00	25	50	125	200	350	425	
1912 . . . . .(700) . .4,400,000		7.00	8.00	10	20	50	85	185	250	500
1912S 708,000		7.00	15.00	35	75	125	165	350	650	
1913 . . . . .(613) . . . 484,000		25.00	35.00	75	150	350	400	550	600	500
1913D 1,450,800		7.00	8.00	20	40	65	125	200	250	
1913S 40,000	1,000.00		2,000.00	3,750	6,500	9,000	10,000	12,500	15,500	

QUARTER DOLLARS

	Mintage	G-4	VG-8	F-12	VF-20	EF-40	AU-50	MS-60	MS-63	PF-63
1914 . . . . . .(380). . . .	6,244,230	$7.00	$8.00	$10.00	$20	$35	$85	$185	$250	$500
1914D	3,046,000	7.00	8.00	10.00	20	35	85	185	250	
1914S	264,000	65.00	125.00	300.00	450	800	1,000	1,500	2,500	
1915 . . . . . .(450). . . .	3,480,000	7.00	8.00	10.00	20	35	85	185	250	500
1915D	3,694,000	7.00	8.00	10.00	20	35	85	185	250	
1915S	704,000	20.00	30.00	45.00	55	75	150	200	350	
1916	1,788,000	7.00	8.00	10.00	20	35	85	185	250	
1916D	6,540,800	7.00	8.00	10.00	20	35	85	185	250	

STANDING LIBERTY (1916–1930)

This design is by Hermon A. MacNeil, whose initial M is above and to the right of the date. Liberty bears a shield of protection in her left arm, while the right hand holds the olive branch of peace. There was a modification in 1917. The reverse had a new arrangement of stars and the eagle was higher. After 1924 the date was "recessed," thereby giving it greater protection from the effects of circulation. A centennial gold issue was struck in 2016.

G-4 Good: Date and lettering legible. Top of date worn. Liberty's right leg and toes worn off. Much wear evident on left leg and drapery lines.

VG-8 Very Good: Distinct date. Toes faintly visible. Drapery lines visible above Liberty's left leg.

F-12 Fine: High curve of right leg flat from thigh to ankle. Only slight wear evident on left leg. Drapery lines over right thigh seen only at sides of leg.

VF-20 Very Fine: Garment line across right leg worn, but visible at sides.

EF-40 Extremely Fine: Flattened only at high spots. Liberty's toes are sharp. Drapery lines across right leg evident.

AU-50 About Uncirculated: Slight trace of wear on head, kneecap, shield's center, and highest point on eagle's body.

MS-60 Uncirculated: No trace of wear, but contact marks, surface spots, or faded luster possible.

MS-63 Choice Uncirculated: No trace of wear. Light blemishes. Attractive mint luster.

Variety 1 – No Stars Below Eagle (1916–1917)

Mintmark location is on obverse, to left of date.

	Mintage	G-4	VG-8	F-12	VF-20	EF-40	AU-50	MS-60	MS-63
1916	52,000	$3,250	$4,500	$5,000	$5,750	$7,500	$8,500	$10,500	$14,000
1917, Variety 1	8,740,000	16	35	45	70	100	135	200	275
1917D, Variety 1 . . .	1,509,200	18	50	65	85	110	175	225	300
1917S, Variety 1 . . .	1,952,000	25	55	75	115	135	200	250	300

Variety 2 – Stars Below Eagle (1917–1930)
Pedestal Date (1917–1924)

1918-S, 8 Over 7

See next page for chart.

	Mintage	G-4	VG-8	F-12	VF-20	EF-40	AU-50	MS-60	MS-63
1917, Variety 2 13,880,000		$15	$30	$38	$45	$75	$100	$145	$210
1917D, Variety 2 6,224,400		30	50	75	100	110	150	200	275
1917S, Variety 2 5,552,000		30	50	70	90	110	145	200	250
1918 14,240,000		11	15	20	25	35	60	125	200
1918D 7,380,000		16	30	52	70	100	135	200	290
1918S, Normal Date . . .11,072,000		11	16	20	26	40	65	185	200
1918S, 8 Over 7 . . . .*		1,200	1,850	2,500	3,000	5,250	7,500	15,000	20,000
1919 11,324,000		24	35	45	50	60	85	150	225
1919D 1,944,000		60	110	160	320	475	675	1,350	2,000
1919S 1,836,000		55	100	150	300	500	750	1,750	2,450
1920 27,860,000		11	15	20	25	35	70	150	225
1920D 3,586,400		80	100	110	135	175	250	500	850
1920S 6,380,000		11	16	20	25	55	130	300	800
1921 1,916,000		120	145	240	375	525	800	1,250	1,650
1923 9,716,000		10	15	22	26	40	70	150	225
1923S 1,360,000		225	350	450	575	1,000	1,650	2,250	3,000
1924 10,920,000		11	15	16	25	35	75	150	225
1924D 3,112,000		35	45	75	100	140	175	200	275
1924S 2,860,000		18	25	30	45	85	200	350	750

* Included in number above.

Recessed Date (1925–1930)

	Mintage	G-4	VG-8	F-12	VF-20	EF-40	AU-50	MS-60	MS-63
1925 12,280,000		$6	$6.50	$7.50	$10	$26	$60	$125	$200
1926 11,316,000		6	6.50	7.50	10	25	55	125	200
1926D 1,716,000		8	12.00	18.00	34	70	95	125	200
1926S 2,700,000		6	6.50	12.00	30	80	185	360	900
1927 11,912,000		6	6.50	7.50	10	25	55	125	200
1927D 976,000		11	15.00	22.00	55	110	200	240	285
1927S 396,000		45	65.00	100.00	200	750	2,000	5,000	7,500
1928 6,336,000		6	6.50	7.50	10	25	65	125	200
1928D 1,627,600		6	6.50	7.50	10	26	60	125	200
1928S 2,644,000		6	6.50	7.50	10	26	60	125	200
1929 11,140,000		6	6.50	7.50	10	25	55	125	200
1929D 1,358,000		6	6.50	7.50	10	26	60	125	200
1929S 1,764,000		6	6.50	7.50	10	25	55	125	200
1930 5,632,000		6	6.50	7.50	10	25	55	125	200
1930S 1,556,000		6	6.50	7.50	10	26	60	125	200

WASHINGTON (1932 TO DATE)

This type was intended to be a commemorative issue marking the 200th anniversary of President Washington's birth. John Flanagan, a New York sculptor, was the designer. The initials JF are found at the base of the neck. The mintmark is on the reverse below the wreath for coins from 1932 to 1964. Starting in 1968, the mintmark was moved to the obverse at the right of the ribbon.

F-12 Fine: Hair lines about Washington's ear visible. Tiny feathers on eagle's breast faintly visible.
VF-20 Very Fine: Most hair details visible. Wing feathers clear.
EF-40 Extremely Fine: Hair lines sharp. Wear spots confined to top of eagle's legs and center of breast.
MS-60 Uncirculated: No trace of wear, but many contact marks, surface spotting, or faded luster possible.
MS-63 Choice Uncirculated: No trace of wear. Light blemishes. Attractive mint luster.
MS-64 Uncirculated: A few scattered contact marks. Good eye appeal and attractive luster.
MS-65 Gem Uncirculated: Only light, scattered, non-distracting marks. Strong luster, good eye appeal.
PF-65 Gem Proof: Hardly any blemishes, and no flaws.

QUARTER DOLLARS

Silver Coinage (1932–1964)

	Mintage	VG-8	F-12	VF-20	EF-40	MS-60	MS-63	MS-65	PF-63
1932	5,404,000	$4.50	$6.00	$7.00	$8.00	$22.00	$32.50	$200	
1932D	436,800	55.00	75.00	100.00	155.00	725.00	1,250.00	7,500	
1932S	408,000	55.00	70.00	75.00	90.00	285.00	425.00	2,000	
1934	31,912,052	4.50	6.00	7.00	8.00	25.00	35.00	55	
1934D	3,527,200	4.50	5.00	7.00	20.00	120.00	165.00	300	
1935	32,484,000	4.50	4.75	7.00	8.00	15.00	22.00	50	
1935D	5,780,000	4.50	7.00	11.00	25.00	150.00	200.00	250	
1935S	5,660,000	5.50	6.00	8.00	15.00	60.00	75.00	150	
1936 (3,837)	41,300,000	4.50	4.75	6.50	8.50	20.00	22.00	55	$650
1936D	5,374,000	4.50	7.00	20.00	45.00	425.00	475.00	700	
1936S	3,828,000	4.50	4.75	8.00	15.00	75.00	90.00	180	
1937 (5,542)	19,696,000	4.50	4.75	7.00	8.50	25.00	30.00	70	225
1937D	7,189,600	5.50	6.00	8.00	15.00	50.00	60.00	90	
1937S	1,652,000	4.50	7.00	12.00	22.50	110.00	175.00	235	
1938 (8,045)	9,472,000	4.50	4.75	7.00	16.00	75.00	90.00	120	125
1938S	2,832,000	4.50	4.75	7.00	18.50	55.00	90.00	125	
1939 (8,795)	33,540,000	4.50	4.75	6.50	7.00	16.00	18.00	45	105
1939D	7,092,000	5.50	6.00	7.00	9.00	30.00	37.50	65	
1939S	2,628,000	4.50	4.75	8.00	18.00	55.00	90.00	165	

	Mintage	F-12	VF-20	EF-40	MS-60	MS-63	MS-65	PF-65
1940 (11,246)	35,704,000	$4.75	$7.00	$8.00	$22.00	$23.00	$25	$100
1940D	2,797,600	5.50	6.00	27.50	100.00	125.00	150	
1940S	8,244,000	5.50	6.00	9.00	25.00	32.50	40	
1941 (15,287)	79,032,000	4.50	4.75	5.00	7.00	11.00	18	75
1941D	16,714,800	4.50	4.75	6.00	32.50	40.00	50	
1941S	16,080,000	4.50	4.75	5.00	27.50	35.00	55	
1942 (21,123)	102,096,000	4.50	4.75	5.00	7.00	7.50	10	75
1942D	17,487,200	4.50	4.75	5.00	14.00	15.00	35	
1942S	19,384,000	4.50	4.75	8.00	55.00	65.00	70	
1943	99,700,000	4.50	4.75	5.00	6.00	7.50	18	
1943D	16,095,600	4.50	4.75	7.00	20.00	30.00	45	
1943S	21,700,000	4.50	4.75	6.00	27.50	32.50	45	
1944	104,956,000	4.50	4.75	5.00	6.00	7.50	13	
1944D	14,600,800	4.50	4.75	5.00	9.00	12.50	15	
1944S	12,560,000	4.50	4.75	5.00	9.00	12.50	15	
1945	74,372,000	4.50	4.75	5.00	6.50	7.50	17	
1945D	12,341,600	4.50	4.75	5.00	6.50	18.00	24	
1945S	17,004,001	4.50	4.75	5.00	6.50	9.00	12	
1946	53,436,000	4.50	4.75	5.00	6.50	7.50	15	
1946D	9,072,800	4.50	4.75	5.00	6.50	9.00	12	
1946S	4,204,000	4.50	4.75	5.00	6.50	7.50	12	
1947	22,556,000	4.50	4.75	5.00	6.50	12.50	15	

Chart continued on next page.

	Mintage	F-12	VF-20	EF-40	MS-60	MS-63	MS-65	PF-65
1947D	15,338,400	$4.50	$4.75	$5	$6.50	$12.00	$14.00	
1947S	5,532,000	4.50	4.75	5	6.50	11.00	15.00	
1948	35,196,000	4.50	4.75	5	6.50	7.50	10.00	
1948D	16,766,800	4.50	4.75	5	6.50	12.50	20.00	
1948S	15,960,000	4.50	4.75	5	6.50	8.00	15.00	
1949	9,312,000	4.50	4.75	7	25.00	30.00	45.00	
1949D	10,068,400	4.50	4.75	7	12.50	22.50	35.00	
1950 (51,386)	24,920,126	4.50	4.75	5	6.00	11.00	20.00	$42.50
1950D	21,075,600	4.50	4.75	5	6.00	12.50	15.00	
1950D, D Over S	*	40.00	60.00	85	175.00	500.00	2,250.00	
1950S	10,284,004	4.50	4.75	5	6.50	10.00	25.00	
1950S, S Over D	*	45.00	80.00	150	275.00	350.00	850.00	
1951 (57,500)	43,448,102	4.50	4.75	5	6.00	7.50	22.00	35.00
1951D	35,354,800	4.50	4.75	5	6.00	8.00	22.00	
1951S	9,048,000	4.50	4.75	5	6.00	15.00	26.00	
1952 (81,980)	38,780,093	4.50	4.75	5	6.00	9.00	22.00	35.00
1952D	49,795,200	4.50	4.75	5	6.00	8.00	20.00	
1952S	13,707,800	4.50	4.75	5	7.00	12.50	26.00	
1953 (128,800)	18,536,120	4.50	4.75	5	6.00	8.00	16.50	30.00
1953D	56,112,400	4.50	4.75	5	6.00	9.00	25.00	
1953S	14,016,000	4.50	4.75	5	7.00	7.50	20.00	
1954 (233,300)	54,412,203	4.50	4.75	5	5.25	5.50	11.00	12.50
1954D	42,305,500	4.50	4.75	5	5.25	5.50	16.50	
1954S	11,834,722	4.50	4.75	5	5.25	5.50	13.50	
1955 (378,200)	18,180,181	4.50	4.75	5	5.25	5.50	20.00	12.50
1955D	3,182,400	4.50	4.75	5	6.00	6.50	22.50	
1956 (669,384)	44,144,000	4.50	4.75	5	5.25	5.50	11.00	9.00
1956D	32,334,500	4.50	4.75	5	5.25	5.50	13.50	
1957 (1,247,952)	46,532,000	4.50	4.75	5	5.25	5.50	11.00	9.00
1957D	77,924,160	4.50	4.75	5	5.25	5.50	18.50	
1958 (875,652)	6,360,000	4.50	4.75	5	5.25	5.50	11.00	9.00
1958D	78,124,900	4.50	4.75	5	5.25	5.50	20.00	
1959 (1,149,291)	24,384,000	4.50	4.75	5	5.25	5.50	11.00	9.00
1959D	62,054,232	4.50	4.75	5	5.25	5.50	11.00	
1960 (1,691,602)	29,164,000	4.50	4.75	5	5.25	5.50	11.00	7.00
1960D	63,000,324	4.50	4.75	5	5.25	5.50	14.50	
1961 (3,028,244)	37,036,000	4.50	4.75	5	5.25	5.50	16.50	7.00
1961D	83,656,928	4.50	4.75	5	5.25	5.50	20.00	
1962 (3,218,019)	36,156,000	4.50	4.75	5	5.25	5.50	20.00	7.00
1962D	127,554,756	4.50	4.75	5	5.25	5.50	18.00	
1963 (3,075,645)	74,316,000	4.50	4.75	5	5.25	5.50	18.00	7.00
1963D	135,288,184	4.50	4.75	5	5.25	5.50	18.00	
1964 (3,950,762)	560,390,585	4.50	4.75	5	5.25	5.50	18.00	7.00
1964D	704,135,528	4.50	4.75	5	5.25	5.50	16.50	

* Included in number above.

Clad Coinage and Silver Proofs (1965 to Date)

	Mintage	MS-63	MS-65	PF-65		Mintage	MS-63	MS-65	PF-65
1965	1,819,717,540	$0.30	$4.00		1968D	101,534,000	$0.30	$3.00	
1966	821,101,500	0.30	3.00		1968S	(3,041,506)			$1
1967	1,524,031,848	0.30	3.00		1969	176,212,000	0.75	3.50	
1968	220,731,500	0.50	3.50		1969D	114,372,000	0.50	4.00	

	Mintage	MS-63	MS-65	PF-65
1969S	(2,934,631)			$1
1970	136,420,000	$0.25	$3	
1970D	417,341,364	0.25	2	
1970S	(2,632,810)			1
1971	109,284,000	0.30	2	
1971D	258,634,428	0.30	2	
1971S	(3,220,733)			1
1972	215,048,000	0.30	2	

	Mintage	MS-63	MS-65	PF-65
1972D	311,067,732	$0.30	$2	
1972S	(3,260,996)			$1
1973	346,924,000	0.30	2	
1973D	232,977,400	0.30	2	
1973S	(2,760,339)			1
1974	801,456,000	0.30	2	
1974D	353,160,300	0.30	3	
1974S	(2,612,568)			1

Bicentennial (1776–1976)

	Mintage	MS-63	MS-65	PF-65
1776–1976, Copper-Nickel Clad	809,784,016	$0.30	$2	
1776–1976D, Copper-Nickel Clad	860,118,839	0.30	2	
1776–1976S, Copper-Nickel Clad	(7,059,099)			$1
1776–1976S, Silver Clad	11,000,000	2.50	3	
1776–1976S, Silver Clad	(4,000,000)			3

Note: Mintage figures for 1976-S silver clad coins are approximate; many were melted in 1982.

Eagle Reverse Resumed (1977–1998)
(Dies Slightly Modified to Lower Relief)

	Mintage	MS-63	MS-65	PF-65
1977	468,556,000	$0.27		
1977D	256,524,978	0.27	$1.00	
1977S	(3,251,152)			$1
1978	521,452,000	0.27	1.50	
1978D	287,373,152	0.27	1.50	
1978S	(3,127,781)			1
1979	515,708,000	0.28	1.50	
1979D	489,789,780	0.27	1.25	
1979S	(3,677,175)			
Type 1				1
Type 2				2
1980P	635,832,000	0.27	1.50	
1980D	518,327,487	0.27	1.25	
1980S	(3,554,806)			1
1981P	601,716,000	0.27	1.50	
1981D	575,722,833	0.27	1.00	
1981S	(4,063,083)			
Type 1				3
Type 2				6
1982P	500,931,000	1.50	10.00	
1982D	480,042,788	1.50	8.00	
1982S	(3,857,479)			1
1983P	673,535,000	8.00	25.00	

	Mintage	MS-63	MS-65	PF-65
1983D	617,806,446	$3.00	$20	
1983S	(3,279,126)			$1
1984P	676,545,000	0.30	3	
1984D	546,483,064	0.30	3	
1984S	(3,065,110)			1
1985P	775,818,962	0.50	5	
1985D	519,962,888	0.35	3	
1985S	(3,362,821)			1
1986P	551,199,333	1.00	4	
1986D	504,298,660	2.00	9	
1986S	(3,010,497)			1
1987P	582,499,481	0.27	3	
1987D	655,594,696	0.27	1	
1987S	(4,227,728)			1
1988P	562,052,000	0.50	5	
1988D	596,810,688	0.50	4	
1988S	(3,262,948)			1
1989P	512,868,000	0.30	5	
1989D	896,535,597	0.27	1	
1989S	(3,220,194)			1
1990P	613,792,000	0.27	4	
1990D	927,638,181	0.28	4	
1990S	(3,299,559)			1

Chart continued on next page.   **111**

	Mintage	MS-63	MS-65	PF-65
1991P	570,968,000	$0.30	$4	
1991D	630,966,693	0.30	4	
1991S	(2,867,787)			$1.25
1992P	384,764,000	0.35	5	
1992D	389,777,107	0.35	5	
1992S	(2,858,981)			1.25
1992S, Silver	(1,317,579)			5.00
1993P	639,276,000	0.30	2	
1993D	645,476,128	0.30	2	
1993S	(2,633,439)			1.25
1993S, Silver	(761,353)			5.00
1994P	825,600,000	0.30	4	
1994D	880,034,110	0.30	4	
1994S	(2,484,594)			1.25
1994S, Silver	(785,329)			5.00
1995P	1,004,336,000	0.30	4	

	Mintage	MS-63	MS-65	PF-65
1995D	1,103,216,000	$0.30	$3	
1995S	(2,117,496)			$3.00
1995S, Silver	(679,985)			5.00
1996P	925,040,000	0.25	3	
1996D	906,868,000	0.25	3	
1996S	(1,750,244)			2.00
1996S, Silver	(775,021)			5.00
1997P	595,740,000	0.25	3	
1997D	599,680,000	0.25	3	
1997S	(2,055,000)			2.00
1997S, Silver	(741,678)			5.00
1998P	896,268,000	0.25	2	
1998D	821,000,000	0.25	2	
1998S	(2,086,507)			2.50
1998S, Silver	(878,792)			5.00

State Quarters (1999–2008)

The United States Mint 50 State Quarters® Program, which began in 1999, produced a series of 50 quarter dollar coins with special designs honoring each state. Five different designs were issued each year during the period 1999 through 2008. States were commemorated in the order of their entrance into statehood.

These are all legal-tender coins of standard weight and composition. The obverse side depicting President George Washington was modified to include some of the wording previously used on the reverse. The modification was authorized by special legislation, and carried out by Mint sculptor-engraver William Cousins, whose initials were added to the truncation of Washington's neck adjacent to those of the original designer, John Flanagan.

Each state theme was proposed, and the design approved, by the governor of the state. Final designs were created by Mint personnel.

Circulation coins were made at the Philadelphia and Denver mints. Proof coins were made in San Francisco. Both copper-nickel and silver Proof coins were made each year.

	Mintage	AU-50	MS-63	PF-65
Delaware				
1999P	373,400,000	$0.25	$0.50	
1999D	401,424,000	0.25	0.50	
1999S	(3,713,359)			$1.75
1999S, Silver	(804,565)			15.00
Pennsylvania				
1999P	349,000,000	0.25	0.50	
1999D	358,332,000	0.25	0.50	
1999S	(3,713,359)			1.75
1999S, Silver	(804,565)			15.00

	Mintage	AU-50	MS-63	PF-65
New Jersey				
1999P	363,200,000	$0.25	$0.30	
1999D	299,028,000	0.25	0.35	
1999S	(3,713,359)			$1.75
1999S, Silver	(804,565)			15.00
Georgia				
1999P	451,188,000	0.25	0.30	
1999D	488,744,000	0.25	0.30	
1999S	(3,713,359)			1.75
1999S, Silver	(804,565)			15.00

QUARTER DOLLARS

	Mintage	AU-50	MS-63	PF-65
Connecticut				
1999P	688,744,000	$0.25	$0.30	
1999D	657,880,000	0.25	0.30	

	Mintage	AU-50	MS-63	PF-65
Connecticut				
1999S	(3,713,359)			$1.75
1999S, Silver	(804,565)			15.00

	Mintage	AU-50	MS-63	PF-65
Massachusetts				
2000P	628,600,000	$0.25	$0.30	
2000D	535,184,000	0.25	0.30	
2000S	(4,020,172)			$1.50
2000S, Silver	(965,421)			6.00
Maryland				
2000P	678,200,000	0.25	0.30	
2000D	556,532,000	0.25	0.30	
2000S	(4,020,172)			1.50
2000S, Silver	(965,421)			6.00
South Carolina				
2000P	742,576,000	0.25	0.32	
2000D	566,208,000	0.25	0.32	

	Mintage	AU-50	MS-63	PF-65
South Carolina				
2000S	(4,020,172)			$1.50
2000S, Silver	(965,421)			6.00
New Hampshire				
2000P	673,040,000	$0.25	$0.30	
2000D	495,976,000	0.25	0.30	
2000S	(4,020,172)			1.50
2000S, Silver	(965,421)			6.00
Virginia				
2000P	943,000,000	0.25	0.30	
2000D	651,616,000	0.25	0.30	
2000S	(4,020,172)			1.50
2000S, Silver	(965,421)			6.00

	Mintage	AU-50	MS-63	PF-65
New York				
2001P	655,400,000	$0.25	$0.30	
2001D	619,640,000	0.25	0.30	
2001S	(3,094,140)			$1.50
2001S, Silver	(889,697)			8.00
North Carolina				
2001P	627,600,000	0.25	0.30	
2001D	427,876,000	0.25	0.30	
2001S	(3,094,140)			1.50
2001S, Silver	(889,697)			8.00
Rhode Island				
2001P	423,000,000	0.25	0.30	
2001D	447,100,000	0.25	0.30	

	Mintage	AU-50	MS-63	PF-65
Rhode Island				
2001S	(3,094,140)			$1.50
2001S, Silver	(889,697)			8.00
Vermont				
2001P	423,400,000	$0.25	$0.30	
2001D	459,404,000	0.25	0.30	
2001S	(3,094,140)			1.50
2001S, Silver	(889,697)			8.00
Kentucky				
2001P	353,000,000	0.25	0.30	
2001D	370,564,000	0.25	0.30	
2001S	(3,094,140)			1.50
2001S, Silver	(889,697)			8.00

QUARTER DOLLARS

	Mintage	AU-50	MS-63	PF-65
Tennessee				
2002P	361,600,000	$0.30	$0.40	
2002D	286,468,000	0.25	0.40	

	Mintage	AU-50	MS-63	PF-65
Tennessee				
2002S	(3,084,245)			$1.50
2002S, Silver . . .	(892,229)			8.00

	AU-50	MS-63
Any P-Mint, 2002–2008 (except TN)*	$0.25	$0.35
Any D-Mint, 2002–2008 (except TN)*	0.25	0.35

	PF-65
Any S-Mint, 2002–2008 (except TN and HI)* . . .	$3.00
Any S-Mint, Silver, 2002–2008 (except TN)* . . .	6.00

* See above for Tennessee values; 2008-S, Hawaii, clad Proof, is valued at $3 in PF-65.

	Mintage
Ohio	
2002P	217,200,000
2002D	414,832,000
2002S	(3,084,245)
2002S, Silver . . .	892,229
Louisiana	
2002P	362,000,000
2002D	402,204,000
2002S	(3,084,245)
2002S, Silver . . .	(892,229)
Indiana	
2002P	362,600,000
2002D	327,200,000
2002S	(3,084,245)
2002S, Silver . . .	(892,229)
Mississippi	
2002P	290,000,000
2002D	289,600,000
2002S	(3,084,245)
2002S, Silver . . .	(892,229)
Illinois	
2003P	225,800,000
2003D	237,400,000
2003S	(3,408,516)
2003S, Silver . .	(1,125,755)
Alabama	
2003P	225,000,000
2003D	232,400,000
2003S	(3,408,516)
2003S, Silver . .	(1,125,755)
Maine	
2003P	217,400,000
2003D	231,400,000
2003S	(3,408,516)
2003S, Silver . .	(1,125,755)
Missouri	
2003P	225,000,000
2003D	228,200,000
2003S	(3,408,516)
2003S, Silver . .	(1,125,755)
Arkansas	
2003P	228,000,000
2003D	229,800,000

	Mintage
Arkansas	
2003S	(3,408,516)
2003S, Silver . .	(1,125,755)
Michigan	
2004P	233,800,000
2004D	225,800,000
2004S	(2,740,684)
2004S, Silver . .	(1,769,786)
Florida	
2004P	240,200,000
2004D	241,600,000
2004S	(2,740,684)
2004S, Silver . .	(1,769,786)
Texas	
2004P	278,800,000
2004D	263,000,000
2004S	(2,740,684)
2004S, Silver . .	(1,769,786)
Iowa	
2004P	213,800,000
2004D	251,400,000
2004S	(2,740,684)
2004S, Silver . .	(1,769,786)
Wisconsin	
2004P	226,400,000
2004D	226,800,000
2004S	(2,740,684)
2004S, Silver . .	(1,769,786)
California	
2005P	257,200,000
2005D	263,200,000
2005S	(3,262,960)
2005S, Silver . .	(1,678,649)
Minnesota	
2005P	239,600,000
2005D	248,400,000
2005S	(3,262,960)
2005S, Silver . .	(1,678,649)
Oregon	
2005P	316,200,000
2005D	404,000,000
2005S	(3,262,960)
2005S, Silver . .	(1,678,649)

	Mintage
Kansas	
2005P	263,400,000
2005D	300,000,000
2005S	(3,262,960)
2005S, Silver . .	(1,678,649)
West Virginia	
2005P	365,400,000
2005D	356,200,000
2005S	(3,262,960)
2005S, Silver . .	(1,678,649)
Nevada	
2006P	277,000,000
2006D	312,800,000
2006S	(2,882,428)
2006S, Silver . .	(1,585,008)
Nebraska	
2006P	318,000,000
2006D	273,000,000
2006S	(2,882,428)
2006S, Silver . .	(1,585,008)
Colorado	
2006P	274,800,000
2006D	294,200,000
2006S	(2,882,428)
2006S, Silver . .	(1,585,008)
North Dakota	
2006P	305,800,000
2006D	359,000,000
2006S	(2,882,428)
2006S, Silver. .	(1,585,008)
South Dakota	
2006P	245,000,000
2006D	265,800,000
2006S	(2,882,428)
2006S, Silver . .	(1,585,008)
Montana	
2007P	257,000,000
2007D	256,240,000
2007S	(2,374,778)
2007S, Silver . .	(1,313,481)
Washington	
2007P	265,200,000
2007D	280,000,000

	Mintage
Washington	
2007S	(2,374,778)
2007S, Silver . .	(1,313,481)
Idaho	
2007P	294,600,000
2007D	286,800,000
2007S	(2,374,778)
2007S, Silver . .	(1,313,481)
Wyoming	
2007P	243,600,000
2007D	320,800,000
2007S	(2,374,778)
2007S, Silver . .	(1,313,481)
Utah	
2007P	255,000,000
2007D	253,200,000
2007S	(2,374,778)
2007S, Silver . .	(1,313,481)
Oklahoma	
2008P	222,000,000
2008D	194,600,000
2008S	(2,078,112)
2008S, Silver . .	(1,192,908)
New Mexico	
2008P	244,200,000
2008D	244,400,000
2008S	(2,078,112)
2008S, Silver . .	(1,192,908)
Arizona	
2008P	244,600,000
2008D	265,000,000
2008S	(2,078,112)
2008S, Silver . .	(1,192,908)
Alaska	
2008P	251,800,000
2008D	254,000,000
2008S	(2,078,112)
2008S, Silver . .	(1,192,908)
Hawaii	
2008P	254,000,000
2008D	263,600,000
2008S	(2,078,112)
2008S, Silver . .	(1,192,908)

Some State quarters were accidentally made with misaligned dies and are valued higher than ordinary pieces. Normal United States coins have dies oriented in "coin alignment," such that the reverse appears upside down when the coin is rotated from right to left. Values for the rotated-die quarters vary according to the amount of shifting. The most valuable are those that are shifted 180 degrees, so that both sides appear upright when the coin is turned over (called *medal alignment*).

Manufacturing varieties showing die doubling or other minor, unintentional characteristics are of interest to collectors and are often worth premium prices.

District of Columbia and U.S. Territories Quarters (2009)

At the ending of the U.S. Mint 50 State Quarters® Program a new series of quarter-dollar reverse designs was authorized to recognize the District of Columbia and the five U.S. territories: the Commonwealth of Puerto Rico, Guam, American Samoa, the U.S. Virgin Islands, and the Commonwealth of the Northern Mariana Islands. Each of these coins, issued sequentially during 2009, has the portrait

of George Washington, as in the past, and is made of the same weight and composition. Each coin commemorates the history, geography, or traditions of the place it represents.

	Mintage	AU-50	MS-63	PF-65
District of Columbia				
2009P	83,600,000	$0.25	$0.30	
2009D	88,800,000	0.25	0.30	
2009S	(2,113,478)			$1.50
2009S, Silver	(996,548)			6.00
Puerto Rico				
2009P	53,200,000	0.25	0.30	
2009D	86,000,000	0.25	0.30	
2009S	(2,113,478)			1.50
2009S, Silver	(996,548)			6.00
Guam				
2009P	45,000,000	0.25	0.30	
2009D	42,600,000	0.25	0.30	
2009S	(2,113,478)			1.50
2009S, Silver	(996,548)			6.00

	Mintage	AU-50	MS-63	PF-65
American Samoa				
2009P	42,600,000	$0.25	$0.30	
2009D	39,600,000	0.25	0.30	
2009S	(2,113,478)			$1.50
2009S, Silver	(996,548)			6.00
U.S. Virgin Islands				
2009P	41,000,000	0.25	0.40	
2009D	41,000,000	0.25	0.40	
2009S	(2,113,478)			1.50
2009S, Silver	(996,548)			6.00
Northern Mariana Islands				
2009P	35,200,000	0.25	0.30	
2009D	37,600,000	0.25	0.30	
2009S	(2,113,478)			1.50
2009S, Silver	(996,548)			6.00

America the Beautiful™ Quarters Program (2010–2021)

Following up on the popularity of the 50 State Quarters® Program, Congress authorized the production of new circulating commemorative quarters from 2010 to 2021. The coins honor a site of "natural or historic significance" from each of the 50 states, five U.S. territories, and the District of Columbia. They continue to bear George Washington's portrait on the obverse.

Five designs were released each year from 2010 through 2020, in the order the coins' featured locations were designated national parks or national sites. The 56th and final coin of the series was issued in early 2021. The West Point Mint produced circulation strikes in 2019 and 2020 as part of an effort to stimulate public interest in coin collecting.

In addition to the circulating quarters, a series of five-ounce silver bullion pieces were coined each year with designs nearly identical to those of the America the Beautiful™ quarters, with two main exceptions: the size, which is three inches in diameter; and the edge, which is marked .999 FINE SILVER 5.0 OUNCE, rather than reeded as on the standard quarters.

	AU-50	MS-63	PF-65
Any P-Mint, 2010–2021	$0.25	$0.30	
Any D-Mint, 2010–2021	0.25	0.30	
Any S-Mint, 2010–2021 **(a)**		0.30	$0.35

	MS-63	PF-65
Any S-Mint, Silver, 2010–2018		$3.00
Any S-Mint, Silver, 2019–2021 **(b)**		3.00
Any W-Mint, 2020		6.00

a. Uncirculated strikes were made at the San Francisco Mint starting in 2012. Not intended for circulation, they were sold to collectors in rolls and bags at a premium above face value. **b.** In 2019, the fineness of all silver Proofs was changed from .900 to .999.

Mintage	Mintage	Mintage	Mintage
Hot Springs Nat'l Park (AR)	**Glacier Nat'l Park (MT)**	**Hawai'i Volcanoes**	**Ft. McHenry Nat'l Mon.**
2010P 35,600,000	2011S, Silver . . . . (722,076)	**National Park (HI)**	**and Historic Shrine (MD)**
2010D 34,000,000	**Olympic Nat'l Park (WA)**	2012P 46,200,000	2013S 1,313,680
2010S . . . . (1,402,889)	2011P 30,400,000	2012D 78,600,000	2013S . . . . (946,380)
2010S, Silver . . . (859,417)	2011D 30,600,000	2012S 1,409,120	2013S, Silver . . . . (467,691)
Yellowstone National	2011S . . . . . . (1,268,231)	2012S . . . . (962,447)	**Mount Rushmore National**
Park (WY)	2011S, Silver . . . . (722,076)	2012S, Silver . . . . (608,060)	**Memorial (SD)**
2010P 33,600,000	**Vicksburg National**	**Denali National Park and**	2013P 231,800,000
2010D 34,800,000	**Military Park (MS)**	**Preserve (AK)**	2013D 272,400,000
2010S . . . . (1,404,259)	2011P 30,800,000	2012P 135,400,000	2013S 1,373,260
2010S, Silver . . . (859,417)	2011D 33,400,000	2012D 166,600,000	2013S . . . . (958,853)
Yosemite Nat'l Park (CA)	2011S . . . . . . (1,268,623)	2012S 1,409,220	2013S, Silver . . . . (467,691)
2010P 35,200,000	2011S, Silver . . . . (722,076)	2012S . . . . (959,602)	**Great Smoky Mountains**
2010D 34,800,000	**Chickasaw National**	2012S, Silver . . . . (608,060)	**National Park (TN)**
2010S . . . . (1,401,522)	**Recreation Area (OK)**	**White Mountain National**	2014P 73,200,000
2010S, Silver . . . (859,417)	2011P 73,800,000	**Forest (NH)**	2014D 99,400,000
Grand Canyon National	2011D 69,400,000	2013P 68,800,000	2014S 1,360,780
Park (AZ)	2011S . . . . . . (1,266,825)	2013D 107,600,000	2014S . . . . (884,381)
2010P 34,800,000	2011S, Silver . . . . (722,076)	2013S 1,606,900	2014S, Silver . . . . (591,358)
2010D 35,400,000	**El Yunque Nat'l Forest (PR)**	2013S . . . . (989,803)	**Shenandoah Nat'l Park (VA)**
2010S . . . . (1,401,462)	2012P 25,800,000	2013S, Silver . . . . (467,691)	2014P 112,800,000
2010S, Silver . . . (859,417)	2012D 25,000,000	**Perry's Victory and Int'l**	2014D 197,800,000
Mount Hood National	2012S 1,680,140	**Peace Memorial (OH)**	2014S 1,266,720
Forest (OR)	2012S . . . . (1,012,094)	2013P 107,800,000	2014S . . . . (847,191)
2010P 34,400,000	2012S, Silver . . . . (608,060)	2013D 131,600,000	2014S, Silver . . . . (591,358)
2010D 34,400,000	**Chaco Culture National**	2013S 1,425,860	**Arches National Park (UT)**
2010S . . . . (1,398,106)	**Historical Park (NM)**	2013S . . . . (947,815)	2014P 214,200,000
2010S, Silver . . . (859,417)	2012P 22,000,000	2013S, Silver . . . . (467,691)	2014D 251,400,000
Gettysburg National	2012D 22,000,000	**Great Basin Nat'l Park (NV)**	2014S 1,235,940
Military Park (PA)	2012S 1,389,020	2013P 122,400,000	2014S . . . . (845,699)
2011P 30,800,000	2012S . . . . (961,464)	2013D 141,400,000	2014S, Silver . . . . (591,358)
2011D 30,400,000	2012S, Silver . . . . (608,060)	2013S 1,316,500	**Great Sand Dunes**
2011S . . . . . . (1,273,068)	**Acadia National Park (ME)**	2013S . . . . (945,777)	**National Park (CO)**
2011S, Silver . . . . (722,076)	2012P 24,800,000	2013S, Silver . . . . (467,691)	2014P 159,600,000
Glacier Nat'l Park (MT)	2012D 21,606,000	**Ft. McHenry Nat'l Mon.**	2014D 171,800,000
2011P 30,400,000	2012S 1,409,120	**and Historic Shrine (MD)**	2014S 1,176,760
2011D 31,200,000	2012S . . . . (962,038)	2013P 120,000,000	2014S . . . . (843,959)
2011S . . . . . . (1,269,422)	2012S, Silver . . . . (608,060)	2013D 151,400,000	2014S, Silver . . . . (591,358)

QUARTER DOLLARS

	Mintage
Everglades Nat'l Park (FL)	
2014P	157,601,200
2014D	142,400,000
2014S	1,180,900
2014S	(857,805)
2014S, Silver	(591,358)
Homestead National	
Mon. of America (NE)	
2015P	214,400,000
2015D	248,600,000
2015S	1,153,840
2015S	(831,503)
2015S, Silver	(490,829)
Kisatchie Nat'l Forest (LA)	
2015P	397,200,000
2015D	379,600,000
2015S	1,099,380
2015S	(762,407)
2015S, Silver	(490,829)

	Mintage
Blue Ridge Parkway (NC)	
2015P	325,616,000
2015D	505,200,000
2015S	1,096,620
2015S	(762,407)
2015S, Silver	(490,829)
Bombay Hook National	
Wildlife Refuge (DE)	
2015P	275,000,000
2015D	206,400,000
2015S	1,013,920
2015S	(762,407)
2015S, Silver	(490,829)
Saratoga National	
Historical Park (NY)	
2015P	223,000,000
2015D	215,800,000
2015S	1,045,500
2015S	(791,347)

	Mintage
Saratoga National	
Historical Park (NY)	
2015S, Silver	(490,829)
Shawnee Nat'l Forest (IL)	
2016P	155,600,000
2016D	151,800,000
2016S	1,081,914
2016S	(732,039)
2016S, Silver	(515,205)
Cumberland Gap National	
Historical Park (KY)	
2016P	215,400,000
2016D	223,200,000
2016S	1,036,093
2016S	(701,831)
2016S, Silver	(515,205)
Harpers Ferry National	
Historical Park (WV)	
2016P	434,630,000

	Mintage
Harpers Ferry National	
Historical Park (WV)	
2016D	424,000,000
2016S	1,050,185
2016S	(701,203)
2016S, Silver	(515,205)
Theodore Roosevelt	
National Park (ND)	
2016P	231,600,000
2016D	223,200,000
2016S	1,073,092
2016S	(716,236)
2016S, Silver	(515,205)
Ft. Moultrie at Ft. Sumter	
Nat'l Monument (SC)	
2016P	154,400,000
2016D	142,200,000
2016S	979,566
2016S	(703,742)
2016S, Silver	(515,205)

	Mintage	SP-69	SP-70
2016W, Gold **(a)**	(91,752)	$450	$500

a. In 2016 the Mint issued a centennial version of the Standing Liberty quarter in gold.

119

	Mintage
Effigy Mounds National Monument (IA)	
2017P	271,200,000
2017D	210,800,000
2017S	*945,853*
2017S	*(692,129)*
2017S	*(496,618)*
Frederick Douglass National Historic Site (DC)	
2017P	184,800,000
2017D	185,800,000
2017S	*950,503*
2017S	*(657,587)*
2017S, Silver	*(496,618)*
Ozark National Scenic Riverways (MO)	
2017P	203,000,000
2017D	200,000,000
2017S	*921,747*
2017S	*(657,587)*
2017S	*(496,618)*
Ellis Island (Statue of Liberty National Monument, NJ)	
2017P	234,000,000
2017D	254,000,000
2017S	*973,147*
2017S	*(657,587)*
2017S, Silver	*(496,618)*
George Rogers Clark Nat'l Historical Park (IN)	
2017P	191,600,000
2017D	180,800,000
2017S	*933,150*
2017S	*(675,757)*
2017S, Silver	*(496,618)*

	Mintage
Pictured Rocks National Lakeshore (MI)	
2018P	186,714,000
2018D	182,600,000
2018S	*931,220*
2018S	*(653,176)*
2018S, Silver	*(461,048)*
Apostle Islands National Lakeshore (WI)	
2018P	223,200,000
2018D	216,600,000
2018S	*889,080*
2018S	*(618,988)*
2018S, Silver	*(461,048)*
Voyageurs Nat'l Park (MN)	
2018P	237,400,000
2018D	197,800,000
2018S	*867,400*
2018S	*(619,013)*
2018S, Silver	*(461,048)*
Cumberland Island National Seashore (GA)	
2018P,	138,000,000
2018D	151,600,000
2018S	*880,940*
2018S	*(618,725)*
2018S, Silver	*(461,048)*
Block Island National Wildlife Refuge (RI)	
2018P	159,600,000
2018D	159,600,000
2018S	*854,940*
2018S	*(636,372)*
2018S, Silver	*(461,048)*
Lowell National Historical Park (MA)	
2019P	165,800,000
2019D	182,200,000
2019S	*909,080*
2019S	*(821,610)*
2019S, Silver	*(539,710)*
2019W	2,000,000

	Mintage
American Memorial Park (N. Mariana Islands)	
2019P	142,800,000
2019D	182,600,000
2019S	*904,880*
2019S	*(749,279)*
2019S, Silver	*(539,710)*
2019W	2,000,000
War in the Pacific Nat'l Historical Park (Guam)	
2019P	116,600,000
2019D	114,400,000
2019S	*924,380*
2019S	*(749,283)*
2019S, Silver	*(539,710)*
2019W	2,000,000
San Antonio Missions Nat'l Historical Park (TX)	
2019P	142,800,000
2019D	129,400,000
2019S	*931,580*
2019S	*(749,258)*
2019S, Silver	*(539,710)*
2019W	2,000,000
Franch Church River of No Return Wilderness (ID)	
2019P	223,400,000
2019D	251,600,000
2019S	*901,920*
2019S	*(768,340)*
2019S, Silver	*(539,710)*
2019W	2,000,000
Nat'l Park of American Samoa (American Samoa)	
2020P	*286,0*00,000
2020D	212,200,000
2020S	*939,760*
2020S	*(573,615)*
2020S, Silver	*(427,256)*
2020W (a)	2,000,000

	Mintage
Weir Farm National Historic Site (CT)	
2020P	125,600,000
2020D	155,000,000
2020S	*945,820*
2020S	*(544,309)*
2020S, Silver	*(427,256)*
2020W (a)	2,000,000
Salt River Bay National Historical Park and Ecological Preserve (USVI)	
2020P	580,200,000
2020D	515,000,000
2020S	*930,960*
2020S	*(544,287)*
2020S, Silver	*(427,256)*
2020W (a)	2,000,000
Marsh-Billings-Rockefeller Nat'l Historical Park (VT)	
2020P	304,600,000
2020D	345,800,000
2020S	*928,940*
2020S	*(544,249)*
2020S, Silver	*(427,256)*
2020W (a)	2,000,000
Tallgrass Prairie National Preserve (KS)	
2020P	101,200,000
2020D	142,400,000
2020S	*931,060*
2020S	*(561,030)*
2020S, Silver	*(427,256)*
2020W (a)	2,000,000
Tuskegee Airmen National Historic Site (AL)	
2021P	160,400,000
2021D	304,000,000
2021S	*305,680*
2021S	*(528,201)*
2021S, Silver	*(350,323)*

a. The 2020-W quarters have a "V75" privy mark on the obverse commemorating the 75th anniversary of the end of World War II.

Crossing the Delaware (2021)

The America's Beautiful National Parks Quarter Dollar Coin Act of 2008 specified what would happen to the coin after that program ended in 2021: "The reverse of the quarter dollar shall contain an image of General Washington crossing the Delaware River prior to the Battle of Trenton," and the obverse would "revert to the same design containing an image of President Washington" that was used before the State quarters program started in 1999.

	Mintage	AU-50	MS-63
2021P	998,800,000	$0.25	$0.30
2021D	1,169,400,000	0.25	0.30

	Mintage	PF-65
2021S	(512,729)	$1.50
2021S, Silver	(350,323)	6.50

American Women (2022–2025)

The Circulating Collectible Coin Redesign Act of 2020, signed into law January 13, 2021, brought wide-ranging changes involving all of America's circulating coins. In particular, it scheduled the quarter dollar as the venue for several new educational coin programs, including the American Women Quarters program.

Scan to learn more about the program honorees.

From 2022 to 2025, the quarter commemorates prominent American women and the ratification of the Nineteenth Amendment granting women the right to vote. Five coins are being issued per year, each featuring a new reverse design honoring a woman selected from fields and accomplishments such as "suffrage, civil rights, abolition, government, humanities, science, space, and arts."

Common obverse design by Laura Gardin Fraser.

	Mintage	AU-50	MS-63	PF-65
2022P, Maya Angelou	237,600,000	$0.25	$0.30	
2022D, Maya Angelou	258,200,000	0.25	0.30	
2022S, Maya Angelou (a)	(442,828) 303,520		0.50	$1.50
2022S, Maya Angelou, Silver	(352,834)			6.50

a. Uncirculated strikes were made at the San Francisco Mint starting in 2012. Not intended for circulation, they were sold to collectors in rolls and bags at a premium above face value.

	Mintage	AU-50	MS-63	PF-65
2022P, Dr. Sally Ride	275,200,000	$0.25	$0.30	
2022D, Dr. Sally Ride	278,000,000	0.25	0.30	
2022S, Dr. Sally Ride **(a)**	(442,828) 304,120		0.50	$1.50
2022S, Dr. Sally Ride, Silver	(352,834)			6.50
2022P, Wilma Mankiller	310,000,000	0.25	0.30	
2022D, Wilma Mankiller	296,800,000	0.25	0.30	
2022S, Wilma Mankiller **(a)**	(442,828) 304,640		0.50	1.50
2022S, Wilma Mankiller, Silver	(352,834)			6.50
2022P, Nina Otero-Warren	225,000,000	0.25	0.30	
2022D, Nina Otero-Warren	219,200,000	0.25	0.30	
2022S, Nina Otero-Warren **(a)**	(442,828) 305,560		0.50	1.50
2022S, Nina Otero-Warren, Silver	(352,834)			6.50
2022P, Anna May Wong	226,800,000	0.25	0.30	
2022D, Anna May Wong	240,800,000	0.25	0.30	
2022S, Anna May Wong **(a)**	(442,828) 304,680		0.50	1.50
2022S, Anna May Wong, Silver	(352,834)			6.50

a. Uncirculated strikes were made at the San Francisco Mint starting in 2012. Not intended for circulation, they were sold to collectors in rolls and bags at a premium above face value.

	Mintage	AU-50	MS-63	PF-65
2023P, Bessie Coleman		$0.25	$0.30	
2023D, Bessie Coleman		0.25	0.30	
2023S, Bessie Coleman **(a)**			0.50	$1.50
2023S, Bessie Coleman, Silver				6.50
2023P, Edith Kanaka'ole		0.25	0.30	
2023D, Edith Kanaka'ole		0.25	0.30	
2023S, Edith Kanaka'ole **(a)**			0.50	1.50
2023S, Edith Kanaka'ole, Silver				6.50
2023P, Eleanor Roosevelt		0.25	0.30	
2023D, Eleanor Roosevelt		0.25	0.30	
2023S, Eleanor Roosevelt **(a)**			0.50	1.50
2023S, Eleanor Roosevelt, Silver				6.50
2023P, Jovita Idar		0.25	$0.30	
2023D, Jovita Idar		0.25	0.30	
2023S, Jovita Idar **(a)**			0.50	1.50
2023S, Jovita Idar, Silver				6.50
2023P, Maria Tallchief		0.25	0.30	

a. Uncirculated strikes were made at the San Francisco Mint starting in 2012. Not intended for circulation, they were sold to collectors in rolls and bags at a premium above face value.

	Mintage	AU-50	MS-63	PF-65
2023D, Maria Tallchief	$0.25	$0.30		
2023S, Maria Tallchief **(a)**			0.50	$1.50
2023S, Maria Tallchief, Silver				6.50

a. Uncirculated strikes were made at the San Francisco Mint starting in 2012. Not intended for circulation, they were sold to collectors in rolls and bags at a premium above face value.

	Mintage	AU-50	MS-63	PF-65
2024P, Rev. Dr. Pauli Murray	$0.25	$0.30		
2024D, Rev. Dr. Pauli Murray	0.25	0.30		
2024S, Rev. Dr. Pauli Murray **(a)**			0.50	$1.50
2024S, Rev. Dr. Pauli Murray, Silver				6.50
2024P, Patsy Takemoto Mink	0.25	0.30		
2024D, Patsy Takemoto Mink	0.25	0.30		
2024S, Patsy Takemoto Mink **(a)**			0.50	1.50
2024S, Patsy Takemoto Mink, Silver				6.50
2024P, Dr. Mary Edwards Walker	0.25	0.30		
2024D, Dr. Mary Edwards Walker	0.25	0.30		
2024S, Dr. Mary Edwards Walker **(a)**			0.50	1.50
2024S, Dr. Mary Edwards Walker, Silver				6.50
2024P, Celia Cruz	0.25	0.30		
2024D, Celia Cruz	0.25	0.30		
2024S, Celia Cruz **(a)**			0.50	1.50
2024S, Celia Cruz, Silver				6.50
2024P, Zitkala-Ša	0.25	0.30		
2024D, Zitkala-Ša	0.25	0.30		
2024S, Zitkala-Ša **(a)**			0.50	1.50
2024S, Zitkala-Ša, Silver				6.50

a. Uncirculated strikes were made at the San Francisco Mint starting in 2012. Not intended for circulation, they were sold to collectors in rolls and bags at a premium above face value.

The half dollar, authorized by the Act of April 2, 1792, was not minted until December 1794. The weight of the half dollar was 208 grains and its fineness .8924 when first issued. This standard was not changed until 1837 when the Act of January 18, 1837, specified 206-1/4 grains, .900 fine. This fineness continued in use until 1965.

Arrows at the date in 1853 indicate the reduction of weight to 192 grains. During that year only, rays were added to the reverse. Arrows remained in 1854 and 1855. In 1873 the weight was raised by .9 grains and arrows were again placed at the date.

FLOWING HAIR (1794–1795)

AG-3 About Good: Clear enough to identify.
G-4 Good: Date and letters sufficient to be legible. Main devices outlined, but lacking in detail.
VG-8 Very Good: Major details discernible. Letters well formed but worn.
F-12 Fine: Hair ends distinguishable. Top hair lines visible, but otherwise worn smooth.
VF-20 Very Fine: Some detail visible in hair in center; other details more bold.
EF-40 Extremely Fine: Hair above head and down neck detailed, with slight wear.
AU-50 About Uncirculated: All hair visible; slight wear on bust of Liberty and on top edges of eagle's wings, head, and breast.

1795, 2 Leaves Under Each Wing

1795, 3 Leaves Under Each Wing

	Mintage	AG-3	G-4	VG-8	F-12	VF-20	EF-40	AU-50
1794	23,464	$1,350	$2,500	$3,500	$6,000	$9,500	$25,000	$50,000
1795	299,680	500	1,000	1,300	1,500	2,500	5,000	10,000
1795, Recut Date	*	500	1,350	1,400	1,650	5,000	8,500	25,000
1795, 3 Leaves Under Each Wing	*	800	1,500	2,000	3,500	5,000	12,000	25,000

* Included in number above.

DRAPED BUST (1796–1807)

AG-3 About Good: Clear enough to identify.
G-4 Good: Date and letters sufficiently clear to be legible. Main devices outlined, but lacking in detail.
VG-8 Very Good: Major details discernible. Letters well formed but worn.
F-12 Fine: Hair ends distinguishable. Top hair lines visible, but otherwise worn smooth.
VF-20 Very Fine: Right side of drapery slightly worn. Left side to curls smooth.
EF-40 Extremely Fine: All lines in drapery on bust distinctly visible around to hair curls.
AU-50 About Uncirculated: Slight trace of wear on cheek, hair, and shoulder.

Small Eagle Reverse (1796–1797)

1796, 16 Stars

1797, 15 Stars

HALF DOLLARS

	Mintage	AG-3	G-4	VG-8	F-12	VF-20	EF-40	AU-50
1796, All kinds. 3,918								
1796, 15 Stars		$13,500	$25,000	$32,500	$37,500	$45,000	$85,000	$125,000
1796, 16 Stars		13,500	25,000	32,500	37,500	45,000	85,000	125,000
1797, 15 Stars		13,500	25,000	32,500	37,500	45,000	85,000	125,000

Heraldic Eagle Reverse (1801–1807)

1805, 5 Over 4

1806, 6 Over 5

	Mintage	G-4	VG-8	F-12	VF-20	EF-40	AU-50	MS-60
1801 30,289		$750	$1,250	$1,700	$2,000	$4,500	$10,000	$65,000
1802 29,890		1,150	1,500	2,000	2,500	4,500	12,500	55,000
1803 188,234		275	350	400	650	1,500	2,500	17,500
1805, All kinds. 211,722								
1805, 5 Over 4		350	625	900	1,250	2,350	5,750	25,000
1805, Normal Date		200	275	350	475	1,350	3,000	18,500
1806, All kinds. 839,576								
1806, Normal Date		200	250	300	475	1,150	1,750	11,000
1806, 6 Over 5		225	300	400	550	1,800	2,750	9,500
1806, 6 Over Inverted 6.		250	325	700	1,050	3,000	5,500	20,000
1807 301,076		200	250	300	475	1,100	1,750	5,500

CAPPED BUST, LETTERED EDGE (1807–1836)

John Reich designed this capped-head concept of Liberty. Reich's design of Liberty facing left was used on all U.S. silver denominations for the next 30 years.

G-4 Good: Date and letters legible. Bust worn smooth with outline distinct.

VG-8 Very Good: LIBERTY faint. Legends distinguishable. Clasp at shoulder visible; curl above it nearly smooth.

F-12 Fine: Clasp and adjacent curl clearly outlined with slight details.

VF-20 Very Fine: Clasp at shoulder clear. Wear visible on highest point of curl. Hair over brow distinguishable.

EF-40 Extremely Fine: Clasp and adjacent curl fairly sharp. Brow and hair above distinct. Curls well defined.

AU-50 About Uncirculated: Trace of wear on hair over eye and over ear.

MS-60 Uncirculated: No trace of wear. Light blemishes. Possible slide marks from storage handling.

MS-63 Choice Uncirculated: Some distracting contact marks or blemishes in prime focal areas. Impaired luster possible.

First Style (1807–1808)

See next page for chart.

125

	Mintage	G-4	VG-8	F-12	VF-20	EF-40	AU-50	MS-60	MS-63
1807 750,500		$150	$165	$350	$475	$750	$1,800	$5,250	$10,000
1808, 8 Over 7 . . . . *		80	120	190	260	500	1,000	3,750	7,000
1808 1,368,600		55	65	85	115	250	750	2,500	5,000

* Included in number below.

Remodeled Portrait and Eagle (1809–1836)

	Mintage	G-4	VG-8	F-12	VF-20	EF-40	AU-50	MS-60	MS-63
1809 1,405,810		$65	$100	$125	$180	$400	$700	$2,000	$4,500
1810 1,276,276		55	75	95	150	325	500	1,800	3,750
1811 1,203,644		55	75	95	150	325	600	1,500	2,500

1812, 2 Over 1			1813, 50 C. Over UNI			1814, 4 Over 3			
	Mintage	G-4	VG-8	F-12	VF-20	EF-40	AU-50	MS-60	MS-63
1812, All kinds 1,628,059									
1812, 2 Over 1		$95	$110	$150	$225	$500	$900	$2,500	$6,500
1812		55	75	95	125	325	550	1,350	2,250
1813 1,241,903		50	70	90	125	325	575	2,000	3,250
1813, 50 C. Over UNI. . . . . . . *		90	125	200	325	600	1,100	2,250	5,750
1814, All kinds 1,039,075									
1814, 4 Over 3		125	170	250	350	775	1,300	3,250	8,000
1814		70	90	110	170	425	625	1,450	3,250

* Included in number above.

1817, 7 Over 3			1817, 7 Over 4			1817, "Punctuated" Date			
	Mintage	G-4	VG-8	F-12	VF-20	EF-40	AU-50	MS-60	MS-63
1815, 5 Over 2 47,150		$1,500	$2,250	$2,750	$3,000	$4,500	$7,000	$15,000	$35,000
1817, All kinds 1,215,567									
1817, 7 Over 3		135	200	350	475	900	2,000	5,500	18,000
1817, 7 Over 4 *(8 known)* . .			135,000	175,000	250,000				
1817, Dated 181.7		100	135	180	225	600	2,000	8,000	
1817		85	100	115	180	300	750	1,750	4,250

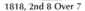

1818, 2nd 8 Over 7

1819, 9 Over 8

1820, 20 Over 19

	Mintage	G-4	VG-8	F-12	VF-20	EF-40	AU-50	MS-60	MS-63
1818, 2nd 8 Over 7 . . . . *		$60	$70	$110	$160	$450	$950	$2,500	$5,500
1818	1,960,322	45	55	70	115	250	475	1,450	3,000
1819, 9 Over 8 . . . . *		55	60	75	120	300	425	1,700	6,000
1819	2,208,000	45	55	75	130	225	425	1,500	3,250
1820, 20 Over 19 . . . . *		65	90	110	180	600	850	4,000	8,500
1820	751,122	55	80	110	160	375	675	2,500	5,250
1821	1,305,797	55	60	70	110	250	400	1,250	2,500
1822	1,559,573	45	55	70	110	250	350	1,100	1,550
1823	1,694,200	45	55	70	100	200	400	1,000	2,000

* Included in number below.

"Various Dates"
Probably 4 Over 2 Over 0.

1824, 4 Over 1

1828, Curl Base, Knob 2

1828, Square Base 2

	Mintage	G-4	VG-8	F-12	VF-20	EF-40	AU-50	MS-60	MS-63
1824, All kinds.	3,504,954								
1824, 4 Over Various Dates		$55	$65	$90	$115	$325	$850	$2,400	$4,500
1824, 4 Over 1		65	90	110	125	250	425	1,750	5,000
1824		45	50	60	65	125	240	900	1,600
1825	2,943,166	45	50	60	65	125	240	675	1,350
1826	4,004,180	45	50	60	65	125	240	675	1,450
1827, All kinds.	5,493,400								
1827, 7 Over 6		70	90	110	140	300	500	1,450	3,000
1827		45	50	60	70	140	250	675	1,500
1828, All kinds.	3,075,200								
1828, Curl Base No Knob 2		45	50	60	70	125	250	900	1,800
1828, Curl Base Knob 2.		50	60	85	115	180	450	1,650	3,000
1828, Square Base 2.		45	50	60	70	140	250	825	1,600
1829, 9 Over 7 . . . . *		50	60	90	125	250	500	1,100	2,500
1829	3,712,156	45	50	60	70	125	225	650	1,200
1830	4,764,800	45	50	60	70	125	225	650	1,200
1831	5,873,660	45	50	60	70	125	225	650	1,200
1832	4,797,000	45	50	60	70	125	225	650	1,200
1833	5,206,000	45	50	60	70	125	225	650	1,200
1834	6,412,004	45	50	60	70	125	225	650	1,200
1835	5,352,006	45	50	60	70	125	225	650	1,200
1836	6,545,000	45	50	60	70	125	225	650	1,200
1836, 50 Over 00 . . . . **		90	110	150	240	325	550	2,000	3,500

* Included in number below. ** Included in number above.

CAPPED BUST, REEDED EDGE (1836–1839)

G-4 Good: LIBERTY barely discernible on headband.
VG-8 Very Good: Some letters in LIBERTY clear.
F-12 Fine: LIBERTY complete but faint.
VF-20 Very Fine: LIBERTY sharp. Shoulder clasp clear.
EF-40 Extremely Fine: LIBERTY sharp and strong. Hair details visible.
AU-50 About Uncirculated: Slight trace of wear on cap, cheek, and hair above forehead, and on eagle's claws, wing tops, and head.
MS-60 Uncirculated: No trace of wear. Light blemishes.
MS-63 Choice Uncirculated: Some distracting marks or blemishes in focal areas. Impaired luster possible.

Reverse 50 CENTS (1836–1837)

	Mintage	G-4	VG-8	F-12	VF-20	EF-40	AU-50	MS-60	MS-63
1836	*1,200+*	$850	$1,000	$1,500	$2,000	$3,000	$3,500	$7,500	$15,000
1837	3,629,820	50	55	65	90	150	325	825	2,000

Reverse HALF DOL. (1838–1839)

On half dollars of 1838 and 1839, the mintmark appears on the obverse; on those thereafter, through 1915, it is on the reverse.

	Mintage	G-4	VG-8	F-12	VF-20	EF-40	AU-50	MS-60	MS-63
1838	3,546,000	$50	$55	$65	$90	$150	$325	$825	$2,250
1838O	*20*					250,000	300,000	350,000	
1839	1,392,976	50	55	65	95	190	375	1,050	2,500
1839O	116,000	500	650	1,000	1,350	2,000	2,750	7,000	12,500

LIBERTY SEATED (1839–1891)

G-4 Good: Scant rim. LIBERTY on shield worn off. Date and letters legible.
VG-8 Very Good: Rim fairly defined. Some letters in LIBERTY evident.
F-12 Fine: LIBERTY complete, but weak.
VF-20 Very Fine: LIBERTY mostly sharp.
EF-40 Extremely Fine: LIBERTY entirely sharp. Scroll edges and clasp distinct.
AU-50 About Uncirculated: Slight wear on Liberty's breast and knees; eagle's head, claws, and wing tops.
MS-60 Uncirculated: No trace of wear. Light blemishes.
MS-63 Choice Uncirculated: Some distracting blemishes in prime focal areas. Impaired luster possible.
PF-63 Choice Proof: Reflective surfaces with only a few blemishes in secondary focal places. No major flaws.

Variety 1 – No Motto Above Eagle (1839–1853)

1842, Small Date

1842, Medium Date

No Drapery
From Elbow

Drapery
From Elbow
(Starting 1839)

	Mintage	G-4	VG-8	F-12	VF-20	EF-40	AU-50	MS-60	MS-63
1839, No Drapery From Elbow.....*		$250	$325	$450	$700	$1,600	$2,650	$7,500	$20,000
1839, Drapery 1,972,400		40	55	75	100	225	450	1,250	2,500
1840 1,435,008		60	85	100	125	250	350	750	1,450
18400 855,100		40	50	70	125	225	350	1,750	4,000
1841 310,000		50	65	85	125	275	500	1,150	2,000
18410 401,000		50	65	85	125	300	600	1,100	2,500
1842, Small Date.......2,012,764		50	60	75	100	175	350	1,100	2,500
1842, Medium Date........... **		40	55	65	90	150	325	900	1,650
18420, Small Date 957,000		650	900	1,250	1,650	2,750	5,500	12,000	22,500
18420, Medium Date.......... **		40	50	65	100	150	500	850	1,650
1843 3,844,000		35	40	55	65	125	250	700	1,500
18430 2,268,000		50	55	65	75	160	350	1,100	2,500
1844 1,766,000		35	40	50	100	125	300	650	1,500
18440 2,005,000		35	40	60	115	190	350	1,250	2,500
1845 589,000		35	50	60	100	160	450	900	2,750
18450 2,094,000		35	50	65	90	140	550	750	2,500
1846 2,210,000		35	40	50	65	130	325	800	1,250
1846, 6 Over Horizontal 6 .... **		200	300	450	800	1,350	2,000	3,500	7,500
18460 2,304,000		35	45	75	115	200	350	1,350	3,750
1847 1,156,000		35	40	65	80	150	250	550	1,500
18470 2,584,000		35	40	50	70	125	350	1,000	3,500
1848 580,000		35	40	90	140	240	500	1,000	2,250
18480 3,180,000		35	40	55	100	200	350	1,150	1,850
1849 1,252,000		35	55	65	100	125	275	750	1,650
18490 2,310,000		40	50	55	70	275	500	1,000	2,250
1850 227,000		350	450	500	600	725	1,000	1,500	3,000
18500 2,456,000		35	40	50	80	150	250	750	1,450
1851 200,750		650	700	850	1,000	1,500	2,000	2,750	3,500
18510 402,000		50	75	115	125	375	650	1,100	2,500
1852 77,130		375	450	550	850	1,350	1,750	2,750	3,750
18520 144,000		350	400	450	650	1,000	1,500	3,500	10,000
18530 (4 known)...............		150,000	225,000	300,000					

* Included in number below. **Included in number above.

Variety 2 – Arrows at Date, Rays Around Eagle (1853)

	Mintage	G-4	VG-8	F-12	VF-20	EF-40	AU-50	MS-60	MS-63
1853	3,532,708	$45	$60	$85	$115	$250	$425	$1,100	$2,750
1853O	1,328,000	45	60	85	115	325	650	2,250	4,500

Variety 3 – Arrows at Date, No Rays (1854–1855)

	Mintage	G-4	VG-8	F-12	VF-20	EF-40	AU-50	MS-60	MS-63
1854	2,982,000	$35	$40	$55	$65	$125	$200	$450	$1,000
1854O	5,240,000	35	40	55	65	125	200	450	1,000
1855, Over 1854	*	65	110	155	250	400	725	1,500	3,000
1855	759,500	35	40	50	65	135	275	700	1,250
1855O	3,688,000	35	40	50	65	135	200	450	1,000
1855S	129,950	375	900	1,000	1,250	2,750	4,750	27,500	45,000

* Included in number below.

Variety 1 Resumed, With Weight Standard of Variety 2 (1856–1866)

	Mintage	G-4	VG-8	F-12	VF-20	EF-40	AU-50	MS-60	MS-63	PF-63
1856	938,000	$35	$40	$50	$65	$115	$200	$450	$1,150	
1856O	2,658,000	35	40	50	65	140	250	400	1,100	
1856S	211,000	125	175	300	450	900	1,500	4,000	8,500	
1857	1,988,000	35	40	50	65	115	200	400	850	
1857O	818,000	35	40	50	65	165	350	1,250	3,000	
1857S	158,000	150	200	275	400	900	1,500	2,750	7,000	
1858 . . . . . . (300+) . . .	4,225,700	35	40	50	65	100	225	400	850	$1,350
1858O	7,294,000	35	40	50	65	110	225	400	1,000	
1858S	476,000	40	60	100	175	250	450	1,500	3,250	
1859 . . . . . . (800)	747,200	35	40	50	65	100	200	400	850	1,350
1859O	2,834,000	35	50	55	70	110	225	500	1,500	
1859S	566,000	45	60	70	135	200	450	1,000	2,750	
1860 . . . . (1,000) . . .	302,700	35	40	50	65	125	250	500	850	1,000
1860O	1,290,000	35	45	50	75	130	250	550	850	
1860S	472,000	45	65	100	115	225	350	1,250	4,000	
1861 . . . . (1,000) . . .	2,887,400	38	45	50	75	150	250	500	1,000	1,000
1861O	2,532,633	50	85	125	175	350	600	1,250	2,750	
1861S	939,500	40	50	85	100	300	550	900	2,500	
1862 . . . . . (550) . . .	253,000	55	75	115	165	300	550	850	1,350	1,000
1862S	1,352,000	45	60	65	115	200	325	950	2,000	
1863 . . . . . . (460) . . .	503,200	50	80	125	180	275	500	675	1,150	1,000
1863S	916,000	45	60	85	120	225	400	1,000	1,500	
1864 . . . . . . (470) . . .	379,100	50	80	115	250	375	650	1,200	1,750	1,000
1864S	658,000	65	100	150	200	350	550	1,500	4,000	
1865 . . . . . (500) . . .	511,400	80	90	120	200	500	900	1,750	2,250	1,000
1865S	675,000	90	125	150	200	450	650	1,800	3,250	
1866S, No Motto	60,000	500	600	700	850	1,500	2,000	7,000	12,500	

Variety 4 – Motto Above Eagle (1866–1873)

	Mintage	G-4	VG-8	F-12	VF-20	EF-40	AU-50	MS-60	MS-63	PF-63
1866 . . . . . . (725) 744,900		$45	$55	$65	$85	$150	$225	$550	$1,500	$900
1866S 994,000		50	60	75	135	225	325	950	2,250	
1867 . . . . . . (625) 449,300		55	75	115	175	250	400	750	1,100	900
1867S 1,196,000		45	55	75	100	200	400	1,350	2,500	
1868 . . . . . . (600) 417,600		60	75	100	140	225	400	700	1,500	900
1868S 1,160,000		40	45	60	100	185	275	1,000	2,250	
1869 . . . . . . (600) 795,300		45	55	65	75	150	250	525	1,000	900
1869S 656,000		50	60	70	80	180	350	900	2,250	
1870 . . . . (1,000) 633,900		35	45	55	70	140	275	525	1,150	900
1870CC 54,617		1,100	2,250	3,500	4,500	7,500	22,500	55,000	—	
1870S 1,004,000		50	70	90	125	400	500	2,000	3,000	
1871 . . . . . . (960) . . . 1,203,600		35	45	50	65	110	200	550	1,000	900
1871CC 153,950		500	700	1,000	1,500	2,750	4,500	25,000	55,000	
1871S 2,178,000		35	45	50	60	130	200	750	1,650	
1872 . . . . . . (950) 880,600		35	45	50	60	125	200	600	1,000	900
1872CC 257,000		250	500	650	1,000	1,850	3,250	18,000	50,000	
1872S 580,000		35	45	75	130	225	450	1,450	2,750	
1873 . . . . . . (600) 801,200		35	45	55	100	125	225	675	1,150	900
1873CC 122,500		275	450	800	1,500	2,600	4,500	9,500	25,000	

Variety 5 – Arrows at Date (1873–1874)

	Mintage	G-4	VG-8	F-12	VF-20	EF-40	AU-50	MS-60	MS-63	PF-63
1873 . . . . . . (800) 1,815,200		$35	$40	$50	$70	$160	$300	$650	$1,350	$1,500
1873CC 214,560		200	350	450	750	1,500	2,500	7,000	12,500	
1873S 228,000		55	110	150	200	450	600	2,500	6,000	
1874 . . . . . . (700) 2,359,600		35	40	55	70	160	300	650	1,350	1,500
1874CC 59,000		850	1,350	2,250	3,250	4,500	6,000	12,500	25,000	
1874S 394,000		65	130	155	175	300	500	1,250	2,000	

Chart continued on next page.

Variety 4 Resumed, With Weight Standard of Variety 5 (1875–1891)

	Mintage	G-4	VG-8	F-12	VF-20	EF-40	AU-50	MS-60	MS-63	PF-63
1875 . . . . . . (700)	6,026,800	$35	$40	$50	$65	$90	$150	$300	$600	$900
1875CC	1,008,000	65	115	200	300	500	750	1,500	2,750	
1875S	3,200,000	35	40	50	60	100	150	300	600	
1876 . . . . (1,150)	8,418,000	35	40	50	60	100	150	300	600	900
1876CC	1,956,000	65	85	165	225	550	800	1,350	2,750	
1876S	4,528,000	35	40	50	60	90	150	350	750	
1877 . . . . . . (510)	8,304,000	35	40	50	60	90	150	300	600	900
1877CC	1,420,000	60	70	100	175	275	350	1,000	2,000	
1877S	5,356,000	35	40	50	60	90	150	300	600	
1878 . . . . . . (800)	1,377,600	45	70	85	95	150	200	350	1,000	900
1878CC	62,000	1,000	1,250	1,850	2,250	3,000	3,500	10,000	16,000	
1878S	12,000	25,000	35,000	42,500	50,000	60,000	65,000	85,000	125,000	
1879 . . . . (1,100)	4,800	200	250	300	400	600	700	850	1,000	900
1880 . . . . (1,355)	8,400	225	350	425	500	650	750	850	1,150	900
1881 . . . . . . (975)	10,000	225	250	325	425	600	700	950	1,250	900
1882 . . . . (1,100)	4,400	225	250	325	425	600	700	850	1,100	900
1883 . . . . (1,039)	8,000	225	300	325	425	650	700	850	1,500	900
1884 . . . . . . (875)	4,400	275	300	325	550	800	850	1,000	1,500	900
1885 . . . . . . (930)	5,200	250	275	325	400	600	700	850	1,500	900
1886 . . . . . . (886)	5,000	275	350	375	400	600	725	850	1,100	900
1887 . . . . . . (710)	5,000	350	400	425	475	600	700	850	1,500	900
1888 . . . . . . (832)	12,001	200	250	325	375	600	700	850	1,100	900
1889 . . . . . . (711)	12,000	180	250	325	375	625	725	900	1,750	900
1890 . . . . . . (590)	12,000	180	250	325	375	500	700	850	1,000	900
1891 . . . . . . (600)	200,000	40	60	100	110	160	250	350	900	900

BARBER (1892–1915)

Like the dime and quarter dollar, this type was designed by U.S. Mint chief engraver Charles E. Barber, whose initial B is on the truncation of the neck.

G-4 Good: Date and legends legible. LIBERTY worn off headband.
VG-8 Very Good: Some letters legible in LIBERTY.
F-12 Fine: LIBERTY nearly completely legible, but worn.
VF-20 Very Fine: All letters in LIBERTY evenly plain.
EF-40 Extremely Fine: LIBERTY bold, and its ribbon distinct.
AU-50 About Uncirculated: Slight trace of wear above forehead, leaf tips, and cheek, and on eagle's head, tail, and wing tips.
MS-60 Uncirculated: No trace of wear. Light blemishes.
MS-63 Choice Uncirculated: Some distracting contact marks or blemishes in prime focal areas. Impaired luster possible.
PF-63 Choice Proof: Reflective surfaces with only a few blemishes in secondary focal places. No major flaws.

Mintmark location on reverse, below eagle.

	Mintage	G-4	VG-8	F-12	VF-20	EF-40	AU-50	MS-60	MS-63	PF-63
1892 . . . . (1,245)	934,000	$25	$30	$50	$125	$200	$275	$450	$650	$750
1892O	390,000	225	350	450	550	650	750	1,000	1,500	

	Mintage	G-4	VG-8	F-12	VF-20	EF-40	AU-50	MS-60	MS-63	PF-63
1892S	1,029,028	$200	$250	$325	$450	$600	$750	$1,100	$1,850	
1893 . . . . . .(792). . . .	1,826,000	20	25	55	125	200	275	500	750	$750
1893O	1,389,000	30	55	100	185	275	350	600	850	
1893S	740,000	100	250	450	650	1,100	1,350	2,000	3,500	
1894 . . . . . .(972). . . .	1,148,000	30	55	100	165	275	350	600	850	750
1894O	2,138,000	25	30	65	125	225	275	450	750	
1894S	4,048,690	20	24	40	75	135	225	550	1,100	
1895 . . . . . .(880). . . .	1,834,338	18	20	40	75	125	225	450	750	750
1895O	1,766,000	22	36	70	125	175	250	600	1,200	
1895S	1,108,086	22	48	100	150	200	275	650	1,200	
1896 . . . . . .(762).	950,000	30	33	55	100	150	225	550	950	750
1896O	924,000	30	33	125	300	1,250	2,250	5,500	10,000	
1896S	1,140,948	65	125	200	450	850	1,100	1,850	2,500	
1897 . . . . . .(731). . . .	2,480,000	13	15	30	70	125	225	500	700	750
1897O	632,000	100	120	300	500	750	850	2,000	3,000	
1897S	933,900	100	145	250	400	850	1,000	2,150	2,750	
1898 . . . . . .(735). . . .	2,956,000	13	15	30	70	125	225	450	700	750
1898O	874,000	20	65	145	250	400	550	1,150	2,000	
1898S	2,358,550	15	20	55	100	225	350	1,150	1,750	
1899 . . . . . .(846). . . .	5,538,000	13	15	30	70	140	225	450	650	750
1899O	1,724,000	13	20	40	115	200	300	800	1,350	
1899S	1,686,411	13	20	50	100	135	275	700	1,700	
1900 . . . . . .(912). . . .	4,762,000	10	11	30	70	125	225	450	700	750
1900O	2,744,000	10	11	45	125	225	325	1,500	3,250	
1900S	2,560,322	10	11	35	75	175	225	650	1,500	
1901 . . . . . .(813). . . .	4,268,000	10	11	30	70	125	225	450	650	750
1901O	1,124,000	10	15	40	150	850	1,100	1,650	3,250	
1901S	847,044	45	65	200	350	1,000	1,350	2,750	5,000	
1902 . . . . . .(777). . . .	4,922,000	10	11	30	70	125	225	450	650	750
1902O	2,526,000	10	11	30	70	125	325	700	1,500	
1902S	1,460,670	10	11	30	90	175	225	1,100	2,000	
1903 . . . . . .(755). . . .	2,278,000	10	11	30	70	125	225	450	900	750
1903O	2,100,000	10	11	30	70	125	225	525	1,100	
1903S	1,920,772	10	11	30	75	150	300	650	1,600	
1904 . . . . . .(670). . . .	2,992,000	10	11	30	70	125	225	450	650	750
1904O	1,117,600	10	12	45	125	325	550	1,500	3,000	
1904S	553,038	45	100	275	650	1,650	4,500	10,000	13,500	
1905 . . . . . .(727).	662,000	10	12	50	110	150	225	550	900	750
1905O	505,000	10	20	60	125	200	225	800	1,350	
1905S	2,494,000	10	11	30	75	125	225	550	1,100	
1906 . . . . . .(675). . . .	2,638,000	10	11	30	70	125	225	450	650	750
1906D	4,028,000	10	11	30	70	125	225	450	650	
1906O	2,446,000	10	11	30	70	125	225	700	1,200	
1906S	1,740,154	10	11	30	70	125	225	650	1,100	
1907 . . . . . .(575). . . .	2,598,000	10	11	30	70	125	225	450	650	750
1907D	3,856,000	10	11	30	70	125	225	450	650	
1907O	3,946,600	10	11	30	70	125	225	450	650	
1907S	1,250,000	10	20	40	100	225	425	2,000	3,750	
1908 . . . . . .(545). . . .	1,354,000	10	11	30	70	125	225	450	650	750
1908D	3,280,000	10	11	30	70	125	225	450	650	
1908O	5,360,000	10	11	30	70	125	225	450	650	
1908S	1,644,828	10	11	40	100	175	225	850	1,450	

Chart continued on next page.

	Mintage	G-4	VG-8	F-12	VF-20	EF-40	AU-50	MS-60	MS-63	PF-63
1909......(650)....	2,368,000	$10	$11	$30	$70	$125	$225	$450	$650	$750
1909O.............	925,400	10	11	40	110	250	475	900	1,200	
1909S.............	1,764,000	10	11	35	70	125	225	500	950	
1910......(551)......	418,000	12	15	45	110	200	225	500	900	750
1910S.............	1,948,000	10	12	30	70	125	225	650	1,000	
1911......(543)...	1,406,000	10	11	30	70	125	225	450	650	750
1911D.............	695,080	10	11	30	70	125	225	450	650	
1911S.............	1,272,000	10	11	30	70	125	225	800	1,250	
1912......(700)....	1,550,000	10	11	30	70	125	225	450	650	750
1912D.............	2,300,800	10	11	30	70	125	225	450	650	
1912S.............	1,370,000	10	11	30	70	125	225	450	750	
1913......(627)......	188,000	40	50	125	275	400	525	1,500	2,000	750
1913D.............	534,000	15	18	30	70	125	225	450	650	
1913S.............	604,000	15	18	30	70	125	225	750	1,200	
1914......(380)......	124,230	65	100	200	325	475	650	1,500	2,000	750
1914S.............	992,000	9	11	30	70	125	225	550	1,000	
1915......(450)......	138,000	50	75	185	225	350	550	1,100	2,000	750
1915D.............	1,170,400	10	11	30	70	125	225	450	650	
1915S.............	1,604,000	10	11	30	70	125	225	450	650	

LIBERTY WALKING (1916–1947)

This type was designed by American sculptor Adolph A. Weinman, whose monogram, AW, appears under the tip of the tail feathers. On the 1916 coins and some of the 1917 coins, the mintmark is located on the obverse below the motto. A centennial gold issue was struck in 2016.

G-4 Good: Rims defined. Motto IN GOD WE TRUST legible.

VG-8 Very Good: Motto distinct. About half of skirt lines at left clear.

F-12 Fine: All skirt lines evident, but worn in spots. Clear details in sandal below motto.

VF-20 Very Fine: Skirt lines sharp, including leg area. Little wear on breast and right arm.

EF-40 Extremely Fine: All skirt lines bold.

AU-50 About Uncirculated: Slight trace of wear on Liberty's head, knee, and breast tips and on eagle's claws and head.

MS-60 Uncirculated: No trace of wear. Light blemishes.

MS-63 Choice Uncirculated: Some distracting contact marks or blemishes in prime focal areas. Impaired luster possible.

PF-63 Choice Proof: Reflective surfaces with only a few blemishes in secondary focal places. No major flaws.

PF-65 Gem Proof: Brilliant surfaces with no noticeable blemishes or flaws. A few scattered, barely noticeable marks or hairlines possible.

Mintmark Locations

1916–1917   *1917–1947*

Coin dealers often pay more than the Mint State prices shown for choice Uncirculated examples that are well struck.

	Mintage	G-4	VG-8	F-12	VF-20	EF-40	AU-50	MS-60	MS-63
1916......................	608,000	$35.00	$40	$65	$125	$175	$275	$600	$850
1916D, Obverse Mintmark....	1,014,400	32.00	45	65	115	185	275	550	800
1916S, Obverse Mintmark......	508,000	70.00	115	225	375	650	1,000	2,000	3,400
1917..................	12,292,000	10.00	12	14	16	30	65	150	300

Mintage		G-4	VG-8	F-12	VF-20	EF-40	AU-50	MS-60	MS-63
1917D, Obverse Mintmark	765,400	$20	$35.00	$70	$110	$250	$350	$750	$1,200
1917D, Reverse Mintmark	1,940,000	15	20.00	40	100	210	400	1,000	1,500
1917S, Obverse Mintmark	952,000	22	40.00	125	300	750	1,350	3,500	4,500
1917S, Reverse Mintmark	5,554,000	9	10.00	20	45	125	225	750	1,350
1918	6,634,000	9	10.00	18	50	100	225	600	1,000
1918D	3,853,040	13	18.00	40	115	250	450	1,250	2,000
1918S	10,282,000	9	14.00	18	30	85	200	550	1,150
1919	962,000	22	35.00	65	225	500	900	2,200	3,250
1919D	1,165,000	22	55.00	140	275	1,000	2,000	5,000	6,500
1919S	1,552,000	18	30.00	65	275	850	1,850	5,500	8,000
1920	6,372,000	9	10.00	16	30	65	175	450	750
1920D	1,551,000	15	20.00	70	250	650	1,350	3,000	4,750
1920S	4,624,000	9	10.00	20	85	200	550	1,200	2,500
1921	246,000	80	150.00	350	750	1,850	3,250	6,000	7,500
1921D	208,000	200	325.00	550	1,100	3,500	5,000	9,000	10,000
1921S	548,000	75	90.00	250	650	3,000	7,500	20,000	35,000
1923S	2,178,000	14	18.00	40	175	800	1,650	3,500	5,000
1927S	2,392,000	10	11.00	20	45	285	650	1,350	2,000
1928S	1,940,000	10	11.00	20	75	250	850	2,000	3,000
1929D	1,001,200	10	11.00	20	30	75	185	500	850
1929S	1,902,000	10	11.00	20	22	100	225	500	850
1933S	1,786,000	10	10.50	15	25	65	200	600	1,000
1934	6,964,000	9	9.50	10	11	13	20	55	85
1934D	2,361,000	9	9.50	10	14	22	55	100	250
1934S	3,652,000	9	9.50	10	11	32	65	250	750
1935	9,162,000	9	9.50	10	11	22	30	40	60
1935D	3,003,800	9	9.50	10	13	22	45	100	250
1935S	3,854,000	9	9.50	10	11	26	70	240	450

Mintage		G-4	VG-8	F-12	VF-20	EF-40	AU-50	MS-60	MS-63	PF-63	PF-65
1936 (3,901)	12,614,000	$8.75	$9.00	$9.50	$10.00	$14	$17	$25	$65	$1,200	$2,350
1936D	4,252,400	8.75	9.00	9.50	10.00	16	30	65	125		
1936S	3,884,000	8.75	9.00	9.50	10.00	22	45	100	200		
1937 (5,728)	9,522,000	8.75	9.00	9.50	10.00	14	17	30	75	375	600
1937D	1,676,000	8.75	9.00	9.50	14.00	32	70	160	250		
1937S	2,090,000	8.75	9.00	9.50	10.00	18	45	115	200		
1938 (8,152)	4,110,000	8.75	9.00	9.50	12.00	14	25	50	125	350	550
1938D	491,600	30.00	36.00	55.00	70.00	100	160	340	650		
1939 (8,808)	6,812,000	8.75	9.00	9.50	10.00	12	22	40	65	325	500
1939D	4,267,800	8.75	9.00	9.50	10.00	13	17	34	75		
1939S	2,552,000	8.75	9.00	9.50	10.00	18	55	100	150		
1940 (11,279)	9,156,000		8.75	9.00	9.50	10	18	25	45	325	450
1940S	4,550,000		8.75	9.00	9.50	13	25	35	55		
1941 (15,412)	24,192,000		8.75	9.00	9.50	10	12	25	45	280	350
1941D	11,248,400		8.75	9.00	9.50	10	12	28	60		
1941S	8,098,000		8.75	9.00	9.50	11	20	55	100		
1942 (21,120)	47,818,000		8.75	9.00	9.50	10	12	25	45	280	350

Chart continued on next page.

	Mintage	VG-8	F-12	VF-20	EF-40	AU-50	MS-60	MS-63
1942D	10,973,800	$8.75	$9	$9.50	$10	$12	$28	$65
1942S	12,708,000	8.75	9	9.50	10	18	28	65
1943	53,190,000	8.75	9	9.50	10	13	30	55
1943D	11,346,000	8.75	9	9.50	10	16	30	55
1943S	13,450,000	8.75	9	9.50	10	18	30	65
1944	28,206,000	8.75	9	9.50	10	12	25	45
1944D	9,769,000	8.75	9	9.50	10	16	28	45
1944S	8,904,000	8.75	9	9.50	10	20	34	65
1945	31,502,000	8.75	9	9.50	10	12	25	45
1945D	9,966,800	8.75	9	9.50	10	12	25	45
1945S	10,156,000	8.75	9	9.50	10	20	25	45
1946	12,118,000	8.75	9	9.50	10	12	25	45
1946D	2,151,000	8.75	9	9.50	14	23	25	45
1946S	3,724,000	8.75	9	9.50	13	27	40	45
1947	4,094,000	8.75	9	9.50	13	16	35	45
1947D	3,900,600	8.75	9	9.50	13	22	35	45

FRANKLIN (1948–1963)

The Benjamin Franklin half dollar and the Roosevelt dime were both designed by U.S. Mint chief engraver John R. Sinnock. His initials appear below the shoulder.

VF-20 Very Fine: At least half of the lower and upper incused lines on rim of Liberty Bell on reverse visible.

EF-40 Extremely Fine: Wear spots at top of end of Franklin's curls and hair at back of ears. Wear evident at top and on lettering of Liberty Bell.

MS-60 Uncirculated: No trace of wear. Light blemishes.

MS-63 Choice Uncirculated: Some distracting contact marks or blemishes in prime focal areas. Impaired luster possible.

MS-65 Gem Uncirculated: Only light, scattered contact marks that are not distracting. Strong luster, good eye appeal.

PF-63 Choice Proof: Reflective surfaces with only a few blemishes in secondary focal places. No major flaws.

PF-65 Gem Proof: Brilliant surfaces with no noticeable blemishes or flaws. A few scattered, barely noticeable marks or hairlines possible.

Coin dealers usually pay more than the Mint State prices shown for well-struck Uncirculated halves with full bell lines.

Mintmark Location

	Mintage	VF-20	EF-40	MS-60	MS-63	MS-65	PF-63	PF-65
1948	3,006,814	$8.75	$9	$14.00	$16.00	$50		
1948D	4,028,600	8.75	9	13.00	15.00	65		
1949	5,614,000	8.75	9	22.00	26.00	90		
1949D	4,120,600	8.75	9	34.00	35.00	180		
1949S	3,744,000	8.75	9	55.00	60.00	90		
1950 . . . . . (51,386). . . .	7,742,123	8.75	9	14.00	16.00	60	$300	$450
1950D	8,031,600	8.75	9	18.00	22.00	125		
1951 . . . . . (57,500). . .	16,802,102	8.75	9	10.00	11.00	35	225	290
1951D	9,475,200	8.75	9	22.00	25.00	115		

	Mintage	VF-20	EF-40	MS-60	MS-63	MS-65	PF-63	PF-65
1951S 13,696,000		$8.75	$9	$15.00	$18.00	40		
1952 . . . . . (81,980). . . 21,192,093		8.75	9	10.00	11.00	35	$130	$180
1952D 25,395,600		8.75	9	10.00	11.00	80		
1952S 5,526,000		8.75	9	37.50	42.50	75		
1953 . . . . (128,800). . . . 2,668,120		8.75	9	10.00	16.00	50	95	135
1953D 20,900,400		8.75	9	10.00	11.00	60		
1953S 4,148,000		8.75	9	20.00	22.00	34		
1954 . . . . (233,300). . . 13,188,202		8.75	9	10.00	11.00	28	45	65
1954D 25,445,580		8.75	9	10.00	11.00	55		
1954S 4,993,400		8.75	9	12.00	14.00	22		
1955 . . . . (378,200). . . . 2,498,181		8.75	9	12.00	14.00	30	45	60
1956 . . . . (669,384). . . . 4,032,000		8.75	9	10.00	11.00	22	22	25
1957 . . . (1,247,952). . . . 5,114,000		8.75	9	10.00	12.00	15	16	22
1957D 19,966,850		8.75	9	10.00	12.00	20		
1958 . . . (875,652). . . . 4,042,000		8.75	9	10.00	12.00	15	20	24
1958D 23,962,412		8.75	9	10.00	12.00	15		
1959 . . . (1,149,291). . . . 6,200,000		8.75	9	10.00	12.00	25	16	18
1959D 13,053,750		8.75	9	10.00	12.00	40		
1960 . . . (1,691,602). . . . 6,024,000		8.75	9	10.00	12.00	45	16	18
1960D 18,215,812		8.75	9	10.00	12.00	100		
1961 . . . (3,028,244). . . . 8,290,000		8.75	9	10.00	12.00	20	16	18
1961D 20,276,442		8.75	9	10.00	12.00	60		
1962 . . . (3,218,019). . . . 9,714,000		8.75	9	10.00	12.00	40	16	18
1962D 35,473,281		8.75	9	10.00	12.00	35		
1963 . . . (3,075,645). . . 22,164,000		8.75	9	10.00	12.00	15	16	18
1963D 67,069,292		8.75	9	10.00	12.00	15		

KENNEDY (1964 TO DATE)

Gilroy Roberts, chief engraver of the U.S. Mint from 1948 to 1964, designed the obverse of this coin, a tribute to President John F. Kennedy, who was assassinated in November 1963. Roberts's stylized initials are on the truncation of the bust of Kennedy. The reverse, which uses as its motif the eagle from the Seal of the President of the United States, is the work of assistant engraver Frank Gasparro. The Kennedy half dollar was minted in 90% silver in its first year of issue, 1964. From 1965 to 1970 its fineness was reduced to 40% silver. Since 1971 the coin has been struck in copper-nickel (except for certain silver Proofs, 1992 to date). Dates after 2001 have not been released into general circulation, instead being made available in 20-coin rolls, 200-coin bags, and coin sets sold by the Mint. In 2014 a .999 fine gold version was made for collectors, dual-dated 1964–2014 to mark the coin's 50th anniversary.

In the early 1970s an open contest was held to select a new reverse design for the Kennedy half dollar, to celebrate the nation's bicentennial. Seth G. Huntington's winning entry featured a view of Independence Hall in Philadelphia. The Bicentennial half dollars bear the dual date 1776–1976.

Mintmark Location (1964)

Mintmark Location (1968 to Date)

Silver Coinage (1964)

	Mintage	MS-63	PF-63	PF-65
1964 . . . . (3,950,762) 273,304,004		$10	$10	$13
1964D 156,205,446		10		

Silver Clad Coinage (1965–1970)

	Mintage	MS-63	PF-63	PF-65
1965	65,879,366	$4.75		
1966	108,984,932	4.75		
1967	295,046,978	4.75		
1968D	246,951,930	4.75		
1968S	(3,041,506)		$3	$3.25
1969D	129,881,800	$4.75		
1969S	(2,934,631)		$3.50	$4.50
1970D	2,150,000	10.00		
1970S	(2,632,810)		3.50	4.50

Clad Coinage and Silver Proofs (1971 to Date)

	Mintage	MS-63	PF-63	PF-65
1971	155,164,000	$0.75		
1971D	302,097,424	0.75		
1971S	(3,220,733)		$1.25	$1.75
1972	153,180,000	0.75		
1972D	141,890,000	0.75		
1972S	(3,260,996)		1.25	1.75
1973	64,964,000	$0.75		
1973D	83,171,400	0.75		
1973S	(2,760,339)		$1.25	$1.75
1974	201,596,000	0.75		
1974D	79,066,300	0.75		
1974S	(2,612,568)		1.00	1.50

Bicentennial (1776–1976)

	Mintage	MS-63	PF-63	PF-65
1776–1976, Clad. 234,308,000		$0.75		
1776–1976D, Clad 287,565,248		0.75		
1776–1976S, Clad. . . . . (7,059,099).			$1.25	$1.75
1776–1976S, Silver. *11,000,000*		4.00		
1776–1976S, Silver. . . . . *(4,000,000)*.			4.50	8.00

Note: Mintage figures for 1976-S silver coins are approximate; many were melted in 1982.

HALF DOLLARS

Eagle Reverse Resumed (1977 to Date)

	Mintage	MS-63	PF-63	PF-65
1977	43,598,000	$0.75		
1977D	31,449,106	0.75		
1977S	(3,251,152)		$2.00	$3.50
1978	14,350,000	0.75		
1978D	13,765,799	0.75		
1978S	(3,127,781)		1.25	1.50
1979	68,312,000	0.75		
1979D	15,815,422	0.75		
1979S	(3,677,175)			
Type 1			1.00	1.75
Type 2			5.00	7.50
1980P	44,134,000	0.75		
1980D	33,456,449	0.75		
1980S	(3,554,806)		2.00	3.50
1981P	29,544,000	0.75		
1981D	27,839,533	0.75		
1981S	(4,063,083)			
Type 1			1.00	1.25
Type 2			7.50	12.00
1982P	10,819,000	0.75		
1982D	13,140,102	4.50		
1982S	(3,857,479)		1.00	1.50
1983P	34,139,000	4.00		
1983D	32,472,244	0.75		
1983S	(3,279,126)		1.00	2.75
1984P	26,029,000	0.75		
1984D	26,262,158	0.75		
1984S	(3,065,110)		1.00	1.25
1985P	18,706,962	0.75		
1985D	19,814,034	0.75		
1985S	(3,362,821)		1.00	1.25
1986P	13,107,633	1.00		
1986D	15,336,145	0.75		
1986S	(3,010,497)		1.00	1.75
1987P **(a)**	2,890,758	2.00		
1987D **(a)**	2,890,758	2.00		
1987S	(4,227,728)		1.00	1.75
1988P	13,626,000	0.75		
1988D	12,000,096	0.75		
1988S	(3,262,948)		1.00	1.50
1989P	24,542,000	0.75		
1989D	23,000,216	0.75		
1989S	(3,220,194)		1.25	1.75
1990P	22,278,000	0.75		
1990D	20,096,242	0.75		
1990S	(3,299,559)		1.25	1.75
1991P	14,874,000	0.75		
1991D	15,054,678	0.75		
1991S	(2,867,787)		1.25	1.75
1992P	17,628,000	0.75		

	Mintage	MS-63	PF-63	PF-65
1992D	17,000,106	$0.75		
1992S	(2,858,981)		$1.25	$1.75
1992S, Silver . . .	(1,317,579)		7.00	9.50
1993P	15,510,000	0.75		
1993D	15,000,006	0.75		
1993S	(2,633,439)		1.25	1.75
1993S, Silver	(761,353)		7.00	9.50
1994P	23,718,000	0.75		
1994D	23,828,110	0.75		
1994S	(2,484,594)		3.00	4.00
1994S, Silver	(785,329)		7.00	9.50
1995P	26,496,000	0.75		
1995D	26,288,000	0.75		
1995S	(2,117,496)		6.00	8.00
1995S, Silver	(679,985)		7.50	10.50
1996P	24,442,000	0.75		
1996D	24,744,000	0.75		
1996S	(1,750,244)		1.50	2.75
1996S, Silver	(775,021)		8.00	11.50
1997P	20,882,000	0.75		
1997D	19,876,000	0.75		
1997S	(2,055,000)		2.00	3.75
1997S, Silver	(741,678)		8.00	11.50
1998P	15,646,000	0.75		
1998D	15,064,000	0.75		
1998S	(2,086,507)		2.00	3.75
1998S, Silver	(878,792)		8.00	11.50
1998S, Silver, Matte Finish . . .	(62,000)		75.00	100.00
1999P	8,900,000	0.75		
1999D	10,682,000	0.75		
1999S	(2,543,401)		2.00	3.75
1999S, Silver	(804,565)		10.00	14.50
2000P	22,600,000	0.75		
2000D	19,466,000	0.75		
2000S	(3,082,483)		2.00	3.75
2000S, Silver	(965,421)		8.00	11.50
2001P	21,200,000	0.75		
2001D	19,504,000	0.75		
2001S	(2,294,909)		2.00	3.75
2001S, Silver	(889,697)		8.00	11.50
2002P **(a)**	3,100,000	0.75		
2002D **(a)**	2,500,000	0.75		
2002S	(2,319,766)		2.00	3.75
2002S, Silver	(892,229)		7.00	9.50
2003P **(a)**	2,500,000	0.75		
2003D **(a)**	2,500,000	0.75		
2003S	(2,172,684)		1.75	2.75
2003S, Silver . . .	(1,125,755)		7.00	9.50
2004P **(a)**	2,900,000	0.75		

a. Not issued for circulation.

	Mintage	MS-63	PF-63	PF-65
2004D (a)	2,900,000	$0.75		
2004S	(1,789,488)		$2.00	$3.75
2004S, Silver	(1,175,934)		7.00	9.50
2005P (a)	3,800,000	0.75		
2005D (a)	3,500,000	0.75		
2005S	(2,275,000)		1.00	1.50
2005S, Silver	(1,069,679)		7.00	9.50
2006P (a)	2,400,000	0.75		
2006D (a)	2,000,000	0.75		
2006S	(2,000,428)		2.00	3.75
2006S, Silver	(1,054,008)		7.00	9.50
2007P (a)	2,400,000	0.75		
2007D (a)	2,400,000	0.75		
2007S	(1,702,116)		2.00	3.75
2007S, Silver	(875,050)		8.00	10.00
2008P (a)	1,700,000	0.75		
2008D (a)	1,700,000	0.75		
2008S	(1,405,674)		3.50	5.50
2008S, Silver	(763,887)		7.00	9.50
2009P (a)	1,900,000	0.75		
2009D (a)	1,900,000	0.75		
2009S	(1,482,502)		1.00	1.50
2009S, Silver	(697,365)		7.00	9.50
2010P (a)	1,800,000	0.75		
2010D (a)	1,700,000	0.75		
2010S	(1,103,815)		6.00	10.00
2010S, Silver	(585,401)		10.00	12.00
2011P (a)	1,750,000	0.75		
2011D (a)	1,700,000	0.75		
2011S	(1,098,835)		3.50	4.75
2011S, Silver	(574,175)		7.00	9.50
2012P (a)	1,800,000	0.75		

	Mintage	MS-63	PF-63	PF-65
2012D (a)	1,700,000	$0.75		
2012S	(843,705)		$5	$7.50
2012S, Silver	(445,612)		45	55.00
2013P (a)	5,000,000	0.75		
2013D (a)	4,600,000	0.75		
2013S	(854,785)		3	3.75
2013S, Silver	(467,691)		7	9.50
2014P (a)	2,500,000	1.00		
2014P, High Relief (b)	197,608	1.00		
2014P, Silver (c)	(219,173)		7	9.50
2014D (a)	2,100,000	1.00		
2014D, High Relief (b)	197,608	1.00		
2014D, Silver (c)	219,173	18.00		
2014S, Silver Enh. Unc. (c)	219,173	20.00		
2014S	(777,357)		3	4.50
2014S, Silver	(472,107)		7	9.50
2014W, Reverse Proof, Silver (c)	(219,173)		20	25.00
2014W, 50th Anniversary, Gold (d)	(73,722)		1,350	1,500.00
2015P (a)	2,300,000	0.75		
2015D (a)	2,300,000	0.75		
2015S	(662,854)		7	10.00
2015S, Silver	(387,310)		10	13.00
2016P (a)	2,100,000	0.75		
2016D (a)	2,100,000	0.75		
2016S	(641,775)		9	12.50
2016S, Silver	(419,496)		7	9.50

a. Not issued for circulation. b. To celebrate the 50th anniversary of the Kennedy half dollar, the U.S. Mint issued an Uncirculated two-coin set featuring a Kennedy half dollar from Philadelphia and one from Denver. c. Featured in the 2014 half dollar silver-coin collection released by the U.S. Mint to commemorate the 50th anniversary of the Kennedy half dollar. d. First gold half dollar offered by the U.S. Mint. It commemorates the 50th anniversary of the first release of the Kennedy half dollar in 1964.

	Mintage	SP-69	SP-70
2016W, Gold (a)	65,509	$950	$1,050

a. In 2016 the Mint issued a centennial version of the Liberty Walking half dollar in gold.

	Mintage	MS-63	PF-63	PF-65
2017P **(a)**	1,800,000	$0.75		
2017D **(a)**	2,900,000	0.75		
2017S	(621,390)		$10	$14.00
2017S, Silver	(406,986)		11	15.00
2018P **(a)**	4,800,000	0.75		
2018D **(a)**	6,100,000	0.75		
2018S	(568,804)		7	9.50
2018S, Silver	(381,748)		10	13.50
2019P **(a)**	1,700,000	0.75		
2019D **(a)**	1,700,000	0.75		
2019S	(673,650)		4	5.50
2019S, Silver	(461,125)		7	10.00
2019S, Enhanced RevPf **(b)**	(99,998)		7	10.00
2020P **(a)**	2,300,000	0.75		
2020D **(a)**	3,400,000	0.75		
2020S	(510,726)		4	5.50

	Mintage	MS-63	PF-63	PF-65
2020S, Silver	(363,244)		$7	$10
2021P	5,400,000	$0.75		
2021D	7,700,000	0.75		
2021S	(512,729)		4	7
2021S, Silver	(350,323)		7	10
2022P	4,800,000	0.75		
2022D	4,900,000	0.75		
2022S	(400,007)		4	7
2022S, Silver	(295,153)		7	10
2023P		0.75		
2023D		0.75		
2023S			4	7
2023S, Silver			7	10
2024P **(a)**		0.75		
2024D **(a)**		0.75		
2024S			4	7
2024S, Silver			7	10

a. Not issued for circulation. **b.** In 2019, an Enhanced Reverse Proof half dollar from the San Francisco Mint was included in the Apollo 11 50th Anniversary Half Dollar Set.

The silver dollar was authorized by Congress April 2, 1792. Its weight was specified at 416 grains and its fineness at .8924. The first issues appeared in 1794, and until 1804 all silver dollars had the value stamped on the edge: HUNDRED CENTS, ONE DOLLAR OR UNIT. After a lapse in coinage of the silver dollar during the period 1804 to 1835, coins were made with either plain (1836 only) or reeded edges and the value was placed on the reverse side.

Mintages shown here are as reported by the Mint for calendar years and do not necessarily refer to the dates on the coins.

The weight was changed by the law of January 18, 1837, to 412-1/2 grains, fineness .900. The coinage was discontinued by the Act of February 12, 1873, and reauthorized by the Act of February 28, 1878. The silver dollar was again discontinued after 1935, and since then copper-nickel and other base-metal pieces have been coined for circulation. (See also "$1 American Silver Eagle Coins" starting on page 245.)

FLOWING HAIR (1794–1795)

AG-3 About Good: Clear enough to identify.
G-4 Good: Date and letters legible. Main devices outlined, but lacking in detail.
VG-8 Very Good: Major details discernible. Letters well formed but worn.
F-12 Fine: Hair ends distinguishable. Top hair lines visible, but otherwise worn smooth.
VF-20 Very Fine: Some detail visible in hair in center. Other details more bold.
EF-40 Extremely Fine: Hair well defined but with some wear.
AU-50 About Uncirculated: Slight trace of wear on tips of highest curls; breast feathers usually weak.
MS-60 Uncirculated: No trace of wear. Light blemishes.

	Mintage	AG-3	G-4	VG-8	F-12	VF-20	EF-40	AU-50	MS-60
1794 1,758		$32,500	$55,000	$85,000	$105,000	$145,000	$275,000	$475,000	$850,000
1795 160,295		900	2,400	2,800	4,000	5,500	9,000	15,000	50,000

DRAPED BUST (1795–1804)
Small Eagle Reverse (1795–1798)

AG-3 About Good: Clear enough to identify.
G-4 Good: Bust outlined, no detail. Date legible, some leaves evident.
VG-8 Very Good: Drapery worn except deepest folds. Hair lines smooth.
F-12 Fine: All drapery lines distinguishable. Some detail visible in hair lines near cheek and neck.
VF-20 Very Fine: Left side of drapery worn smooth.
EF-40 Extremely Fine: Drapery distinctly visible. Hair well outlined and detailed.
AU-50 About Uncirculated: Slight trace of wear on the bust shoulder and hair to left of forehead, as well as on eagle's breast and top edges of wings.
MS-60 Uncirculated: No trace of wear. Light blemishes.

Mintage	AG-3	G-4	VG-8	F-12	VF-20	EF-40	AU-50	MS-60
1795, Bust Type. . *42,738*	$700	$1,850	$2,200	$2,850	$3,750	$6,500	$10,000	$37,500
1796 79,920	700	1,850	2,200	2,850	3,750	6,500	10,000	37,500
1797 7,776	700	1,850	2,200	2,850	3,750	6,500	10,000	42,000
1798 . . . .*40,000*	850	1,850	2,200	3,250	4,500	6,500	12,000	85,000

Heraldic Eagle Reverse (1798–1804)

G-4 Good: Letters and date legible. E PLURIBUS UNUM illegible.

VG-8 Very Good: Motto partially legible. Only deepest drapery details visible. All other lines smooth.

F-12 Fine: All drapery lines distinguishable. Some detail visible in hair lines near cheek and neck.

VF-20 Very Fine: Left side of drapery worn smooth.

EF-40 Extremely Fine: Drapery distinct. Hair well detailed.

AU-50 About Uncirculated: Slight trace of wear on the bust shoulder and hair to left of forehead, as well as on eagle's breast and top edges of wings.

MS-60 Uncirculated: No trace of wear. Light blemishes.

Mintage	G-4	VG-8	F-12	VF-20	EF-40	AU-50	MS-60
1798, Heraldic Eagle . . . .*	$800	$1,100	$1,650	$2,000	$3,000	$5,000	$17,500
1799 423,515	800	1,200	1,650	2,000	3,000	5,000	17,500
1800 220,920	800	1,200	1,650	2,000	3,000	5,000	17,500
1801 54,454	825	1,200	1,750	2,250	3,250	5,500	18,500
1802 41,650	850	1,350	1,750	2,250	3,000	5,000	17,500
1803 85,634	900	1,350	1,850	2,500	3,250	7,500	25,000
1804, Class I, First Rev (0 Above Cloud) **(a)** *(8 known)*				Proof: $3,500,000			
1804, Class II, Second Rev (0 Above Space Between Clouds, Plain Edge) **(b)** . . .				*(unique, in Smithsonian collection)*			
1804, Class III, Second Rev (0 Above Space Between Clouds, Lettered Edge) **(a)** *(6 known)*				Proof: $3,500,000			

* Included in number above. **a.** Numerous counterfeits exist. **b.** Electrotype copies exist, made at the Mint from their specimen.

GOBRECHT (1836–1839)

Silver dollars of 1836, 1838, and 1839 were mostly made as patterns and restrikes, but some dated 1836 were made for general circulation.

	VF-20	EF-40	AU-50	PF-60
1836, C. GOBRECHT F. on base. Reverse eagle flying upward amid stars. Plain edge. Although scarce, this is the most common variety and was issued for circulation as regular coinage....	$8,500	$12,500	$13,500	$23,500
1838, Similar obverse, designer's name omitted, stars added around border. Reverse eagle flying left in plain field. Reeded edge....	15,000	17,500	25,000	
1839, Obverse as above. Reverse eagle in plain field. Reeded edge. Issued for circulation as regular coinage....	10,000	12,500	15,000	25,000

LIBERTY SEATED (1840–1873)

Starting again in 1840, silver dollars were issued for general circulation, continuing to about 1850, after which their main use was in the export trade to China. The seated figure of Liberty was adopted for the obverse, and a heraldic eagle for the reverse.

VG-8 Very Good: Any three letters of LIBERTY at least two-thirds complete.
F-12 Fine: All seven letters of LIBERTY visible, though weak.
VF-20 Very Fine: LIBERTY strong, but slight wear visible on its ribbon.
EF-40 Extremely Fine: Horizontal lines of shield complete. Eagle's eye plain.
AU-50 About Uncirculated: Traces of light wear on only the high points of the design. Half of mint luster present.
MS-60 Uncirculated: No trace of wear. Light marks or blemishes.
PF-60 Proof: Several contact marks, hairlines, or light rubs possible on surface. Luster possibly dull and eye appeal lacking.
PF-63 Choice Proof: Reflective surfaces with only a few blemishes in secondary focal places. No major flaws.

No Motto (1840–1865)

Location of mintmark, when present, is on reverse, below eagle.

SILVER AND RELATED DOLLARS

	Mintage	VG-8	F-12	VF-20	EF-40	AU-50	MS-60	PF-60	PF-63
1840 61,005		$275	$350	$425	$650	$1,200	$4,000	$9,500	$25,000
1841 173,000		275	350	400	600	950	2,500	25,000	50,000
1842 184,618		250	350	400	600	750	2,250	11,000	35,000
1843 165,100		250	350	400	550	750	1,850	10,000	35,000
1844 20,000		275	350	425	750	1,200	3,850	13,500	30,000
1845 24,500		350	450	550	850	1,250	4,250	10,000	25,000
1846 110,600		275	350	375	550	800	1,600	8,500	20,000
1846O 59,000		275	350	400	600	1,000	5,000		
1847 140,750		275	350	400	525	750	2,250	10,000	20,000
1848 15,000		350	500	600	1,250	1,650	5,000	10,000	20,000
1849 62,600		275	400	450	750	1,000	2,250	12,500	30,000
1850 7,500		550	650	750	1,650	2,500	4,500	10,000	20,000
1850O 40,000		325	450	550	1,250	2,500	8,000		
1851 1,300		8,500	10,000	12,500	18,500	25,000	37,500	17,500	25,000
1852 1,100		11,000	14,000	20,000	25,000	27,500	35,000	20,000	25,000
1853 46,110		500	650	850	1,500	2,000	3,250	20,000	25,000
1854 33,140		1,500	2,500	3,000	5,500	6,500	10,000	9,500	12,500
1855 26,000		1,450	1,850	3,000	4,500	6,500	8,500	8,500	12,500
1856 63,500		650	1,100	1,200	2,250	3,000	6,000	4,000	10,000
1857 94,000		600	950	1,500	2,000	3,000	4,500	3,500	9,500
1858 . . . . (210)		2,500	3,000	3,500	4,500	6,000	6,250	6,500	8,500
1859 . . . . (800) 255,700		450	500	600	850	1,250	3,000	1,650	3,500
1859O 360,000		300	350	400	550	750	1,350		
1859S 20,000		550	750	1,000	1,500	3,000	5,500		
1860 . . . . . . (1,330) 217,600		300	375	450	650	850	2,000	1,650	3,500
1860O 515,000		275	375	400	550	750	1,500		
1861 . . . . . . (1,000) 77,500		1,000	1,650	2,250	3,000	4,000	5,500	1,650	3,500
1862 . . . . (550) 11,540		550	900	1,500	2,750	4,000	5,500	1,650	3,500
1863 . . . . (460) 27,200		800	1,100	1,600	2,250	2,750	3,750	1,650	3,500
1864 . . . . (470) 30,700		450	650	1,000	1,500	2,750	4,000	1,650	3,500
1865 . . . . (500) 46,500		550	700	1,200	2,000	2,500	4,000	1,650	3,500

With Motto IN GOD WE TRUST (1866–1873)

Motto IN GOD WE TRUST on Reverse (1866–1873)

	Mintage	VG-8	F-12	VF-20	EF-40	AU-50	MS-60	PF-60	PF-63
1866 . . . . (725) 48,900		$300	$375	$500	$850	$1,100	$2,000	$1,650	$3,250
1867 . . . . (625) 46,900		450	550	750	1,000	1,500	3,250	1,650	3,250
1868 . . . . (600) 162,100		325	400	550	850	1,200	2,250	1,650	3,250
1869 . . . . (600) 423,700		325	375	500	750	1,000	2,000	1,650	3,250

Chart continued on next page.

	Mintage	VG-8	F-12	VF-20	EF-40	AU-50	MS-60	PF-60	PF-63
1870 ... (1,000)... 415,000		$300	$350	$375	$600	$650	$1,850	$1,650	$3,250
1870CC 11,758		1,500	2,000	3,000	4,000	6,000	20,000		
1870S 175,000		250,000	350,000	450,000	800,000	1,250,000			
1871 ..... (960) ..1,073,800		275	325	375	550	650	1,500	1,650	3,250
1871CC 1,376		3,800	5,000	7,500	11,000	17,500	65,000		
1872 ..... (950) ..1,105,500		275	325	375	500	600	1,500	1,650	3,250
1872CC 3,150		2,250	2,850	3,500	6,500	10,000	17,500		
1872S 9,000		650	850	1,250	1,850	3,000	9,000		
1873 ..... (600)... 293,000		300	350	375	500	1,000	2,500	1,650	3,250
1873CC 2,300		12,500	15,000	18,000	30,000	50,000	100,000		

TRADE DOLLARS (1873–1885)

This trade dollar was issued for circulation in Asia to compete with dollar-size coins of other countries. It weighed 420 grains compared to 412-1/2 grains, the weight of the regular silver dollar.

VG-8 Very Good: About half of mottoes IN GOD WE TRUST (on Liberty's pedestal) and E PLURIBUS UNUM (on obverse ribbon) visible. Rim on both sides well defined.

F-12 Fine: Mottoes and LIBERTY legible but worn.

EF-40 Extremely Fine: Mottoes and LIBERTY sharp. Only slight wear on rims.

AU-50 About Uncirculated: Slight trace of wear on Liberty's left breast and left knee and on hair above ear, as well as on eagle's head, knee, and wing tips.

MS-60 Uncirculated: No trace of wear. Light blemishes.

MS-63 Choice Uncirculated: Some distracting contact marks or blemishes in prime focal areas. Impaired luster possible.

PF-63 Choice Proof: Reflective surfaces with only a few blemishes in secondary focal places. No major flaws.

1875-S, S Over CC

	Mintage	VG-8	F-12	EF-40	AU-50	MS-60	MS-63	PF-63
1873 .... (600) 396,900		$160	$175	$375	$450	$950	$2,350	$2,200
1873CC 124,500		400	580	1,650	2,200	6,000	20,000	
1873S 703,000		180	240	450	525	1,100	2,800	
1874 .... (700) 987,100		150	185	375	450	975	1,900	2,200
1874CC 1,373,200		260	310	700	900	1,700	4,350	
1874S 2,549,000		145	170	300	325	750	1,500	
1875 .... (700) 218,200		290	360	850	1,050	1,800	3,250	2,200
1875CC 1,573,700		275	330	725	900	2,200	3,500	
1875S 4,487,000		145	175	250	325	750	1,100	
1875S, S Over CC .... *		375	475	1,100	1,300	4,000	12,500	
1876 ...... (1,150) 455,000		160	190	340	400	750	1,450	2,200
1876CC 509,000		475	535	1,100	1,450	4,500	12,500	

* Included in number above.

	Mintage	VG-8	F-12	EF-40	AU-50	MS-60	MS-63	PF-63
1876S	5,227,000	$145	$175	$300	$340	$800	$1,300	
1877	(510)....3,039,200	145	185	300	390	825	1,300	$2,500
1877CC	.534,000	360	450	975	1,350	3,350	7,500	
1877S	9,519,000	145	175	300	325	750	1,100	
1878	(900)			850				2,250
1878CC **(a)**	.97,000	800	1,150	3,600	5,000	12,500	22,500	
1878S	4,162,000	145	175	300	330	750	1,100	
1879	(1,541)			850				2,250
1880	(1,987)			900				2,250
1881	(960)			900				2,250
1882	(1,097)			900				2,250
1883	(979)			900				2,250
1884 **(b)**	(10)							325,000
1885 **(b)**	(5)							1,500,000

a. 44,148 trade dollars were melted on July 19, 1878. Many of these may have been 1878-CC. **b.** The trade dollars of 1884 and 1885 were unknown to collectors until 1908. None are listed in the Mint director's report, and numismatists believe that they are not a part of the regular Mint issue.

MORGAN (1878–1921)

George T. Morgan, formerly a pupil of William Wyon at the Royal Mint in London, designed the new dollar. His initial M is found at the truncation of the neck, at the last tress. It also appears on the reverse on the left-hand loop of the ribbon.

Sharply struck prooflike coins have a highly reflective surface and usually command substantial premiums.

The 1921 Silver Dollar Coin Anniversary Act authorized the Mint to produce coins celebrating the 2021 centennial of the last Morgan dollar.

VF-20 Very Fine: Two thirds of hair lines from top of forehead to ear visible. Ear well defined. Feathers on eagle's breast worn.

EF-40 Extremely Fine: All hair lines strong and ear bold. Eagle's feathers all plain but with slight wear on breast and wing tips.

AU-50 About Uncirculated: Slight trace of wear on the bust shoulder and hair left of forehead, and on eagle's breast and top edges of wings.

MS-60 Uncirculated: No trace of wear. Full mint luster present, but may be noticeably marred by scuff marks or bag abrasions.

MS-63 Choice Uncirculated: No trace of wear; full mint luster; few noticeable surface marks.

MS-64 Uncirculated: A few scattered contact marks. Good eye appeal and attractive luster.

MS-65 Gem Uncirculated: Only light, scattered contact marks that are not distracting. Strong luster, good eye appeal.

8 Tail Feathers, 1878, Philadelphia Only
Mintmark location on reverse, below wreath.

Most Proof Morgan dollars, where indicated in mintage records (quantity shown in parentheses), are valued by coin dealers approximately as follows:
Proof-60 – $600; Proof-63 – $1,400; Proof-65 – $3,000.

Most Uncirculated silver dollars have scratches or nicks because of handling of mint bags in shipping and storage. Coin dealers usually pay more than the listed prices for choice sharply struck pieces with full brilliance and without blemishes.

	Mintage	VF-20	EF-40	AU-50	MS-60	MS-63	MS-65
1878, 8 Feathers.........(500).....*749,500*		$65	$75	$100	$185	$350	$1,350
1878, 7 Feathers.........(250)...*9,759,300*		38	40	55	75	150	475
1878, 7 Over 8 Tail Feathers, Strong........*		38	40	100	200	375	1,800
1878, 7 Over 8 Tail Feathers, Weak........*		38	40	60	95	210	500
1878CC......................2,212,000		130	165	225	300	450	1,400
1878S......................9,774,000		38	39	42	65	105	275
1879..............(1,100)..14,806,000		32	34	42	55	95	350
1879CC, CC Over CC..............756,000		450	1,300	2,350	4,000	7,000	18,500
1879O......................2,887,000		32	35	50	90	350	1,750
1879S......................9,110,000		32	34	43	55	85	150
1880..............(1,355)..12,600,000		32	34	39	47	72	275
1880CC......................*591,000*		190	225	275	525	600	950
1880O......................5,305,000		32	34	50	100	475	7,500
1880S......................8,900,000		32	34	39	45	60	150
1881..............(984)...9,163,000		32	34	39	47	70	350
1881CC......................296,000		300	330	375	500	600	800
1881O......................5,708,000		32	34	39	45	75	650
1881S......................12,760,000		32	34	39	45	60	150
1882..............(1,100)..11,100,000		32	34	39	47	75	260
1882CC......................1,133,000		125	155	190	235	275	400
1882O......................6,090,000		32	34	39	50	65	400
1882S......................9,250,000		32	34	39	45	60	150
1883..............(1,039)..12,290,000		32	34	39	47	60	150
1883CC......................1,204,000		125	155	195	235	275	400
1883O......................8,725,000		32	34	39	47	70	150
1883S......................6,250,000		35	70	185	1,000	2,250	20,000
1884..............(875)..14,070,000		32	34	39	47	63	150
1884CC......................1,136,000		125	155	190	235	275	400
1884O......................9,730,000		32	33	39	45	60	150
1884S......................3,200,000		45	90	320	7,000	25,000	175,000
1885..............(930)..17,787,000		32	34	39	47	63	150
1885CC......................228,000		425	475	500	550	650	1,000
1885O......................9,185,000		32	34	39	47	63	150
1885S......................1,497,000		36	65	120	285	450	1,350
1886..............(886)..19,963,000		32	34	39	47	63	150
1886O......................10,710,000		34	70	135	1,000	2,500	135,000
1886S......................750,000		60	95	160	375	550	1,350
1887..............(710)..20,290,000		32	34	39	47	63	150
1887O......................11,550,000		32	34	55	105	210	1,500
1887S......................1,771,000		34	40	65	150	325	1,150
1888..............(833)..19,183,000		32	34	39	47	63	150
1888O......................12,150,000		32	34	39	55	82	225
1888S......................657,000		100	115	180	300	625	1,500
1889..............(811)..21,726,000		32	34	39	47	67	200
1889CC......................350,000		1,500	3,500	6,750	20,000	35,000	220,000
1889O......................11,875,000		34	45	110	325	500	1,850

* Included in number above.

SILVER AND RELATED DOLLARS

	Mintage	VF-20	EF-40	AU-50	MS-60	MS-63	MS-65
1889S	.700,000	$50	$60	$105	$245	$375	$1,200
1890 . . . . (590). . .	16,802,000	32	34	39	50	72	550
1890CC	2,309,041	135	215	315	600	1,100	3,750
1890O	10,701,000	32	34	40	90	165	800
1890S	8,230,373	32	34	40	75	155	550
1891 . . . . (650). . .	8,693,556	32	34	39	72	180	1,600
1891CC	1,618,000	125	215	290	575	800	3,000
1891O	7,954,529	50	80	110	200	375	3,250
1891S	5,296,000	32	34	50	85	250	1,150
1892 . . . . . . (1,245). . .	1,036,000	36	70	130	375	625	2,200
1892CC	1,352,000	315	525	675	1,300	2,150	5,500
1892O	2,744,000	32	63	130	360	525	2,250
1892S	1,200,000	125	425	1,800	40,000	85,000	175,000
1893 . . . . (792). . .	.378,000	300	500	675	1,350	1,850	4,500
1893CC	.677,000	700	1,850	2,850	4,500	7,500	75,000
1893O	.300,000	375	625	1,000	4,000	7,350	150,000
1893S	.100,000	4,500	8,500	20,000	170,000	300,000	525,000
1894 . . . . (972). . . .	.110,000	650	950	1,350	2,850	4,000	27,500
1894O	1,723,000	37	125	225	1,800	3,750	32,500
1894S	1,260,000	100	215	450	1,000	1,500	4,500
1895 . . . . (880).		35,000 (a)	36,500 (a)	45,000 (a)	47,500 (a)	65,000 (a)
1895O	.450,000	325	550	1,400	10,000	40,000	165,000
1895S	.400,000	650	1,250	2,000	4,250	6,000	15,000
1896 . . . . (762). . .	9,976,000	32	34	39	48	65	155
1896O	4,900,000	40	65	150	1,450	4,250	145,000
1896S	5,000,000	110	375	1,000	2,500	3,250	8,500
1897 . . . . (731). . .	2,822,000	32	34	39	48	105	200
1897O	4,004,000	37	55	85	1,000	3,000	45,000
1897S	5,825,000	32	34	45	82	170	450
1898 . . . . (735). . .	5,884,000	32	34	39	48	72	150
1898O	4,440,000	32	34	39	48	68	150
1898S	4,102,000	37	60	130	400	775	1,700
1899 . . . . (846). . . .	.330,000	80	90	125	200	300	650
1899O	12,290,000	32	34	39	48	68	150
1899S	2,562,000	50	90	225	475	800	1,650
1900 . . . . (912). . .	8,830,000	32	34	39	48	68	160
1900O	12,590,000	32	34	39	48	68	160
1900S	3,540,000	35	65	130	375	650	1,000
1901 . . . . (813). . .	6,962,000	65	160	340	3,650	7,500	300,000
1901O	13,320,000	32	34	39	48	68	150
1901S	2,284,000	45	60	235	525	1,000	2,500
1902 . . . . (777). . .	7,994,000	35	37	50	100	225	325
1902O	8,636,000	32	34	39	48	65	155
1902S	1,530,000	120	125	275	450	800	1,800
1903 . . . . (755). . .	4,652,000	36	37	45	65	100	200
1903O	4,450,000	335	350	375	500	650	775
1903S	1,241,000	175	525	2,000	5,750	8,000	11,500
1904 . . . . (650). . .	2,788,000	32	37	55	115	400	1,500
1904O	3,720,000	32	33	39	48	65	150
1904S	2,304,000	115	325	1,100	2,700	4,000	6,250
1921	44,690,000	28	29	30	33	40	115
1921D	20,345,000	28	29	30	53	145	425
1921S	21,695,000	28	29	30	54	115	625

a. Values are for Proofs.

PEACE (1921–1935)

Anthony de Francisci, a medalist, designed this dollar. His monogram is located in the field of the coin under the neck of Liberty.

The 1921 Silver Dollar Coin Anniversary Act authorized the Mint to produce coins celebrating the 2021 centennial of the first Peace dollar.

VF-20 Very Fine: Hair over eye well worn. Some strands over ear well defined. Some eagle feathers on top and outside edge of right wing visible.

EF-40 Extremely Fine: Hair lines over brow and ear are strong, though slightly worn. Outside wing feathers at right and those at top visible but faint.

AU-50 About Uncirculated: Slight trace of wear. Most luster present, although marred by contact marks.

MS-60 Uncirculated: No trace of wear. Full mint luster, but possibly noticeably marred by stains, surface marks, or bag abrasions.

MS-63 Choice Uncirculated: Some distracting contact marks or blemishes in prime focal areas. Impaired luster possible.

MS-64 Uncirculated: A few scattered contact marks. Good eye appeal and attractive luster.

MS-65 Gem Uncirculated: Only light, scattered, non-distracting contact marks. Strong luster, good eye appeal.

PF-65 Choice Proof: Satin surfaces, no noticeable blemishes or flaws.

Most Uncirculated silver dollars have scratches or nicks because of handling of mint bags in shipping and storage. Coin dealers usually pay more than the listed prices for choice sharply struck pieces with full brilliance and without blemishes.

Mintmark location on reverse, below ONE.

	Mintage	VF-20	EF-40	AU-50	MS-60	MS-63	MS-65	PF-65
1921	1,006,473	$135	$200	$250	$450	$750	$2,150	$115,000
1922	51,737,000	24	26	28	30	45	85	160,000
1922D	15,063,000	24	26	32	38	85	400	
1922S	17,475,000	24	26	32	45	85	950	
1923	30,800,000	24	26	28	30	45	85	
1923D	6,811,000	24	26	45	90	200	800	
1923S	19,020,000	24	26	32	55	85	1,750	
1924	11,811,000	24	26	28	34	45	150	
1924S	1,728,000	32	40	67	225	450	4,000	
1925	10,198,000	24	26	32	34	45	95	
1925S	1,610,000	30	38	54	125	250	14,500	
1926	1,939,000	24	27	42	82	110	400	
1926D	2,348,700	24	27	50	130	290	825	
1926S	6,980,000	24	26	32	72	75	600	
1927	848,000	30	42	50	100	200	1,100	
1927D	1,268,900	34	65	110	260	525	2,500	
1927S	866,000	34	55	82	250	550	3,500	
1928	360,649	175	200	250	350	600	3,200	
1928S	1,632,000	33	55	90	220	500	12,500	
1934	954,057	29	40	60	140	200	600	
1934D	1,569,500	35	50	62	125	275	1,300	
1934S	1,011,000	50	100	275	2,350	4,750	6,750	
1935	1,576,000	35	42	55	110	175	525	
1935S	1,964,000	36	48	95	250	440	1,100	

EISENHOWER (1971–1978)
Eagle Reverse (1971–1974)

Honoring both President Dwight D. Eisenhower and the first landing of man on the moon, this design is the work of Chief Engraver Frank Gasparro, whose initials are on the truncation of the President's neck and below the eagle. The reverse is an adaptation of the official *Apollo 11* insignia.

Mintmark location is above date.

	Mintage	EF-40	MS-63	PF-63	PF-65
1971, Copper-Nickel Clad	47,799,000	$1.20	$2.00		
1971D, Copper-Nickel Clad	68,587,424	1.20	1.75		
1971S, Silver Clad	(4,265,234)......6,868,530		9.00	$9.50	$12.00
1972, Copper-Nickel Clad	75,890,000	1.20	1.75		
1972D, Copper-Nickel Clad	92,548,511	1.20	1.75		
1972S, Silver Clad	(1,811,631)......2,193,056		9.00	9.50	12.00
1973, Copper-Nickel Clad **(a)**	2,000,056	1.20	3.50		
1973D, Copper-Nickel Clad **(a)**	2,000,000	1.20	3.50		
1973S, Copper-Nickel Clad	(2,760,339)			2.50	7.00
1973S, Silver Clad	(1,013,646)......1,883,140		10.00	22.00	27.00
1974, Copper-Nickel Clad	27,366,000	1.20	1.75		
1974D, Copper-Nickel Clad	45,517,000	1.20	1.75		
1974S, Copper-Nickel Clad	(2,612,568)			2.50	3.75
1974S, Silver Clad	(1,306,579)......1,900,156		9.00	12.00	14.00

a. 1,769,258 of each sold only in sets and not released for circulation. Unissued coins destroyed at mint.

Bicentennial (1776–1976)

| Obverse | Reverse Variety 2 | Reverse Variety 1 |

Variety 1: Design in low relief, bold lettering on reverse.
Variety 2: Sharp design, delicate lettering on reverse.

See next page for chart.   151

	Mintage	EF-40	MS-63	PF-63	PF-65
1776–1976, Copper-Nickel Clad, Variety 1	4,019,000	$1.20	$3.00		
1776–1976, Copper-Nickel Clad, Variety 2	113,318,000	1.20	1.75		
1776–1976D, Copper-Nickel Clad, Variety 1	21,048,710	1.20	1.75		
1776–1976D, Copper-Nickel Clad, Variety 2	82,179,564	1.20	1.75		
1776–1976S, Copper-Nickel Clad, Variety 1	(2,845,450)			$3	$5.50
1776–1976S, Copper-Nickel Clad, Variety 2	(4,149,730)			3	4.00
1776–1976S, Silver Clad, Variety 1	11,000,000		9.00		
1776–1976S, Silver Clad, Variety 1	(4,000,000)			12	13.00

Eagle Reverse Resumed (1977–1978)

	Mintage	EF-40	MS-63	PF-63	PF-65
1977, Copper-Nickel Clad	12,596,000	$1.20	$1.75		
1977D, Copper-Nickel Clad	32,983,006	1.20	1.75		
1977S, Copper-Nickel Clad	(3,251,152)			$3	$5
1978, Copper-Nickel Clad	25,702,000	1.20	1.75		
1978D, Copper-Nickel Clad	33,012,890	1.20	1.75		
1978S, Copper-Nickel Clad	(3,127,781)			3	5

SUSAN B. ANTHONY (1979–1999)

Filled S   Clear S

	Mintage	MS-63
1979P, Narrow Rim	360,222,000	$1.10
1979P, Wide Rim	*	27.00
1979D	288,015,744	1.10
1979S	109,576,000	1.10

* Included in number above.

	Mintage	MS-65	PF-63	PF-65
1979S, Proof, Type 1	(3,677,175)	$2.50	$4	
1979S, Proof, Type 2	*	20.00	40	
1980P	27,610,000	$1.10		
1980D	41,628,708	1.10		
1980S	20,422,000	1.10		
1980S, Proof	(3,554,806)		2.50	3
1981P	3,000,000	2.00		

	Mintage	MS-65	PF-63	PF-65
1981D	3,250,000	$2.00		
1981S	3,492,000	2.00		
1981S, Proof, Type 1	(4,063,083)		$2.50	$4
1981S, Proof, Type 2	*		35.00	75
1999P	29,592,000	2.50		
1999P, Proof	(750,000)		13.00	16
1999D	11,776,000	2.50		

* Included in number above.

SACAGAWEA (2000–2008)

The design of this coin was selected in national competition from among 120 submissions that were considered by a panel appointed by Treasury Secretary Robert Rubin. The adopted motif depicts Sacagawea, a young Native American Shoshone, as rendered by artist Glenna Goodacre. On her back she carries Jean Baptiste, her infant son. The reverse shows an eagle in flight, designed by Mint engraver Thomas D. Rogers Sr.

The composition exemplifies the spirit of Liberty, Peace, and Freedom shown by Sacagawea in her conduct as interpreter and guide to explorers Meriwether Lewis and William Clark during their famed journey westward from St. Louis to the Pacific.

These coins have a distinctive golden color and a plain edge to distinguish them from other denominations or coins of a similar size. The change in composition and appearance was mandated under the United States Dollar Coin Act of 1997.

Several distinctive finishes can be identified on the Sacagawea dollars as a result of the Mint attempting to adjust the dies, blanks, strikes, or finishing to produce coins with minimal spotting and a better surface color. One group of 5,000 pieces dated 2000 with a special finish were presented to sculptor Glenna Goodacre in payment for the obverse design. Unexplained error coins made from mismatched dies (a State quarter obverse combined with a Sacagawea dollar reverse) are extremely rare.

	Mintage	MS-65	PF-63	PF-65		Mintage	MS-65	PF-63	PF-65
2000P	767,140,000	$1.10			2004S	(2,965,422)		$3	$5
2000D	518,916,000	1.10			2005P (a)	2,520,000	$1.50		
2000S	(4,097,904)		$3	$5	2005D (a)	2,520,000	1.50		
2001P	62,468,000	1.10			2005S	(3,344,679)		3	5
2001D	70,939,500	1.10			2006P (a)	4,900,000	1.50		
2001S	(3,183,740)		7	9	2006D (a)	2,800,000	1.50		
2002P (a)	3,865,610	1.25			2006S	(3,054,436)		3	5
2002D (a)	3,732,000	1.25			2007P (a)	3,640,000	1.50		
2002S	(3,211,995)		3	5	2007D (a)	3,920,000	1.50		
2003P (a)	3,080,000	1.50			2007S	(2,577,166)		3	5
2003D (a)	3,080,000	1.50			2008P (a)	1,820,000	2.00		
2003S	(3,298,439)		3	5	2008D (a)	1,820,000	2.00		
2004P (a)	2,660,000	1.50			2008S	(2,169,561)		6	8
2004D (a)	2,660,000	1.50							

a. Not issued for circulation.

PRESIDENTIAL (2007–2016, 2020)

Four different coins, each bearing the image of a former U.S. president, were issued each year in the order that the presidents served. The size and composition of these coins is the same as that of the Native American dollars that are also made each year. A companion series of ten-dollar gold bullion coins (listed in the Bullion section) honors the spouse of each president.

Presidential Dollars Reverse

Date, Mintmark, and Motto Incused on Edge (Motto Moved to Obverse in 2009)

The 2016 Ronald Reagan issues brought the regular production of Presidential dollars to a close. In 2020, the Mint produced a new coin to honor President George H.W. Bush (d. November 30, 2018), along with a gold bullion coin honoring Barbara Bush, his late wife.

	Mintage	MS-65	PF-65
2007P, Washington	176,680,000	$1.10	
2007D, Washington	163,680,000	1.10	
2007S, Washington	(3,965,989)		$1.50
2007P, J. Adams	112,420,000	1.10	
2007D, J. Adams	112,140,000	1.10	
2007S, J. Adams	(3,965,989)		2.00

	Mintage	MS-65	PF-65
2007P, Jefferson	100,800,000	$1.10	
2007D, Jefferson	102,810,000	1.10	
2007S, Jefferson	(3,965,989)		$2
2007P, Madison	84,560,000	1.10	
2007D, Madison	87,780,000	1.10	
2007S, Madison	(3,965,989)		2

	Mintage	MS-65	PF-65
2008P, Monroe	64,260,000	$1.10	
2008D, Monroe	60,230,000	1.10	
2008S, Monroe	(3,083,940)		$2
2008P, J.Q. Adams	57,540,000	1.10	
2008D, J.Q. Adams	57,720,000	1.10	
2008S, J.Q. Adams	(3,083,940)		2

	Mintage	MS-65	PF-65
2008P, Jackson	61,180,000	$1.10	
2008D, Jackson	61,070,000	1.10	
2008S, Jackson	(3,083,940)		$2
2008P, Van Buren	51,520,000	1.10	
2008D, Van Buren	50,960,000	1.10	
2008S, Van Buren	(3,083,940)		2

	Mintage	MS-65	PF-65
2009P, Harrison	43,260,000	$1.10	
2009D, Harrison	55,160,000	1.10	
2009S, Harrison	(2,809,452)		$2
2009P, Tyler	43,540,000	1.10	
2009D, Tyler	43,540,000	1.10	
2009S, Tyler	(2,809,452)		2

	Mintage	MS-65	PF-65
2009P, Polk	46,620,000	$1.10	
2009D, Polk	41,720,000	1.10	
2009S, Polk	(2,809,452)		$2
2009P, Taylor	41,580,000	1.10	
2009D, Taylor	36,680,000	1.10	
2009S, Taylor	(2,809,452)		2

Note: Errors have been reported in the Presidential dollar series, including coins minted without edge lettering. Depending on their rarity, dealers may pay a premium for such errors.

	Mintage	MS-65	PF-65
2010P, Fillmore	37,520,000	$1.10	
2010D, Fillmore	36,960,000	1.10	
2010S, Fillmore	(2,224,827)		$2
2010P, Pierce	38,220,000	1.10	
2010D, Pierce	38,360,000	1.10	
2010S, Pierce	(2,224,827)		2

	Mintage	MS-65	PF-65
2010P, Buchanan	36,820,000	$1.10	
2010D, Buchanan	36,540,000	1.10	
2010S, Buchanan	(2,224,827)		$2
2010P, Lincoln	49,000,000	1.10	
2010D, Lincoln	48,020,000	1.10	
2010S, Lincoln	(2,224,827)		3

	Mintage	MS-65	PF-65
2011P, A. Johnson	35,560,000	$1.10	
2011D, A. Johnson	37,100,000	1.10	
2011S, A. Johnson	(1,972,863)		$2
2011P, Grant	38,080,000	1.10	
2011D, Grant	37,940,000	1.10	
2011S, Grant	(1,972,863)		2

	Mintage	MS-65	PF-65
2011P, Hayes	37,660,000	$1.10	
2011D, Hayes	36,820,000	1.10	
2011S, Hayes	(1,972,863)		$2
2011P, Garfield	37,100,000	1.10	
2011D, Garfield	37,100,000	1.10	
2011S, Garfield	(1,972,863)		2

	Mintage	MS-65	PF-65
2012P, Arthur (a)	6,020,000	$1.10	
2012D, Arthur (a)	4,060,000	1.10	
2012S, Arthur	(1,438,743)		$3
2012P, Cleveland, Variety 1 (a)	5,460,000	1.10	
2012D, Cleveland, Variety 1 (a)	4,060,000	1.10	
2012S, Cleveland, Variety 1	(1,438,743)		3

	Mintage	MS-65	PF-65
2012P, Harrison (a)	5,640,001	$1.10	
2012D, Harrison (a)	4,200,000	1.10	
2012S, Harrison	(1,438,743)		$3
2012P, Cleveland, Variety 2 (a)	10,680,000	1.10	
2012D, Cleveland, Variety 2	3,920,000	1.10	
2012S, Cleveland, Variety 2	(1,438,743)		3

a. Not issued for circulation.

	Mintage	MS-65	PF-65
2013P, McKinley (a)	4,760,000	$1.10	
2013D, McKinley (a)	3,365,100	1.10	
2013S, McKinley	(1,488,798)		$2
2013P, T. Roosevelt (a)	5,310,700	1.10	
2013D, T. Roosevelt (a)	3,920,000	1.10	
2013S, T. Roosevelt	(1,503,943)		2

a. Not issued for circulation.

	Mintage	MS-65	PF-65
2013P, Taft (a)	4,760,000	$1.10	
2013D, Taft (a)	3,360,000	1.10	
2013S, Taft	(1,488,798)		$2
2013P, Wilson (a)	4,620,000	1.10	
2013D, Wilson (a)	3,360,000	1.10	
2013S, Wilson	(1,488,798)		2

	Mintage	MS-65	PF-65
2014P, Harding (a)	6,160,000	$1.10	
2014D, Harding (a)	3,780,000	1.10	
2014S, Harding	(1,373,569)		$3
2014P, Coolidge (a)	4,480,000	1.10	
2014D, Coolidge (a)	3,780,000	1.10	
2014S, Coolidge	(1,373,569)		3

a. Not issued for circulation.

	Mintage	MS-65	PF-65
2014P, Hoover (a)	4,480,000	$1.10	
2014D, Hoover (a)	3,780,000	1.10	
2014S, Hoover	(1,373,569)		$3
2014P, F.D. Roosevelt (a)	4,760,000	1.10	
2014D, F.D. Roosevelt (a)	3,920,000	1.10	
2014S, F.D. Roosevelt	(1,392,619)		3

	Mintage	MS-65	PF-65
2015P, Truman (a)	4,900,000	$1.10	
2015P, Truman, RevPf	(16,812)		$18
2015D, Truman (a)	3,500,000	1.10	
2015S, Truman	(1,272,232)		3
2015P, Eisenhower (a)	4,900,000	1.10	
2015P, Eisenhower, RevPf	(16,744)		18
2015D, Eisenhower (a)	3,645,998	1.10	
2015S, Eisenhower	(1,272,232)		3

a. Not issued for circulation.

	Mintage	MS-65	PF-65
2015P, Kennedy (a)	6,160,000	$1.10	
2015P, Kennedy, RevPf	(49,051)		$18
2015D, Kennedy (a)	5,180,000	1.10	
2015S, Kennedy	(1,272,232)		3
2015P, L. Johnson (a)	7,840,000	1.10	
2015P, L. Johnson, RevPf	(23,905)		18
2015D, L. Johnson (a)	4,200,000	1.10	
2015S, L.B. Johnson	(1,272,232)		3

SILVER AND RELATED DOLLARS

	Mintage	MS-65	PF-65
2016P, Nixon **(a)**	5,460,000	$1.10	
2016D, Nixon **(a)**	4,340,000	1.10	
2016S, Nixon	(1,196,582)		$3
2016P, Ford **(a)**	5,460,000	1.10	
2016P, Ford **(a)**	5,040,000	1.10	
2016S, Ford	(1,196,582)		3
2016P, Reagan **(a)**	7,140,000	1.10	

	Mintage	MS-65	PF-65
2016D, Reagan **(a)**	5,880,000	$1.10	
2016S, Reagan	(1,196,582)		$3
2016S, Reagan, RevPf	(47,447)		18
2020P, G.H.W. Bush **(a)**	*1,458,725*	1.10	
2020D, G.H.W. Bush **(a)**	*1,444,700*	1.10	
2020S, G.H.W. Bush, RevPf	*(11,305)*		18

a. Not issued for circulation.

NATIVE AMERICAN (2009 TO DATE)

Obverse

Three Sisters (2009)

Great Law of Peace (2010)

Wampanoag Treaty (2011)

Trade Routes in the 17th Century (2012)

Treaty With the Delawares (2013)

Native Hospitality (2014)

Mohawk Ironworkers (2015)

Code Talkers (2016)

Sequoyah (2017)

Jim Thorpe (2018)

American Indians in Space (2019)

Entry continued on next page.

Elizabeth Peratrovich and Alaska's Anti-Discrimination Law (2020)

American Indians in the U.S. Military (2021)

Ely S. Parker (2022)

Maria Tallchief and American Indians in Ballet (2023)

Indian Citizenship Act of 1924 Centennial (2024)

	Mintage	MS-65	PF-65
2009P, Three Sisters	39,200,000	$1.25	
2009D, Three Sisters	35,700,000	1.25	
2009S, Three Sisters	(2,179,867)		$3
2010P, Great Law	32,060,000	1.75	
2010D, Great Law	48,720,000	1.75	
2010S, Great Law	(1,689,216)		3
2011P, Wampanoag	29,400,000	2.00	
2011D, Wampanoag	48,160,000	2.00	
2011S, Wampanoag	(1,673,010)		3
2012P, Trade Routes (a)	2,800,000	1.75	
2012D, Trade Routes (a)	3,080,000	1.75	
2012S, Trade Routes	(1,189,445)		7
2013P, Treaty, Delawares (a)	1,820,000	1.50	
2013D, Treaty, Delawares (a)	1,820,000	1.50	
2013S, Treaty, Delawares	(1,222,180)		3
2014P, Native Hospitality (a)	3,080,000	1.50	
2014D, Native Hospitality (a)	2,800,000	1.50	
2014D, Native Hospitality, Enhanced Uncirculated	50,000	8.75	
2014S, Native Hospitality	(1,144,154)		3
2015P, Mohawk Ironworkers (a)	2,800,000	1.50	
2015D, Mohawk Ironworkers (a)	2,240,000	1.50	
2015S, Mohawk Ironworkers	(1,050,164)		3
2015W, Mohawk Ironworkers, Enhanced Uncirculated	88,805	8.75	
2016P, Code Talkers (a)	2,800,000	1.50	
2016D, Code Talkers (a)	2,100,000	1.50	
2016S, Code Talkers, Enh. Unc.	50,737	8.75	
2016S, Code Talkers	(965,033)		3
2017P, Sequoyah (a)	1,820,000	1.50	
2017D, Sequoyah (a)	1,540,000	1.50	
2017S, Sequoyah	(926,763)		3
2018P, Jim Thorpe (a)	1,400,000	1.50	
2018D, Jim Thorpe (a)	1,400,000	1.50	

	Mintage	MS-65	PF-65
2018S, Jim Thorpe	(849,321)		$3
2018S, Jim Thorpe, RevPf	199,116		3
2019P, Am. Indians / Space (a)	1,400,000	$1.50	
2019P, Am. Indians / Space, Enhanced Uncirculated	46,964	8.75	
2019D, Am. Indians /Space (a)	1,540,000	1.50	
2019S, Am. Indians in Space	(1,056,828)		3
2020P, E. Peratrovich / Alaska's Anti-Discrimination Law (a)	1,400,000	1.50	
2020D, E. Peratrovich / Alaska's Anti-Discrimination Law (a)	1,260,000	1.50	
2020S, E. Peratrovich / Alaska's Anti-Discrimination Law	(777,381)		3
2021P, American Indians in the U.S. Military (a)	1,260,000	1.50	
2021D, American Indians in the U.S. Military (a)	1,260,000	1.50	
2021S, American Indians in the U.S. Military	(814,340)		3
2022P, Ely S. Parker (a)	980,000	1.50	
2022D, Ely S. Parker (a)	980,000	1.50	
2022S, Ely S. Parker	(646,177)		3
2023P, Maria Tallchief and Am. Indians in Ballet (a)	1,120,000	1.50	
2023D, Maria Tallchief and Am. Indians in Ballet (a)	1,120,000	1.50	
2023S, Maria Tallchief and Am. Indians in Ballet			3
2024P, Indian Citizenship Act of 1924 Centennial (a)		1.50	
2024D, Indian Citizenship Act of 1924 Centennial (a)		1.50	
2024S, Indian Citizenship Act of 1924 Centennial			3

a. Not issued for circulation.

AMERICAN INNOVATION (2018–2032)

In 2018, the U.S. Mint inaugurated a new, 15-year coin series: the American Innovation $1 Coin Program. Each of the golden dollars in the program features a reverse design that "symbolizes quintessentially American traits—the willingness to explore, to discover, and to create one's own destiny." Four new designs, in Uncirculated and Proof finishes, are issued each year from 2019 through 2032—one for each state, in the order in which the states ratified the Constitution or were admitted to the Union, and then for the District of Columbia and each of the five U.S. territories (Puerto Rico, Guam, American Samoa, the U.S. Virgin Islands, and the Northern Mariana Islands). Like all dollar coins minted after 2011, they are issued for numismatic sales only; none are distributed for circulation.

Obverse   American Innovators (2018)

Privy Marks

2019   2020   2021

2022   2023   2024

Delaware: Classifying the Stars (2019)

Pennsylvania: Polio Vaccine (2019)

New Jersey: Light Bulb (2019)

Georgia: Trustees' Garden (2019)

Connecticut: Gerber Variable Scale (2020)

Massachusetts: Telephone (2020)

Maryland: The Hubble Space Telescope (2020)

South Carolina: Septima Clark (2020)

New Hampshire: Ralph Baer (2021)

Virginia: Chesapeake Bay Bridge-Tunnel (2021)

New York: Erie Canal (2021)

North Carolina: Higher Learning (2021)

Entry continued on next page.

| Rhode Island: Nautical Innovation (2022) | Vermont: Snowboarding (2022) | Kentucky: Bluegrass Music (2022) | Tennessee: Tennessee Valley Authority (2022) |

| Ohio: Underground Railroad (2023) | Louisiana: Higgins Boat (2023) | Indiana: Automobile Industry (2023) | Mississippi: First Human Lung Transplant (2023) |

| Illinois: Steel Plow (2024) | Alabama: *Saturn V* Rocket (2024) | Maine: Direct Current Defibrillator (2024) | Missouri: George Washington Carver (2024) |

	Mintage	MS-65	PF-65
2018P, Innovators (a)	856,475	$1.50	
2018D, Innovators (a)	929,450	1.50	
2018S, Innovators	(252,862)		$3
2018S, Innovators, RevPf	(74,720)		5
2019P, Delaware (a)	541,575	1.50	
2019D, Delaware (a)	540,625	1.50	
2019S, Delaware	(147,454)		3
2019S, Delaware, RevPf	(70,346)		5
2019P, Pennsylvania (a)	610,425	1.50	
2019D, Pennsylvania (a)	507,675	1.50	
2019S, Pennsylvania	(147,454)		3
2019S, Pennsylvania, RevPf	(54,819)		5
2019P, New Jersey (a)	610,150	1.50	
2019D, New Jersey (a)	548,775	1.50	
2019S, New Jersey	(147,454)		3
2019S, New Jersey, RevPf	(50,333)		5
2019P, Georgia (a)	538,325	1.50	
2019D, Georgia (a)	512,675	1.50	
2019S, Georgia	(147,454)		3

	Mintage	MS-65	PF-65
2019S, Georgia, RevPf	(46,915)		$5
2020P, Connecticut (a)	436,000	$1.50	
2020D, Connecticut (a)	435,325	1.50	
2020S, Connecticut	(107,052)		3
2020S, Connecticut, RevPf	(46,556)		5
2020P, Massachusetts (a)	436,750	1.50	
2020D, Massachusetts (a)	436,425	1.50	
2020S, Massachusetts	(107,052)		3
2020S, Massachusetts, RevPf	(48,529)		5
2020P, Maryland (a)	434,825	1.50	
2020D, Maryland (a)	435,475	1.50	
2020S, Maryland	(107,052)		3
2020S, Maryland, RevPf	(49,731)		5
2020P, South Carolina (a)	432,850	1.50	
2020D, South Carolina (a)	397,775	1.50	
2020S, South Carolina	(107,052)		3
2020S, South Carolina, RevPf	(41,083)		5
2021P, New Hampshire (a)	454,325	1.50	
2021D, New Hampshire (a)	454,450	1.50	

a. Not issued for circulation.

	Mintage	MS-65	PF-65
2021S, New Hampshire	(84,604)		$3
2021S, New Hampshire, RevPf	(49,541)		5
2021P, Virginia (a)	454,975	$1.50	
2021D, Virginia (a)	453,850	1.50	
2021S, Virginia	(84,604)		3
2021S, Virginia, RevPf	(49,541)		5
2021P, New York (a)	453,750	1.50	
2021D, New York (a)	453,825	1.50	
2021S, New York	(84,604)		3
2021S, New York, RevPf	(49,541)		5
2021P, North Carolina (a)	454,150	1.50	
2021D, North Carolina (a)	454,450	1.50	
2021S, North Carolina	(84,604)		3
2021S, North Carolina, RevPf	(49,541)		5
2022P, Rhode Island (a)	454,150	1.50	
2022D, Rhode Island (a)	453,775	1.50	
2022S, Rhode Island	(77,766)		3
2022S, Rhode Island, RevPf	(49,478)		5
2022P, Vermont (a)	454,275	1.50	
2022D, Vermont (a)	452,875	1.50	
2022S, Vermont	(77,766)		3
2022S, Vermont, RevPf	(49,478)		5
2022P, Kentucky (a)	451,900	1.50	
2022D, Kentucky (a)	452,625	1.50	
2022S, Kentucky	(77,766)		3
2022S, Kentucky, RevPf	(49,478)		5
2022P, Tennessee (a)	452,325	1.50	
2022D, Tennessee (a)	452,275	1.50	
2022S, Tennessee	(77,766)		3
2022S, Tennessee, RevPf	(49,478)		5
2023P, Ohio (a)		1.50	

	Mintage	MS-65	PF-65
2023D, Ohio (a)		$1.50	
2023S, Ohio			$3
2023S, Ohio, RevPf			5
2023P, Louisiana (a)		1.50	
2023D, Louisiana (a)		1.50	
2023S, Louisiana			3
2023S, Louisiana, RevPf			5
2023P, Indiana (a)		1.50	
2023D, Indiana (a)		1.50	
2023S, Indiana			3
2023S, Indiana, RevPf			5
2023P, Mississippi (a)		1.50	
2023D, Mississippi (a)		1.50	
2023S, Mississippi			3
2023S, Mississippi, RevPf			5
2024P, Illinois (a)		1.50	
2024D, Illinois (a)		1.50	
2024S, Illinois			3
2024S, Illinois, RevPf			5
2024P, Alabama (a)		1.50	
2024D, Alabama (a)		1.50	
2024S, Alabama			3
2024S, Alabama, RevPf			5
2024P, Maine (a)		1.50	
2024D, Maine (a)		1.50	
2024S, Maine			3
2024S, Maine, RevPf			5
2024P, Missouri (a)		1.50	
2024D, Missouri (a)		1.50	
2024S, Missouri			3
2024S, Missouri, RevPf			5

a. Not issued for circulation.

1921 SILVER DOLLAR ANNIVERSARY COINS (2021 TO DATE)

Congress passed the 1921 Silver Dollar Coin Anniversary Act "to mint and issue $1 coins in recognition of the 100th anniversary of completion of coinage of the Morgan dollar and the 100th anniversary of commencement of coinage of the Peace dollar." The resulting products, first minted in 2021, are not precise copies of the older coins, but, in the words of the legislation, "honor" the originals with "renditions" of the designs used on the original Morgan and Peace silver dollars.

The Mint's artists use modern technology and historical Mint assets to create the modern designs.

Some of the first-year-of-issue Morgan anniversary coins were minted in Philadelphia with "CC" and "O" privy marks to represent the historical mintages of Carson City and New Orleans.

In November 2021 the Mint announced plans to produce the coins as recurring products, in various finishes and using multiple Mint facilities. Because of a shortage of silver planchets, none were issued in 2022.

"CC" privy mark

"O" privy mark

	Mintage	Uncertified	MS-69	MS-70	PF-69DC	PF-70DC
2021(P), Morgan, No Privy Mark	174,498	$120	$135	$225		
2021(P), Morgan, CC Privy Mark	173,781	190	210	300		
2021(P), Morgan, O Privy Mark	173,530	120	135	225		
2021D, Morgan	174,661	120	135	600		
2021S, Morgan	174,850	125	140	230		
2021(P), Peace	199,543	145	160	250		
2023(P), Morgan		70	75	80		
2023S, Morgan		70			$75	$90
2023(P), Peace		70	75	80		
2023S, Peace		70			75	90
Two-Coin Set. 2023-S Morgan and						
Peace Reverse Proof silver dollars.		180			210	240

The Coinage Act of 1792 established the independent monetary system of the United States, with the dollar as its basic monetary unit. Silver dollar coins were made starting in 1794. Coinage of a gold dollar coin, however, was not authorized until the Act of March 3, 1849. Its weight was set at 25.8 grains, fineness .900.

The first type, struck until 1854, is known as the Liberty Head. In 1854 the gold dollar was made larger in diameter and thinner, while keeping the same weight. Along with that modification, the design was changed to a female wearing a feather headdress, generally referred to as the Indian Princess Head type. In 1856 this was changed slightly by enlarging the size of the head.

LIBERTY HEAD (1849–1854)

VF-20 Very Fine: LIBERTY on headband complete and legible. Knobs on coronet defined.
EF-40 Extremely Fine: Slight wear on Liberty's hair. Knobs on coronet sharp.
AU-50 About Uncirculated: Trace of wear on headband. Nearly full luster.
AU-55 Choice About Uncirculated: Evidence of friction on design high points.
MS-60 Uncirculated: No trace of wear. Light marks and blemishes.
MS-63 Choice Uncirculated: Some distracting contact marks or blemishes in prime focal areas. Impaired luster possible.

	Mintage	VF-20	EF-40	AU-50	AU-55	MS-60	MS-63
1849, Open Wreath, No L on Truncation	688,567	$240	$275	$285	$325	$700	$1,200
1849, Close Wreath	*	240	275	285	300	425	750
1849C, Open Wreath	11,634	165,000	200,000	265,000	300,000		
1849C, Close Wreath	*	1,450	2,000	3,000	3,250	7,500	15,000
1849D	21,588	1,450	1,950	2,500	2,950	4,250	15,000
1849O	215,000	250	285	300	425	850	2,250
1850	481,953	240	265	285	300	325	460
1850C	6,966	1,450	2,000	3,200	3,500	5,000	22,500
1850D	8,382	1,600	2,250	3,250	4,000	8,000	30,000
1850O	14,000	255	800	1,000	1,100	2,500	5,500
1851	3,317,671	240	265	285	300	325	460
1851C	41,267	1,200	1,400	1,650	1,950	2,750	4,500
1851D	9,882	1,600	2,000	2,650	3,000	4,500	15,000
1851O	290,000	245	265	300	325	600	1,350
1852	2,045,351	240	265	285	300	325	460
1852C	9,434	1,350	1,500	2,000	2,450	4,000	10,000
1852D	6,360	1,500	1,950	2,750	3,250	6,750	27,500
1852O	140,000	245	265	350	550	950	3,000
1853	4,076,051	240	265	285	300	325	475
1853C	11,515	1,400	1,650	2,250	2,750	4,250	13,500
1853D	6,583	1,600	1,950	3,000	3,500	6,500	17,500
1853O	290,000	245	265	300	325	475	1,250
1854	855,502	240	265	285	300	325	475
1854D	2,935	2,500	4,000	5,500	6,500	8,500	32,500
1854S	14,632	375	650	1,100	1,350	2,850	6,000

* Included in number above.

INDIAN PRINCESS HEAD, SMALL HEAD (1854–1856)

VF-20 Very Fine: Feather-curl tips on headdress outlined but details worn.

EF-40 Extremely Fine: Slight wear on tips of feather curls on headdress.

AU-50 About Uncirculated: Trace of wear on feathers, nearly full luster.

AU-55 Choice About Uncirculated: Evidence of friction on design high points. Most of original mint luster present.

MS-60 Uncirculated: No trace of wear. Light marks and blemishes.

MS-63 Choice Uncirculated: Some distracting contact marks or blemishes in prime focal areas. Impaired luster possible.

PF-63 Choice Proof: Reflective surfaces with only a few blemishes in secondary focal areas. No major flaws.

	Mintage	VF-20	EF-40	AU-50	AU-55	MS-60	MS-63	PF-63
1854	783,943	$350	$450	$500	$575	$1,150	$3,500	$135,000
1855	758,269	350	450	500	575	1,150	3,500	115,000
1855C	9,803	2,750	4,500	4,750	6,500	17,500		
1855D	1,811	17,500	20,000	25,000	32,500	50,000	80,000	
1855O	55,000	600	1,000	1,500	2,000	6,000	22,000	
1856S	24,600	650	1,250	1,850	2,500	6,000	17,500	

INDIAN PRINCESS HEAD, LARGE HEAD (1856–1889)

VF-20 Very Fine: Slight detail in curled feathers in headdress. Details worn smooth at eyebrow, hair below headdress, and behind ear and bottom curl.

EF-40 Extremely Fine: Slight wear above and to right of eye and on top of curled feathers.

AU-50 About Uncirculated: Trace of wear on feathers, nearly full luster.

AU-55 Choice About Uncirculated: Evidence of friction on design high points. Most of original mint luster present.

MS-60 Uncirculated: No trace of wear. Light marks and blemishes.

MS-63 Choice Uncirculated: Some distracting contact marks or blemishes in prime focal areas. Impaired luster possible.

PF-63 Choice Proof: Reflective surfaces with only a few blemishes in secondary focal places. No major flaws.

	Mintage	VF-20	EF-40	AU-50	AU-55	MS-60	MS-63	PF-63
1856	1,762,936	$275	$295	$305	$315	$350	$600	$25,000
1856D	1,460	4,500	6,500	8,000	9,500	25,000	57,500	
1857	774,789	275	295	305	315	325	600	10,000
1857C	13,280	1,450	1,750	3,000	3,500	7,000		
1857D	3,533	1,750	2,750	3,250	4,750	15,000	65,000	
1857S	10,000	450	800	1,100	1,250	4,000	16,500	
1858	117,995	275	295	305	315	325	800	9,500
1858D	3,477	1,450	2,650	3,800	4,250	7,500	18,500	

1873, Close 3

1873, Open 3

	Mintage	VF-20	EF-40	AU-50	AU-55	MS-60	MS-63	PF-63
1858S 10,000		$300	$650	$950	$1,350	$4,250	$12,500	
1859 . . . . (80) 168,244		275	295	305	315	325	650	$8,500
1859C 5,235		1,850	2,750	3,500	4,000	6,000	27,500	
1859D 4,952		1,550	2,000	3,000	3,500	6,750	17,500	
1859S 15,000		275	500	1,000	1,350	4,000	15,000	
1860 . . . . (154) . . .36,514		275	295	305	325	450	850	8,000
1860D 1,566		3,500	5,500	8,000	9,500	20,000	45,000	
1860S 13,000		325	400	650	850	2,000	4,500	
1861 . . . . (349) . . .527,150		275	295	305	325	385	600	7,500
1861D *1,250*		35,000	47,500	60,000	65,000	85,000	150,000	
1862 . . . . (35) . . 1,361,355		275	295	305	325	350	650	7,500
1863 . . . . (50) 6,200		1,200	1,750	3,000	3,500	6,000	9,500	10,000
1864 . . . . (50) 5,900		600	1,000	1,250	1,350	2,500	5,500	10,000
1865 . . . . (25) 3,700		450	1,000	1,350	1,500	2,750	4,500	10,000
1866 . . . . (30) 7,100		350	500	650	850	1,150	2,000	10,000
1867 . . . . (50) 5,200		350	500	750	850	1,100	2,000	10,000
1868 . . . . (25) 10,500		325	500	575	625	850	2,000	10,000
1869 . . . . (25) 5,900		325	500	575	625	1,000	1,750	10,000
1870 . . . . (35) 6,300		325	500	575	675	750	1,450	10,000
1870S 3,000		650	1,000	1,450	1,550	3,250	7,000	
1871 . . . . (30) 3,900		275	375	425	525	700	1,350	9,500
1872 . . . . (30) 3,500		275	375	425	475	875	2,000	9,500
1873, Close 3 . . . (25) 1,800		350	550	675	775	1,250	2,850	11,500
1873, Open 3 123,300		275	295	305	315	325	600	
1874 . . . . (20) 198,800		275	295	305	315	325	600	10,000
1875 . . . . (20) 400		3,000	4,500	5,750	6,250	10,000	15,500	25,000
1876 . . . . (45) 3,200		300	350	550	600	850	1,250	7,500
1877 . . . . (20) 3,900		300	350	500	525	750	1,350	6,500
1878 . . . . (20) 3,000		300	350	500	525	675	1,100	6,500
1879 . . . . (30) 3,000		275	325	375	425	650	1,100	6,500
1880 . . . . (36) 1,600		275	350	375	425	475	1,100	5,500
1881 . . . . (87) 7,620		275	325	375	425	475	700	5,000
1882 . . . . (125) 5,000		275	325	350	375	525	750	5,000
1883 . . . . (207) . . .10,800		275	325	350	375	475	650	4,500
1884 . . . . (1,006) 5,230		275	300	325	345	475	650	4,500
1885 . . . . (1,105) . . .11,156		275	300	325	345	450	650	4,000
1886 . . . . (1,016) 5,000		275	300	325	345	450	650	4,000
1887 . . . . (1,043) 7,500		275	300	325	345	450	650	4,000
1888 . . . . (1,079) . . .15,501		275	300	325	345	450	650	4,000
1889 . . . . (1,779) . . .28,950		275	300	305	325	450	650	4,000

Although authorized by the Act of April 2, 1792, coinage of quarter eagles ($2.50 gold coins) was not begun until 1796.

CAPPED BUST TO RIGHT (1796–1807)

F-12 Fine: Hair worn smooth on high spots. E PLURIBUS UNUM on ribbon weak but legible.
VF-20 Very Fine: Some wear on high spots.
EF-40 Extremely Fine: Only slight wear on Liberty's hair and cheek.
AU-50 About Uncirculated: Trace of wear on cap, hair, cheek, and drapery.
AU-55 Choice About Uncirculated: Evidence of friction on design high points. Some original mint luster.
MS-60 Uncirculated: No trace of wear. Light blemishes.

No Stars on Obverse (1796)

Stars on Obverse (1796–1807)

	Mintage	F-12	VF-20	EF-40	AU-50	AU-55	MS-60
1796, No Stars on Obverse 963		$50,000	$75,000	$105,000	$125,000	$185,000	$300,000
1796, Stars on Obverse 432		47,500	60,000	75,000	100,000	125,000	155,000
1797 427		20,000	27,500	40,000	85,000	110,000	200,000
1798 1,094		5,500	7,500	13,500	22,500	30,000	85,000
1802, 2 Over 1 3,035		5,000	7,000	10,500	12,500	16,500	27,500
1804, 13-Star Reverse . . . . *		45,000	70,000	125,000	175,000	325,000	
1804, 14-Star Reverse 3,327		6,000	7,250	11,500	15,000	20,000	30,000
1805 1,781		5,000	6,500	10,000	13,000	16,000	30,000
1806, 6/4, 8 Stars Left, 5 Right 1,136		5,500	6,500	11,500	15,000	25,000	42,500
1806, 6/5, 7 Stars Left, 6 Right 480		5,500	7,000	12,500	25,000	35,000	75,000
1807 6,812		5,000	6,500	10,000	12,500	16,000	27,500

* Included in number below.

DRAPED BUST TO LEFT, LARGE SIZE (1808)

F-12 Fine: E PLURIBUS UNUM on reverse, and LIBERTY on headband, legible but weak.
VF-20 Very Fine: Motto and LIBERTY clear.
EF-40 Extremely Fine: All details of hair plain.
AU-50 About Uncirculated: Trace of wear above eye, on top of cap, and on cheek and hair.
AU-55 Choice About Uncirculated: Evidence of friction on design high points. Some original mint luster present.
MS-60 Uncirculated: No trace of wear. Light blemishes.

	Mintage	F-12	VF-20	EF-40	AU-50	AU-55	MS-60
1808 2,710		$42,500	$55,000	$100,000	$125,000	$150,000	$225,000

CAPPED HEAD TO LEFT (1821–1834)

Those dated 1829 to 1834 are smaller in diameter than the 1821 to 1827 pieces.

Large Diameter   Reduced Diameter

	Mintage	F-12	VF-20	EF-40	AU-50	AU-55	MS-60
1821	6,448	$6,000	$7,500	$10,500	$12,500	$15,000	$26,500
1824, 4 Over 1	2,600	6,000	7,000	10,000	12,500	15,000	27,500
1825	4,434	6,000	7,000	10,000	12,500	16,500	28,500
1826, 6 Over 6	760	10,000	15,000	22,500	30,000	40,000	75,000
1827	2,800	6,000	7,000	10,000	11,500	17,000	25,000
1829	3,403	5,000	6,000	8,500	11,500	13,500	20,000
1830	4,540	5,000	6,000	8,500	11,500	13,500	20,000
1831	4,520	5,000	6,000	8,500	11,500	13,500	20,000
1832	4,400	5,000	6,000	8,500	11,500	13,500	20,000
1833	4,160	5,000	6,000	8,500	11,500	13,500	20,000
1834, With Motto	4,000	25,000	32,500	55,000	100,000	135,000	165,000

CLASSIC HEAD, NO MOTTO ON REVERSE (1834–1839)

In 1834, the quarter eagle was redesigned. A ribbon binding the hair, bearing the word LIBERTY, replaced the Liberty cap. The motto was omitted from the reverse.

F-12 Fine: LIBERTY on headband legible and complete. Curl under ear outlined but no detail.
VF-20 Very Fine: LIBERTY plain; detail in hair curl.
EF-40 Extremely Fine: Small amount of wear on top of hair and below L in LIBERTY. Wear evident on wing.
AU-50 About Uncirculated: Trace of wear on coronet and hair above ear.
AU-55 Choice About Uncirculated: Evidence of friction on design high points. Some of original mint luster present.
MS-60 Uncirculated: No trace of wear. Light blemishes.
MS-63 Choice Uncirculated: Some distracting contact marks or blemishes in prime focal areas. Impaired luster possible.

Mintmark location.

	Mintage	F-12	VF-20	EF-40	AU-50	AU-55	MS-60	MS-63
1834, No Motto	112,234	$475	$550	$750	$1,000	$1,500	$2,750	$6,000
1835	131,402	475	550	750	1,000	1,500	2,850	9,000
1836	547,986	475	550	750	1,000	1,550	2,850	6,500
1837	45,080	500	650	850	1,100	1,850	4,000	10,000
1838	47,030	500	650	800	1,250	1,650	2,650	7,500
1838C	7,880	3,750	4,750	7,000	9,500	12,000	25,000	55,000
1839	27,021	600	950	1,750	3,000	4,000	8,500	40,000
1839C	18,140	3,000	4,250	6,000	7,500	10,000	20,000	60,000
1839D	13,674	3,000	4,250	6,500	8,500	11,000	25,000	70,000
1839O	17,781	1,100	1,650	3,000	4,000	6,500	11,000	35,000

LIBERTY HEAD (1840–1907)

Mintmark location.

4 Plain 4

4 Crosslet 4

	Mintage	VF-20	EF-40	AU-50	AU-55	MS-60	MS-63
1840	18,859	$700	$800	$1,500	$2,750	$5,750	$12,000
1840C	12,822	1,450	2,750	2,950	4,000	8,000	22,500
1840D	3,532	4,500	8,500	13,500	22,500	60,000	
1840O	33,580	600	1,500	2,000	3,000	7,500	22,500

Chart continued on next page.　　　　　　　　　　　　　　　　　　　　　　　　**167**

	Mintage	VF-20	EF-40	AU-50	AU-55	MS-60	MS-63
1841 . . . . (unknown)		$50,000	$85,000	$110,000	$130,000		
1841C 10,281		2,000	2,750	3,750	4,500	$17,500	$50,000
1841D 4,164		3,500	6,000	7,500	10,000	32,500	70,000
1842 2,823		1,850	4,000	5,500	9,000	15,500	40,000
1842C 6,729		1,700	3,000	6,000	8,000	17,500	47,500
1842D 4,643		2,500	4,250	7,000	8,250	30,000	
1842O 19,800		600	950	1,650	3,250	7,000	18,500
1843 100,546		450	500	600	850	1,800	7,500
1843C, Large Date. 23,076		1,500	2,250	2,750	3,000	6,000	17,000
1843C, Small Date. 2,988		3,000	4,500	6,000	7,750	20,000	
1843D 36,209		1,600	2,250	3,000	3,500	5,500	30,000
1843O 364,002		500	550	600	675	1,500	6,500
1844 6,784		650	950	2,000	3,000	7,500	22,500
1844C 11,622		1,500	2,500	3,750	4,500	12,000	35,000
1844D 17,332		1,500	1,950	3,000	4,000	7,000	20,000
1845 91,051		450	500	525	575	1,250	4,000
1845D 19,460		1,600	2,150	2,750	3,500	7,500	35,000
1845O 4,000		2,750	5,500	7,500	12,000	25,000	80,000
1846 21,598		550	625	750	1,000	3,500	17,500
1846C 4,808		1,600	2,750	4,500	7,500	17,500	35,000
1846D 19,303		1,750	2,250	2,750	4,000	8,500	26,500
1846O 62,000		550	650	1,000	1,500	5,000	15,000
1847 29,814		450	550	750	800	2,500	10,000
1847C 23,226		1,500	1,850	2,500	3,000	4,500	12,000
1847D 15,784		1,600	1,850	2,500	3,750	7,000	20,000
1847O 124,000		550	600	1,000	1,350	4,500	15,000
1848 6,500		750	1,200	2,250	3,500	5,000	12,500

CAL. Gold Quarter Eagle (1848)

In 1848, about 230 ounces of gold were sent to Secretary of War William L. Marcy by Colonel R.B. Mason, military governor of California. The gold was turned over to the Mint and made into quarter eagles. The distinguishing mark CAL. was punched above the eagle on the reverse side while the coins were in the die.

CAL. Above Eagle on Reverse (1848)

	Mintage	VF-20	EF-40	AU-50	AU-55	MS-60	MS-63
1848, CAL. Above Eagle. 1,389		$35,000	$50,000	$60,000	$65,000	$80,000	$150,000
1848C 16,788		2,000	2,650	3,000	4,000	9,500	35,000
1848D 13,771		1,550	2,150	3,000	3,500	7,000	23,500
1849 23,294		550	700	850	1,000	2,350	6,000
1849C 10,220		1,500	2,400	4,250	5,000	11,000	30,000
1849D 10,945		1,750	2,500	2,750	4,000	12,000	
1850 252,923		450	500	525	550	700	3,500
1850C 9,148		1,450	2,500	3,250	4,500	10,000	32,500
1850D 12,148		1,600	2,500	3,500	4,250	10,000	32,000

QUARTER EAGLES ($2.50)

	Mintage	VF-20	EF-40	AU-50	AU-55	MS-60	MS-63	PF-63
1850O 84,000		$500	$600	$800	$1,000	$3,500	$18,500	
1851 1,372,748		400	450	475	525	575	850	
1851C 14,923		1,500	2,150	3,000	3,500	7,000	30,000	
1851D 11,264		1,600	2,500	3,500	5,000	15,000	27,500	
1851O 148,000		425	600	750	1,000	3,000	10,000	
1852 1,159,681		400	450	475	550	600	850	
1852C 9,772		1,250	2,000	3,000	4,250	7,500	27,500	
1852D 4,078		1,500	2,750	5,500	6,500	15,000	40,000	
1852O 140,000		500	550	700	900	3,750	9,000	
1853 1,404,668		400	425	450	525	575	800	
1853D 3,178		1,900	3,000	5,000	6,000	12,000	47,500	
1854 596,258		400	450	475	485	550	1,000	
1854C 7,295		1,750	2,500	3,500	4,500	9,000	60,000	
1854D 1,760		3,000	6,000	8,500	14,500	25,000	65,000	
1854O 153,000		500	550	600	750	1,250	8,000	
1854S 246		300,000	400,000	450,000				
1855 235,480		400	450	500	525	575	1,500	
1855C 3,677		2,000	3,000	4,500	5,500	16,500	40,000	
1855D 1,123		3,750	7,500	15,000	19,500	45,000	75,000	
1856 384,240		400	450	500	525	575	1,000	$65,000
1856C 7,913		1,600	2,500	3,500	5,000	10,000	25,000	
1856D 874		20,000	30,000	50,000	67,500	100,000		
1856O 21,100		550	800	1,350	2,250	7,000		
1856S 72,120		450	500	700	1,000	3,500	10,000	
1857 214,130		400	450	475	485	550	1,100	55,000
1857D 2,364		1,500	2,250	4,000	6,500	10,000	25,000	
1857O 34,000		500	550	850	1,200	4,000	12,000	
1857S 69,200		400	450	800	1,300	3,500	10,000	
1858 47,377		400	450	475	485	900	3,000	35,000
1858C 9,056		1,500	2,250	3,000	3,500	6,250	20,000	
1859 . . . . (80) 39,364		400	450	600	650	1,000	4,000	25,000
1859D 2,244		2,250	3,500	5,000	7,000	17,500		
1859S 15,200		400	850	1,500	2,150	4,250	15,000	
1860 . . . . (112) 22,563		400	450	500	750	1,100	3,000	17,500
1860C 7,469		1,550	2,500	3,000	5,500	12,500	27,500	
1860S 35,600		375	525	1,100	1,450	3,250	13,500	
1861 . . . . (90) . . . 1,283,788		400	450	500	575	650	1,150	17,500
1861S 24,000		700	950	3,250	4,500	15,000		
1862, 2 Over 1 . . . . *		700	1,500	2,750	3,750	8,000	22,500	
1862 . . . . (35) 98,508		400	475	1,250	1,750	3,500	8,000	17,500
1862S 8,000		2,000	4,000	4,750	5,500	15,000	35,000	
1863, Proof only (30)								65,000
1863S 10,800		1,500	2,750	4,000	5,500	12,500	25,000	
1864 . . . . (50) 2,774		17,500	32,500	55,000	67,500	125,000		17,500
1865 . . . . (25) 1,520		4,000	8,000	15,000	27,500	65,000		17,500
1865S 23,376		600	1,250	1,750	2,250	4,000	16,500	
1866 . . . . (30) 3,080		850	2,750	4,500	6,500	11,500	25,000	17,500
1866S 38,960		375	500	900	1,500	6,500	20,000	
1867 . . . . (50) 3,200		500	850	1,250	2,000	5,500	15,000	17,500
1867S 28,000		375	500	1,000	1,250	3,500	12,000	
1868 . . . . (25) 3,600		375	425	650	675	2,000	10,000	17,500

* Included in number below.

Chart continued on next page.

	Mintage	VF-20	EF-40	AU-50	AU-55	MS-60	MS-63	PF-63
1868S 34,000		$375	$425	$750	$1,000	$2,500	$6,500	
1869 . . . . (25). 4,320		375	425	650	900	2,500	8,500	$17,500
1869S 29,500		375	450	550	775	2,250	8,500	
1870 . . . . (35). 4,520		375	425	700	1,150	3,250	9,500	17,500
1870S 16,000		375	425	625	1,100	3,250	12,500	
1871 . . . . (30). 5,320		375	450	600	750	1,500	4,000	17,500
1871S 22,000		375	425	450	650	1,500	3,750	
1872 . . . . (30). 3,000		425	700	1,500	2,250	3,750	15,000	17,500
1872S 18,000		375	425	625	900	3,500	8,500	
1873 . . . . (25). 178,000		375	385	400	405	465	600	17,500
1873S 27,000		375	425	500	750	1,350	5,000	
1874 . . . . (20). 3,920		375	425	550	700	1,650	4,500	25,000
1875 . . . . (20). 400		6,500	11,000	15,000	17,500	30,000	125,000	30,000
1875S 11,600		375	425	500	1,000	2,750	5,000	
1876 . . . . (45). 4,176		500	600	800	1,100	2,750	7,500	12,000
1876S 5,000		375	425	750	1,100	2,000	7,500	
1877 . . . . (20). 1,632		425	800	1,250	1,500	2,500	10,000	12,000
1877S 35,400		350	385	400	405	500	1,750	
1878 . . . . (20). 286,240		350	385	400	405	425	550	12,000
1878S 178,000		350	385	400	405	425	850	
1879 . . . . (30). 88,960		350	385	400	405	425	550	12,000
1879S 43,500		350	385	400	405	1,250	4,000	
1880 . . . . (36). 2,960		350	425	550	1,000	1,500	3,000	9,500
1881 . . . . (51). 640		2,000	3,000	5,000	5,500	10,000	25,000	8,500
1882 . . . . (67). 4,000		400	450	475	550	1,000	2,250	6,000
1883 . . . . (82). 1,920		650	1,150	2,500	4,250	6,500	10,000	6,000
1884 . . . . (73). 1,950		400	475	500	750	1,500	2,750	6,000
1885 . . . . (87). 800		800	2,000	3,250	4,000	5,500	10,000	6,000
1886 . . . . (88). 4,000		375	450	500	650	1,000	3,000	6,000
1887 . . . . (122). 6,160		375	385	500	550	700	1,100	5,500
1888 . . . . (97). 16,001		375	385	400	405	425	750	5,500
1889 . . . . (48). 17,600		375	385	400	405	425	650	5,500
1890 . . . . (93). 8,720		375	385	400	405	425	1,350	5,500
1891 . . . . (80). 10,960		375	385	400	405	425	1,000	5,500
1892 . . . . (105). 2,440		375	385	400	450	700	1,850	5,500
1893 . . . . (106). 30,000		375	385	400	405	425	525	5,500
1894 . . . . (122). 4,000		400	425	500	550	600	1,750	5,500
1895 . . . . (119). 6,000		350	385	400	405	425	1,000	5,500
1896 . . . . (132). 19,070		350	385	400	405	425	525	5,500
1897 . . . . (136). 29,768		350	385	400	405	425	500	5,500
1898 . . . . (165). 24,000		350	385	400	405	425	500	5,500
1899 . . . . (150). 27,200		350	385	400	405	425	450	5,500
1900 . . . . (205). 67,000		350	385	400	405	425	450	5,000
1901 . . . . (223). 91,100		350	385	400	405	425	450	5,000
1902 . . . . (193). 133,540		350	385	400	405	425	450	5,000
1903 . . . . (197). 201,060		350	385	400	405	425	450	5,000
1904 . . . . (170). 160,790		350	385	400	405	425	450	5,000
1905 . . . . (144). 217,800		350	385	400	405	425	450	5,000
1906 . . . . (160). 176,330		350	385	400	405	425	450	5,000
1907 . . . . (154). 336,294		350	385	400	405	425	450	5,000

INDIAN HEAD (1908–1929)

American sculptor Bela Lyon Pratt, a former student of Augustus Saint-Gaudens, designed this coin and the similar five-dollar gold piece. It features no raised rim, and the main devices and legends are in sunken relief below the surface of the coin. President Theodore Roosevelt, who sought to improve the overall aesthetic quality of American coinage, was enthusiastic about the innovative new design. Collectors and the public were not as pleased. Some feared that the recessed design would collect dirt and germs—an unfounded concern. Over time the design has been recognized as a classic, and part of the early 20th-century renaissance of American coinage.

VF-20 Very Fine: Hair-cord knot distinct. Feathers at top of head clear. Cheekbone worn.

EF-40 Extremely Fine: Cheekbone, war bonnet, and headband feathers slightly worn.

AU-50 About Uncirculated: Trace of wear on cheekbone and headdress.

MS-60 Uncirculated: No trace of wear. Light blemishes.

MS-63 Choice Uncirculated: Some distracting contact marks or blemishes in prime focal areas. Impaired luster possible.

MS-64 Uncirculated: A few scattered contact marks visible. Good eye appeal and attractive luster.

Matte PF-63 Choice Proof: Few blemishes in secondary focal areas. No major flaws. Matte surfaces.

Mintmark location is on reverse, to left of arrows.

	Mintage	VF-20	EF-40	AU-50	MS-60	MS-63	MS-64	MATTE PF-63
1908 . . . .(236). 564,821		$325	$350	$375	$400	$1,000	$1,650	$10,000
1909 . . . .(139). 441,760		325	350	375	400	1,500	2,500	10,000
1910 . . . .(682). 492,000		325	350	375	400	1,100	1,650	10,000
1911 . . . .(191). 704,000		325	350	375	400	950	1,600	10,000
1911D 55,680		1,750	2,750	3,250	5,500	10,000	16,500	
1912 . . . .(197). 616,000		325	350	375	400	1,500	3,000	10,000
1913 . . . .(165). 722,000		325	350	375	400	1,000	1,500	10,000
1914 . . . .(117). 240,000		325	350	375	500	2,250	3,500	10,000
1914D 448,000		325	350	375	400	1,500	2,750	
1915 . . . .(100). 606,000		325	350	375	400	950	1,500	10,000
1925D 578,000		325	350	375	400	475	550	
1926 446,000		325	350	375	400	475	550	
1927 388,000		325	350	375	400	475	550	
1928 416,000		325	350	375	400	475	550	
1929 532,000		325	350	375	400	475	550	

The three-dollar gold piece was authorized by the Act of February 21, 1853. Coinage was struck beginning in 1854. It was never popular and saw very little circulation.

VF-20 Very Fine: Eyebrow, hair about forehead and ear, and bottom curl all worn smooth. Faint details visible on curled feather-ends of headdress.

EF-40 Extremely Fine: Light wear above and to right of eye, and on top of curled feathers.

AU-50 About Uncirculated: Trace of wear on top of curled feathers and in hair above and to right of eye.

AU-55 Choice About Uncirculated: Evidence of friction on design high points. Much of original mint luster present.

MS-60 Uncirculated: No trace of wear. Light blemishes.

MS-63 Choice Uncirculated: Some distracting contact marks or blemishes in prime focal areas. Impaired luster possible.

PF-63 Choice Proof: Reflective surfaces with only a few blemishes in secondary focal places. No major flaws.

Mintmark location is on reverse, below wreath.

	Mintage	VF-20	EF-40	AU-50	AU-55	MS-60	MS-63	PF-63
1854	138,618	$675	$900	$1,100	$1,250	$2,000	$4,500	$65,000
1854D	1,120	20,000	36,500	47,500	5,500	115,000		
1854O	24,000	1,500	2,500	3,500	4,250	40,000	85,000	
1855	50,555	750	1,000	1,100	1,500	2,000	4,750	45,000
1855S	6,600	1,100	2,500	4,250	8,000	35,000	85,000	
1856	26,010	750	1,000	1,200	1,350	2,500	5,500	40,000
1856S	34,500	850	1,500	2,500	5,000	10,000	26,500	
1857	20,891	750	1,000	1,250	1,650	2,500	4,750	35,000
1857S	14,000	850	1,750	4,000	6,500	20,000	50,000	
1858	2,133	1,050	2,200	3,250	4,500	12,500	18,500	25,000
1859	(80)...15,558	800	1,000	1,500	1,650	2,500	6,500	17,500
1860	(119)....7,036	800	1,150	2,000	2,250	4,500	6,500	12,500
1860S	7,000	950	4,250	7,000	8,750	30,000	100,000	
1861	(113)....5,959	1,400	3,250	4,750	5,750	8,500	12,500	13,500
1862	(35)....5,750	1,400	3,250	4,750	5,750	8,500	13,500	13,500
1863	(39)....5,000	1,150	2,000	3,000	4,500	8,500	10,000	13,500
1864	(50)....2,630	1,250	3,000	4,250	5,000	8,500	12,000	13,500
1865	(25)....1,140	2,250	4,250	7,500	8,000	13,500	20,000	16,500
1866	(30)....4,000	950	1,100	1,650	2,150	4,500	7,500	13,500
1867	(50)....2,600	1,050	1,850	2,750	3,000	7,500	12,000	13,500
1868	(25)....4,850	950	1,200	1,450	2,000	5,000	7,000	13,500
1869	(25)....2,500	950	1,750	2,500	2,850	4,750	10,000	13,500
1870	(35)....3,500	1,000	1,250	1,850	2,000	5,000	10,000	13,500
1870S (unique)		—						
1871	(30)....1,300	1,000	1,750	2,250	2,450	6,500	10,000	15,000
1872	(30)....2,000	1,000	2,000	2,500	2,750	5,750	10,000	13,500
1873, Open 3 (Original)	(25)........		10,000	13,500				45,000
1873, Close 3		3,750	7,500	9,000	12,500	25,000	40,000	45,000
1874	(20)...41,800	725	900	1,000	1,200	2,000	4,500	24,000
1875, Proof only	(20)........			50,000	65,000			125,000
1876, Proof only	(45)........			20,000	25,000			55,000
1877	(20)....1,468	3,750	6,750	10,000	12,500	25,000	40,000	17,500
1878	(20)...82,304	700	900	1,200	1,250	2,000	4,250	17,500
1879	(30)....3,000	875	1,200	1,500	2,000	3,500	5,500	13,000
1880	(36)....1,000	1,150	1,750	3,000	3,500	5,500	7,500	13,000
1881	(54)......500	2,000	4,750	7,500	8,500	12,500	15,000	13,000
1882	(76)....1,500	1,150	2,000	2,500	2,850	5,000	7,500	11,000
1883	(89)......900	1,350	2,250	3,000	3,250	6,000	7,500	11,000
1884	(106)....1,000	1,350	2,250	3,250	3,500	7,500	9,500	11,000
1885	(110)......800	1,350	2,200	2,800	3,000	6,500	9,000	11,000
1886	(142)....1,000	1,150	2,100	2,750	3,000	5,000	10,000	11,000
1887	(160)....6,000	875	1,500	1,850	2,000	3,500	5,000	11,000
1888	(291)....5,000	875	1,500	1,800	1,950	3,500	4,500	11,000
1889	(129)....2,300	875	1,475	2,000	2,150	3,500	4,500	11,000

STELLA (1879–1880)

These pattern pieces were first suggested by the Hon. John A. Kasson, then U.S. envoy extraordinary and minister plenipotentiary to Austria-Hungary. It was through the efforts of Dr. W.W. Hubbell, who patented the alloy goloid (used in making another pattern piece, the goloid metric dollar) that we have these beautiful and interesting coins.

The four-dollar Stella—so called because of the five-pointed star on the reverse—was envisioned by Kasson as America's answer to various foreign gold coins popular in the international market. The British sovereign, Italy's 20 lire, and the 20 pesetas of Spain were three such coins: each smaller than a U.S. five-dollar gold piece, they were used widely in international trade.

The Stella was one of many proposals made to Congress for an international trade coin, and one of only several that made it to pattern coin form (others include the 1868 five dollar and 1874 Bickford ten dollar).

Odds were stacked against the Stella from the start. The denomination of four U.S. dollars didn't match any of the coin's European counterparts, and at any rate the U.S. double eagle (twenty-dollar coin)—already used in international commerce—was a more convenient medium of exchange. The Stella was never minted in quantities for circulation.

There are two distinct types in both years of issue. Charles E. Barber is thought to have designed the Flowing Hair type, and George T. Morgan the Coiled Hair. They were struck as patterns in gold, aluminum, copper, and white metal. Only those struck in gold are listed.

Flowing Hair   **Coiled Hair**

	Mintage	EF-40	AU-50	PF-60	PF-63	PF-65
1879, Flowing Hair	(425+)	$75,000	$85,000	$100,000	$140,000	$185,000
1879, Coiled Hair *(12 known)*				250,000	400,000	1,000,000
1880, Flowing Hair *(17 known)*	100,000	125,000	135,000	165,000	350,000
1880, Coiled Hair *(8 known)*				500,000	700,000	1,250,000

While the 1856 Flying Eagle cent, the 1879 and 1880 four-dollar Stellas, and a few other patterns are listed in this book, there are more than 1,800 other trial pieces that were minted from 1792 to the present. These are listed in Whitman's *United States Pattern Coins* book and are a fascinating numismatic specialty. Most patterns are rare, and most were made in Proof formats.

The half eagle (five-dollar gold coin) was the first gold coin struck for the United States. It was authorized to be coined by the Act of April 2, 1792. The first type weighed 135 grains, of .91667 fineness. The weight was changed by the Act of June 28, 1834, to 129 grains, of .899225 fineness. Fineness became .900 by the Act of January 18, 1837.

CAPPED BUST TO RIGHT (1795–1807)

F-12 Fine: Liberty's hair worn smooth but with distinct outline. For heraldic type, E PLURIBUS UNUM faint but legible.

VF-20 Very Fine: Slight to noticeable wear on high spots such as hair, turban, and eagle's head and wings.

EF-40 Extremely Fine: Slight wear on hair and highest part of cheek.

AU-50 About Uncirculated: Trace of wear on cap, hair, cheek, and drapery.

MS-60 Uncirculated: No trace of wear. Light blemishes.

MS-63 Choice Uncirculated: Some distracting marks or blemishes in focal areas. Impaired luster possible.

Small Eagle Reverse (1795–1798)

1795 Obverse · 1795 Reverse · 1796, 6 Over 5 · 1797, 15 Stars · 1797, 16 Stars

	Mintage	F-12	VF-20	EF-40	AU-50	AU-55	MS-60	MS-63
1795, Small Eagle 8,707		$20,000	$25,000	$35,000	$42,500	$52,500	$80,000	$165,000
1796, 6 Over 5 6,196		20,000	25,000	35,000	50,000	60,000	90,000	175,000
1797, 15 Stars. 3,609		25,000	32,500	60,000	100,000	145,000	200,000	
1797, 16 Stars. . . . . *		25,000	32,500	60,000	100,000	135,000	250,000	
1798, Small Eagle *(6 known)*.			200,000	450,000	1,000,000	1,500,000	—	

* Included in number above.

Heraldic Eagle Reverse (1795–1807)

	Mintage	F-12	VF-20	EF-40	AU-50	AU-55	MS-60	MS-63
1795, Heraldic Eagle . . . . *		$12,500	$20,000	$32,500	$65,000	$75,000	$85,000	$175,000
1797, 7 Over 5 . . . . *		27,500	30,000	37,500	55,000	100,000	150,000	
1798, Large 8, 13-Star Reverse. . 24,867		4,000	4,500	8,500	12,500	13,500	20,000	
1798, Large 8, 14-Star Reverse. . . . . . **		4,500	5,000	8,500	17,500	27,500	85,000	
1799 7,451		3,500	4,500	8,000	10,000	12,500	20,000	55,000
1800 37,628		3,500	4,500	6,500	7,500	8,500	10,000	32,500

* Included in number below. ** Included in number above.

HALF EAGLES ($5)

	Mintage	F-12	VF-20	EF-40	AU-50	AU-55	MS-60	MS-63
1802, 2 Over 1 53,176		$3,500	$4,250	$6,000	$7,500	$8,500	$10,000	$25,000
1803, 3 Over 2 33,506		3,500	4,250	6,000	7,500	8,500	10,000	25,000
1804 30,475		3,500	4,250	6,000	7,500	8,500	10,000	30,000
1805 33,183		3,500	4,250	6,000	7,500	8,500	10,000	20,000
1806 64,093		3,500	4,250	6,000	7,500	8,500	10,000	20,000
1807 32,488		3,500	4,250	6,000	7,500	8,500	10,000	20,000

DRAPED BUST TO LEFT (1807–1812)

F-12 Fine: LIBERTY on cap legible but partly weak.
VF-20 Very Fine: Headband edges slightly worn.
LIBERTY bold.
EF-40 Extremely Fine: Slight wear on highest
portions of hair; 80% of major curls plain.
AU-50 About Uncirculated: Trace of wear above eye
and on top of cap, cheek, and hair.
AU-55 Choice About Uncirculated: Evidence of
friction on design high points. Some mint luster present.
MS-60 Uncirculated: No trace of wear. Light
blemishes.
MS-63 Choice Uncirculated: Some distracting contact marks or blemishes in prime focal areas. Impaired
luster possible.

	Mintage	F-12	VF-20	EF-40	AU-50	AU-55	MS-60	MS-63
1807 51,605		$3,250	$4,000	$5,250	$7,000	$8,000	$9,500	$17,500
1808, All kinds. 55,578								
1808, 8 Over 7		3,500	4,500	5,750	7,500	9,000	12,000	25,000
1808		3,250	4,000	5,250	7,000	8,000	9,500	20,000
1809, 9 Over 8 33,875		3,250	4,000	5,250	7,000	8,000	9,500	18,500
1810 100,287		3,250	4,000	5,250	7,000	8,000	9,500	16,500
1811 99,581		3,250	4,000	5,250	7,000	8,000	9,500	18,000
1812 58,087		3,250	4,000	5,250	7,000	8,000	9,500	16,500

CAPPED HEAD TO LEFT (1813–1834)

Large Diameter   Reduced Diameter

Large Diameter (1813–1829)

	Mintage	F-12	VF-20	EF-40	AU-50	AU-55	MS-60	MS-63
1813 95,428		$3,500	$4,250	$6,500	$8,000	$8,500	$10,000	$20,000
1814, 4 Over 3 15,454		4,500	5,500	7,500	9,500	12,000	16,500	35,000
1815 635		37,500	75,000	165,000	185,000	200,000	225,000	300,000
1818 48,588		4,500	5,000	12,000	12,500	13,500	17,500	37,500
1819 51,723		22,500	32,500	50,000	57,500	60,000	65,000	90,000
1820 263,806		4,000	5,500	11,500	12,500	14,000	18,500	35,000
1821 34,641		25,000	37,500	55,000	95,000	125,000	165,000	250,000
1822 *(3 known)*. 17,796				7,500,000				
1823 14,485		4,500	5,500	10,000	13,000	16,000	22,500	45,000

Chart continued on next page.

	Mintage	F-12	VF-20	EF-40	AU-50	AU-55	MS-60	MS-63
1824	17,340	$7,500	$10,000	$27,500	$30,000	$35,000	$50,000	$75,000
1825, 5 Over Partial 4	29,060	8,500	12,500	25,000	35,000	40,000	75,000	125,000
1825, 5 Over 4 *(2 known)*	*				600,000			
1826	18,069	5,500	10,000	20,000	25,000	32,500	55,000	125,000
1827	24,913	7,500	12,500	22,000	30,000	35,000	45,000	115,000
1828, 8 Over 7 *(5 known)*	**	15,000	25,000	50,000	65,000	80,000	150,000	250,000
1828	28,029	12,000	20,000	30,000	45,000	55,000	100,000	200,000
1829, Large Date	57,442	12,500	25,000	50,000	65,000	75,000	120,000	275,000

* Included in number above. ** Included in number below.

Reduced Diameter (1829–1834)

	Mintage	F-12	VF-20	EF-40	AU-50	AU-55	MS-60	MS-63
1829, Small Date	*	$25,000	$45,000	$60,000	$95,000	$125,000	$250,000	$375,000
1830	126,351	16,500	27,500	42,500	50,000	57,500	65,000	100,000
1831	140,594	16,500	27,500	42,500	50,000	57,500	65,000	125,000
1832, Curved-Base 2, 12 Stars *(5 known)*	157,487	75,000	125,000	175,000	250,000			
1832, Square-Base 2, 13 Stars	**	16,000	27,500	42,500	50,000	57,500	65,000	100,000
1833	193,630	16,000	27,500	42,500	50,000	57,500	65,000	100,000
1834	50,141	16,000	27,500	42,500	50,000	57,500	65,000	100,000

* Included in mintage for 1829, Large Date (previous chart). ** Included in number above.

CLASSIC HEAD, NO MOTTO (1834–1838)

	Mintage	F-12	VF-20	EF-40	AU-50	AU-55	MS-60	MS-63
1834	657,460	$550	$650	$900	$1,350	$1,800	$3,000	$10,000
1835	371,534	550	650	900	1,350	1,800	3,000	10,000
1836	553,147	550	650	900	1,350	1,800	3,000	10,000
1837	207,121	600	700	1,200	1,650	2,000	5,000	18,500
1838	286,588	600	700	1,250	1,650	2,000	4,750	10,000
1838C	17,179	4,250	6,250	12,000	15,000	22,500	60,000	200,000
1838D	20,583	3,750	5,000	9,000	15,000	22,500	30,000	100,000

LIBERTY HEAD (1839–1908)
Variety 1 – No Motto Above Eagle (1839–1866)

VF-20 Very Fine: LIBERTY on coronet bold. Major lines show in curls on neck.

EF-40 Extremely Fine: Details clear in curls on neck. Slight wear on top and lower part of coronet and on hair.

AU-50 About Uncirculated: Trace of wear on coronet and hair above eye.

AU-55 Choice About Uncirculated: Evidence of friction on design high points. Some original mint luster.

MS-60 Uncirculated: No trace of wear. Light blemishes.

MS-63 Choice Uncirculated: Some distracting contact marks or blemishes in prime focal areas. Impaired luster possible.

Mintmark: 1839, above date; 1840–1908, below eagle.

PF-63 Choice Proof: Attractive reflective surfaces with only a few blemishes in secondary focal places. No major flaws.

HALF EAGLES ($5)

1842, Large Date

Small Letters

Large Letters

	Mintage	VF-20	EF-40	AU-50	AU-55	MS-60	MS-63	PF-63
1839	118,143	$575	$950	$1,500	$2,000	$6,000	$25,000	
1839C	17,205	3,750	6,500	13,500	17,500	27,500	50,000	
1839D	18,939	5,000	7,500	12,500	25,000	37,500		
1840	137,382	500	650	800	1,250	3,000	7,500	
1840C	18,992	1,700	3,250	5,000	6,500	17,500	45,000	
1840D	22,896	2,250	3,250	5,000	6,000	12,500	40,000	
1840O	40,120	750	1,100	2,000	2,500	10,000	32,500	
1841	15,833	500	750	1,450	1,650	3,500	10,000	
1841C	21,467	1,500	2,000	4,000	5,250	12,500	30,000	
1841D	29,392	1,600	2,650	4,250	5,250	10,000	20,000	
1842, Small Letters	27,578	550	1,000	2,250	3,250	10,000	15,000	
1842, Large Letters	*	600	1,500	2,500	3,000	8,500	16,000	
1842C, Small Date	27,432	7,000	15,000	22,500	30,000	70,000	100,000	
1842C, Large Date	*	1,800	2,200	3,250	4,500	9,500	25,000	
1842D, Small Date	59,608	2,150	2,250	4,000	4,750	12,500	30,000	
1842D, Large Date	*	4,000	7,500	10,000	15,000	40,000		
1842O	16,400	2,000	3,000	8,000	9,000	20,000	35,000	
1843	611,205	500	525	550	600	1,250	8,000	
1843C	44,277	1,500	2,200	3,000	3,750	8,000	25,000	
1843D	98,452	2,150	3,000	3,500	5,000	8,500	25,000	
1843O, Small Letters	19,075	800	1,750	3,000	4,250	15,000	30,000	
1843O, Large Letters	82,000	550	750	2,250	4,000	10,000	22,500	
1844	340,330	500	525	550	650	1,500	7,500	
1844C	23,631	1,850	2,750	4,500	5,250	12,000	26,000	
1844D	88,982	2,000	2,750	3,500	3,750	7,500	25,000	
1844O	364,600	500	650	800	1,250	3,750	17,500	
1845	417,099	500	525	550	600	1,500	7,000	
1845D	90,629	2,800	3,250	4,500	5,500	7,500	23,500	
1845O	41,000	750	1,500	3,250	4,750	12,500	55,000	
1846, Large Date	395,942	500	525	575	750	1,750	10,000	
1846, Small Date	*	500	525	600	850	2,500	10,000	
1846C	12,995	1,750	3,250	4,500	6,000	12,500	50,000	
1846D	80,294	1,650	2,000	2,750	4,000	10,000	35,000	
1846O	58,000	850	1,750	3,000	4,250	11,000	45,000	
1847	915,981	500	525	550	650	1,100	4,000	
1847C	84,151	1,500	2,000	2,750	3,500	8,000	25,000	
1847D	64,405	2,000	3,000	3,750	4,500	8,500	22,500	
1847O	12,000	4,000	8,500	11,000	15,000	25,000		
1848	260,775	500	525	550	650	1,350	8,500	
1848C	64,472	1,600	2,000	2,750	4,000	12,500	32,500	
1848D	47,465	1,750	2,500	3,500	5,000	10,000	25,000	
1849	133,070	500	525	550	1,350	2,000	12,000	
1849C	64,823	1,500	1,750	3,250	4,000	7,500	20,000	
1849D	39,036	2,500	3,250	4,500	5,500	13,500	40,000	
1850	64,491	500	525	950	1,000	2,500	15,000	

* Included in number above.

Chart continued on next page.

177

	Mintage	VF-20	EF-40	AU-50	AU-55	MS-60	MS-63	PF-63
1850C	63,591	$1,500	$1,750	$3,000	$3,250	$8,500	$16,500	
1850D	43,984	1,600	2,000	3,750	4,250	20,000		
1851	377,505	500	525	650	700	1,500	7,500	
1851C	49,176	1,850	2,250	2,850	4,250	9,500	30,000	
1851D	62,710	2,500	3,000	4,000	5,000	9,500	20,000	
1851O	41,000	800	2,000	3,250	5,250	8,500	20,000	
1852	573,901	500	525	550	650	1,200	4,000	
1852C	72,574	2,000	3,000	3,600	4,250	6,000	20,000	
1852D	91,584	1,850	2,500	3,000	4,250	8,000	25,000	
1853	305,770	500	525	550	650	1,050	5,000	
1853C	65,571	2,000	2,750	3,500	4,500	7,000	18,000	
1853D	89,678	1,950	2,750	3,500	4,250	7,000	15,000	
1854	160,675	500	525	550	650	1,500	6,500	
1854C	39,283	1,500	2,250	3,250	3,750	10,000	32,500	
1854D	56,413	1,850	2,500	3,500	4,500	6,500	22,500	
1854O	46,000	550	750	1,500	3,250	6,000	20,000	
1854S (2 known)	268		3,000,000					
1855	117,098	500	525	550	650	1,500	5,500	
1855C	39,788	1,500	2,000	2,750	4,000	8,500	37,500	
1855D	22,432	1,750	3,000	3,500	4,500	11,500	32,500	
1855O	11,100	1,250	2,750	4,500	5,500	17,500		
1855S	61,000	1,000	1,500	2,500	3,500	10,000		
1856	197,990	500	525	550	650	1,250	6,000	—
1856C	28,457	1,500	2,000	2,750	3,500	10,000	40,000	
1856D	19,786	1,750	2,500	3,000	4,250	8,000	25,000	
1856O	10,000	1,200	1,750	3,500	6,500	12,000	100,000	
1856S	105,100	550	750	1,200	2,000	7,500	27,500	
1857	98,188	500	525	550	650	1,600	5,500	—
1857C	31,360	1,550	2,400	3,000	4,000	8,500	30,000	
1857D	17,046	2,000	2,800	3,750	4,750	12,000	37,500	
1857O	13,000	1,500	2,500	4,000	5,250	11,000	40,000	
1857S	87,000	550	625	1,500	2,500	7,500	25,000	
1858	15,136	650	950	1,250	1,650	3,000	7,500	—
1858C	38,856	1,800	2,800	3,250	5,000	7,500	25,000	
1858D	15,362	2,000	2,600	3,250	5,000	11,000	45,000	
1858S	18,600	1,500	3,750	5,000	7,000	25,000		
1859 (80)	16,734	850	1,100	1,500	2,500	5,000	18,500	$65,000
1859C	31,847	1,450	1,850	2,600	4,000	8,500	32,500	
1859D	10,366	2,500	3,000	4,400	5,500	12,000	35,000	
1859S	13,220	1,850	4,000	6,000	7,500	25,000		
1860 (62)	19,763	650	1,000	1,500	1,850	5,500	16,500	35,000
1860C	14,813	2,250	3,250	5,000	6,500	10,000	22,500	
1860D	14,635	2,250	3,500	4,250	5,500	9,000	45,000	
1860S	21,200	2,400	4,500	7,500	12,000	25,000		
1861 (66)	688,084	500	525	550	650	1,300	4,250	35,000
1861C	6,879	6,500	11,000	17,500	20,000	32,500	100,000	
1861D	1,597	25,000	40,000	47,500	60,000	90,000	250,000	
1861S	18,000	3,500	7,500	10,000	12,500			
1862 (35)	4,430	2,500	5,500	8,500	12,500	25,000	30,000	35,000
1862S	9,500	5,500	10,000	16,500	20,000	37,500		
1863 (30)	2,442	5,500	10,000	20,000	30,000	50,000		30,000
1863S	17,000	4,000	7,000	17,500	22,500	40,000		
1864 (50)	4,170	5,500	10,000	15,000	20,000	27,500		30,000
1864S	3,888	32,500	55,000	85,000	125,000	200,000		
1865 (25)	1,270	15,000	25,000	32,500	37,500	45,000		30,000
1865S	27,612	3,000	5,000	7,500	8,500	16,500	45,000	
1866S	9,000	2,500	5,000	9,000	12,000	35,000		

Variety 2 – Motto Above Eagle (1866–1908)

VF-20 Very Fine: Half of hair lines above coronet missing. Hair curls under ear evident, but worn. Motto and its ribbon sharp.

EF-40 Extremely Fine: Small amount of wear on top of hair and below L in LIBERTY. Wear evident on wing tips and neck of eagle.

AU-50 About Uncirculated: Trace of wear on tip of coronet and hair above eye.

AU-55 Choice About Uncirculated: Evidence of friction on design high points. Some original mint luster present.

MS-60 Uncirculated: No trace of wear. Light blemishes.

MS-63 Choice Uncirculated: Some distracting contact marks or blemishes in prime focal areas. Impaired luster possible.

PF-63 Choice Proof: Reflective surfaces with only a few blemishes in secondary focal places. No major flaws.

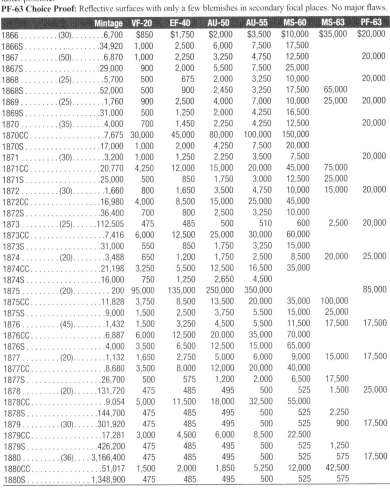

	Mintage	VF-20	EF-40	AU-50	AU-55	MS-60	MS-63	PF-63
1866 . . . .(30). 6,700		$850	$1,750	$2,000	$3,500	$10,000	$35,000	$20,000
1866S 34,920		1,000	2,500	6,000	7,500	17,500		
1867 . . . .(50). 6,870		1,000	2,250	3,250	4,750	12,500		20,000
1867S 29,000		900	2,000	5,500	7,500	25,000		
1868 . . . .(25). 5,700		500	675	2,000	3,250	10,000		20,000
1868S 52,000		500	900	2,450	3,250	17,500	65,000	
1869 . . . .(25). 1,760		900	2,500	4,000	7,000	10,000	25,000	20,000
1869S 31,000		500	1,250	2,000	4,250	16,500		
1870 . . . .(35). 4,000		700	1,450	2,250	4,250	12,500		20,000
1870CC 7,675		30,000	45,000	80,000	100,000	150,000		
1870S 17,000		1,000	2,000	4,250	7,500	20,000		
1871 . . . .(30). 3,200		1,000	1,250	2,250	3,500	7,500		20,000
1871CC 20,770		4,250	12,000	15,000	20,000	45,000	75,000	
1871S 25,000		500	850	1,750	3,000	12,500	25,000	
1872 . . . .(30). 1,660		800	1,650	3,500	4,750	10,000	15,000	20,000
1872CC 16,980		4,000	8,500	15,000	25,000	45,000		
1872S 36,400		700	800	2,500	3,250	10,000		
1873 . . . .(25). 112,505		475	485	500	510	600	2,500	20,000
1873CC 7,416		6,000	12,500	25,000	30,000	60,000		
1873S 31,000		550	850	1,750	3,250	15,000		
1874 . . . .(20). 3,488		650	1,200	1,750	2,500	8,500	20,000	25,000
1874CC 21,198		3,250	5,500	12,500	16,500	35,000		
1874S 16,000		750	1,250	2,650	4,500			
1875 . . . .(20). 200		95,000	135,000	250,000	350,000			85,000
1875CC 11,828		3,750	8,500	13,500	20,000	35,000	100,000	
1875S 9,000		1,500	2,500	3,750	5,500	15,000	25,000	
1876 . . . .(45). 1,432		1,500	3,250	4,500	5,500	11,500	17,500	17,500
1876CC 6,887		6,000	12,500	20,000	35,000	70,000		
1876S 4,000		3,500	6,500	12,500	15,000	65,000		
1877 . . . .(20). 1,132		1,650	2,750	5,000	6,000	9,000	15,000	17,500
1877CC 8,680		3,500	8,000	12,000	20,000	40,000		
1877S 26,700		500	575	1,200	2,000	6,500	17,500	
1878 . . . .(20). 131,720		475	485	495	500	525	1,500	25,000
1878CC 9,054		5,000	11,500	18,000	32,500	55,000		
1878S 144,700		475	485	495	500	525	2,250	
1879 . . . .(30). 301,920		475	485	495	500	525	900	17,500
1879CC 17,281		3,000	4,500	6,000	8,500	22,500		
1879S 426,200		475	485	495	500	525	1,250	
1880 . . . .(36). . . .3,166,400		475	485	495	500	525	575	17,500
1880CC 51,017		1,500	2,000	1,850	5,250	12,000	42,500	
1880S 1,348,900		475	485	495	500	525	575	

Chart continued on next page.

	Mintage	VF-20	EF-40	AU-50	AU-55	MS-60	MS-63	PF-63
1881 . . . . (42). . . .	5,708,760	$475	$485	$495	$500	$525	$575	$17,500
1881CC.	13,886	3,000	5,500	8,000	12,000	20,000	40,000	
1881S	969,000	475	485	495	500	525	575	
1882 . . . . (48). . . .	2,514,520	475	485	495	500	525	575	15,000
1882CC.	82,817	1,000	1,750	2,250	4,500	10,000	35,000	
1882S	969,000	475	485	495	500	525	575	
1883 . . . . (61).	233,400	475	485	495	500	525	1,000	15,000
1883CC.	12,598	2,000	4,000	5,500	7,000	16,500	45,000	
1883S	83,200	475	485	495	500	525	1,100	
1884 . . . . (48).	191,030	475	485	495	500	525	1,100	15,000
1884CC.	16,402	1,750	3,000	4,250	6,750	18,500		
1884S	177,000	475	485	495	500	525	800	
1885 . . . . (66).	601,440	475	485	495	500	525	600	13,500
1885S	1,211,500	475	485	495	500	525	550	
1886 . . . . (72).	388,360	475	485	495	500	525	550	13,500
1886S	3,268,000	475	485	495	500	525	550	
1887, Proof only (87).								37,500
1887S	1,912,000	475	485	495	500	525	600	
1888 . . . . (95).	18,201	475	485	495	500	525	1,500	12,000
1888S	293,900	475	485	495	500	650	2,750	
1889 . . . . (45).	7,520	475	550	600	650	1,250	3,250	12,000
1890 . . . . (88).	4,240	550	650	1,250	1,450	2,500	5,000	12,000
1890CC.	53,800	650	1,050	1,350	1,600	2,000	6,000	
1891 . . . . (53).	61,360	475	485	495	500	525	900	12,000
1891CC.	208,000	650	850	1,500	1,650	2,000	3,500	
1892 . . . . (92).	753,480	475	485	495	500	525	575	12,000
1892CC.	82,968	650	950	1,650	1,850	2,850	9,500	
1892O	10,000	1,650	3,000	4,000	4,250	6,500	25,000	
1892S	298,400	475	485	495	500	525	1,250	
1893 . . . . (77). . . .	1,528,120	475	485	495	500	525	575	12,000
1893CC.	60,000	750	1,650	2,500	2,500	3,250	10,000	
1893O	110,000	475	525	650	650	1,000	5,000	
1893S	224,000	475	485	495	500	525	600	
1894 . . . . (75).	957,880	475	485	495	500	525	575	12,000
1894O	16,600	550	575	600	750	1,500	8,500	
1894S	55,900	475	485	495	600	2,000	7,500	
1895 . . . . (81). . . .	1,345,855	475	485	495	500	525	575	12,000
1895S	112,000	475	485	495	500	750	3,750	
1896 . . . . (103).	58,960	475	485	495	500	525	575	10,000
1896S	155,400	475	485	495	500	600	3,000	
1897 . . . . (83).	867,800	475	485	495	500	525	575	10,000
1897S	354,000	475	485	495	500	600	2,750	
1898 . . . . (75).	633,420	475	485	495	500	525	575	10,000
1898S	1,397,400	475	485	495	500	525	575	
1899 . . . . (99). . . .	1,710,630	475	485	495	500	525	575	10,000
1899S	1,545,000	475	485	495	500	525	575	
1900 . . . . (230). . . .	1,405,500	475	485	495	500	525	575	10,000
1900S	329,000	475	485	495	500	525	575	
1901 . . . . (140).	615,900	475	485	495	500	525	575	10,000
1901S, 1 Over 0	3,648,000	475	485	495	500	525	650	
1901S . . . . *		475	485	495	500	525	575	
1902 . . . . (162).	172,400	475	485	495	500	525	575	10,000
1902S	939,000	475	485	495	500	525	575	
1903 . . . . (154).	226,870	475	485	495	500	525	575	10,000
1903S	1,855,000	475	485	495	500	525	575	

* Included in number above.

	Mintage	VF-20	EF-40	AU-50	AU-55	MS-60	MS-63	PF-63
1904 . . . .(136). 392,000		$500	$510	$515	$520	$550	$575	$10,000
1904S 97,000		500	510	515	520	550	2,250	
1905 . . . .(108). 302,200		500	510	515	520	550	575	10,000
1905S 880,700		500	510	515	520	550	950	
1906 . . . .(85). 348,735		500	510	515	520	550	575	10,000
1906D 320,000		500	510	515	520	550	575	
1906S 598,000		500	510	515	520	550	575	
1907 . . . .(92). 626,100		500	510	515	520	550	575	10,000
1907D 888,000		500	510	515	520	550	575	
1908 421,874		500	510	515	520	550	575	

INDIAN HEAD (1908–1929)

This type conforms in design to the quarter eagle of the same date. The sunken-relief designs and lettering make the Indian Head a unique series, along with the quarter eagle, in United States coinage.

VF-20 Very Fine: Noticeable wear on large middle feathers and tip of eagle's wing.

EF-40 Extremely Fine: Cheekbone, war bonnet, and head-band feathers slightly worn. Feathers on eagle's upper wing show considerable wear.

AU-50 About Uncirculated: Trace of wear on cheekbone and headdress.

AU-55 Choice About Uncirculated: Evidence of friction on design high points. Much of original mint luster present.

MS-60 Uncirculated: No trace of wear. Light blemishes.

MS-63 Choice Uncirculated: Some distracting contact marks or blemishes in prime focal areas. Impaired luster possible.

Mintmark Location

Matte PF-63 Choice Proof: Matte surfaces with few blemishes in secondary focal places. No major flaws.

Coin dealers usually pay higher prices than those listed for scarcer coins with well-struck mintmarks.

	Mintage	VF-20	EF-40	AU-50	AU-55	MS-60	MS-63	MATTE PF-63
1908 . . . .(167). 577,845		$485	$525	$535	$550	$600	$1,350	$17,500
1908D 148,000		485	525	535	550	600	1,450	
1908S 82,000		485	675	1,100	1,500	4,750	10,000	
1909 . . . .(78). 627,060		485	525	535	550	600	1,450	17,500
1909D 3,423,560		485	525	535	550	600	800	
1909O 34,200		4,500	7,000	8,500	11,500	18,500	70,000	
1909S 297,200		550	600	650	700	1,500	10,000	
1910 . . . .(250). 604,000		485	525	535	550	600	1,350	17,500
1910D 193,600		485	525	535	550	600	2,650	
1910S 770,200		485	525	535	550	850	8,500	
1911 . . . .(139). 915,000		485	525	535	550	600	1,350	17,500
1911D 72,500		650	1,000	1,450	1,550	5,250	22,500	
1911S 1,416,000		485	525	535	550	800	4,000	
1912 . . . .(144). 790,000		485	525	535	550	600	1,500	17,500
1912S 392,000		485	525	535	550	1,250	12,000	
1913 . . . .(99). 915,901		485	525	535	550	600	1,350	17,500
1913S 408,000		485	525	535	550	1,650	10,000	
1914 . . . .(125). 247,000		485	525	535	550	600	1,500	17,500
1914D 247,000		485	525	535	550	600	2,250	
1914S 263,000		485	525	535	550	1,500	8,500	
1915 . . . .(75). 588,000		485	525	535	550	600	1,450	18,500
1915S 164,000		525	550	535	550	2,000	10,000	
1916S 240,000		485	525	550	575	1,000	4,500	
1929 662,000		12,500	15,000	17,000	18,500	25,000	30,000	

Coinage authorization, specified weights, and fineness of the eagle coins conform to those of the half eagle. The Small Eagle reverse was used until 1797, when the large, Heraldic Eagle replaced it.

CAPPED BUST TO RIGHT (1795–1804)

F-12 Fine: Details on turban and head obliterated.
VF-20 Very Fine: Hair lines in curls on neck and details under turban and over forehead worn but distinguishable.
EF-40 Extremely Fine: Definite wear on hair to left of eye and strand of hair across and around turban, as well as on eagle's wing tips.
AU-50 About Uncirculated: Trace of wear on cap, hair, cheek, and drapery.
AU-55 Choice About Uncirculated: Evidence of friction on design high points. Most of original mint luster present.
MS-60 Uncirculated: No trace of wear. Light blemishes.
MS-63 Choice Uncirculated: Some distracting contact marks or blemishes in prime focal areas. Impaired luster possible.

Small Eagle Reverse (1795–1797)

	Mintage	F-12	VF-20	EF-40	AU-50	AU-55	MS-60	MS-63
1795	5,583	$25,000	$35,000	$50,000	$60,000	$85,000	$100,000	$325,000
1796	4,146	27,500	35,000	50,000	65,000	85,000	105,000	375,000
1797, Small Eagle	3,615	35,000	50,000	70,000	85,000	120,000	200,000	

Heraldic Eagle Reverse (1797–1804)

	Mintage	F-12	VF-20	EF-40	AU-50	AU-55	MS-60	MS-63
1797, Large Eagle	10,940	$9,000	$13,500	$20,000	$27,500	$32,500	$50,000	$165,000
1798, 8 Over 7, 9 Stars Left, 4 Right	900	12,000	20,000	30,000	45,000	70,000	125,000	
1798, 8 Over 7, 7 Stars Left, 6 Right	842	37,500	65,000	85,000	165,000	225,000	375,000	
1799	37,449	8,500	10,000	12,000	15,000	17,000	25,000	55,000
1800	5,999	8,500	10,000	12,000	15,000	17,000	22,500	65,000
1801	44,344	8,500	10,000	12,000	15,000	17,000	25,000	55,000
1803	15,017	8,500	10,000	12,000	16,500	18,500	27,500	55,000
1804	3,757	18,500	25,000	32,500	45,000	65,000	95,000	300,000

LIBERTY HEAD, NO MOTTO ABOVE EAGLE (1838–1866)

In 1838 the weight and diameter of the eagle were reduced and the obverse and reverse were redesigned. Liberty now faced left and the word LIBERTY was placed on the coronet.

VF-20 Very Fine: Hair lines above coronet partly worn. Curls under ear worn but defined.

EF-40 Extremely Fine: Small amount of wear on top of hair and below L in LIBERTY. Wear evident on wing tips and neck of eagle.

AU-50 About Uncirculated: Trace of wear on tip of coronet and hair above eye.

AU-55 Choice About Uncirculated: Evidence of friction on design high points. Some of original mint luster present.

MS-60 Uncirculated: No trace of wear. Light blemishes.

Mintmark is on reverse, below eagle.

MS-63 Choice Uncirculated: Some distracting contact marks or blemishes in prime focal areas. Impaired luster possible.

PF-63 Choice Proof: Attractive reflective surfaces with only a few blemishes in secondary focal places. No major flaws.

	Mintage	VF-20	EF-40	AU-50	AU-55	MS-60	MS-63	PF-63
1838 7,200		$2,750	$7,000	$12,500	$22,500	$55,000	$90,000	
1839, Large Letters 25,801		1,500	4,250	5,500	7,500	25,000	85,000	
1839, Small Letters 12,447		4,500	8,000	10,000	20,000	55,000	115,000	
1840 47,338		1,000	1,500	2,000	3,250	13,500		
1841 63,131		900	950	1,250	2,000	10,000	45,000	
1841O 2,500		8,500	16,500	35,000	65,000			
1842 81,507		900	925	1,500	2,500	11,500	25,000	
1842O 27,400		1,350	2,250	4,500	8,000	45,000	225,000	
1843 75,462		1,000	1,050	1,750	3,250	20,000		
1843O 175,162		1,000	1,250	2,150	5,000	13,500	75,000	
1844 6,361		2,500	4,000	7,000	15,000	22,500	75,000	
1844O 118,700		1,200	1,350	2,000	3,000	12,000	75,000	
1845 26,153		1,100	1,650	2,250	3,750	15,000		
1845O 47,500		1,250	2,000	3,250	5,000	18,500	55,000	
1846 20,095		1,200	1,650	3,750	6,000	27,500		
1846O 81,780		1,300	2,250	3,250	5,500	25,000	65,000	
1847 862,258		900	925	975	1,000	3,000	20,000	
1847O 571,500		1,000	1,100	1,500	1,750	5,500	30,000	
1848 145,484		900	925	975	1,000	5,000	25,000	
1848O 35,850		1,350	3,000	3,750	5,500	15,000	40,000	
1849 653,618		900	925	975	1,250	3,000	17,500	
1849O 23,900		2,500	3,500	4,750	8,000	35,000		
1850 291,451		900	950	1,200	2,000	5,500	27,500	
1850O 57,500		1,500	2,000	3,250	5,500	18,500	45,000	
1851 176,328		900	925	1,200	1,500	4,250	30,000	
1851O 263,000		1,100	1,200	1,450	2,000	12,000	35,000	
1852 263,106		900	925	950	1,200	2,750	20,000	
1852O 18,000		1,650	4,000	5,500	10,000	85,000		
1853, 3 Over 2 201,253		1,000	1,350	1,850	2,500	12,500		
1853 . . . .*		900	925	950	1,050	3,250	20,000	
1853O 51,000		1,100	1,500	1,750	3,750	17,500		
1854 54,250		900	1,100	1,250	2,250	5,500	25,000	
1854O 52,500		1,100	1,450	2,250	3,250	13,500	35,000	
1854S 123,826		1,100	1,350	1,850	3,000	16,500	25,000	
1855 121,701		900	925	1,000	1,100	3,250	16,500	
1855O 18,000		1,650	3,250	5,500	8,500	22,500		

* Included in number above.

Chart continued on next page.

	Mintage	VF-20	EF-40	AU-50	AU-55	MS-60	MS-63	PF-63
1855S 9,000		$3,000	$3,750	$5,500	$15,000			
1856 60,490		900	925	950	1,150	$3,250	$16,500	
1856O 14,500		1,500	2,750	4,000	8,000	32,500		
1856S 68,000		1,200	1,250	1,650	2,500	12,500	45,000	
1857 16,606		900	1,000	1,750	2,500	20,000		
1857O 5,500		2,750	5,500	7,500	10,000	20,000		
1857S 26,000		1,500	2,500	3,500	4,500	10,000	30,000	
1858 2,521		4,500	6,000	9,000	12,500	27,500	125,000	$100,000
1858O 20,000		1,100	1,650	2,250	3,500	12,500	40,000	
1858S 11,800		1,650	3,000	7,000	10,000			
1859 . . . . (80) 16,013		900	1,000	1,650	2,500	15,000	60,000	65,000
1859O 2,300		7,500	13,500	22,500	35,000	50,000		
1859S 7,000		4,500	6,500	18,500	20,000	40,000		
1860 . . . . (50) 15,055		900	925	1,250	1,850	8,000	30,000	50,000
1860O 11,100		1,850	3,000	4,000	6,000	18,000		
1860S 5,000		6,000	11,000	16,500	20,000	37,500		
1861 . . . . (69) 113,164		900	950	1,250	2,000	4,750	20,000	50,000
1861S 15,500		4,000	8,500	12,500	15,000	40,000		
1862 . . . . (35) 10,960		2,750	3,750	5,500	6,500	16,500		50,000
1862S 12,500		4,500	7,000	10,000	17,500			
1863 . . . . (30) 1,218		12,500	35,000	45,000	55,000	85,000	150,000	50,000
1863S 10,000		7,500	12,000	16,000	22,500	100,000		
1864 . . . . (50) 3,530		6,500	10,000	22,500	32,500	60,000		50,000
1864S 2,500		55,000	80,000	125,000				
1865 . . . . (25) 3,980		3,750	5,500	17,500	22,500	35,000		50,000
1865S 16,700		6,000	13,500	16,000	32,500	85,000		
1866S 8,500		6,000	13,500	15,000	25,000	55,000		

LIBERTY HEAD, MOTTO ABOVE EAGLE (1866–1907)

VF-20 Very Fine: Half of hair lines over coronet visible. Curls under ear worn but defined. IN GOD WE TRUST and its ribbon sharp.

EF-40 Extremely Fine: Small amount of wear on top of hair and below L in LIBERTY. Wear evident on wing tips and neck of eagle.

AU-50 About Uncirculated: Trace of wear on hair above eye and on coronet.

AU-55 Choice About Uncirculated: Evidence of friction on design high points. Some of original mint luster present.

Mintmark is on reverse, below eagle.

MS-60 Uncirculated: No trace of wear. Light blemishes.

MS-63 Choice Uncirculated: Some distracting marks or blemishes in focal areas. Impaired luster possible.

PF-63 Choice Proof: Reflective surfaces with only a few blemishes in secondary focal areas. No major flaws.

	Mintage	VF-20	EF-40	AU-50	AU-55	MS-60	MS-63	PF-63
1866 . . . . (30) 3,750		$1,650	$3,500	$5,500	$8,000	$32,500		$45,000
1866S 11,500		3,000	5,000	7,000	10,000	22,500		
1867 . . . . (50) 3,090		2,750	4,000	6,500	10,000	27,500		45,000
1867S 9,000		4,250	7,000	10,000	16,500			
1868 . . . . (25) 10,630		1,100	1,250	2,000	3,000	10,000		40,000
1868S 13,500		1,650	2,500	3,500	6,500			
1869 . . . . (25) 1,830		1,600	4,000	6,500	10,500	30,000	$75,000	40,000
1869S 6,430		2,500	4,000	5,500	10,000	27,500		
1870 . . . . (35) 3,990		1,650	2,250	3,000	6,500	26,500		32,500
1870CC 5,908		80,000	100,000	150,000	350,000			
1870S 8,000		2,250	3,500	4,500	12,000	32,500		
1871 . . . . (30) 1,790		1,350	2,750	5,000	7,500	40,000		30,000
1871CC 8,085		5,500	15,000	20,000	27,500	55,000		

EAGLES ($10)

	Mintage	VF-20	EF-40	AU-50	AU-55	MS-60	MS-63	PF-63
1871S 16,500		$1,450	$1,650	$4,250	$8,500			
1872 . . . . (30). 1,620		2,750	5,500	8,500	12,500	$27,500	$45,000	$30,000
1872CC 4,600		10,000	17,500	26,500	37,500			
1872S 17,300		1,000	1,500	2,750	5,500	22,500		
1873 . . . . (25). 800		8,500	16,500	30,000	40,000	75,000		32,500
1873CC 4,543		17,500	32,500	50,000	70,000			
1873S 12,000		1,250	2,750	4,250	6,000	25,000		
1874 . . . . (20). 53,140		925	950	975	1,000	1,200	12,500	32,500
1874CC 16,767		3,250	6,000	12,000	25,000	65,000	165,000	
1874S 10,000		1,100	2,250	4,500	8,000			
1875 . . . . (20). 100		135,000	225,000	450,000	700,000			150,000
1875CC 7,715		6,500	12,500	22,500	45,000	95,000	165,000	
1876 . . . . (45). 687		4,750	8,500	20,000	27,500	65,000		30,000
1876CC 4,696		6,750	12,500	20,000	35,000			
1876S 5,000		2,250	4,500	7,500	20,000			
1877 . . . . (20). 797		3,750	6,250	9,500	17,500	37,500		30,000
1877CC 3,332		8,500	13,500	32,500	70,000			
1877S 17,000		950	1,150	2,000	5,000	25,000		
1878 . . . . (20). 73,780		900	925	950	975	1,000	4,000	30,000
1878CC 3,244		7,500	15,000	25,000	45,000	110,000		
1878S 26,100		900	950	975	1,850	14,500	40,000	
1879 . . . . (30). 384,740		900	925	950	975	1,000	2,500	30,000
1879CC 1,762		17,500	35,000	45,000	55,000			
1879O 1,500		9,500	15,000	25,000	35,000	70,000		
1879S 224,000		900	925	950	975	1,000	5,500	
1880 . . . . (36). . . . 1,644,840		900	925	950	975	1,000	1,500	25,000
1880CC 11,190		1,750	3,000	4,500	7,500	32,500		
1880O 9,200		1,200	2,250	3,250	5,000	15,000	55,000	
1880S 506,250		900	925	950	975	1,000	1,500	
1881 . . . . (40). . . . 3,877,220		900	925	950	975	1,000	1,250	25,000
1881CC 24,015		1,750	2,850	4,000	5,000	7,500	42,500	
1881O 8,350		1,250	2,000	3,000	4,000	10,000		
1881S 970,000		900	925	950	975	1,000	1,650	
1882 . . . . (40). . . . 2,324,440		900	925	950	975	1,000	1,250	22,500
1882CC 6,764		2,000	4,000	6,500	10,000	25,000	65,000	
1882O 10,820		1,000	1,500	1,850	3,000	7,500	35,000	
1882S 132,000		900	925	950	975	1,000	1,650	
1883 . . . . (40). 208,700		900	925	950	975	1,000	1,300	20,000
1883CC 12,000		2,000	3,500	5,500	9,500	30,000		
1883O 800		25,000	42,500	75,000	100,000	150,000		
1883S 38,000		900	925	950	975	1,200	7,000	
1884 . . . . (45). 76,860		900	925	950	975	1,000	2,750	18,500
1884CC 9,925		1,750	3,000	5,250	8,500	17,500	75,000	
1884S 124,250		900	925	950	975	1,000	3,000	
1885 . . . . (65). 253,462		900	925	950	975	1,000	1,300	18,500
1885S 228,000		900	925	950	975	1,000	1,300	
1886 . . . . (60). 236,100		900	925	950	975	1,000	1,650	18,500
1886S 826,000		900	925	950	975	1,000	1,300	
1887 . . . . (80). 53,600		900	925	950	975	1,200	4,500	18,500
1887S 817,000		900	925	950	975	1,000	1,300	
1888 . . . . (75). 132,921		900	925	950	975	1,000	5,000	18,500
1888O 21,335		925	975	1,000	1,050	1,150	5,500	
1888S 648,700		900	925	950	975	1,000	1,300	
1889 . . . . (45). 4,440		1,050	1,350	1,450	1,750	3,000	8,500	18,500
1889S 425,400		900	925	950	975	1,000	1,300	
1890 . . . . (63). 57,980		900	925	950	975	1,050	2,500	15,000
1890CC 17,500		1,250	1,850	2,500	3,500	5,500	20,000	
1891 . . . . (48). 91,820		900	925	950	975	1,000	1,650	15,000

Chart continued on next page.

	Mintage	VF-20	EF-40	AU-50	AU-55	MS-60	MS-63	PF-63
1891CC 103,732		$1,250	$1,750	$2,000	$2,500	$2,750	$6,500	
1892 . . . .(72). 797,480		900	925	950	975	1,000	1,300	$12,500
1892CC 40,000		1,200	1,500	2,150	3,000	6,500	27,500	
1892O 28,688		900	975	1,000	1,050	1,200	7,000	
1892S 115,500		900	925	950	975	1,000	1,500	
1893 . . . .(55). . . . 1,840,840		900	925	950	975	1,000	1,300	12,500
1893CC 14,000		1,500	2,500	4,500	7,500	20,000		
1893O 17,000		925	950	975	1,000	1,150	4,500	
1893S 141,350		900	925	950	975	1,000	1,500	
1894 . . . .(43). . . . 2,470,735		900	925	950	975	1,000	1,300	12,500
1894O 107,500		900	950	975	1,000	1,150	4,500	
1894S 25,000		900	925	950	1,100	3,500		
1895 . . . .(56). 567,770		900	925	950	975	1,000	1,300	12,500
1895O 98,000		925	950	975	1,000	1,100	4,250	
1895S 49,000		900	925	950	1,000	2,500	7,500	
1896 . . . .(78). 76,270		900	925	950	975	1,000	1,300	12,500
1896S 123,750		900	925	950	1,000	1,500	6,000	
1897 . . . .(69). . . . 1,000,090		900	925	950	975	1,000	1,300	12,500
1897O 42,500		900	950	975	1,000	1,100	4,500	
1897S 234,750		900	925	950	975	1,000	4,000	
1898 . . . .(67). 812,130		900	925	950	975	1,000	1,300	12,500
1898S 473,600		900	925	950	975	1,000	1,500	
1899 . . . .(86). . . . 1,262,219		900	925	950	975	1,000	1,300	12,500
1899O 37,047		900	950	975	1,000	1,100	6,500	
1899S 841,000		900	925	950	975	1,000	1,300	
1900 . . . .(120). 293,840		900	925	950	975	1,000	1,300	12,500
1900S 81,000		900	925	950	975	1,000	3,000	
1901 . . . .(85). . . . 1,718,740		900	925	950	975	1,000	1,300	12,500
1901O 72,041		900	950	975	1,000	1,100	2,250	
1901S 2,812,750		900	925	950	975	1,000	1,300	
1902 . . . .(113). 82,400		900	925	950	975	1,000	1,300	12,500
1902S 469,500		900	925	950	975	1,000	1,300	
1903 . . . .(96). 125,830		900	925	950	975	1,000	1,300	12,500
1903O 112,771		900	950	975	1,000	1,200	1,850	
1903S 538,000		900	925	950	975	1,000	1,300	
1904 . . . .(108). 161,930		900	925	950	975	1,000	1,300	12,500
1904O 108,950		900	950	975	1,000	1,200	1,850	
1905 . . . .(86). 200,992		900	925	950	975	1,000	1,300	12,500
1905S 369,250		900	925	950	975	1,000	3,500	
1906 . . . .(77). 165,420		900	925	950	975	1,000	1,300	12,500
1906D 981,000		900	925	950	975	1,000	1,300	
1906O 86,895		900	950	975	1,000	1,350	3,500	
1906S 457,000		900	925	950	975	1,000	1,500	
1907 . . . .(74). . . . 1,203,899		900	925	950	975	1,000	1,300	12,500
1907D 1,030,000		900	925	950	975	1,000	1,300	
1907S 210,500		900	925	950	975	1,000	2,600	

INDIAN HEAD (1907–1933)

VF-20 Very Fine: Bonnet feathers worn near band. Wear visible on high points of hair.

EF-40 Extremely Fine: Slight wear on cheekbone and headdress feathers. Slight wear visible on eagle's eye and left wing.

AU-50 About Uncirculated: Trace of wear on hair above eye and on forehead.

AU-55 Choice About Uncirculated: Evidence of friction on design high points. Much of original mint luster present.

MS-60 Uncirculated: No trace of wear. Light blemishes.

MS-63 Choice Uncirculated: Some distracting contact marks or blemishes in prime focal areas. Impaired luster possible.

Matte PF-63 Choice Proof: Matte surfaces with few blemishes in secondary focal places. No major flaws.

EAGLES ($10)

No Motto
Mintmark is above left tip of branch on 1908-D No Motto.

With Motto IN GOD WE TRUST
Mintmark is at left of arrow points.

Gem Uncirculated (MS-65) coins are rare, and dealers usually pay substantial premiums for them.

	Mintage	VF-20	EF-40	AU-50	AU-55	MS-60	MS-63
1907, Wire Rim, Periods	500	$15,000	$17,500	$27,500	$30,000	$35,000	$45,000
1907, Rounded Rim, Periods Before and After •E•PLURIBUS•UNUM•	50	35,000	40,000	50,000	55,000	85,000	125,000
1907, No Periods	239,406	1,050	1,100	1,125	1,150	1,250	1,850
1908, No Motto	33,500	1,050	1,100	1,125	1,150	1,300	4,000
1908D, No Motto	210,000	1,050	1,100	1,125	1,150	1,300	5,500

Variety 2 – Motto on Reverse (1908–1933)

	Mintage	VF-20	EF-40	AU-50	AU-55	MS-60	MS-63	MATTE PF-63
1908 . . . .(116).	341,370	$1,050	$1,100	$1,125	$1,150	$1,200	$1,650	$17,500
1908D	836,500	1,050	1,100	1,125	1,150	1,200	4,250	
1908S	59,850	1,050	1,200	1,250	1,400	3,750	10,000	
1909 . . . .(74).	184,789	1,050	1,100	1,125	1,150	1,200	2,000	18,500
1909D	121,540	1,050	1,100	1,125	1,150	1,200	3,500	
1909S	292,350	1,050	1,100	1,125	1,150	1,250	4,000	
1910 . . . .(204).	318,500	1,050	1,100	1,125	1,150	1,200	1,500	17,500
1910D	2,356,640	1,050	1,100	1,125	1,150	1,200	1,350	
1910S	811,000	1,050	1,100	1,125	1,150	1,300	5,000	
1911 . . . .(95).	505,500	1,050	1,100	1,125	1,150	1,200	1,350	17,500
1911D	30,100	1,200	1,650	1,850	2,700	6,000	15,000	
1911S	51,000	1,050	1,100	1,125	1,150	3,000	12,000	
1912 . . . .(83).	405,000	1,050	1,100	1,125	1,150	1,200	1,500	17,500
1912S	300,000	1,050	1,100	1,125	1,150	1,250	5,500	
1913 . . . .(71).	442,000	1,050	1,100	1,125	1,150	1,200	1,400	17,500
1913S	66,000	1,050	1,100	1,125	1,250	3,750	15,000	
1914 . . . .(50).	151,000	1,050	1,100	1,125	1,150	1,200	1,500	17,500
1914D	343,500	1,050	1,100	1,125	1,150	1,200	1,650	
1914S	208,000	1,050	1,100	1,125	1,150	1,400	4,500	
1915 . . . .(75).	351,000	1,050	1,100	1,125	1,150	1,200	1,650	18,500
1915S	59,000	1,050	1,150	1,350	1,500	5,000	15,000	
1916S	138,500	1,050	1,100	1,125	1,150	1,200	5,000	
1920S	126,500	22,500	30,000	35,000	36,500	75,000	125,000	
1926	1,014,000	1,050	1,100	1,125	1,150	1,200	1,350	
1930S	96,000	16,000	22,500	25,000	27,500	35,000	50,000	
1932	4,463,000	1,050	1,100	1,125	1,150	1,200	1,350	
1933	312,500			150,000	165,000	175,000	225,000	

This largest denomination of all regular United States issues was authorized to be coined by the Act of March 3, 1849. The coin's weight was set at 516 grains, and its fineness at .900. A single twenty-dollar gold specimen of 1849 resides in the Smithsonian.

LIBERTY HEAD (1850–1907)

VF-20 Very Fine: LIBERTY on crown bold; prongs on crown defined; lower half worn flat. Hair worn about ear.

EF-40 Extremely Fine: Trace of wear on rounded prongs of crown and down hair curls. Minor bagmarks.

AU-50 About Uncirculated: Trace of wear on hair over eye and on coronet.

AU-55 Choice About Uncirculated: Evidence of friction on design high points. Some of original mint luster present.

MS-60 Uncirculated: No trace of wear. Light blemishes.

MS-63 Choice Uncirculated: Some distracting marks or blemishes in focal areas. Impaired luster possible.

PF-63 Choice Proof: Reflective surfaces with only a few blemishes in secondary focal areas. No major flaws.

Without Motto on Reverse (1850–1866)

Mintmark is below eagle.

	Mintage	VF-20	EF-40	AU-50	AU-55	MS-60	MS-63	PF-63
1850	1,170,261	$2,250	$3,000	$3,750	$5,500	$15,000	$60,000	
1850O	141,000	4,000	6,500	10,000	17,500	47,500		
1851	2,087,155	1,950	2,000	2,400	2,750	5,000	25,000	
1851O	315,000	2,450	3,650	4,500	7,000	22,500	100,000	
1852	2,053,026	1,950	2,000	2,250	2,650	3,750	22,500	
1852O	190,000	2,650	3,650	5,500	7,500	25,000	115,000	
1853	1,261,326	1,950	2,000	2,150	2,750	4,500	32,500	
1853O	71,000	3,000	5,500	8,500	13,500	32,500		
1854	757,899	1,950	2,000	2,050	2,500	5,500	27,500	
1854O	3,250	110,000	185,000	275,000	350,000			
1854S	141,468	4,000	6,500	10,000	16,500	22,500	45,000	
1855	364,666	1,950	2,000	2,050	3,000	8,500	45,000	
1855O	8,000	12,500	30,000	42,500	55,000	100,000		
1855S	879,675	1,950	2,000	2,350	2,850	5,500	20,000	
1856	329,878	1,950	2,000	2,250	2,600	6,000	30,000	
1856O	2,250	150,000	200,000	300,000	350,000			
1856S	1,189,750	1,950	2,000	2,050	2,500	5,000	15,000	
1857	439,375	1,950	2,000	2,050	2,500	4,000	30,000	
1857O	30,000	5,000	8,000	11,000	15,000	67,500	200,000	
1857S (a)	970,500	1,950	2,000	2,050	2,250	3,000	5,500	
1858	211,714	1,950	2,500	3,000	4,000	5,000	35,000	
1858O	35,250	6,000	10,000	12,500	22,500	50,000	165,000	
1858S	846,710	1,950	2,000	2,250	2,750	5,000	42,500	
1859	(80)	43,597	3,000	6,000	8,500	12,500	20,000		$125,000
1859O	9,100	15,000	25,000	32,500	50,000	125,000		
1859S	636,445	1,950	2,000	2,200	3,500	6,500	75,000	
1860	(59)	577,611	1,950	2,000	2,200	2,350	4,000	15,000	100,000
1860O	6,600	15,000	30,000	37,500	60,000	120,000		
1860S	544,950	1,950	2,000	2,250	3,250	5,500	35,000	

a. Different size mintmarks exists; the Large S variety is rarest.

DOUBLE EAGLES ($20)

	Mintage	VF-20	EF-40	AU-50	AU-55	MS-60	MS-63	PF-63
1861 . . . . (66). . . . 2,976,387		$1,950	$2,000	$2,050	$2,500	$3,250	$20,000	$100,000
18610 17,741		17,500	27,500	35,000	50,000	200,000		
1861S 768,000		1,950	2,000	2,500	3,250	12,500	50,000	
1862 . . . . (35). 92,098		5,500	10,000	16,500	22,500	32,500	75,000	85,000
1862S 854,173		1,950	2,000	2,650	3,500	9,500	50,000	
1863 . . . . (30). 142,760		4,000	6,500	9,500	13,500	25,000	75,000	85,000
1863S 966,570		1,950	2,000	2,250	3,250	6,000	40,000	
1864 . . . . (50). 204,235		3,250	5,000	7,500	12,500	22,500	65,000	75,000
1864S 793,660		1,950	2,000	2,250	2,750	6,000	40,000	
1865 . . . . (25). 351,175		1,950	2,000	2,750	4,000	6,000	15,000	75,000
1865S 1,042,500		1,950	2,000	2,250	3,000	5,500	13,500	
1866S 120,000		9,000	16,500	25,000	40,000	130,000		

Motto Above Eagle (1866–1907)
Value TWENTY D. (1866–1876)

	Mintage	VF-20	EF-40	AU-50	AU-55	MS-60	MS-63	PF-63
1866 . . . . (30). 698,745		$1,900	$1,925	$3,000	$4,250	$7,500	$50,000	$60,000
1866S 842,250		1,900	2,000	2,400	5,750	10,000		
1867 . . . . (50). 251,015		1,900	1,925	1,950	3,500	4,500	25,000	60,000
1867S 920,750		1,900	1,925	1,950	3,500	7,000		
1868 . . . . (25). 98,575		1,900	2,500	6,500	10,000	15,000	50,000	60,000
1868S 837,500		1,900	1,925	1,950	2,500	4,750	40,000	
1869 . . . . (25). 175,130		1,900	1,925	2,500	4,500	9,500	32,500	60,000
1869S 686,750		1,900	1,925	1,950	2,000	4,500	30,000	
1870 . . . . (35). 155,150		1,900	1,925	2,250	5,000	10,000	40,000	60,000
1870CC 3,789		250,000	375,000	650,000	1,250,000			
1870S 982,000		1,900	1,925	1,950	1,975	4,000	42,500	
1871 . . . . (30). 80,120		1,900	2,150	3,500	5,500	8,500	37,500	50,000
1871CC 17,387		30,000	35,000	50,000	75,000	115,000		
1871S 928,000		1,900	1,925	1,950	1,975	4,500	16,000	
1872 . . . . (30). 251,850		1,900	1,925	1,950	1,975	3,750	20,000	50,000
1872CC 26,900		4,250	8,000	12,500	22,500	85,000		
1872S 780,000		1,900	1,925	1,950	1,975	3,000	22,500	
1873 . . . . (25). . . . 1,709,800		1,900	1,925	1,950	1,975	2,500	5,000	50,000
1873CC 22,410		3,250	8,500	15,000	20,000	45,000		
1873S 1,040,600		1,900	1,925	1,950	1,975	2,500	15,000	
1874 . . . . (20). 366,780		1,900	1,925	1,950	1,975	3,000	15,000	50,000
1874CC 115,085		2,250	3,250	4,250	7,500	15,000	55,000	
1874S 1,214,000		1,900	1,925	1,950	1,975	2,500	20,000	
1875 . . . . (20). 295,720		1,900	1,925	1,950	1,975	2,150	6,000	75,000
1875CC 111,151		2,250	3,250	3,500	5,500	9,000	30,000	
1875S 1,230,000		1,900	1,925	1,950	1,975	2,100	6,500	
1876 . . . . (45). 583,860		1,900	1,925	1,950	1,975	2,500	6,000	50,000
1876CC 138,441		2,500	3,250	4,500	6,500	8,500	40,000	
1876S 1,597,000		1,900	1,925	1,950	1,975	2,150	5,000	

Value TWENTY DOLLARS (1877–1907)

	Mintage	VF-20	EF-40	AU-50	AU-55	MS-60	MS-63	PF-63
1877 . . . . (20) . .397,650		$1,900	$1,925	$1,950	$1,975	$2,050	$11,000	$40,000
1877CC 42,565		2,500	3,750	7,500	10,000	25,000		
1877S 1,735,000		1,900	1,925	1,950	1,975	2,050	10,000	
1878 . . . . (20) . .543,625		1,900	1,925	1,950	1,975	2,050	7,500	40,000
1878CC 13,180		6,500	12,500	17,500	25,000	55,000		
1878S 1,739,000		1,900	1,925	1,950	1,975	2,050	10,000	
1879 . . . . (30) . .207,600		1,900	1,925	1,950	1,975	2,050	15,000	40,000
1879CC 10,708		6,500	11,500	16,500	22,500	45,000		
1879O 2,325		25,000	45,000	55,000	75,000	125,000	225,000	
1879S 1,223,800		1,900	1,925	1,950	1,975	2,050	25,000	
1880 . . . . (36) . . .51,420		1,900	1,925	1,950	1,975	7,500	27,500	40,000
1880S 836,000		1,900	1,925	1,950	1,975	2,250	15,000	
1881 . . . . (61) 2,199		20,000	30,000	40,000	57,500	100,000		40,000
1881S 727,000		1,900	1,925	1,950	1,975	2,050	15,000	
1882 . . . . (59) 571		27,500	55,000	100,000	115,000	125,000	175,000	40,000
1882CC 39,140		2,450	4,000	5,000	6,000	9,000	100,000	
1882S 1,125,000		1,900	1,925	1,950	1,975	2,050	8,000	
1883, Proof only . . . (92)								65,000
1883CC 59,962		2,650	3,500	5,000	6,000	8,750	45,000	
1883S 1,189,000		1,900	1,925	1,950	1,975	2,050	5,000	
1884, Proof only . . . (71)								65,000
1884CC 81,139		2,500	3,000	4,000	4,500	8,000	35,000	
1884S 916,000		1,900	1,925	1,950	1,975	2,050	4,000	
1885 . . . . (77) 751		17,500	25,000	45,000	50,000	70,000	95,000	55,000
1885CC 9,450		5,500	12,000	18,500	25,000	32,500	115,000	
1885S 683,500		1,900	1,925	1,950	1,975	2,050	4,000	
1886 . . . . (106) 1,000		35,000	65,000	75,000	100,000	125,000	135,000	45,000
1887, Proof only . . (121)								65,000
1887S 283,000		1,900	1,925	1,950	1,975	2,050	6,000	
1888 . . . . (105) . .226,161		1,900	1,925	1,950	1,975	2,050	8,500	35,000
1888S 859,600		1,900	1,925	1,950	1,975	2,050	4,000	
1889 . . . . (41) . . .44,070		1,900	1,925	1,950	1,975	2,050	12,500	35,000
1889CC 30,945		2,650	4,250	5,500	6,500	10,000	50,000	
1889S 774,700		1,900	1,925	1,950	1,975	2,050	3,250	
1890 . . . . (55) . . .75,940		1,900	1,925	1,950	1,975	2,050	6,500	35,000
1890CC 91,209		2,250	2,750	3,500	4,500	7,250	35,000	
1890S 802,750		1,900	1,925	1,950	1,975	2,050	4,000	
1891 . . . . (52) 1,390		15,000	22,500	35,000	45,000	72,500	125,000	35,000
1891CC 5,000		11,000	20,000	25,000	35,000	50,000	165,000	
1891S 1,288,125		1,900	1,925	1,950	1,975	2,050	3,500	
1892 . . . . (93) 4,430		3,750	6,500	8,000	12,000	20,000	35,000	3,500

	Mintage	VF-20	EF-40	AU-50	AU-55	MS-60	MS-63	PF-63
1892CC	27,265	$2,350	$3,250	$4,000	$5,500	$10,500	$37,500	
1892S	930,150	1,900	1,925	1,950	1,975	2,050	3,000	
1893 (59)	344,280	1,900	1,925	1,950	1,975	2,050	3,500	$35,000
1893CC	18,402	3,000	5,000	5,500	8,000	10,000	47,500	
1893S	996,175	1,900	1,925	1,950	1,975	2,050	2,500	
1894 (50)	1,368,940	1,900	1,925	1,950	1,975	2,050	2,750	35,000
1894S	1,048,550	1,900	1,925	1,950	1,975	2,050	3,000	
1895 (51)	1,114,605	1,900	1,925	1,950	1,975	2,050	2,250	35,000
1895S	1,143,500	1,900	1,925	1,950	1,975	2,050	3,500	
1896 (128)	792,535	1,900	1,925	1,950	1,975	2,050	3,250	35,000
1896S	1,403,925	1,900	1,925	1,950	1,975	2,050	3,000	
1897 (86)	1,383,175	1,900	1,925	1,950	1,975	2,050	2,200	35,000
1897S	1,470,250	1,900	1,925	1,950	1,975	2,050	2,150	
1898 (75)	170,395	1,900	1,925	1,950	1,975	2,050	3,250	35,000
1898S	2,575,175	1,900	1,925	1,950	1,975	2,050	2,150	
1899 (84)	1,669,300	1,900	1,925	1,950	1,975	2,050	2,150	35,000
1899S	2,010,300	1,900	1,925	1,950	1,975	2,050	3,000	
1900 (124)	1,874,460	1,900	1,925	1,950	1,975	2,050	2,150	35,000
1900S	2,459,500	1,900	1,925	1,950	1,975	2,050	2,400	
1901 (96)	111,430	1,900	1,925	1,950	1,975	2,050	2,150	35,000
1901S	1,596,000	1,900	1,925	1,950	1,975	2,050	2,500	
1902 (114)	31,140	1,900	1,925	1,950	1,975	2,050	7,500	35,000
1902S	1,753,625	1,900	1,925	1,950	1,975	2,050	2,750	
1903 (158)	287,270	1,900	1,925	1,950	1,975	2,050	2,150	35,000
1903S	954,000	1,900	1,925	1,950	1,975	2,050	2,750	
1904 (98)	6,256,699	1,900	1,925	1,950	1,975	2,050	2,150	35,000
1904S	5,134,175	1,900	1,925	1,950	1,975	2,050	2,150	
1905 (92)	58,919	1,900	1,925	1,950	1,975	2,050	6,500	35,000
1905S	1,813,000	1,900	1,925	1,950	1,975	2,050	2,300	
1906 (94)	69,596	1,900	1,925	1,950	1,975	2,050	6,000	35,000
1906D	620,250	1,900	1,925	1,950	1,975	2,050	2,750	
1906S	2,065,750	1,900	1,925	1,950	1,975	2,050	3,000	
1907 (78)	1,451,786	1,900	1,925	1,950	1,975	2,050	2,150	35,000
1907D	842,250	1,900	1,925	1,950	1,975	2,050	2,750	
1907S	2,165,800	1,900	1,925	1,950	1,975	2,050	3,000	

SAINT-GAUDENS (1907–1933)

The twenty-dollar gold piece designed by Augustus Saint-Gaudens is considered by many to be the most beautiful United States coin. The first coins issued were slightly more than 12,000 high-relief pieces struck for general circulation. The relief is much higher than that of later issues and the date 1907 is in Roman numerals. A few of the Proof coins were made using the lettered-edge collar from the Ultra High Relief version. These can be distinguished by a pronounced bottom left serif on the N in UNUM, and other minor differences. Flat-relief double eagles were issued later in 1907 with Arabic numerals, and continued through 1933.

The field of the rare, Ultra High Relief experimental pieces is extremely concave and connects directly with the edge without any border, giving it a sharp knifelike appearance. Liberty's skirt shows two folds on the side of her right leg; the Capitol building in the background at left is very small; the sun, on the reverse side, has 14 rays, as opposed to the regular high-relief coins, which have only 13 rays extending from the sun. High-relief Proofs are trial or experimental pieces.

VF-20 Very Fine: Minor wear on Liberty's legs and toes. Eagle's left wing and breast feathers worn.

EF-40 Extremely Fine: Drapery lines on chest visible. Wear on left breast, knee, and below. Eagle's feathers on breast and right wing bold.

AU-50 About Uncirculated: Trace of wear on nose, breast, and knee. Wear visible on eagle's wings.

AU-55 Choice About Uncirculated: Evidence of friction on design high points. Most of mint luster remains.

MS-60 Uncirculated: No trace of wear. Light marks or blemishes.

MS-63 Select Uncirculated: Some distracting contact marks or blemishes in prime focal areas. Impaired luster possible.

Matte PF-63 Choice Proof: Matte surfaces with only a few blemishes in secondary focal places. No major flaws.

Ultra High Relief Pattern, MCMVII (1907)

	PF-67
1907, Ultra High Relief, Plain Edge *(unique)*.	—
1907, Ultra High Relief, Lettered Edge.	—

No Motto IN GOD WE TRUST (1907–1908) and With Motto IN GOD WE TRUST (1908–1933)

High Relief, MCMVII (1907)

	Mintage	VF-20	EF-40	AU-50	AU-55	MS-60	MS-63	PF
1907, High Relief, Roman Numerals (MCMVII), Wire Rim	12,367	$6,750	$8,250	$9,250	$9,750	$12,500	$20,000	—

Arabic Numerals (1907–1933)   No Motto (1907–1908)   With Motto IN GOD WE TRUST (1908–1933)

Mintmark is on obverse, above date.   1909, 9 Over 8

DOUBLE EAGLES ($20)

	Mintage	VF-20	EF-40	AU-50	AU-55	MS-60	MS-63	MATTE PF-63
1907	361,667	$1,900	$1,925	$1,950	$1,975	$2,100	$2,500	
1908	4,271,551	1,900	1,925	1,950	1,975	2,000	2,100	
1908D	663,750	1,900	1,925	1,950	1,975	2,000	2,500	
1908, With Motto	(101) 156,258	1,900	1,925	1,950	1,975	2,000	2,500	$35,000
1908D, With Motto	349,500	1,900	1,925	1,950	1,975	2,000	2,500	
1908S, With Motto	22,000	2,000	2,750	4,000	4,500	10,000	25,000	
1909, 9 Over 8	*	1,900	1,925	1,950	1,975	2,000	4,250	
1909	(67) 161,282	1,900	1,925	1,950	1,975	2,000	3,000	35,000
1909D	52,500	1,900	1,925	1,950	1,975	3,500	6,500	
1909S	2,774,925	1,900	1,925	1,950	1,975	2,000	2,100	
1910	(167) 482,000	1,900	1,925	1,950	1,975	2,000	2,100	35,000
1910D	429,000	1,900	1,925	1,950	1,975	2,000	2,050	
1910S	2,128,250	1,900	1,925	1,950	1,975	2,000	2,250	
1911	(100) 197,250	1,900	1,925	1,950	1,975	2,000	2,250	35,000
1911D	846,500	1,900	1,925	1,950	1,975	2,000	2,050	
1911S	775,750	1,900	1,925	1,950	1,975	2,000	2,050	
1912	(74) 149,750	1,900	1,925	1,950	1,975	2,000	2,500	35,000
1913	(58) 168,780	1,900	1,925	1,950	1,975	2,000	2,500	35,000
1913D	393,500	1,900	1,925	1,950	1,975	2,000	2,250	
1913S	34,000	1,900	1,925	1,950	2,000	2,650	5,000	
1914	(70) 95,250	1,900	1,925	1,950	1,975	2,150	3,000	35,000
1914D	453,000	1,900	1,925	1,950	1,975	2,000	2,050	
1914S	1,498,000	1,900	1,925	1,950	1,975	2,000	2,050	
1915	(50) 152,000	1,900	1,925	1,950	1,975	2,100	3,000	40,000
1915S	567,500	1,900	1,925	1,950	1,975	2,000	2,050	
1916S	796,000	1,900	1,925	1,950	1,975	2,000	2,050	
1920	228,250	1,900	1,925	1,950	1,975	2,000	2,500	
1920S	558,000	17,500	25,000	30,000	32,500	55,000	85,000	
1921	528,500	28,500	35,000	45,000	55,000	75,000	250,000	
1922	1,375,500	1,900	1,925	1,950	1,975	2,000	2,050	
1922S	2,658,000	2,000	2,100	2,200	2,250	2,500	3,500	
1923	566,000	1,900	1,925	1,950	1,975	2,000	2,050	
1923D	1,702,250	1,900	1,925	1,950	1,975	2,000	2,050	
1924	4,323,500	1,900	1,925	1,950	1,975	2,000	2,050	
1924D	3,049,500	2,250	2,450	2,650	2,850	4,500	7,500	
1924S	2,927,500	2,250	2,450	2,650	2,850	5,000	10,000	
1925	2,831,750	1,900	1,925	1,950	1,975	2,000	2,050	
1925D	2,938,500	2,500	2,600	2,750	3,000	6,000	10,000	
1925S	3,776,500	2,500	2,850	4,000	4,500	7,500	13,500	
1926	816,750	1,900	1,925	1,950	1,975	2,000	2,050	
1926D	481,000	7,000	9,500	10,500	11,000	13,500	30,000	
1926S	2,041,500	2,500	2,750	2,850	3,000	3,750	6,500	
1927	2,946,750	1,900	1,925	1,950	1,975	2,000	2,050	
1927D	180,000					1,000,000	1,500,000	
1927S	3,107,000	5,000	9,500	12,500	13,500	27,500	50,000	
1928	8,816,000	1,900	1,925	1,950	1,975	2,000	2,050	
1929	1,779,750	12,500	15,000	20,000	22,500	32,500	42,500	
1930S	74,000	22,500	35,000	40,000	42,500	65,000	125,000	
1931	2,938,250	15,000	17,500	20,000	22,500	45,000	75,000	
1931D	106,500	15,000	25,000	30,000	32,500	60,000	85,000	
1932	1,101,750	15,000	20,000	22,500	25,000	60,000	110,000	
1933	445,500			*None placed in circulation.*				

* Included in number below.

Collecting United States commemorative coins is like gathering snapshots for an album of important events, places, and people in the nation's history. Because they represent so many different aspects of America—from wars and Olympic games to presidents and historical landmarks, every collector can assemble a set with its own special significance.

All U.S. commemorative coins are issued as legal tender, though in all cases the precious metal of the coins surpasses their face values. The weight and fineness for commemoratives follow those of standard-issue gold, silver, and clad coins.

CLASSIC COMMEMORATIVE SILVER AND GOLD

(1892–1893) World's Columbian Exposition Half Dollar

	Distribution	AU-50	MS-60	MS-63	MS-65
1892, World's Columbian Exposition half dollar	950,000	$12	$22	$40	$250
1893, Same type.	1,550,405	12	22	40	250

(1893) World's Columbian Exposition, Isabella Quarter Dollar

	Distribution	AU-50	MS-60	MS-63	MS-65
1893, World's Columbian Exposition, Chicago, quarter dollar . .	*24,214*	$200	$275	$325	$1,100

(1900) Lafayette Dollar

	Distribution	AU-50	MS-60	MS-63	MS-65
1900, Lafayette silver dollar	36,026	$275	$575	$1,200	$4,500

(1903) Louisiana Purchase Exposition

	Distribution	AU-50	MS-60	MS-63	MS-65
1903, Louisiana Purchase / Thomas Jefferson gold dollar	17,500	$360	$425	$575	$850
1903, Louisiana Purchase / William McKinley gold dollar	17,500	350	425	475	800

(1904–1905) Lewis and Clark Exposition

	Distribution	AU-50	MS-60	MS-63	MS-65
1904, Lewis and Clark Exposition gold dollar	10,025	$550	$600	$800	$2,500
1905, Lewis and Clark Exposition gold dollar	10,041	550	700	900	4,500

(1915) Panama-Pacific Exposition

	Distribution	AU-50	MS-60	MS-63	MS-65
1915S, Panama-Pacific Exposition half dollar	27,134	$300	$400	$600	$1,000
1915S, Panama-Pacific Exposition gold dollar	15,000	375	425	500	950
1915S, Panama-Pacific Exposition gold $2.50	6,749	1,100	1,600	3,200	4,000
1915S, Panama-Pacific Exposition gold $50 Round	483	35,000	45,000	63,000	135,000

Entry continued on next page.

(1915) Panama-Pacific Exposition

	Distribution	AU-50	MS-60	MS-63	MS-65
1915S, Panama-Pacific Exposition gold $50 Octagonal	645	$35,000	$44,000	$60,000	$130,000

(1916–1917) McKinley Memorial

	Distribution	AU-50	MS-60	MS-63	MS-65
1916, McKinley Memorial gold dollar	15,000	$325	$375	$400	$850
1917, McKinley Memorial gold dollar	5,000	340	475	600	1,100

(1918) Illinois Centennial

	Distribution	AU-50	MS-60	MS-63	MS-65
1918, Illinois Centennial half dollar	100,058	$100	$110	$125	$225

(1920) Maine Centennial

	Distribution	AU-50	MS-60	MS-63	MS-65
1920, Maine Centennial half dollar	50,028	$70	$85	$115	$250

COMMEMORATIVES

(1920–1921) Pilgrim Tercentenary

With 1921 in Field
on Obverse

	Distribution	AU-50	MS-60	MS-63	MS-65
1920, Pilgrim Tercentenary half dollar	152,112	$60	$70	$75	$140
1921, Same, With Date Added in Field	20,053	110	120	140	190

(1921) Missouri Centennial

With 2★4 in Field

	Distribution	AU-50	MS-60	MS-63	MS-65
1921, Missouri Centennial half dollar, "2★4" in Field	9,400	$410	$460	$725	$1,200
1921, Missouri Centennial half dollar, Plain	11,400	275	340	550	1,500

(1921) Alabama Centennial

Without 2X2 in Field

	Distribution	AU-50	MS-60	MS-63	MS-65
1921, Alabama Centennial half dollar, With "2X2" in Field of Obverse	6,006	$200	$215	$290	$950
1921, Alabama Centennial half dollar, Plain	16,014	100	135	275	800

Star in Field

(1922) Grant Memorial

	Distribution	AU-50	MS-60	MS-63	MS-65
1922, Grant Memorial, With Star* half dollar 4,256		$610	$825	$1,250	$4,500
1922, Same type, No Star in Obverse Field 67,405		75	85	110	425
1922, Grant Memorial, With Star* gold dollar. 5,016		1,050	1,100	1,200	1,600
1922, Grant Memorial, No Star in Obverse Field 5,016		960	1,000	1,150	1,500

* Fake stars usually have a flattened spot on the reverse.

(1923) Monroe Doctrine Centennial

	Distribution	AU-50	MS-60	MS-63	MS-65
1923S, Monroe Doctrine Centennial half dollar 274,077		$35	$50	$90	$500

(1924) Huguenot-Walloon Tercentenary

	Distribution	AU-50	MS-60	MS-63	MS-65
1924, Huguenot-Walloon Tercentenary half dollar 142,080		$85	$90	$110	$170

COMMEMORATIVES

(1925) Lexington-Concord Sesquicentennial

	Distribution	AU-50	MS-60	MS-63	MS-65
1925, Lexington-Concord Sesquicentennial half dollar.......	162,013	$50	$65	$70	$175

(1925) Stone Mountain Memorial

	Distribution	AU-50	MS-60	MS-63	MS-65
1925, Stone Mountain Memorial half dollar..............	1,314,709	$40	$50	$60	$130

(1925) California Diamond Jubilee

	Distribution	AU-50	MS-60	MS-63	MS-65
1925S, California Diamond Jubilee half dollar..............	86,594	$110	$130	$140	$400

(1925) Fort Vancouver Centennial

	Distribution	AU-50	MS-60	MS-63	MS-65
1925, Fort Vancouver Centennial half dollar	14,994	$200	$225	$250	$500

**(1926) Sesquicentennial
of American Independence**

	Distribution	AU-50	MS-60	MS-63	MS-65
1926, Sesquicentennial of American Independence half dollar	141,120	$50	$70	$90	$1,200
1926, Sesquicentennial of American Independence gold $2.50	46,019	325	350	400	1,350

(1926–1939) Oregon Trail Memorial

	Distribution	AU-50	MS-60	MS-63	MS-65
1926, Oregon Trail Memorial half dollar	47,955	$100	$110	$125	$175
1926S, Same type, S Mint	83,055	100	110	125	175
1928, Oregon Trail Memorial half dollar (same as 1926)	6,028	110	115	125	200
1933D, Oregon Trail Memorial half dollar	5,008	240	250	275	350
1934D, Oregon Trail Memorial half dollar	7,006	120	130	135	225
1936, Oregon Trail Memorial half dollar	10,006	105	115	125	185
1936S, Same type, S Mint	5,006	110	120	125	185
1937D, Oregon Trail Memorial half dollar	12,008	110	125	135	185
1938, Oregon Trail Memorial half dollar (same as 1926)	6,006				
1938D, Same type, D Mint	6,005	Set:	385	425	625
1938S, Same type, S Mint	6,006				
1939, Oregon Trail Memorial half dollar (same as 1926)	3,004				
1939D, Same type, D Mint	3,004	Set:	975	1,075	1,300
1939S, Same type, S Mint	3,005				
Oregon Trail Memorial half dollar, single type coin		100	115	140	180

(1927) Vermont Sesquicentennial

	Distribution	AU-50	MS-60	MS-63	MS-65
1927, Vermont Sesquicentennial (Battle of Bennington) half dollar . .	28,142	$185	$190	$275	$375

(1928) Hawaiian Sesquicentennial

	Distribution	AU-50	MS-60	MS-63	MS-65
1928, Hawaiian Sesquicentennial half dollar	10,008	$1,250	$1,550	$1,700	$2,800
1928, Hawaiian Sesquicentennial, Sandblast Proof Presentation Piece	(50)			10,000	20,000

(1934) Maryland Tercentenary

	Distribution	AU-50	MS-60	MS-63	MS-65
1934, Maryland Tercentenary half dollar	25,015	$95	$110	$120	$140

(1934–1938) Texas Independence Centennial

	Distribution	AU-50	MS-60	MS-63	MS-65
1934, Texas Independence Centennial half dollar	61,463	$88	$90	$100	$140
1935, Texas Independence Centennial half dollar (same as 1934)	9,996				
1935D, Same type, D Mint	10,007	Set:	265	275	425
1935S, Same type, S Mint	10,008				
1936, Texas Independence Centennial half dollar (same as 1934)	8,911				
1936D, Same type, D Mint	9,039	Set:	265	275	425
1936S, Same type, S Mint	9,055				
1937, Texas Independence Centennial half dollar (same as 1934)	6,571				
1937D, Same type, D Mint	6,605	Set:	265	275	425
1937S, Same type, S Mint	6,637				

	Distribution	AU-50	MS-60	MS-63	MS-65
1938, Texas Independence Centennial half dollar (same as 1934)..... 3,780					
1938D, Same type, D Mint 3,775	*Set:*	$460	$480	$850
1938S, Same type, S Mint.................................... 3,814					
Texas Independence Centennial half dollar, single type coin	$88	90	100	140

(1934–1938) Daniel Boone Bicentennial   **1934 Added on Reverse**

	Distribution	AU-50	MS-60	MS-63	MS-65
1934, Daniel Boone Bicentennial half dollar...................... 10,007	$88	$95	$100	$120
1935, Daniel Boone Bicentennial half dollar..................... 10,010					
1935D, Same type, D Mint 5,005	*Set:*	285	300	375
1935S, Same type, S Mint.................................... 5,005					
1935, Same as 1934 but Small 1934 on reverse................. 10,008					
1935D, Same type, D Mint 2,003	*Set:*	500	550	1,100
1935S, Same type, S Mint.................................... 2,004					
1936, Daniel Boone Bicentennial half dollar (same as preceding) 12,012					
1936D, Same type, D Mint 5,005	*Set:*	300	350	500
1936S, Same type, S Mint.................................... 5,006					
1937, Daniel Boone Bicentennial half dollar (same as preceding) 9,810					
1937D, Same type, D Mint 2,506	*Set:*	425	500	675
1937S, Same type, S Mint.................................... 2,506					
1938, Daniel Boone Bicentennial half dollar (same as preceding) 2,100					
1938D, Same type, D Mint 2,100	*Set:*	675	775	1,050
1938S, Same type, S Mint.................................... 2,100					
Daniel Boone Bicentennial half dollar, single type coin	88	95	100	120

(1935) Connecticut Tercentenary

	Distribution	AU-50	MS-60	MS-63	MS-65
1935, Connecticut Tercentenary half dollar 25,018	$140	$145	$150	$250

COMMEMORATIVES

(1935–1939)
Arkansas Centennial

	Distribution	AU-50	MS-60	MS-63	MS-65
1935, Arkansas Centennial half dollar 13,012					
1935D, Same type, D Mint 5,505		*Set:*	$200	$210	$330
1935S, Same type, S Mint. 5,506					
1936, Arkansas Centennial half dollar (same as 1935 but 1936 on rev) 9,660					
1936D, Same type, D Mint 9,660		*Set:*	200	210	350
1936S, Same type, S Mint. 9,662					
1937, Arkansas Centennial half dollar (same as 1935) 5,505					
1937D, Same type, D mint 5,505		*Set:*	215	225	450
1937S, Same type, S mint. 5,506					
1938, Arkansas Centennial half dollar (same as 1935) 3,156					
1938D, Same type, D Mint 3,155		*Set:*	300	325	750
1938S, Same type, S Mint. 3,156					
1939, Arkansas Centennial half dollar (same as 1935) 2,104					
1939D, Same type, D Mint 2,104		*Set:*	475	550	1,600
1939S, Same type, S Mint. 2,105					
Arkansas Centennial half dollar, single type coin		$70	75	85	125

(1936) Arkansas
Centennial – Robinson

	Distribution	AU-50	MS-60	MS-63	MS-65
1936, Arkansas Centennial (Robinson) half dollar 25,265		$75	$80	$90	$130

(1935) Hudson, New
York, Sesquicentennial

	Distribution	AU-50	MS-60	MS-63	MS-65
1935, Hudson, New York, Sesquicentennial half dollar 10,008		$500	$550	$600	$750

(1935–1936) California-Pacific International Exposition

	Distribution	AU-50	MS-60	MS-63	MS-65
1935S, California-Pacific International Exposition half dollar . . .	70,132	$65	$70	$75	$120
1936D, California-Pacific International Exposition half dollar . . .	30,092	65	70	75	135

(1935) Old Spanish Trail

	Distribution	AU-50	MS-60	MS-63	MS-65
1935, Old Spanish Trail half dollar.	10,008	$700	$725	$750	$850

(1936) Providence, Rhode Island, Tercentenary

	Distribution	AU-50	MS-60	MS-63	MS-65
1936, Providence, Rhode Island, Tercentenary half dollar	20,013				
1936D, Same type, D Mint	15,010	*Set:*	$225	$275	$300
1936S, Same type, S Mint.	15,011				
Providence, Rhode Island, Tercentenary half dollar, single type coin . . .		$65	68	72	90

(1936) Cleveland Centennial / Great Lakes Exposition

	Distribution	AU-50	MS-60	MS-63	MS-65
1936, Cleveland Centennial / Great Lakes Exposition half dollar	50,030	$60	$72	$80	$100

(1936) Wisconsin Territorial Centennial

	Distribution	AU-50	MS-60	MS-63	MS-65
1936, Wisconsin Territorial Centennial half dollar	25,015	$110	$120	$130	$160

(1936) Cincinnati Music Center

	Distribution	AU-50	MS-60	MS-63	MS-65
1936, Cincinnati Music Center half dollar	5,005				
1936D, Same type, D Mint	5,005	*Set:*	$550	$700	$950
1936S, Same type, S Mint.	5,006				
Cincinnati Music Center half dollar, single type coin		$190	200	240	300

(1936) Long Island Tercentenary

	Distribution	AU-50	MS-60	MS-63	MS-65
1936, Long Island Tercentenary half dollar 81,826		$50	$60	$65	$130

(1936) York County, Maine, Tercentenary

	Distribution	AU-50	MS-60	MS-63	MS-65
1936, York County, Maine, Tercentenary half dollar.......... 25,015		$100	$110	$120	$140

(1936) Bridgeport, Connecticut, Centennial

	Distribution	AU-50	MS-60	MS-63	MS-65
1936, Bridgeport, Connecticut, Centennial half dollar 25,015		$90	$100	$120	$160

(1936) Lynchburg, Virginia, Sesquicentennial

	Distribution	AU-50	MS-60	MS-63	MS-65
1936, Lynchburg, Virginia, Sesquicentennial half dollar....... 20,013		$145	$155	$175	$200

(1936) Elgin, Illinois, Centennial

	Distribution	AU-50	MS-60	MS-63	MS-65
1936, Elgin, Illinois, Centennial half dollar	20,015	$115	$120	$130	$155

(1936) Albany, New York, Charter

	Distribution	AU-50	MS-60	MS-63	MS-65
1936, Albany, New York, Charter half dollar	17,671	$145	$150	$160	$200

(1936) San Francisco – Oakland Bay Bridge Opening

	Distribution	AU-50	MS-60	MS-63	MS-65
1936S, San Francisco–Oakland Bay Bridge Opening half dollar	71,424	$130	$135	$140	$150

(1936) Delaware Tercentenary

	Distribution	AU-50	MS-60	MS-63	MS-65
1936, Delaware Tercentenary half dollar	20,993	$135	$140	$150	$185

(1936) Columbia, South Carolina, Sesquicentennial

	Distribution	AU-50	MS-60	MS-63	MS-65
1936, Columbia, South Carolina, Sesquicentennial half dollar 9,007					
1936D, Same type, D Mint 8,009	*Set:*	$425	$450	$550
1936S, Same type, S Mint. 8,007					
Columbia, South Carolina, Sesquicentennial half dollar, single type coin	$120	140	145	175

(1936) Battle of Gettysburg Anniversary

	Distribution	AU-50	MS-60	MS-63	MS-65
1936, Battle of Gettysburg Anniversary half dollar 26,928	$340	$350	$385	$525

(1936) Norfolk, Virginia, Bicentennial

	Distribution	AU-50	MS-60	MS-63	MS-65
1936, Norfolk, Virginia, Bicentennial half dollar 16,936	$200	$215	$225	$235

(1937) Roanoke Island, North Carolina, 350th Anniversary

	Distribution	AU-50	MS-60	MS-63	MS-65
1937, Roanoke Island, NC, 350th Anniversary half dollar.	29,030	$120	$125	$130	$160

(1937) Battle of Antietam Anniversary

	Distribution	AU-50	MS-60	MS-63	MS-65
1937, Battle of Antietam Anniversary half dollar	18,028	$400	$425	$450	$475

(1938) New Rochelle, New York, 250th Anniversary

	Distribution	AU-50	MS-60	MS-63	MS-65
1938, New Rochelle, NY, 250th Anniversary half dollar	15,266	$200	$210	$220	$260

(1946) Iowa Centennial

	Distribution	AU-50	MS-60	MS-63	MS-65
1946, Iowa Centennial half dollar	100,057	$45	$50	$60	$80

(1946–1951) Booker T. Washington Memorial

	Distribution	AU-50	MS-60	MS-63	MS-65
1946, Booker T. Washington Memorial half dollar (a)	700,546				
1946D, Same type, D Mint	50,000	Set:	$40	$48	$110
1946S, Same type, S Mint.	500,279				
1947, Booker T. Washington Memorial half dollar (same as 1946)	6,000				
1947D, Same type, D Mint	6,000	Set:	55	110	140
1947S, Same type, S Mint.	6,000				
1948, Booker T. Washington Memorial half dollar (same as 1946)	8,005				
1948D, Same type, D Mint	8,005	Set:	55	120	155
1948S, Same type, S Mint.	8,005				
1949, Booker T. Washington Memorial half dollar (same as 1946)	6,004				
1949D, Same type, D Mint	6,004	Set:	90	120	300
1949S, Same type, S Mint.	6,004				
1950, Booker T. Washington Memorial half dollar (same as 1946)	6,004				
1950D, Same type, D Mint	6,004	Set:	55	105	185
1950S, Same type, S Mint.	62,091				
1951, Booker T. Washington Memorial half dollar (same as 1946) . .	210,082				
1951D, Same type, D Mint	7,004	Set:	60	105	165
1951S, Same type, S Mint.	7,004				
Booker T. Washington Memorial, single type coin		$12	13	15	40

a. Minted; quantity melted unknown.

(1951–1954) Carver/Washington Commemorative

	Distribution	AU-50	MS-60	MS-63	MS-65
1951, Carver/Washington half dollar	20,018				
1951D, Same type, D Mint	10,004	Set:	$45	$70	$225
1951S, Same type, S Mint.	10,004				
1952, Carver/Washington half dollar (same as 1951)	1,106,292				
1952D, Same type, D Mint	8,006	Set:	55	70	190
1952S, Same type, S Mint.	8,006				

	Distribution	AU-50	MS-60	MS-63	MS-65
1953, Carver/Washington half dollar (same as 1951) 8,003					
1953D, Same type, D Mint 8,003		Set:	$60	$75	$170
1953S, Same type, S Mint. 88,020					
1954, Carver/Washington half dollar (same as 1951) 12,006					
1954D, Same type, D Mint 12,006		Set:	50	60	130
1954S, Same type, S Mint. 42,024					
Carver/Washington half dollar, single type coin		$12	13	15	40

MODERN COMMEMORATIVES

(1982) George Washington 250th Anniversary of Birth

	Distribution	Mint Pkg
1982D, George Washington 250th Anniversary silver half dollar, Uncirculated 2,210,458		$9
1982S, George Washington 250th Anniversary silver half dollar, Proof. . . . . (4,894,044)		8

(1983–1984) Los Angeles Olympiad

See next page for chart.

	Distribution	Mint Pkg
1983P, Discus Thrower silver dollar, Uncirculated	294,543	$15
1983D, Discus Thrower silver dollar, Uncirculated	174,014	15
1983S, Discus Thrower silver dollar, Uncirculated	174,014	15
1983S, Discus Thrower silver dollar, Proof	(1,577,025)	16
1984P, Olympic Coliseum silver dollar, Uncirculated	217,954	15
1984D, Olympic Coliseum silver dollar, Uncirculated	116,675	15
1984S, Olympic Coliseum silver dollar, Uncirculated	116,675	15
1984S, Olympic Coliseum silver dollar, Proof	(1,801,210)	16
1984P, Olympic Torch Bearers gold $10, Proof	(33,309)	900
1984D, Olympic Torch Bearers gold $10, Proof	(34,533)	900
1984S, Olympic Torch Bearers gold $10, Proof	(48,551)	900
1984W, Olympic Torch Bearers gold $10, Uncirculated	75,886	900
1984W, Olympic Torch Bearers gold $10, Proof	(381,085)	900
1983–1984 2-coin set. Both Proof silver dollars		32
1983–1984 6-coin set. One each of Proof and Uncirculated silver dollars, Proof and Uncirculated gold $10 (a)		1,850
1983 3-piece Collector set. P, D, and S Uncirculated silver dollars		48
1984 3-piece Collector set. P, D, and S Uncirculated silver dollars		50
1983–1984 Gold and Silver set. Uncirculated 1983 and 1984 silver dollars and Uncirculated gold $10		932
1983–1984 Gold and Silver set. Proof 1983 and 1984 silver dollars and Proof gold $10		932

Note: Proof Los Angeles Olympiad silver dollars for 1983 and 1984 were also included in Prestige Sets; see page 239.
a. Packaged in a cherrywood box.

(1986) Statue of Liberty Centennial

	Distribution	Mint Pkg
1986D, Statue of Liberty Centennial clad half dollar, Uncirculated	928,008	$1
1986S, Statue of Liberty Centennial clad half dollar, Proof	(6,925,627)	1
1986P, Statue of Liberty Centennial silver dollar, Uncirculated	723,635	15
1986S, Statue of Liberty Centennial silver dollar, Proof	(6,414,638)	16
1986W, Statue of Liberty Centennial gold $5, Uncirculated	95,248	450
1986W, Statue of Liberty Centennial gold $5, Proof	(404,013)	450
2-coin set. Uncirculated silver dollar and clad half dollar		22
2-coin set. Uncirculated and Proof gold $5		900

Note: Proof Statue of Liberty Centennial clad half dollars and silver dollars were also included in Prestige Sets; see page 239.

	Distribution	Mint Pkg
2-coin set. Proof silver dollar and clad half dollar		$16
3-coin set. Uncirculated silver dollar, clad half dollar, and gold $5.		470
3-coin set. Proof silver dollar, clad half dollar, and gold $5.		470
6-coin set. One each of Proof and Uncirculated clad half dollar, silver dollar, and gold $5 **(a)**		950

Note: Proof Statue of Liberty Centennial clad half dollars and silver dollars were also included in Prestige Sets; see page 239. **a.** Packaged in a cherrywood box.

(1987) U.S. Constitution Bicentennial

	Distribution	Mint Pkg
1987P, U.S. Constitution Bicentennial silver dollar, Uncirculated. 451,629		$15
1987S, U.S. Constitution Bicentennial silver dollar, Proof. . . . . (2,747,116)		16
1987W, U.S. Constitution Bicentennial gold $5, Uncirculated 214,225		440
1987W, U.S. Constitution Bicentennial gold $5, Proof. . . . . (651,659)		440
2-coin set. Uncirculated silver dollar and gold $5		465
2-coin set. Proof silver dollar and gold $5		465
4-coin set. One each of Proof and Uncirculated silver dollar and gold $5 **(a)**.		960

Note: Proof U.S. Constitution Bicentennial silver dollars were also included in Prestige Sets; see page 239. **a.** Packaged in a cherrywood box.

(1988) Seoul Olympiad

	Distribution	Mint Pkg
1988D, Seoul Olympiad silver dollar, Uncirculated 191,368		$15
1988S, Seoul Olympiad silver dollar, Proof. . . . . (1,359,366)		15
1988W, Seoul Olympiad gold $5, Uncirculated. 62,913		440
1988W, Seoul Olympiad gold $5, Proof . . . . (281,465)		440
2-coin set. Uncirculated silver dollar and gold $5		465
2-coin set. Proof silver dollar and gold $5		465
4-coin set. One each of Proof and Uncirculated silver dollar and gold $5 **(a)**.		930

Note: Proof Seoul Olympiad silver dollars were also included in Prestige Sets; see page 239. **a.** Packaged in a cherrywood box.

(1989) Congress Bicentennial

	Distribution	Mint Pkg
1989D, Congress Bicentennial clad half dollar, Uncirculated 163,753		$3
1989S, Congress Bicentennial clad half dollar, Proof . . . . (767,897)		4
1989D, Congress Bicentennial silver dollar, Uncirculated 135,203		15
1989S, Congress Bicentennial silver dollar, Proof . . . . (762,198)		16
1989W, Congress Bicentennial gold $5, Uncirculated 46,899		440
1989W, Congress Bicentennial gold $5, Proof . . . . (164,690)		440
2-coin set. Proof clad half dollar and silver dollar		20
3-coin set. Proof clad half dollar, silver dollar, and gold $5		470
2-coin set. Uncirculated clad half dollar and silver dollar		20
3-coin set. Uncirculated clad half dollar, silver dollar, and gold $5		470
6-coin set. One each of Proof and Uncirculated clad half dollar, silver dollar, and gold $5 **(a)**		940

Note: Proof Congress Bicentennial clad half dollars and silver dollars were also included in Prestige Sets; see page 239.
a. Packaged in a cherrywood box.

(1990) Eisenhower Centennial

	Distribution	Mint Pkg
1990W, Eisenhower Centennial silver dollar, Uncirculated 241,669		$20
1990P, Eisenhower Centennial silver dollar, Proof . . . . (1,144,461)		18

Note: Proof Eisenhower Centennial silver dollars were also included in Prestige Sets; see page 239.

(1991) Mount Rushmore Golden Anniversary

	Distribution	Mint Pkg
1991D, Mount Rushmore Golden Anniversary clad half dollar, Uncirculated 172,754		$8
1991S, Mount Rushmore Golden Anniversary clad half dollar, Proof . . . . (753,257)		6
1991P, Mount Rushmore Golden Anniversary silver dollar, Uncirculated 133,139		25
1991S, Mount Rushmore Golden Anniversary silver dollar, Proof . . . . (738,419)		18
1991W, Mount Rushmore Golden Anniversary gold $5, Uncirculated 31,959		440
1991W, Mount Rushmore Golden Anniversary gold $5, Proof . . . . (111,991)		440
2-coin set. Uncirculated clad half dollar and silver dollar		30
2-coin set. Proof clad half dollar and silver dollar		25
3-coin set. Uncirculated clad half dollar, silver dollar, and gold $5		480
3-coin set. Proof clad half dollar, silver dollar, and gold $5		475
6-coin set. One each of Proof and Uncirculated clad half dollar, silver dollar, and gold $5 (a)		965

Note: Proof Mount Rushmore Golden Anniversary clad half dollars and silver dollars were also included in Prestige Sets; see page 239. **a.** Packaged in a cherrywood box.

(1991) Korean War Memorial

	Distribution	Mint Pkg
1991D, Korean War Memorial silver dollar, Uncirculated 213,049		$20
1991P, Korean War Memorial silver dollar, Proof . . . . (618,488)		16

(1991) United Service Organizations

	Distribution	Mint Pkg
1991D, United Service Organizations silver dollar, Uncirculated.	124,958	$20
1991S, United Service Organizations silver dollar, Proof.	(321,275)	18

(1992) XXV Olympiad

	Distribution	Mint Pkg
1992P, XXV Olympiad clad half dollar, Uncirculated	161,607	$5
1992S, XXV Olympiad clad half dollar, Proof.	(519,645)	4
1992D, XXV Olympiad silver dollar, Uncirculated	187,552	18
1992S, XXV Olympiad silver dollar, Proof	(504,505)	18
1992W, XXV Olympiad gold $5, Uncirculated	27,732	450
1992W, XXV Olympiad gold $5, Proof.	(77,313)	450
2-coin set. Uncirculated clad half dollar and silver dollar.		20
2-coin set. Proof clad half dollar and silver dollar		22
3-coin set. Uncirculated clad half dollar, silver dollar, and gold $5.		460
3-coin set. Proof clad half dollar, silver dollar, and gold $5.		460
6-coin set. One each of Proof and Uncirculated clad half dollar, silver dollar, and gold $5 **(a)**		940

Note: Proof XXV Olympiad half dollars and silver dollars were also included in Prestige Sets; see page 239. **a.** Packaged in a cherrywood box.

(1992) White House 200th Anniversary

	Distribution	Mint Pkg
1992D, White House 200th Anniversary silver dollar, Uncirculated......	123,803	$25
1992W, White House 200th Anniversary silver dollar, Proof..............	(375,851)	27

(1992) Christopher Columbus Quincentenary

	Distribution	Mint Pkg
1992D, Christopher Columbus Quincentenary clad half dollar, Uncirculated...............	135,702	$8
1992S, Christopher Columbus Quincentenary clad half dollar, Proof	(390,154)	8
1992D, Christopher Columbus Quincentenary silver dollar, Uncirculated	106,949	24
1992P, Christopher Columbus Quincentenary silver dollar, Proof	(385,241)	22
1992W, Christopher Columbus Quincentenary gold $5, Uncirculated.....................	24,329	440
1992W, Christopher Columbus Quincentenary gold $5, Proof...........................	(79,730)	440
2-coin set. Uncirculated clad half dollar and silver dollar...........................		32
2-coin set. Proof clad half dollar and silver dollar		30
3-coin set. Uncirculated clad half dollar, silver dollar, and gold $5..................		480
3-coin set. Proof clad half dollar, silver dollar, and gold $5........................		475
6-coin set. One each of Proof and Uncirculated clad half dollar, silver dollar, and gold $5 **(a)**		955

a. Packaged in a cherrywood box.

217

(1993) Bill of Rights

	Distribution	Mint Pkg
1993W, Bill of Rights silver half dollar, Uncirculated.. 193,346		$12
1993S, Bill of Rights silver half dollar, Proof... (586,315)		10
1993D, Bill of Rights silver dollar, Uncirculated 98,383		20
1993S, Bill of Rights silver dollar, Proof.. (534,001)		18
1993W, Bill of Rights gold $5, Uncirculated 23,266		440
1993W, Bill of Rights gold $5, Proof.. (78,651)		440
2-coin set. Uncirculated silver half dollar and silver dollar		32
2-coin set. Proof silver half dollar and silver dollar...		30
3-coin set. Uncirculated silver half dollar, silver dollar, and gold $5		485
3-coin set. Proof silver half dollar, silver dollar, and gold $5..................................		480
6-coin set. One each of Proof and Uncirculated silver half dollar, silver dollar, and gold $5 **(a)**		960
Young Collector set. Uncirculated silver half dollar...		10
Coin and Medal set. Silver half dollar and bronze James Madison Peace medal replica..............		10
Coin and Stamp set. Proof silver half dollar and themed 25¢ postage stamp.....................		10

Note: Proof Bill of Rights half dollars and silver dollars were also included in Prestige Sets; see page 239. **a.** Packaged in a cherrywood box.

(1993) 50th Anniversary of World War II, 1991–1995

	Distribution	Mint Pkg
(1993P) 1991–1995 World War II clad half dollar, Uncirculated 197,072		$10
(1993P) 1991–1995 World War II clad half dollar, Proof............................... (317,396)		10

(1993) 50th Anniversary of World War II, 1991–1995

	Distribution	Mint Pkg
(1993D) 1991–1995 World War II silver dollar, Uncirculated 107,240		$24
(1993W) 1991–1995 World War II silver dollar, Proof. . . . . (342,041)		26
(1993W) 1991–1995 World War II gold $5, Uncirculated 23,672		450
(1993W) 1991–1995 World War II gold $5, Proof. . . . . (67,026)		450
2-coin set. Uncirculated clad half dollar and silver dollar.		32
2-coin set. Proof clad half dollar and silver dollar		34
3-coin set. Uncirculated clad half dollar, silver dollar, and gold $5		485
3-coin set. Proof clad half dollar, silver dollar, and gold $5.		485
6-coin set. One each of Proof and Uncirculated clad half dollar, silver dollar, and gold $5 **(a)**		980
Young Collector's set. Uncirculated clad half dollar		10
Victory Medal set. Uncirculated clad half dollar and bronze Victory medal replica		10

a. Packaged in a cherrywood box.

(1994) Thomas Jefferson 250th Anniversary of Birth, 1993

	Distribution	Mint Pkg
1993P (1994) Thomas Jefferson 250th Anniversary of Birth, 1993 silver dollar, Uncirculated . . 266,927		$18
1993S (1994) Thomas Jefferson 250th Anniversary of Birth, 1993 silver dollar, Proof . . . . (332,891)		18
Coinage and Currency set (issued in 1994). Uncirculated silver dollar,		
Matte Finish 1994P Jefferson nickel, and $2 Federal Reserve Note.		40

(1994) World Cup Tournament

	Distribution	Mint Pkg
1994D, World Cup Tournament clad half dollar, Uncirculated	168,208	$6
1994P, World Cup Tournament clad half dollar, Proof	(609,354)	5
1994D, World Cup Tournament silver dollar, Uncirculated	81,524	16
1994S, World Cup Tournament silver dollar, Proof	(577,090)	16
1994W, World Cup Tournament gold $5, Uncirculated	22,447	450
1994W, World Cup Tournament gold $5, Proof	(89,614)	450
2-coin set. Uncirculated clad half dollar and silver dollar.		22
2-coin set. Proof clad half dollar and silver dollar		22
3-coin set. Uncirculated clad half dollar, silver dollar, and gold $5		470
3-coin set. Proof clad half dollar, silver dollar, and gold $5.		470
6-coin set. One each of Proof and Uncirculated clad half dollar, silver dollar, and gold $5 (a)		950
Young Collector set. Uncirculated clad half dollar.		10
Special Edition set. Proof clad half dollar and silver dollar		25

Note: Proof World Cup Tournament half dollars and silver dollars were also included in Prestige Sets; see page 240. The Mint also issued other minor sets under this program; they are not listed here. **a.** Packaged in a cherrywood box.

(1994) Vietnam Veterans Memorial

	Distribution	Mint Pkg
1994W, Vietnam Veterans Memorial silver dollar, Uncirculated.	57,290	$32
1994P, Vietnam Veterans Memorial silver dollar, Proof.	(227,671)	25

COMMEMORATIVES

	Distribution	Mint Pkg
U.S. Veterans set. Uncirculated Vietnam, POW, and Women in Military Service silver dollars **(a)**.		$75
U.S. Veterans set. Proof Vietnam, POW, and Women in Military Service silver dollars **(a)**		75

a. Same set as listed under U.S. Prisoner of War Museum and Women in Military Service Memorial.

(1994) U.S. Prisoner of War Museum

	Distribution	Mint Pkg
1994W, U.S. Prisoner of War Museum silver dollar, Uncirculated 54,893		$32
1994P, U.S. Prisoner of War Museum silver dollar, Proof . . . . (224,449)		24
U.S. Veterans set. Uncirculated POW, Vietnam, and Women in Military Service silver dollars **(a)**.		75
U.S. Veterans set. Proof POW, Vietnam, and Women in Military Service silver dollars **(a)**		75

a. Same set as listed under Vietnam Veterans Memorial and Women in Military Service Memorial.

(1994) Women in Military Service Memorial

	Distribution	Mint Pkg
1994W, Women in Military Service Memorial silver dollar, Uncirculated 69,860		$21
1994P, Women in Military Service Memorial silver dollar, Proof . . . . (241,278)		23
U.S. Veterans set. Uncirculated Women in Military Service, POW, and Vietnam silver dollars **(a)**.		75
U.S. Veterans set. Proof Women in Military Service, POW, and Vietnam silver dollars **(a)**		75

a. Same set as listed under Vietnam Veterans Memorial and U.S. Prisoner of War Museum.

(1994) U.S. Capitol Bicentennial

	Distribution	Mint Pkg
1994D, U.S. Capitol Bicentennial silver dollar, Uncirculated	68,332	$16
1994S, U.S. Capitol Bicentennial silver dollar, Proof	(279,579)	18

(1995) Civil War Battlefield Preservation

	Distribution	Mint Pkg
1995S, Civil War Battlefield Preservation clad half dollar, Uncirculated	119,520	$20
1995S, Civil War Battlefield Preservation clad half dollar, Proof	(330,002)	22
1995P, Civil War Battlefield Preservation silver dollar, Uncirculated	45,866	34
1995S, Civil War Battlefield Preservation silver dollar, Proof	(437,114)	25
1995W, Civil War Battlefield Preservation gold $5, Uncirculated	12,735	450
1995W, Civil War Battlefield Preservation gold $5, Proof	(55,246)	450
2-coin set. Uncirculated clad half dollar and silver dollar		55
2-coin set. Proof clad half dollar and silver dollar		55
3-coin set. Uncirculated clad half dollar, silver dollar, and gold $5		500
3-coin set. Proof clad half dollar, silver dollar, and gold $5		500
6-coin set. One each of Proof and Uncirculated clad half dollar, silver dollar, and gold $5 **(a)**		1,000
Young Collector set. Uncirculated clad half dollar		22
2-coin Union set. Proof clad half dollar and silver dollar in photo case		60
3-coin Union set. Proof clad half dollar, silver dollar, and gold $5 in photo case		520

Note: Proof Civil War Battlefield Preservation half dollars and silver dollars were also included in Prestige Sets; see page 240. **a.** Packaged in a cherrywood box.

(1995–1996) Atlanta Centennial Olympic Games

	Distribution	Mint Pkg
1995S, Basketball clad half dollar, Uncirculated	171,001	$10.00
1995S, Basketball clad half dollar, Proof	(169,655)	10.50
1995S, Baseball clad half dollar, Uncirculated	164,605	11.00
1995S, Baseball clad half dollar, Proof	(118,087)	11.00
1996S, Swimming clad half dollar, Uncirculated	49,533	45.00
1996S, Swimming clad half dollar, Proof	(114,315)	13.00
1996S, Soccer clad half dollar, Uncirculated	52,836	27.00
1996S, Soccer clad half dollar, Proof	(112,412)	27.00
1995D, Gymnastics silver dollar, Uncirculated	42,497	28.00
1995P, Gymnastics silver dollar, Proof	(182,676)	17.00
1995D, Paralympics silver dollar, Uncirculated	28,649	80.00
1995P, Paralympics silver dollar, Proof	(138,337)	23.00
1995D, Track and Field silver dollar, Uncirculated	24,976	37.00
1995P, Track and Field silver dollar, Proof	(136,935)	22.00
1995D, Cycling silver dollar, Uncirculated	19,662	60.00
1995P, Cycling silver dollar, Proof	(118,795)	24.00
1996D, Tennis silver dollar, Uncirculated	15,983	60.00
1996P, Tennis silver dollar, Proof	(92,016)	37.00
1996D, Paralympics silver dollar, Uncirculated	14,497	65.00
1996P, Paralympics silver dollar, Proof	(84,280)	23.00
1996D, Rowing silver dollar, Uncirculated	16,258	85.00
1996P, Rowing silver dollar, Proof	(151,890)	33.00
1996D, High Jump silver dollar, Uncirculated	15,697	100.00
1996P, High Jump silver dollar, Proof	(124,502)	24.00
1995W, Torch Runner gold $5, Uncirculated	14,675	450.00
1995W, Torch Runner gold $5, Proof	(57,442)	450.00
1995W, Stadium gold $5, Uncirculated	10,579	450.00
1995W, Stadium gold $5, Proof	(43,124)	450.00
1996W, Flag Bearer gold $5, Uncirculated	9,174	450.00
1996W, Flag Bearer gold $5, Proof	(32,886)	450.00

Note: Proof Atlanta Centennial Olympic Games half dollars and silver dollars were also included in Prestige Sets; see page 240.

Chart continued on next page.

	Distribution	Mint Pkg
1996W, Cauldron gold $5, Uncirculated	9,210	$475
1996W, Cauldron gold $5, Proof	(38,555)	450
2-coin set #1. Proof silver dollars (Gymnastics, Paralympics)		50
4-coin set #1. Uncirculated clad half dollar (Basketball), silver dollars (Gymnastics, Paralympics), and gold $5 (Torch Bearer)		550
4-coin set #2. Proof clad half dollar (Basketball), silver dollars (Gymnastics, Paralympics), and gold ($5 Torch Bearer)		490
4-coin set #3. Proof clad half dollar (Baseball), silver dollars (Cyclist, Track Runner), and gold $5 (Olympic Stadium)		515
Young Collector's set #1. Uncirculated Basketball clad half dollar		15
Young Collector's set #2. Uncirculated Baseball clad half dollar		15
Young Collector's set #3. Uncirculated Swimming clad half dollar		65
Young Collector's set #4. Uncirculated Soccer clad half dollar		60
1995–1996 16-coin set. One each of all Uncirculated coins **(a)**		2,500
1995–1996 16-coin set. One each of all Proof coins **(a)**		2,200
1995–1996 8-coin set. One each of all Proof silver dollars		240
1995–1996 32-coin set. One each of all Uncirculated and Proof coins **(a)**		4,850

Note: Proof Atlanta Centennial Olympic Games half dollars and silver dollars were also included in Prestige Sets; see page 240. **a.** Packaged in a cherrywood box.

(1995) **Special Olympics World Games**

	Distribution	Mint Pkg
1995W, Special Olympics World Games silver dollar, Uncirculated	89,301	$25
1995P, Special Olympics World Games silver dollar, Proof	(351,764)	26
2-coin set. Proof silver dollar and 1995S Kennedy half dollar		35

(1996) **National Community Service**

	Distribution	Mint Pkg
1996S, National Community Service silver dollar, Uncirculated	23,500	$45
1996S, National Community Service silver dollar, Proof	(101,543)	18
Coin and Stamp set. Proof silver dollar and 3¢ Saint-Gaudens postage stamp		30

(1996) Smithsonian Institution 150th Anniversary

	Distribution	Mint Pkg
1996D, Smithsonian Institution 150th Anniversary silver dollar, Uncirculated	31,320	$30
1996P, Smithsonian Institution 150th Anniversary silver dollar, Proof	(129,152)	34
1996W, Smithsonian Institution 150th Anniversary gold $5, Uncirculated	9,068	450
1996W, Smithsonian Institution 150th Anniversary gold $5, Proof	(21,772)	450
2-coin set. Proof silver dollar and gold $5		480
4-coin set. One each of Proof and Uncirculated silver dollars and gold $5 **(a)**		950
Young Collector's set. Proof silver dollar		30

a. Packaged in a cherrywood box.

(1997) U.S. Botanic Garden

	Distribution	Mint Pkg
1997P, U.S. Botanic Garden silver dollar, Uncirculated	58,505	$18
1997P, U.S. Botanic Garden silver dollar, Proof	(189,671)	28
Coinage and Currency set. Uncirculated silver dollar, Matte Finish 1997P Jefferson nickel, and $1 Federal Reserve Note		60

Note: Proof U.S. Botanic Garden silver dollars were also included in Prestige Sets; see page 240.

(1997) Jackie Robinson

	Distribution	Mint Pkg
1997S, Jackie Robinson silver dollar, Uncirculated	30,180	$40
1997S, Jackie Robinson silver dollar, Proof	(110,002)	38
1997W, Jackie Robinson gold $5, Uncirculated	5,174	500
1997W, Jackie Robinson gold $5, Proof	(24,072)	450
2-coin set. Proof silver dollar and gold $5		490
4-coin set. One each of Proof and Uncirculated silver dollars and gold $5 **(a)**		1,000
Legacy set. Proof gold $5, baseball card, and pin **(a)**		450

a. Packaged in a cherrywood box.

(1997) Franklin D. Roosevelt

	Distribution	Mint Pkg
1997W, Franklin D. Roosevelt gold $5, Uncirculated	11,894	$450
1997W, Franklin D. Roosevelt gold $5, Proof	(29,474)	450
2-coin set. One each of Proof and Uncirculated gold $5		900

(1997) National Law Enforcement Officers Memorial

	Distribution	Mint Pkg
1997P, National Law Enforcement Officers Memorial silver dollar, Uncirculated	28,575	$70
1997P, National Law Enforcement Officers Memorial silver dollar, Proof	(110,428)	35
Insignia set. Proof silver dollar, lapel pin, and patch		45

(1998) Robert F. Kennedy

	Distribution	Mint Pkg
1998S, Robert F. Kennedy silver dollar, Uncirculated 106,422		$22
1998S, Robert F. Kennedy silver dollar, Proof. . . . . (99,020)		34
2-coin Collector's set. Uncirculated RFK silver dollar and Matte Finish 1998S JFK silver half dollar.		105
2-coin set. Proof and Uncirculated RFK silver dollars		55

(1998) Black Revolutionary War Patriots

	Distribution	Mint Pkg
1998S, Black Revolutionary War Patriots silver dollar, Uncirculated 37,210		$45
1998S, Black Revolutionary War Patriots silver dollar, Proof. . . . . (75,070)		35
2-coin set. Proof and Uncirculated silver dollars		80
Young Collector set. Uncirculated silver dollar		30
Coin and Stamp set. Proof silver dollar and four themed postage stamps (10¢, 13¢, 15¢, and 25¢)		32

(1999) Dolley Madison

See next page for chart.

227

	Distribution	Mint Pkg
1999P, Dolley Madison silver dollar, Uncirculated	89,104	$20
1999P, Dolley Madison silver dollar, Proof	(224,403)	20
2-coin set. Proof and Uncirculated silver dollars		40

(1999) George Washington Death Bicentennial

	Distribution	Mint Pkg
1999W, George Washington Death Bicentennial gold $5, Uncirculated	22,511	$450
1999W, George Washington Death Bicentennial gold $5, Proof	(41,693)	450
2-coin set. One each of Proof and Uncirculated gold $5		900

(1999) Yellowstone National Park

	Distribution	Mint Pkg
1999P, Yellowstone National Park silver dollar, Uncirculated	82,563	$25
1999P, Yellowstone National Park silver dollar, Proof	(187,595)	25
2-coin set. One each of Proof and Uncirculated gold $5		50

(2000) Library of Congress Bicentennial

COMMEMORATIVES

	Distribution	Mint Pkg
2000P, Library of Congress Bicentennial silver dollar, Uncirculated	53,264	$16
2000P, Library of Congress Bicentennial silver dollar, Proof	(198,503)	18
2000W, Library of Congress Bicentennial bimetallic (gold/platinum) $10, Uncirculated	7,261	800
2000W, Library of Congress Bicentennial bimetallic (gold/platinum) $10, Proof	(27,445)	750

(2000) Leif Ericson Millennium

	Distribution	Mint Pkg
2000P, Leif Ericson Millennium silver dollar, Uncirculated	28,150	$45
2000P, Leif Ericson Millennium silver dollar, Proof	(144,748)	32
2-coin set. Proof silver dollar and Icelandic 1,000 krónur		60

(2001) American Buffalo Commemorative

	Distribution	Mint Pkg
2001D, American Buffalo silver dollar, Uncirculated	227,131	$75
2001P, American Buffalo silver dollar, Proof	(272,869)	75
2-coin set. One each of Proof and Uncirculated silver dollars		150
Coinage and Currency set. Uncirculated silver dollar, face reprint of 1899 $5 Indian Chief Silver Certificate, 1987 Chief Red Cloud 10¢ stamp, and 2001 Bison 21¢ stamp		85

(2001) Capitol Visitor Center

	Distribution	Mint Pkg
2001P, U.S. Capitol Visitor Center clad half dollar, Uncirculated 99,157		$12
2001P, U.S. Capitol Visitor Center clad half dollar, Proof . . . . (77,962)		14
2001P, U.S. Capitol Visitor Center silver dollar, Uncirculated 35,380		16
2001P, U.S. Capitol Visitor Center silver dollar, Proof . . . . (143,793)		24
2001W, U.S. Capitol Visitor Center gold $5, Uncirculated 6,761		450
2001W, U.S. Capitol Visitor Center gold $5, Proof . . . . (27,652)		450
3-coin set. Proof clad half dollar, silver dollar, and gold $5		490

(2002) Salt Lake Olympic Games

	Distribution	Mint Pkg
2002P, Salt Lake Olympic Games silver dollar, Uncirculated 40,257		$21
2002P, Salt Lake Olympic Games silver dollar, Proof . . . . (166,864)		18
2002W, Salt Lake Olympic Games gold $5, Uncirculated 10,585		450
2002W, Salt Lake Olympic Games gold $5, Proof . . . . (32,877)		450
2-coin set. Proof silver dollar and gold $5		470
4-coin set. One each of Proof and Uncirculated silver dollar and gold $5		940

(2002) West Point Bicentennial

	Distribution	Mint Pkg
2002W, West Point Bicentennial silver dollar, Uncirculated............................	103,201	$16
2002W, West Point Bicentennial silver dollar, Proof................................	(288,293)	28

(2003) First Flight Centennial

	Distribution	Mint Pkg
2003P, First Flight Centennial clad half dollar, Uncirculated........................	57,122	$13
2003P, First Flight Centennial clad half dollar, Proof...............................	(109,710)	15
2003P, First Flight Centennial silver dollar, Uncirculated...........................	53,533	25
2003P, First Flight Centennial silver dollar, Proof................................	(190,240)	26
2003W, First Flight Centennial gold $10, Uncirculated..............................	10,009	900
2003W, First Flight Centennial gold $10, Proof....................................	(21,676)	900
3-coin set. Proof clad half dollar, silver dollar, and gold $10.....................		940

(2004) Thomas Alva Edison

	Distribution	Mint Pkg
2004P, Thomas Alva Edison silver dollar, Uncirculated 92,510		$17
2004P, Thomas Alva Edison silver dollar, Proof. . . . . (211,055)		17
Collector's set. Uncirculated silver dollar in case with functioning light bulb		20

(2004) Lewis and Clark Bicentennial

	Distribution	Mint Pkg
2004P, Lewis and Clark Bicentennial silver dollar, Uncirculated 142,015		$16
2004P, Lewis and Clark Bicentennial silver dollar, Proof. . . . . (351,989)		18
Coin and Pouch set. Proof silver dollar and beaded pouch.		25
Coinage and Currency set. Uncirculated silver dollar, 2004D Sacagawea dollar, 2005P and 2005D		
nickels, Series of 1901 $10 Bison note replica, silver-plated Thomas Jefferson Peace Medal		
replica, three themed 37¢ postage stamps, and two booklets		22

(2005) Chief Justice John Marshall

	Distribution	Mint Pkg
2005P, Chief Justice John Marshall silver dollar, Uncirculated 67,096		$16
2005P, Chief Justice John Marshall silver dollar, Proof. . . . . (196,753)		16
Coin and Chronicles set. Uncirculated silver dollar, booklet, and BEP intaglio portrait.		20
American Legacy set. Proof Marine Corps and John Marshall dollars, 11-piece Proof set **(a)**		60

a. Same set as listed under Marine Corps 230th Anniversary.

(2005) Marine Corps 230th Anniversary

	Distribution	Mint Pkg
2005P, Marine Corps 230th Anniversary silver dollar, Uncirculated 49,671		$35
2005P, Marine Corps 230th Anniversary silver dollar, Proof . . . . (548,810)		40
Coin and Stamp set. Uncirculated silver dollar and themed 3¢ postage stamp		40
American Legacy set. Proof Marine Corps and John Marshall silver dollars, 11-piece Proof set **(a)**.		60

a. Same set as listed under Chief Justice James Marshall.

(2006) Benjamin Franklin Tercentenary

	Distribution	Mint Pkg
2006P, Benjamin Franklin "Scientist" silver dollar, Uncirculated. 58,000		$17
2006P, Benjamin Franklin "Scientist" silver dollar, Proof . . . . (142,000)		20

Chart continued on next page.   **233**

	Distribution	Mint Pkg
2006P, Benjamin Franklin "Founding Father" silver dollar, Uncirculated	58,000	$18
2006P, Benjamin Franklin "Founding Father" silver dollar, Proof	(142,000)	22
Coin and Chronicles set. Uncirculated "Scientist" silver dollar, four themed 39¢ postage stamps, *Poor Richard's Almanack* replica, and intaglio print		18
American Legacy set. Proof "Founding Father" silver dollar; Proof San Francisco Old Mint silver dollar; and Proof cent, nickel, dime, quarter, half dollar, and Sacagawea dollar **(a)**		50

a. Same set as listed under San Francisco Old Mint Centennial.

(2006) San Francisco Old Mint Centennial

	Distribution	Mint Pkg
2006S, San Francisco Old Mint Centennial silver dollar, Uncirculated	67,100	$28
2006S, San Francisco Old Mint Centennial silver dollar, Proof	(160,870)	30
2006S, San Francisco Old Mint Centennial gold $5, Uncirculated	17,500	450
2006S, San Francisco Old Mint Centennial gold $5, Proof	(44,174)	450
American Legacy set. Proof San Francisco Old Mint silver dollar; Proof "Founding Father" silver dollar; and Proof cent, nickel, dime, quarter, half dollar, and Sacagawea dollar **(a)**		48
2007P, Jamestown 400th Anniversary silver dollar, Uncirculated	81,034	17
2007P, Jamestown 400th Anniversary silver dollar, Proof	(260,363)	24
2007W, Jamestown 400th Anniversary gold $5, Uncirculated	18,623	450
2007W, Jamestown 400th Anniversary gold $5, Proof	(47,123)	450
American Legacy set. Proof Jamestown silver dollar; Proof Little Rock Central High School Desegregation silver dollar; and 14-piece Proof Set **(b)**		50
2007P, Little Rock Central High School Desegregation silver dollar, Uncirculated	66,093	16
2007P, Little Rock Central High School Desegregation silver dollar, Proof	(124,678)	16
Coin and Medal set. Uncirculated silver dollar, bronze medal		18
American Legacy set. Proof Little Rock Central High School Desegregation silver dollar; Proof Jamestown silver dollar; and 14-piece Proof Set **(c)**		55
2008S, Bald Eagle Recovery and National Emblem clad half dollar, Uncirculated	120,180	11
2008S, Bald Eagle Recovery and National Emblem clad half dollar, Proof	(220,577)	12
2008P, Bald Eagle Recovery and National Emblem silver dollar, Uncirculated	119,204	18
2008P, Bald Eagle Recovery and National Emblem silver dollar, Proof	(294,601)	16
2008W, Bald Eagle Recovery and National Emblem gold $5, Uncirculated	15,009	450
2008W, Bald Eagle Recovery and National Emblem gold $5, Proof	(59,269)	450
3-coin set. Proof clad half dollar, silver dollar, and gold $5		480
Coin and Medal set. Uncirculated silver dollar and bronze Bald Eagle medal		18
Young Collector set. Uncirculated clad half dollar		12
American Legacy set. Proof Bald Eagle silver dollar and 14-piece Proof Set		55

a. Same set as listed under Benjamin Franklin Tercentenary. b. Same set as listed under Little Rock Central High School Desegregation. c. Same set as listed under Jamestown 400th Anniversary.

COMMEMORATIVES

	Distribution	Mint Pkg
2009P, Louis Braille Bicentennial silver dollar, Uncirculated	82,639	$16
2009P, Louis Braille Bicentennial silver dollar, Proof	(135,235)	16
Education set. Uncirculated silver dollar in tri-fold package		20
2009P, Abraham Lincoln Bicentennial silver dollar, Uncirculated	125,000	25
2009P, Abraham Lincoln Bicentennial silver dollar, Proof	(325,000)	27
Coin and Chronicles set. Proof silver dollar and the four Proof 2009S Lincoln Bicentennial cents		30
2010W, American Veterans Disabled for Life silver dollar, Uncirculated	78,301	24
2010W, American Veterans Disabled for Life silver dollar, Proof	(202,770)	28
2010P, Boy Scouts of America Centennial silver dollar, Uncirculated	105,020	25
2010P, Boy Scouts of America Centennial silver dollar, Proof	(244,963)	24
2011S, Medal of Honor silver dollar, Uncirculated	44,752	30
2011P, Medal of Honor silver dollar, Proof	(112,833)	32
2011P, Medal of Honor gold $5, Uncirculated	8,233	450
2011W, Medal of Honor gold $5, Proof	(17,999)	450
2011D, U.S. Army clad half dollar, Uncirculated	39,442	18
2011S, U.S. Army clad half dollar, Proof	(68,332)	42
2011S, U.S. Army silver dollar, Uncirculated	43,512	30
2011P, U.S. Army silver dollar, Proof	(119,829)	27
2011P, U.S. Army gold $5, Uncirculated	8,052	450
2011W, U.S. Army gold $5, Proof	(17,148)	450
2012W, Infantry Soldier silver dollar, Uncirculated	44,348	28
2012W, Infantry Soldier silver dollar, Proof	(161,151)	32
2012P, Star-Spangled Banner silver dollar, Uncirculated	41,686	28
2012P, Star-Spangled Banner silver dollar, Proof	(169,065)	28
2012W, Star-Spangled Banner gold $5, Uncirculated	7,027	450
2012W, Star-Spangled Banner gold $5, Proof	(18,313)	450
2-coin set. Proof silver dollar and gold $5		480
2013W, Girl Scouts of the U.S.A. Centennial silver dollar, Uncirculated	37,462	27
2013W, Girl Scouts of the U.S.A. Centennial silver dollar, Proof	(86,355)	27
Young Collectors set. Uncirculated silver dollar		30
2013D, 5-Star Generals clad half dollar, Uncirculated	38,095	14
2013S, 5-Star Generals clad half dollar, Proof	(47,326)	25
2013W, 5-Star Generals silver dollar, Uncirculated	34,638	36
2013P, 5-Star Generals silver dollar, Proof	(69,283)	40
2013P, 5-Star Generals gold $5, Uncirculated	5,667	450
2013W, 5-Star Generals gold $5, Proof	(15,844)	450
3-coin set. Proof clad half dollar, silver dollar, and gold $5		520
Profile Collection. Unc. half dollar and silver dollar, bronze MacArthur Congressional Gold Medal replica		50
2014D, National Baseball Hall of Fame clad half dollar, Uncirculated (d)	142,405	18
2014S, National Baseball Hall of Fame clad half dollar, Proof (d)	(249,049)	22
2014P, National Baseball Hall of Fame silver dollar, Uncirculated (d)	131,910	32
2014P, National Baseball Hall of Fame silver dollar, Proof (d)	(267,847)	35
2014W, National Baseball Hall of Fame gold $5, Uncirculated (d)	17,674	450
2014W, National Baseball Hall of Fame gold $5, Proof (d)	(32,428)	450
Young Collectors set. Uncirculated clad half dollar (d)		25

d. The obverse of each denomination is concave; the reverse is convex.

Chart continued on next page.   **235**

	Distribution	Mint Pkg
2014P, Civil Rights Act of 1964 silver dollar, Uncirculated 24,720		$38
2014P, Civil Rights Act of 1964 silver dollar, Proof. . . . . (61,992)		42
2015D, U.S. Marshals Service 225th Anniversary clad half dollar, Uncirculated 30,231		15
2015S, U.S. Marshals Service 225th Anniversary clad half dollar, Proof. . . . . (76,549)		18
2015P, U.S. Marshals Service 225th Anniversary silver dollar, Uncirculated 38,149		36
2015P, U.S. Marshals Service 225th Anniversary silver dollar, Proof . . . . (124,329)		34
2015W, U.S. Marshals Service 225th Anniversary gold $5, Uncirculated 6,743		450
2015W, U.S. Marshals Service 225th Anniversary gold $5, Proof. . . . . (24,959)		450
3-coin set. Proof clad half dollar, silver dollar, and gold $5.		575
2015P, March of Dimes 75th Anniversary silver dollar, Uncirculated. 24,742		$35
2015W, March of Dimes 75th Anniversary silver dollar, Proof. . . . . (32,030)		26
Special Silver set. Proof silver dollar, silver Proof and Reverse Proof dimes		32
2016P, Mark Twain silver dollar, Uncirculated. 26,291		35
2016P, Mark Twain silver dollar, Proof . . . . (78,549)		26
2016W, Mark Twain gold $5, Uncirculated. 5,701		450
2016W, Mark Twain gold $5, Proof . . . . (13,271)		450
2016D, National Park Service 100th Anniversary clad half dollar, Uncirculated 21,328		18
2016S, National Park Service 100th Anniversary clad half dollar, Proof . . . . (54,946)		20
2016P, National Park Service 100th Anniversary silver dollar, Uncirculated 20,979		26
2016P, National Park Service 100th Anniversary silver dollar, Proof. (77,319)		28
2016W, National Park Service 100th Anniversary gold $5, Uncirculated. 5,195		450
2016W, National Park Service 100th Anniversary gold $5, Proof . . . . (19,503)		450
3-coin set. Proof clad half dollar, silver dollar, and gold $5.		500
2017P, Lions Club International Century of Service silver dollar, Uncirculated 68,330		36
2017P, Lions Club International Century of Service silver dollar, Proof . . . . (17,224)		40
2017S, Boys Town Centennial clad half dollar, Uncirculated. 15,561		20
2017D, Boys Town Centennial clad half dollar, Proof . . . . (23,212)		22
2017P, Boys Town Centennial silver dollar, Uncirculated 12,307		35
2017P, Boys Town Centennial silver dollar, Proof . . . . (31,648)		38
2017W, Boys Town Centennial gold $5, Uncirculated. 2,939		450
2017W, Boys Town Centennial gold $5, Proof . . . . (7,377)		450
3-coin set. Proof clad half dollar, silver dollar, and gold $5.		500
2018P, World War I Centennial silver silver dollar, Uncirculated 22,338		36
2018P, World War I Centennial silver dollar, Proof. . . . . (127,867)		38
Air Service Medal set. Proof silver dollar and silver Air Service medal		80
Army Medal set. Proof silver dollar and silver Army medal		80
Coast Guard Medal set. Proof silver dollar and silver Coast Guard medal.		80
Marine Corps Medal set. Proof silver dollar and silver Marine Corps medal		80
Navy Medal set. Proof silver dollar and silver Navy medal		80
2018D, Breast Cancer Awareness clad half dollar, Uncirculated. 11,301		18
2018S, Breast Cancer Awareness clad half dollar, Proof . . . . (22,391)		20
2018P, Breast Cancer Awareness silver dollar, Uncirculated. 12,521		42
2018P, Breast Cancer Awareness silver dollar, Proof . . . . (34,548)		40
2018W, Breast Cancer Awareness gold $5, Uncirculated (e) 4,477		450
2018W, Breast Cancer Awareness gold $5, Proof (e). . . . . (10,381)		450
Coin and Stamp set. Proof clad half dollar and themed First Class postage stamp.		60

e. Produced in "rose pink" gold, composed of .850 gold, .148 copper, and .002 zinc.

	Distribution	Mint Pkg
2019D, Apollo 11 50th Anniversary clad half dollar, Uncirculated **(d)**	41,748	$20
2019S, Apollo 11 50th Anniversary clad half dollar, Proof **(d)**	(181,735)	18
2019P, Apollo 11 50th Anniversary silver dollar, Uncirculated **(d)**	59,711	38
2019P, Apollo 11 50th Anniversary silver dollar, Proof **(d)**	(224,010)	40
2019P, Apollo 11 50th Anniversary 5-oz. silver dollar, Proof **(d,f)**	(68,308)	160
2019W, Apollo 11 50th Anniversary gold $5, Uncirculated **(d)**	12,035	450
2019W, Apollo 11 50th Anniversary gold $5, Proof **(d)**	(34,036)	450
Half dollar set. Uncirculated and Proof clad half dollars **(d)**		40
2019D, American Legion 100th Anniversary clad half dollar, Uncirculated	11,429	$25
2019S, American Legion 100th Anniversary clad half dollar, Proof	(27,286)	26
2019P, American Legion 100th Anniversary silver dollar, Uncirculated	13,790	40
2019P, American Legion 100th Anniversary silver dollar, Proof	(63,100)	40
2019W, American Legion 100th Anniversary gold $5, Uncirculated	2,929	450
2019W, American Legion 100th Anniversary gold $5, Proof	(10,916)	450
3-coin set. Proof clad half dollar, silver dollar **(d)**, and gold $5.		500
Silver Dollar and Medal set. Proof silver dollar **(d)** and silver American Veterans medal		50
2020D, Naismith Mem. Basketball Hall of Fame 60th Anniv. clad half dollar, Uncirculated **(d)**	13,639	20
2020S, Naismith Mem. Basketball Hall of Fame 60th Anniv. clad half dollar, Enh. Unc.	22,565	15
2020S, Naismith Mem. Basketball Hall of Fame 60th Anniv. clad half dollar, Proof **(d)**	(26,584)	18
2020S, Naismith Mem. Basketball Hall of Fame 60th Anniv. clad half dollar, Proof, Colorized **(d)**	(32,614)	50
2020P, Naismith Mem. Basketball Hall of Fame 60th Anniv. silver dollar, Uncirculated **(d)**	21,328	40
2020P, Naismith Mem. Basketball Hall of Fame 60th Anniv. silver dollar, Proof **(d)**	(68,778)	40
2020P, Naismith Mem. Basketball Hall of Fame 60th Anniv. silver dollar, Proof, Colorized **(d)**	(25,735)	75
2020W, Naismith Mem. Basketball Hall of Fame 60th Anniv. gold $5, Uncirculated **(d)**	3,263	450
2020W, Naismith Mem. Basketball Hall of Fame 60th Anniv. gold $5, Proof **(d)**	(8,075)	450
Kids set. Enhanced Uncirculated clad half dollar **(d)**		45
2020P, Women's Suffrage Centennial silver dollar, Uncirculated	12,625	35
2020P, Women's Suffrage Centennial silver dollar, Proof	(43,479)	40
Coin and Medal set. Proof silver dollar and silver medal		40
2021P, Christa McAuliffe silver dollar, Uncirculated	16,025	50
2021P, Christa McAuliffe silver dollar, Proof	(54,222)	55
2021D, National Law Enforcement Memorial and Museum clad half dollar, Uncirculated	10,171	20
2021S, National Law Enforcement Memorial and Museum clad half dollar, Proof	(27,698)	24
2021P, National Law Enforcement Memorial and Museum silver dollar, Uncirculated	9,422	50
2021P, National Law Enforcement Memorial and Museum silver dollar, Proof	(34,092)	55
2021W, National Law Enforcement Memorial and Museum gold $5, Uncirculated	1,753	450
2021W, National Law Enforcement Memorial and Museum gold $5, Proof	(5,864)	450
3-coin set. Proof clad half dollar, silver dollar **(c)**, and gold $5.		550
2022D, National Purple Heart Hall of Honor clad half dollar, Uncirculated	12,264	20
2022S, National Purple Heart Hall of Honor clad half dollar, Proof	(27,799)	24
2022W, National Purple Heart Hall of Honor silver dollar, Uncirculated	14,168	50
2022W, National Purple Heart Hall of Honor silver dollar, Proof	(53,325)	55
2022W, National Purple Heart Hall of Honor silver dollar, Proof, colorized	(24,871)	80
2022W, National Purple Heart Hall of Honor gold $5, Uncirculated	1,677	450
2022W, National Purple Heart Hall of Honor gold $5, Proof	(7,675)	450
3-coin set. Proof clad half dollar, silver dollar, and gold $5.		500

d. The obverse of each denomination is concave; the reverse is convex. **f.** Identical in design to the regular-issue dollar coin, but enlarged to 3 inches in diameter.

Chart continued on next page.

	Distribution	Mint Pkg
2022D, Negro Leagues Baseball clad half dollar, Uncirculated	*9,792*	$20
2022S, Negro Leagues Baseball clad half dollar, Proof	*(22,841)*	24
2022W, Negro Leagues Baseball silver dollar, Uncirculated	*8,445*	40
2022P, Negro Leagues Baseball silver dollar, Proof	*(37,186)*	45
2022P, Negro Leagues Baseball silver dollar, Proof, with privy mark	*(19,687)*	50
2022W, Negro Leagues Baseball gold $5, Uncirculated	*1,507*	450
2022W, Negro Leagues Baseball gold $5, Proof	*(5,357)*	450
3-coin set. Proof clad half dollar, silver dollar, and gold $5		500
Coin and medal set. Proof silver dollar and Jackie Robinson Proof silver medal		100
2024D, Greatest Generation clad half dollar, Uncirculated		
2024S, Greatest Generation clad half dollar, Proof		
2024P, Greatest Generation silver dollar, Uncirculated		
2024P, Greatest Generation silver dollar, Proof		
2024W, Greatest Generation gold $5, Uncirculated		
2024W, Greatest Generation gold $5, Proof		
3-coin set. Proof clad half dollar, silver dollar and gold $5		
2024D, Harriet Tubman Bicentennial clad half dollar, Uncirculated		
2024S, Harriet Tubman Bicentennial clad half dollar, Proof		
2024P, Harriet Tubman Bicentennial silver dollar, Uncirculated		
2024P, Harriet Tubman Bicentennial silver dollar, Proof		
2024W, Harriet Tubman Bicentennial gold $5, Uncirculated		
2024W, Harriet Tubman Bicentennial gold $5, Proof		
3-coin set. Proof clad half dollar, silver dollar and gold $5		

PROOF COINS AND SETS

Proof coins can usually be distinguished by their sharpness of detail, high wire edge, and extremely brilliant, mirrorlike surface. Proofs are sold by the Mint at a premium.

Proof coins were not struck during 1943–1949 or 1965–1967. Sets from 1936 through 1972 include the cent, nickel, dime, quarter, and half dollar; from 1973 through 1981 the dollar was also included. From 1999 on, Proof sets have included the year's multiple quarter dollars, and since 2000 they have included the Mint's golden dollar coins. *Values shown are for original unblemished sets.*

Figures in parentheses represent the total number of full sets minted.

	Mintage	Issue Price	Current Value		Mintage	Issue Price	Current Value
1936	(3,837)	$1.89	$3,000.00	1981S, Type 1	(4,063,083)	$11.00	$4.00
1937	(5,542)	1.89	1,800.00	1981S, Type 2	*	11.00	160.00
1938	(8,045)	1.89	750.00	1982S	(3,857,479)	11.00	5.00
1939	(8,795)	1.89	725.00	1983S	(3,138,765)	11.00	5.00
1940	(11,246)	1.89	700.00	1983S, Prestige set			
1941	(15,287)	1.89	700.00	(Olympic dollar)	(140,361)	59.00	25.00
1942, Both nickels	(21,120)	1.89	700.00	1984S	(2,748,430)	11.00	4.50
1942, One nickel	*	1.89	680.00	1984S, Prestige set			
1950	(51,386)	2.10	520.00	(Olympic dollar)	(316,680)	59.00	20.00
1951	(57,500)	2.10	450.00	1985S	(3,362,821)	11.00	4.50
1952	(81,980)	2.10	200.00	1986S	(2,411,180)	11.00	4.50
1953	(128,800)	2.10	160.00	1986S, Prestige set (Statue			
1954	(233,300)	2.10	80.00	of Liberty half, dollar)	(599,317)	48.50	20.00
1955, Box pack	(378,200)	2.10	75.00	1987S	(3,792,233)	11.00	3.75
1955, Flat pack	*	2.10	75.00	1987S, Prestige set			
1956	(669,384)	2.10	45.00	(Constitution dollar)	(435,495)	45.00	20.00
1957	(1,247,952)	2.10	24.00	1988S	(3,031,287)	11.00	3.75
1958	(875,652)	2.10	25.00	1988S, Prestige set			
1959	(1,149,291)	2.10	20.00	(Olympic dollar)	(231,661)	45.00	20.00
1960, With LgDt cent	(1,691,602)	2.10	20.00	1989S	(3,009,107)	11.00	3.50
1960, With SmDt cent	*	2.10	22.00	1989S, Prestige set			
1961	(3,028,244)	2.10	20.00	(Congressional half,			
1962	(3,218,019)	2.10	20.00	dollar)	(211,807)	45.00	20.00
1963	(3,075,645)	2.10	20.00	1990S	(2,793,433)	11.00	4.00
1964	(3,950,762)	2.10	20.00	1990S, With No S cent	(3,555)	11.00	3,500.00
1968S	(3,041,506)	5.00	5.00	1990S, Prestige set			
1969S	(2,934,631)	5.00	5.00	(Eisenhower dollar)	(506,126)	45.00	20.00
1970S	(2,632,810)	5.00	7.00	1990S, Prestige Set,			
1970S, With SmDt cent	*	5.00	50.00	With No S cent	*	45.00	3,500.00
1971S	(3,220,733)	5.00	3.00	1991S	(2,610,833)	11.00	4.00
1972S	(3,260,996)	5.00	3.00	1991S, Prestige set (Mt.			
1973S	(2,760,339)	7.00	7.00	Rushmore half, dollar)	(256,954)	59.00	25.00
1974S	(2,612,568)	7.00	7.00	1992S	(2,675,618)	11.00	4.00
1975S, With 1976 quarter,				1992S, Prestige set			
half, and dollar	(2,845,450)	7.00	7.50	(Olympic half, dollar)	(183,293)	56.00	22.00
1976S	(4,149,730)	7.00	7.00	1992S, Silver	(1,009,586)	21.00	12.00
1976S, 3-piece set	(3,998,621)	15.00	16.00	1992S, Silver Premier set	(308,055)	37.00	12.00
1977S	(3,251,152)	9.00	7.00	1993S	(2,409,394)	12.50	4.50
1978S	(3,127,781)	9.00	6.50	1993S, Prestige set (Bill			
1979S, Type 1	(3,677,175)	9.00	6.50	of Rights half, dollar)	(224,045)	57.00	28.00
1979S, Type 2	*	9.00	30.00	1993S, Silver	(570,213)	21.00	14.00
1980S	(3,554,806)	10.00	4.00	1993S, Silver Premier set	(191,140)	37.50	16.00

* Included in number above.

239

	Mintage	Issue Price	Current Value
1994S . . . .(2,308,701)		$12.50	$4.00
1994S, Prestige set (World			
Cup half, dollar) . . . . . . (175,893)		57.00	25.00
1994S, Silver . . . . (636,009)		21.00	14.00
1994S, Silver Premier set . (149,320)		37.50	14.00
1995S . . . .(2,010,384)		12.50	7.00
1995S, Prestige set (Civil			
War half, dollar) . . . . . . (107,112)		57.00	45.00
1995S, Silver . . . . (549,878)		21.00	25.00
1995S, Silver Premier set . (130,107)		37.50	25.00
1996S . . . .(1,695,244)		12.50	6.75
1996S, Prestige set			
(Olympic half, dollar). . . . (55,000)		57.00	125.00
1996S, Silver . . . . (623,655)		21.00	15.00
1996S, Silver Premier set . (151,366)		37.50	15.00
1997S . . . .(1,975,000)		12.50	7.00
1997S, Prestige set			
(Botanic dollar) . . . . (80,000)		48.00	30.00
1997S, Silver . . . . (605,473)		21.00	17.00
1997S, Silver Premier set . (136,205)		37.50	17.00
1998S . . . .(2,086,507)		12.50	7.00
1998S, Silver . . . . (638,134)		21.00	14.00
1998S, Silver Premier set . (240,658)		37.50	14.00
1999S, 9-pc set . . . .(2,543,401)		19.95	6.50
1999S, 5-pc qtr. set . . . . .(1,169,958)		13.95	2.50
1999S, Silver 9-pc set . . . (804,565)		31.95	50.00
2000S, 10-pc set . . . . . .(3,082,572)		19.95	6.00
2000S, 5-pc qtr set. . . . . . (937,600)		13.95	3.00
2000S, Silver 10-pc set . . (965,421)		31.95	25.00
2001S, 10-pc set . . . . . .(2,294,909)		19.95	7.00
2001S, 5-pc qtr. set. . . . . . (799,231)		13.95	3.00
2001S, Silver 10-pc set . . (889,697)		31.95	25.00
2002S, 10-pc set . . . . . .(2,319,766)		19.95	6.00
2002S, 5-pc qtr set. . . . . . (764,479)		13.95	3.50
2002S, Silver 10-pc set . . (892,229)		31.95	30.00
2003S, 10-pc set . . . . . .(2,172,684)		19.95	6.00
2003S, 5-pc qtr. set. . . . . .(1,235,832)		13.95	2.00
2003S, Silver 10-pc set .(1,125,755)		31.95	30.00
2004S, 11-pc set . . . . . .(1,789,488)		22.95	7.00
2004S, 5-pc qtr. set. . . . . (951,196)		15.95	3.00
2004S, Silver 11-pc set .(1,175,934)		37.95	28.00
2004S, Silver 5-pc qtr. set. (593,852)		23.95	18.00
2005S, 11-pc set . . . . . .(2,275,000)		22.95	6.00
2005S, 5-pc qtr. set. . . . . . (987,960)		15.95	2.00
2005S, Silver 11-pc set .(1,069,679)		37.95	25.00
2005S, Silver 5-pc qtr. set. (608,970)		23.95	20.00
2006S, 10-pc set . . . . . .(2,000,428)		22.95	6.00
2006S, 5-pc qtr. set. . . . . . (882,000)		15.95	2.00
2006S, Silver 10-pc set .(1,054,008)		37.95	30.00
2006S, Silver 5-pc qtr. set. (531,000)		23.95	18.00
2007S, 14-pc set . . . . . .(1,702,116)		26.95	10.00
2007S, 5-pc qtr set. . . . . . (672,662)		$13.95	$4.00
2007S, 4-pc Pres set . .(1,285,972)		14.95	4.25
2007S, Silver 14-pc set . . (875,050)		44.95	35.00
2007S, Silver 5-pc qtr. set. (672,662)		25.95	18.00
2008S, 14-pc set . . . . . .(1,382,017)		26.95	20.00
2008S, 5-pc qtr. set. . . . . . (672,438)		13.95	8.00
2008S, 4-pc Pres set . . . . (836,730)		14.95	6.00
2008S, Silver 14-pc set . . (763,887)		44.95	30.00
2008S, Silver 5-pc qtr. set. (429,021)		25.95	18.00
2009S, 18-pc set . . . . . .(1,477,967)		29.95	20.00
2009S, 6-pc qtr. set. . . . . . (635,423)		14.95	4.00
2009S, 4-pc Pres set . . . . (627,925)		14.95	5.00
2009S, Silver 18-pc set . . (694,406)		52.95	32.00
2009S, Silver 6-pc qtr. set. (299,164)		29.95	21.00
2009S, 4-pc Lincoln			
Bicentennial set . . . . . . (200,000)		7.95	5.00
2010S, 14-pc set . . . . . .(1,103,950)		31.95	24.00
2010S, 5-pc qtr. set. . . . . . (276,335)		14.95	7.00
2010S, 4-pc Pres set . . . . (535,463)		15.95	7.00
2010S, Silver 14-pc set . . (585,414)		56.95	28.00
2010S, Silver 5-pc qtr. set. (274,003)		32.95	18.00
2011S, 14-pc set . . . . . .(1,098,835)		31.95	22.00
2011S, 5-pc qtr. set. . . . . . (152,302)		14.95	8.00
2011S, 4-pc Pres set . . . . (299,853)		19.95	16.00
2011S, Silver 14-pc set . . (574,175)		67.95	35.00
2011S, Silver 5-pc qtr. set. (147,901)		39.95	20.00
2012S, 14-pc set . . . . (794,002)		31.95	55.00
2012S, 5-pc qtr. set. . . . . . (148,498)		14.95	8.00
2012S, 4-pc Pres set . . . . (249,298)		18.95	30.00
2012S, Silver 14-pc set . . (395,443)		67.95	75.00
2012S, Silver 8-pc			
Limited Edition set . . . . . (50,169)		149.95	100.00
2012S, Silver 5-pc qtr. set. (162,448)		41.95	20.00
2013S, 14-pc set . . . . (802,460)		31.95	24.00
2013S, 5-pc qtr. set. . . . . . (128,377)		14.95	7.00
2013S, 4-pc Pres set . . . . (266,618)		18.95	7.00
2013S, Silver 14-pc set . . (419,720)		67.95	40.00
2013S, Silver 8-pc			
Limited Edition set . . . . . (47,971)		139.95	65.00
2013S, Silver 5-pc qtr. set. (138,451)		41.95	20.00
2014S, 14-pc set . . . . (714,661)		31.95	24.00
2014S, 5-pc qtr. set. . . . . . (115,179)		14.95	9.00
2014S, 4-pc Pres set . . . . (229,415)		18.95	8.00
2014S, Silver 14-pc set . . (429,493)		67.95	38.00
2014S, Silver 8-pc			
Limited Edition set . . . . . (42,614)		139.95	85.00
2014S, Silver 5-pc qtr. set. (119,251)		41.95	20.00
2015S, 14-pc set . . . . (662,854)		32.95	25.00
2015S, 5-pc qtr. set. . . . . . (99,466)		14.95	7.00
2015S, 4-pc Pres set . . . . (222,068)		18.95	8.00
2015S, Silver 14-pc set . . (387,310)		53.95	40.00

PROOF AND MINT SETS

Year	Mintage	Issue Price	Current Value
2015S, Silver 5-pc qtr set . .	(103,311)	$31.95	$20
2016S, 13-piece set	(595,184)	31.95	40
2016S, 5-piece qtr set	(91,674)	14.95	7
2016S, 3-piece Pres set . .	(231,549)	17.95	8
2016S, Silver 13-pc set . .	(369,849)	52.95	45
2016S, Silver 5-pc qtr set . .	(95,709)	31.95	19
2016S, Silver 8-pc Limited Edition set, with 2016W American Silver Eagle . . .	(49,647)	139.95	85
2017S, 10-piece set	(568,678)	31.95	28
2017S, 5-piece qtr set	(88,909)	14.95	8
2017S, Silver 10-pc set . .	(358,085)	52.95	38
2017S, Silver 5-pc qtr set . .	(89,632)	31.95	20
2017S, Silver 8-piece Limited Edition set	(48,901)	139.95	100
2018S, 10-piece set	(517,053)	27.95	25
2018S, 5-piece qtr set	(86,694)	15.95	10
2018S, Silver 10-pc set . .	(332,268)	49.95	30
2018S, Silver 5-pc qtr set . .	(79,300)	33.95	20
2018S, 50th Anniv silver 10-piece RevPf set	(199,116)	54.95	52
2018S, Silver 8-piece Limited Edition set	(49,480)	144.95	115
2019S, 10-piece set, plus 2019W Proof cent	(601,327)	27.95	30
2019S, 5-piece qtr set	(84,120)	15.95	12
2019S, 4-piece American Innovation dollar set . .	(147,454)	20.95	17
2019S, Silver 10-pc set, plus 2019W RevPf cent	(412,708)	54.95	50
2019S, Silver 5-pc qtr set . .	(78,585)	36.95	25
2019S, Silver 8-piece Limited Edition set	(48,417)	149.95	120
2020S, 10-piece set, Plus 2020W Proof nickel . . .	(464,658)	32.00	40
2020S, 5-piece quarter set	(64,242)	18.50	8
2020S, 4-piece American Innovation dollar set . .	(107,052)	24.00	17
2020S, Silver 10-piece set, Plus 2020W Reverse Proof nickel	(313,183)	63.25	100
2020S, Silver 5-pc qtr set . .	(64,012)	$42.50	$45
2020S, Silver 8-piece Limited Edition set	(50,061)	201.00	180
2021S, 7-piece set	(512,729)	32.00	25
2021S, 4-piece American Innovation dollar set . . .	(84,604)	24.00	17
2021S, 4-piece American Innovation dollar RevPf set	(49,541)	28.00	22
2021S, Silver 7-piece set	(301,611)	105.00	80
2021S, Silver 6-piece Limited Edition set	(48,712)	235.00	200
2022S, 10-piece set	(400,007)	32.00	22
2022S, 5-piece quarter set	(42,821)	21.00	15
2022S, 4-piece American Innovation dollar set . . .	(77,766)	24.00	17
2022S, 4-piece American Innovation dollar RevPf set	(49,478)	28.00	22
2022S, Silver 10-piece set	(246,170)	105.00	85
2022S, Silver 5-piece qtr set	(57,681)	73.00	50
2022S, Silver 8-piece Limited Edition set	(48,983)	201.00	150
2023S, 10-piece set		35.00	25
2023S, 5-piece quarter set		23.00	14
2023S, 4-piece American Innovation dollar set		24.00	
2023S, 4-piece American Innovation dollar RevPf set		28.00	
2023S, Silver 10-piece set . .		130.00	
2023S, Silver 5-piece quarter set . .		80.00	
2023S, Silver 8-piece Limited Edition set		220.00	
2024S, 10-piece set		35.00	
2024S, 5-piece quarter set		23.00	
2024S, 4-piece American Innovation dollar set			
2024S, 4-piece American Innovation dollar RevPf set			
2024S, Silver 10-piece set			
2024S, Silver 5-piece quarter set . .		80.00	
2024S, Silver 8-piece Limited Edition set		220.00	

UNCIRCULATED MINT SETS

Official Mint Sets are specially packaged by the government for sale to collectors. They contain Uncirculated specimens of each year's coins for every denomination issued from each mint. Sets from 1947 through 1958 contain two examples of each regular-issue coin. No official sets were produced in 1950, 1982, or 1983. Privately assembled sets are valued according to individual coin prices. Only official sets are included in the following list. Unlike the Proof sets, these are normal coins intended for circulation and are not minted with any special consideration for quality. From

1942 to 1946, groups of two coins from each mint were sold in a cloth shipping bag with only minimal protection. Very few of those mailing packages were saved by collectors.

	Mintage	Issue Price	Current Value
1947 P-D-S	5,000	$4.87	$1,000.00
1948 P-D-S	6,000	4.92	750.00
1949 P-D-S	5,000	5.45	900.00
1951 P-D-S	8,654	6.75	700.00
1952 P-D-S	11,499	6.14	650.00
1953 P-D-S	15,538	6.14	525.00
1954 P-D-S	25,599	6.19	290.00
1955 P-D-S	49,656	3.57	225.00
1956 P-D	45,475	3.34	225.00
1957 P-D	34,324	4.40	225.00
1958 P-D	50,314	4.43	150.00
1959 P-D	187,000	2.40	35.00
1960 P-D	260,485	2.40	30.00
1961 P-D	223,704	2.40	30.00
1962 P-D	385,285	2.40	30.00
1963 P-D	606,612	2.40	30.00
1964 P-D	1,008,108	2.40	30.00
1965*	2,360,000	4.00	9.00
1966*	2,261,583	4.00	7.00
1967*	1,863,344	4.00	8.00
1968 P-D-S	2,105,128	2.50	4.00
1969 P-D-S	1,817,392	2.50	4.00
1970 P-D-S	2,038,134	2.50	10.00
1971 P-D-S	2,193,396	3.50	3.00
1972 P-D-S	2,750,000	3.50	3.00
1973 P-D-S	1,767,691	6.00	9.00
1974 P-D-S	1,975,981	6.00	8.00
1975 P-D	1,921,488	6.00	8.00
1776–1976, 3-piece set	4,908,319	9.00	12.00
1976 P-D	1,892,513	6.00	8.00
1977 P-D	2,006,869	7.00	8.00
1978 P-D	2,162,609	7.00	8.00
1979 P-D	2,526,000	8.00	5.00
1980 P-D-S	2,815,066	9.00	5.00
1981 P-D-S	2,908,145	11.00	5.50
1984 P-D	1,832,857	7.00	2.50
1985 P-D	1,710,571	7.00	2.50
1986 P-D	1,153,536	7.00	5.00
1987 P-D	2,890,758	7.00	3.25
1988 P-D	1,646,204	7.00	3.00
1989 P-D	1,987,915	7.00	2.50

	Mintage	Issue Price	Current Value
1990 P-D	1,809,184	$7.00	$2.50
1991 P-D	1,352,101	7.00	2.50
1992 P-D	1,500,143	7.00	3.00
1993 P-D	1,297,431	8.00	3.00
1994 P-D	1,234,813	8.00	2.50
1995 P-D	1,038,787	8.00	3.00
1996 P-D, Plus 1996W dime	1,457,949	8.00	10.00
1997 P-D	950,473	8.00	4.00
1998 P-D	1,187,325	8.00	3.00
1999 P-D (18 pieces)	1,243,867	14.95	5.00
2000 P-D (20 pieces)	1,490,160	14.95	7.50
2001 P-D (20 pieces)	1,116,915	14.95	7.50
2002 P-D (20 pieces)	1,139,388	14.95	7.50
2003 P-D (20 pieces)	1,001,532	14.95	7.50
2004 P-D (22 pieces)	842,507	16.95	7.50
2005 P-D (22 pieces)	1,160,000	16.95	7.50
2006 P-D (20 pieces)	847,361	16.95	7.50
2007 P-D (28 pieces)	895,628	22.95	16.00
2008 P-D (28 pieces)	745,464	22.95	18.00
2009 P-D (36 pieces)	774,844	27.95	16.00
2010 P-D (28 pieces)	583,912	31.95	16.00
2011 P-D (28 pieces)	533,529	31.95	16.00
2012 P-D (28 pieces)	392,224	27.95	40.00
2013 P-D (28 pieces)	376,844	27.95	22.00
2014 P-D (28 pieces)	345,813	27.95	20.00
2015 P-D (28 pieces)	314,029	28.95	18.00
2016 P-D (28 pieces)	296,582	28.95	24.00
2017 P-D (28 pieces)	286,813	26.95	18.00
2017S, 225th Anniversary Enhanced Uncirculated Set (10 pieces)	210,419	29.95	15.00
2018 P-D (20 pieces)	257,531	20.95	22.00
2019 P-D (20 pieces), Plus 2019W cent	346,117	21.95	25.00
2020 P-D (20 pieces) (a)	211,787	25.25	15.00
2021 P-D (14 pieces)	226,410	25.25	15.00
2022 P-D (20 pieces)	245,234	25.25	25.00
2023 P-D (20 pieces)		29.00	18.00
2024 P-D (20 pieces)		29.00	18.00

Note: Sets issued from 2005 to 2010 have a special Satin Finish that is somewhat different from the finish on Uncirculated coins made for general circulation. * Special Mint Set. **a.** An Uncirculated nickel from the West Point Mint was intended to be a premium for the 2020 Mint Set, but was canceled due to COVID-19.

OTHER COLLECTIBLE SETS

Mint Pkg

(2000) Millennium Coin and Currency Set
3-piece set. Uncirculated Sacagawea dollar, Uncirculated American Silver Eagle bullion coin, and $1 Federal Reserve Note $40

PROOF AND **MINT SETS**

	Mint Pkg

(2003) Legacies of Freedom™
Uncirculated American Silver Eagle bullion coin and Uncirculated 2002 £2 Silver Britannia coin $45

(2004) Westward Journey Nickel Series™
Proof Sacagawea dollar, two 2004 Proof nickels, and silver-plated Peace Medal replica. 30

(2005) Westward Journey Nickel Series™
Proof Sacagawea dollar, two 2005 Proof nickels, and silver-plated Peace Medal replica. 30

(2009) Abraham Lincoln Coin and Chronicles
Proof Abraham Lincoln commemorative silver dollar, four copper Proof Lincoln cents, reproduction
portrait of Abraham Lincoln, and replica of handwritten Gettysburg Address. 28

(2013) Theodore Roosevelt Coin and Chronicles
Uncirculated Presidential dollar, silver Presidential medal, National Wildlife Refuge System
Centennial bronze medal, and Roosevelt print. 90

(2014) Franklin D. Roosevelt Coin and Chronicles
Proof dime and Presidential dollar, bronze Presidential medal, silver Presidential medal,
four themed postage stamps (1¢, 2¢, 3¢, 5¢), and companion booklet. 40

(2014) American $1 Coin and Currency Set
2014D Native American – Native Hospitality Enhanced Uncirculated dollar and
$1 Federal Reserve Note. 35

(2015) Harry S. Truman Coin and Chronicles
Reverse Proof Presidential dollar, silver Presidential medal, 1973 Truman 8¢ postage stamp,
and information booklet. 150

(2015) Dwight D. Eisenhower Coin and Chronicles
Reverse Proof Presidential dollar, silver Presidential medal, 1969 Eisenhower 6¢ postage stamp,
and information booklet. 105

(2015) John F. Kennedy Coin and Chronicles
Reverse Proof Presidential dollar, silver Presidential medal, 1964 Kennedy 5¢ postage stamp,
and information booklet. 40

(2015) Lyndon B. Johnson Coin and Chronicles
Reverse Proof Presidential dollar, silver Presidential medal, 1973 Johnson 8¢ postage stamp,
and information booklet. 40

(2015) American $1 Coin and Currency Set
2015W Native American – Mohawk Ironworkers Enhanced Uncirculated dollar and
$1 Federal Reserve Note. 10

(2016) Ronald Reagan Coin and Chronicles
Reverse Proof Presidential dollar, Proof American Silver Eagle, bronze Ronald and Nancy Reagan
medal, engraved Ronald Reagan Presidential portrait, and information booklet. 50

(2016) American $1 Coin and Currency Set
2016S Native American – Code Talkers Enhanced Uncirculated dollar and $1 Federal Reserve Note . . . 10

(2019) American $1 Coin and Currency Set
2019W Native American – American Indians in Space Enhanced Uncirculated dollar and
$1 Federal Reserve Note. . . . .

(2019) Youth Coin and Currency Set
Five Proof America the Beautiful quarters and $2 Federal Reserve Note . . . .

(2021) George Herbert Walker Bush Coin and Chronicles
Reverse Proof Presidential dollar, silver Presidential medal, 2019 George H.W. Bush "forever"
postage stamp, Barbara Bush bronze medal, and information booklet . . . .

AMERICA THE BEAUTIFUL™ SILVER BULLION COINS

Weight and purity incused on edge
Actual size 3 inches.

	Mintage	MS	SP
25¢ 2010(P), Hot Springs (AR)	33,000	$140	
25¢ 2010P, Hot Springs (AR)	. . . . .(26,788)		$160
25¢ 2010(P), Yellowstone (WY)	33,000	140	
25¢ 2010P, Yellowstone (WY)	. . . .(26,711)		160
25¢ 2010(P), Yosemite (CA)	33,000	140	
25¢ 2010P, Yosemite (CA)	. . . .(26,716)		160
25¢ 2010(P), Grand Canyon (AZ)	. .33,000	140	
25¢ 2010P, Grand Canyon (AZ)	. . .(25,967)		160
25¢ 2010(P), Mount Hood (OR)	33,000	140	
25¢ 2010P, Mount Hood (OR)	. . . .(26,637)		160
25¢ 2011P, Gettysburg (PA)	126,700	140	
25¢ 2011(P), Gettysburg (PA).	. . . . (24,625)		160
25¢ 2011(P), Glacier (MT)	126,700	140	
25¢ 2011P, Glacier (MT)	. . . .(20,856)		160
25¢ 2011(P), Olympic (WA)	104,900	140	
25¢ 2011P, Olympic (WA)	. . . .(18,398)		160
25¢ 2011(P), Vicksburg (MS)	58,100	140	
25¢ 2011P, Vicksburg (MS)	. . . . . .(18,594)		160
25¢ 2011(P), Chickasaw (OK)	48,700	140	
25¢ 2011P, Chickasaw (OK)	. . . . .(16,827)		160
25¢ 2012(P), El Yunque (PR)	24,000	140	
25¢ 2012P, El Yunque (PR)	. . . . . .(17,314)		165
25¢ 2012(P), Chaco (NM)	24,400	140	
25¢ 2012P, Chaco (NM)	. . . .(17,146)		165
25¢ 2012(P), Acadia (ME)	25,400	140	
25¢ 2012P, Acadia (ME)	. . . .(14,978)		160
25¢ 2012(P), Hawai'i Volcanoes (HI)	20,000	200	
25¢ 2012P, Hawai'i Volcanoes (HI)	. . . .(14,863)		240
25¢ 2012(P), Denali (AK)	20,000	140	
25¢ 2012P, Denali (AK)	. . . .(15,225)		170
25¢ 2013(P), White Mountain (NH)	35,000	140	
25¢ 2013P, White Mountain (NH)	. . . .(20,530)		160
25¢ 2013(P), Perry's Victory (OH)	30,000	140	
25¢ 2013P, Perry's Victory (OH)	. .(17,707)		$160
25¢ 2013(P), Great Basin (NV)	30,000	$140	
25¢ 2013P, Great Basin (NV)	. . . . .(17,792)		160
25¢ 2013(P), Ft McHenry (MD)	30,000	140	
25¢ 2013P, Ft McHenry (MD)	. . . .(19,802)		160
25¢ 2013(P), Mt Rush (SD)	35,000	140	
25¢ 2013P, Mt Rush (SD)	. . . . . .(23,547)		160
25¢ 2014(P), Smky Mtns (TN)	33,000	140	
25¢ 2014P, Smky Mtns (TN)	. . . . .(24,710)		160
25¢ 2014(P), Shenand (VA)	25,000	140	
25¢ 2014P, Shenand (VA)	. . . .(28,276)		160
25¢ 2014(P), Arches (UT)	22,000	140	
25¢ 2014P, Arches (UT)	. . . .(28,183)		160
25¢ 2014(P), Sand Dunes (CO)	22,000	140	
25¢ 2014P, Sand Dunes (CO)	. . . .(24,103)		160
25¢ 2014(P), Everglades (FL)	34,000	140	
25¢ 2014P, Everglades (FL)	. . . . . .(19,772)		160
25¢ 2015(P), Homestead (NE)	35,000	140	
25¢ 2015P, Homestead (NE)	. . . . .(21,286)		160
25¢ 2015(P), Kisatchie (LA)	42,000	140	
25¢ 2015P, Kisatchie (LA)	. . . .(19,449)		160
25¢ 2015(P), Blue Ridge (NC)	45,000	140	
25¢ 2015P, Blue Ridge (NC)	. . . . .(17,461)		160
25¢ 2015(P), Bombay Hk (DE)	45,000	140	
25¢ 2015P, Bombay Hk (DE)	. . . . .(17,309)		160
25¢ 2015(P), Saratoga (NY)	45,000	140	
25¢ 2015P, Saratoga (NY)	. . . .(17,563)		160
25¢ 2016(P), Shawnee (IL)	 105,000	140	
25¢ 2016P, Shawnee (IL)	. . . . . . (18,781)		160
25¢ 2016(P), Cumberland (KY)	. . . 75,000	140	
25¢ 2016P, Cumberland (KY)	. . . (18,713)		160
25¢ 2016(P), Harpers Ferry (WV)	. . 75,000	140	
25¢ 2016P, Harpers Ferry (WV)	. . (18,896)		160
25¢ 2016(P), T. Roosevelt (ND)	. . . 40,000	140	
25¢ 2016P, T. Roosevelt (ND)	. . . (18,917)		160
25¢ 2016(P), Fort Moultrie (SC)	. . . 35,000	140	
25¢ 2016P, Fort Moultrie (SC)	. . . (17,882)		160

Note: The U.S. Mint produces the America the Beautiful™ 5-oz. silver coins in bullion and numismatic versions. The bullion version, which lacks the P mintmark, has a brilliant Uncirculated finish and is sold only through dealers. The numismatic version, with the P mintmark, has a matte or burnished finish (although it is not marketed by the Mint as "Burnished"). These coins, designated Specimens (SP) by grading services, are sold directly to the public.

	Mintage	MS	SP		Mintage	MS	SP
25¢ 2017(P), Effigy (IA)	35,000	$140		25¢ 2019(P), Am. Mem. (NMI) . .	80,000	$140	
25¢ 2017P, Effigy (IA)	(17,251)		$160	25¢ 2019P, Am. Mem. (NMI) . .	(16,287)		$160
25¢ 2017(P), Douglass (DC)	20,000	140		25¢ 2019(P), War in			
25¢ 2017P, Douglass (DC).	(17,678)		160	the Pacific (Guam)	72,500	140	
25¢ 2017(P), Ozark (MO).	20,000	140		25¢ 2019P, War in			
25¢ 2017P, Ozark (MO)	(17,694)		160	the Pacific (Guam)	(16,277)		160
25¢ 2017(P), Ellis Island (NJ) . . .	40,000	140		25¢ 2019(P), Church (ID)	25,000	140	
25¢ 2017(P), Ellis Island (NJ). . . .	(17,670)		160	25¢ 2019(P), Church (ID)	(16,310)		160
25¢ 2017P, G.R. Clark (IN)	35,000	140		25¢ 2019(P), San Antonio (TX). .	55,200	140	
25¢ 2017P, G.R. Clark (IN).	(14,731)		160	25¢ 2019P, San Antonio (TX). .	(16,211)		160
25¢ 2018(P), Pictured Rocks (MI). .	30,000	140		25¢ 2020P, Am. Samoa (AS) . . .	45,000	140	
25¢ 2018P, Pictured Rocks (MI)	(17,773)		160	25¢ 2020P, Am. Samoa (AS) .	(15,781)		160
25¢ 2018(P), Apostle (WI)	30,000	140		25¢ 2020(P), Weir Farm (CT) . . .	45,000	140	
25¢ 2018(P), Apostle (WI)	(16,802)		160	25¢ 2020(P), Weir Farm (CT) . . .	(15,326)		160
25¢ 2018(P), Voyageurs (MN) . . .	30,000	140		25¢ 2020P, Salt Riv. Bay (USVI) . . .	45,000	140	
25¢ 2018(P), Voyageurs (MN) . . .	(16,839)		160	25¢ 2020(P), Salt Riv. Bay (USVI)	(13,566)		160
25¢ 2018(P), Cumberland (GA) . .	52,500	140		25¢ 2020P, Marsh (VT)	45,000	140	
25¢ 2018(P), Cumberland (GA) . .	(16,376)		160	25¢ 2020P, Marsh (VT)	(13,544)		160
25¢ 2018(P), Block Island (RI) . .	80,000	140		25¢ 2020(P), Tallgrass (KS)	45,000	140	
25¢ 2018(P), Block Island (RI). . .	(15,912)		160	25¢ 2020(P), Tallgrass (KS) . . .	(13,613)		160
25¢ 2019(P), Lowell (MA)	80,000	140		25¢ 2021P, Tuskegee (AL).	52,900	140	
25¢ 2019P, Lowell (MA)	(16,644)		160	25¢ 2021(P), Tuskegee (AL). . .	(19,815)		160

Note: The U.S. Mint produced the America the Beautiful™ 5-oz. silver coins in bullion and numismatic versions. The bullion version, which lacks the P mintmark, has a brilliant Uncirculated finish and was sold only through dealers. The numismatic version, with the P mintmark, has a matte or burnished finish (although it was not marketed by the Mint as "Burnished"). These coins, designated Specimens (SP) by grading services, were sold directly to the public.

$1 AMERICAN SILVER EAGLE COINS

Values below are based on spot silver value of $25 per ounce.

Reverse, 1986–2021.   **Reverse, 2021 to date.**

See next page for chart.

	Mintage	Unc.	PF
$1 1986	5,393,005	$55	
$1 1986S	(1,446,778)		$65
$1 1987	11,442,335	29	
$1 1987S	(904,732)		65
$1 1988	5,004,646	26	
$1 1988S	(557,370)		65
$1 1989	5,203,327	26	
$1 1989S	(617,694)		65
$1 1990	5,840,110	30	
$1 1990S	(695,510)		65
$1 1991	7,191,066	26	
$1 1991S	(511,925)		65
$1 1992	5,540,068	26	
$1 1992S	(498,654)		65
$1 1993	6,763,762	26	
$1 1993P	(405,913)		68
$1 1994	4,227,319	60	
$1 1994P	(372,168)		90
$1 1995	4,672,051	31	
$1 1995P	(438,511)	38	65
$1 1995W	(30,125)		2,500
$1 1996	3,603,386	50	
$1 1996P	(500,000)		65
$1 1997	4,295,004	26	
$1 1997P	(435,368)		65
$1 1998	4,847,549	26	
$1 1998P	(450,000)		65
$1 1999	7,408,640	31	
$1 1999P	(549,769)		65
$1 2000(W)	9,239,132	26	
$1 2000P	(600,000)		65
$1 2001(W)	9,001,711	26	
$1 2001W	(746,398)		65
$1 2002(W)	10,539,026	26	
$1 2002W	(647,342)		65
$1 2003(W)	8,495,008	26	
$1 2003W	(747,831)		65
$1 2004(W)	8,882,754	26	
$1 2004W	(801,602)		65
$1 2005(W)	8,891,025	26	
$1 2005W	(816,663)		65
$1 2006(W)	10,676,522	26	
$1 2006W, Burnished	468,020	35	
$1 2006W	(1,092,477)		65
$1 2006P, Reverse Proof	(248,875)		70
$1 2007(W)	9,028,036	26	
$1 2007W, Burnished	621,333	35	
$1 2007W	(821,759)		65
$1 2008(W)	20,583,000	$26	
$1 2008W, Burnished	533,757	35	
$1 2008W, Burnished, Reverse of 2007	47,000	300	
$1 2008W	(700,979)		$65
$1 2009(W) (a)	30,459,000	26	
$1 2010(W)	34,764,500	26	
$1 2010W	(849,861)		$65
$1 2011(W)(S)	40,020,000	29	
$1 2011W, Burnished	409,927	35	
$1 2011W	(947,355)		65
$1 2011S, Burnished	99,882	100	
$1 2011P, Reverse Proof	(99,882)		140
$1 2012(W)(S)	33,121,500	26	
$1 2012W, Burnished	226,120	35	
$1 2012W	(869,386)		65
$1 2012S	(285,184)		65
$1 2012S, Reverse Proof	(224,981)		70
$1 2013(W)(S)	42,675,000	26	
$1 2013W, Burnished	222,091	35	
$1 2013W, Enh. Unc.	235,689	85	
$1 2013W	(934,812)		65
$1 2013W, Reverse Proof	(235,689)		65
$1 2014(W)(S)	44,006,000	26	
$1 2014W, Burnished	253,169	35	
$1 2014W	(944,770)		65
$1 2015(W)(P)(S)	47,000,000	26	
$1 2015W, Burnished	201,188	35	
$1 2015W	(707,518)		65
$1 2016(W)(S)	37,701,500	26	
$1 2016W, Burnished	216,501	35	
$1 2016W	(651,453)		65
$1 2017(W)(S)	18,065,500	26	
$1 2017W, Burnished	176,739	35	
$1 2017W	(440,596)		65
$1 2017S	(123,799)		65
$1 2018(W)(S)	15,700,000	26	
$1 2018W, Burnished	138,947	35	
$1 2018W	(430,053)		65
$1 2018S	(197,005)		65
$1 2019(W)	14,863,500	27	
$1 2019W, Burnished	141,030	35	
$1 2019W	(406,924)		65
$1 2019W, Enh. RevPf	(99,675)		75
$1 2019S	(200,696)		65
$1 2019S, Enh. RevPf	(29,909)		800
$1 2020(W)(S)	30,089,500	26	
$1 2020W	154,863	35	

Note: "Burnished" refers to special American Eagle Uncirculated coins in silver, gold, and platinum sold directly by the U.S. Mint. Similar in appearance to ordinary Uncirculated American Eagle bullion coins, these coins can be distinguished by the presence of a mintmark and the use of burnished coin blanks. (Proof coins also have a mintmark but have highly reflective, mirrorlike surfaces.) **a.** No Proof dollars were made in 2009. Beware of alterations made privately outside the Mint.

SILVER BULLION

	Mintage	Unc.	PF
$1 2020W, 75th Anniversary of the End of WWII (with privy mark) . . . . *(74,709)*			$260
$1 2020W . . . . *(414,182)*			65
$1 2020S . . . . *(266,537)*			65
$1 2021(W), Her. Eagle . . . *28,275,000*		$26	
$1 2021W, Her. Eagle . . . . . *(416,044)*			65
$1 2021W, Her. Eagle, RevPf.			100
$1 2021(W)(S), Flying Eagle.		26	
$1 2021W, Flying Eagle, Burnished *154,861*		35	
$1 2021W, Flying Eagle. . . . *(434,488)*			65
$1 2021S, Flying Eagle . . . . *(225,661)*			65

	Mintage	Unc.	PF
$1 2021S, Flying Eagle, RevPf.			$95
$1 2022(W)(S) *16,000,000*		$26	
$1 2022W, Burnished *187,430*		35	
$1 2022W . . . . *(690,943)*			65
$1 2022S . . . . *(365,681)*			65
$1 2023(W)(S)		26	
$1 2023W, Burnished *199,533*		35	
$1 2023W			65
$1 2023S			65
$1 2024(W)(S)		26	
$1 2024W, Burnished		35	
$1 2024W			65
$1 2024S			65

Note: "Burnished" refers to special American Eagle Uncirculated coins in silver, gold, and platinum sold directly by the U.S. Mint. Similar in appearance to ordinary Uncirculated American Eagle bullion coins, these coins can be distinguished by the presence of a mintmark and the use of burnished coin blanks. (Proof coins also have a mintmark but have highly reflective, mirrorlike surfaces.)

American Silver Eagle Sets

1997 Impressions of Liberty Set	$3,850
2006 20th Anniversary Silver Coin Set. Uncirculated, Proof, Reverse Proof	180
2006 20th Anniversary 1-oz. Gold- and Silver-Dollar Set. Uncirculated	2,100
2011 25th Anniversary Five-Coin Set. 2011W Unc., Pf; 2011P RevPf; 2011S Unc.; 2011 Bullion.	500
2012 75th Anniversary of San Francisco Mint Two-Piece Set. S-Mint Pf and RevPf silver dollars	140
2013 75th Anniversary of West Point Depository Two-Coin Set. W-Mint Enhanced Uncirculated and Reverse Proof silver dollars	200
2019 Pride of Two Nations Limited Edition Two-Coin Set. W-Mint Enhanced Reverse Proof and Royal Canadian Mint Silver Maple Leaf modified Proof	140
2021 Reverse Proof Two-Coin Set. W-Mint, Heraldic Eagle, and S-Mint, Flying Eagle, Reverse Proof silver dollars.	160

AMERICAN GOLD EAGLE COINS

Bullion values are based on spot gold at $2,000 per ounce.

Reverse,
1986–2021.

Reverse,
2021 to date.

$5 Tenth-Ounce Gold

	Mintage	Unc.	PF		Mintage	Unc.	PF
$5 MCMLXXXVI (1986).....	912,609	$210		$5 2005W	(49,265)		$235
$5 MCMLXXXVII (1987)	580,266	205		$5 2006	285,006	$205	
$5 MCMLXXXVIII (1988)....	159,500	210		$5 2006W, Burnished	20,643	220	
$5 MCMLXXXVIII (1988)P..	(143,881)		$235	$5 2006W	(47,277)		235
$5 MCMLXXXIX (1989).....	264,790	205		$5 2007	190,010	205	
$5 MCMLXXXIX (1989)P....	(84,647)		235	$5 2007W, Burnished	22,501	210	
$5 MCMXC (1990).......	210,210	205		$5 2007W	(58,553)		235
$5 MCMXC (1990)P.......	(99,349)		235	$5 2008	305,000	205	
$5 MCMXCI (1991)	165,200	210		$5 2008W, Burnished	12,657	250	
$5 MCMXCI (1991)P	(70,334)		235	$5 2008W	(28,116)		235
$5 1992	209,300	205		$5 2009	270,000	205	
$5 1992P	(64,874)		235	$5 2010	435,000	205	
$5 1993	210,709	205		$5 2010W	(54,285)		235
$5 1993P	(58,649)		235	$5 2011	350,000	205	
$5 1994	206,380	205		$5 2011W	(42,697)		235
$5 1994W	(62,849)		235	$5 2012	290,000	205	
$5 1995	223,025	205		$5 2012W	(20,637)		235
$5 1995W	(62,667)		235	$5 2013	555,000	205	
$5 1996	401,964	205		$5 2013W	(21,738)		235
$5 1996W	(57,047)		235	$5 2014	545,000	205	
$5 1997	528,266	205		$5 2014W	(22,725)		235
$5 1997W	(34,977)		235	$5 2015	980,000	205	
$5 1998	1,344,520	205		$5 2015W	(26,769)		235
$5 1998W	(39,395)		235	$5 2016	925,000	205	
$5 1999	2,750,338	205		$5 2016W	(38,889)		235
$5 1999W, Unc. Made from				$5 2017	395,000	205	
unpolished Proof dies.....	14,500	500		$5 2017W	(20,974)		235
$5 1999W	(48,428)		235	$5 2018	230,000	205	
$5 2000	569,153	205		$5 2018W	(22,155)		235
$5 2000W	(49,971)		235	$5 2019	195,000	205	
$5 2001	269,147	205		$5 2019W	(19,612)		235
$5 2001W	(37,530)		235	$5 2020	350,000	205	
$5 2002	230,027	205		$5 2020W	(24,033)		235
$5 2002W	(40,864)		235	$5 2021, Family of Eagles.	490,000	205	
$5 2003	245,029	205		$5 2021W, Family of Eagles.	(20,062)		235
$5 2003W	(40,027)		235	$5 2021, Head of Eagle..........		205	
$5 2004	250,016	205		$5 2021W, Head of Eagle..	(26,342)		235
$5 2004W	(35,131)		235	$5 2022	575,000	205	
$5 2005	300,043	190		$5 2022W	(23,712)		235

GOLD BULLION

	Mintage	Unc.	PF
$5 2023		$205	
$5 2023W	(22,821)		$235

	Mintage	Unc.	PF
$5 2024		$205	
$5 2024W			$235

$10 Quarter-Ounce Gold

	Mintage	Unc.	PF
$10 MCMLXXXVI (1986). . . .	726,031	$510	
$10 MCMLXXXVII (1987) . . .	269,255	510	
$10 MCMLXXXVIII (1988). . . .	49,000	1,200	
$10 MCMLXXXVIII (1988)P. .	(98,028)		$625
$10 MCMLXXXIX (1989).	81,789	1,200	
$10 MCMLXXXIX (1989)P. . .	(54,170)		625
$10 MCMXC (1990).	41,000	1,500	
$10 MCMXC (1990)P.	(62,674)		625
$10 MCMXCI (1991)	36,100	1,500	
$10 MCMXCI (1991)P	(50,839)		625
$10 1992	59,546	950	
$10 1992P	(46,269)		625
$10 1993	71,864	950	
$10 1993P	(46,464)		625
$10 1994	72,650	950	
$10 1994W	(48,172)		625
$10 1995	83,752	950	
$10 1995W	(47,526)		625
$10 1996	60,318	950	
$10 1996W	(38,219)		625
$10 1997	108,805	510	
$10 1997W	(29,805)		625
$10 1998	309,829	510	
$10 1998W	(29,503)		625
$10 1999	564,232	510	
$10 1999W, Unc. Made from unpolished Proof dies	10,000	850	
$10 1999W	(34,417)		625
$10 2000	128,964	510	
$10 2000W	(36,036)		625
$10 2001	71,280	900	
$10 2001W	(25,613)		625
$10 2002	62,027	510	
$10 2002W	(29,242)		625
$10 2003	74,029	510	
$10 2003W	(30,292)		625
$10 2004	72,014	510	
$10 2004W	(28,839)		625
$10 2005	72,015	510	
$10 2005W	(37,207)		625
$10 2006	60,004	510	
$10 2006W, Burnished	15,188	550	

	Mintage	Unc.	PF
$10 2006W	(36,127)		$625
$10 2007	34,004	$510	
$10 2007W, Burnished	12,766	550	
$10 2007W	(46,189)		625
$10 2008	70,000	510	
$10 2008W, Burnished	8,883	650	
$10 2008W	(18,877)		625
$10 2009	110,000	510	
$10 2010	86,000	510	
$10 2010W	(44,507)		625
$10 2011	80,000	510	
$10 2011W	(28,782)		625
$10 2012	90,000	510	
$10 2012W	(13,926)		625
$10 2013	114,500	510	
$10 2013W	(12,782)		625
$10 2014	90,000	510	
$10 2014W	(14,790)		625
$10 2015	158,000	510	
$10 2015W	(15,775)		625
$10 2016	152,000	510	
$10 2016W	(24,405)		625
$10 2017	64,000	510	
$10 2017W	(14,513)		625
$10 2018	62,000	510	
$10 2018W	(12,769)		625
$10 2019	38,000	510	
$10 2019W	(11,861)		625
$10 2020	106,000	510	
$10 2020W	(15,806)		625
$10 2021, Fam. of Eagles . .	162,000	510	
$10 2021W, Fam. of Eagles.	(13,531)		625
$10 2021, Head of Eagle.		510	
$10 2021W, Head of Eagle (a)	7,924	1,250	
$10 2021W, Head of Eagle	(10,865)		625
$10 2022	140,000	510	
$10 2022W	(14,370)		625
$10 2023		510	
$10 2023W	(13,884)		625
$10 2024		510	
$10 2024W			625

a. The Mint reported that 7,924 bullion-strike pieces were made in error with an unfinished Proof obverse die bearing a W mintmark. To date, just over 60 have been found.

$25 Half-Ounce Gold

	Mintage	Unc.	PF
$25 MCMLXXXVI (1986)...	599,566	$1,020	
$25 MCMLXXXVII (1987)..	131,255	1,020	
$25 MCMLXXXVII (1987)P	(143,398)		$1,250
$25 MCMLXXXVIII (1988)...	45,000	2,500	
$25 MCMLXXXVIII (1988)P..	(76,528)		$1,250
$25 MCMLXXXIX (1989)....	44,829	1,500	
$25 MCMLXXXIX (1989)P..	(44,798)		$1,250
$25 MCMXC (1990)......	31,000	3,500	
$25 MCMXC (1990)P.....	(51,636)		1,250
$25 MCMXCI (1991)	24,100	2,500	
$25 MCMXCI (1991)P	(53,125)		1,250
$25 1992	54,404	1,100	
$25 1992P	(40,976)		1,250
$25 1993	73,324	1,500	
$25 1993P	(43,819)		1,250
$25 1994	62,400	1,500	
$25 1994W	(44,584)		1,250
$25 1995	53,474	1,800	
$25 1995W	(45,388)		1,250
$25 1996	39,287	1,800	
$25 1996W	(35,058)		1,250
$25 1997	79,605	1,050	
$25 1997W	(26,344)		1,250
$25 1998	169,029	1,020	
$25 1998W	(25,374)		1,250
$25 1999	263,013	1,020	
$25 1999W	(30,427)		1,250
$25 2000	79,287	1,020	
$25 2000W	(32,028)		1,250
$25 2001	48,047	1,020	
$25 2001W	(23,240)		1,250
$25 2002	70,027	1,020	
$25 2002W	(29,242)		1,250
$25 2003	79,029	1,020	
$25 2003W	(28,270)		1,250
$25 2004	98,040	1,020	
$25 2004W	(27,330)		1,250
$25 2005	80,023	1,020	
$25 2005W	(34,311)		1,250
$25 2006	66,005	1,020	
$25 2006W, Burnished	15,164	1,050	
$25 2006W	(34,322)		$1,250
$25 2007	47,002	$1,020	
$25 2007W, Burnished	11,455	1,050	
$25 2007W	(44,025)		1,250
$25 2008	61,000	1,020	
$25 2008W, Burnished	15,682	1,100	
$25 2008W	(22,602)		1,250
$25 2009	110,000	1,020	
$25 2010	81,000	1,020	
$25 2010W	(44,527)		1,250
$25 2011	70,000	1,020	
$25 2011W	(26,781)		1,250
$25 2012	43,000	1,020	
$25 2012W	(12,919)		1,250
$25 2013	57,000	1,020	
$25 2013W	(12,716)		1,250
$25 2014	35,000	1,020	
$25 2014W	(14,693)		1,250
$25 2015	78,000	1,020	
$25 2015W	(15,820)		1,250
$25 2016	71,000	1,020	
$25 2016W	(23,578)		1,250
$25 2017	*37,000*	1,020	
$25 2017W	(12,715)		1,250
$25 2018	*32,000*	1,020	
$25 2018W	(9,961)		1,250
$25 2019	*30,000*	1,020	
$25 2019W	*(10,703)*		1,250
$25 2020	*70,000*	1,020	
$25 2020W	*(14,020)*		1,250
$25 2021, Fam. of Eagles ...	*95,000*	1,020	
$25 2021W, Fam. of Eagles .	*(12,180)*		1,250
$25 2021, Head of Eagle.........		1,020	
$25 2021W, Head of Eagle			1,250
$25 2022	*75,000*	1,020	
$25 2022W	*(11,876)*		1,250
$25 2023		1,020	
$25 2023W	*(11,408)*		1,250
$25 2024		1,020	
$25 2024W			1,250

$50 One-Ounce Gold

	Mintage	Unc.	PF
$50 MCMLXXXVI (1986)...	1,362,650	$2,050	
$50 MCMLXXXVI (1986)W	(446,290)		$2,400
$50 MCMLXXXVII (1987) ..	1,045,500	2,050	
$50 MCMLXXXVII (1987)W	(147,498)		2,400
$50 MCMLXXXVIII (1988)....	465,000	2,050	
$50 MCMLXXXVIII (1988)W	(87,133)		2,400
$50 MCMLXXXIX (1989).....	415,790	2,050	
$50 MCMLXXXIX (1989)W .	(54,570)		$2,400
$50 MCMXC (1990)......	373,210	$2,050	
$50 MCMXC (1990)W	(62,401)		2,400
$50 MCMXCI (1991)	243,100	2,050	
$50 MCMXCI (1991)W	(50,411)		2,400
$50 1992	275,000	2,050	
$50 1992W	(44,826)		2,400

GOLD BULLION

	Mintage	Unc.	PF
$50 1993	480,192	$2,050	
$50 1993W	(34,369)		$2,400
$50 1994	221,633	2,050	
$50 1994W	(46,674)		2,400
$50 1995	200,636	2,050	
$50 1995W	(46,368)		2,400
$50 1996	189,148	2,050	
$50 1996W	(36,153)		2,400
$50 1997	664,508	2,050	
$50 1997W	(32,999)		2,400
$50 1998	1,468,530	2,050	
$50 1998W	(25,886)		2,400
$50 1999	1,505,026	2,050	
$50 1999W	(31,427)		2,400
$50 2000	433,319	2,050	
$50 2000W	(33,007)		2,400
$50 2001	143,605	2,050	
$50 2001W	(24,555)		2,400
$50 2002	222,029	2,050	
$50 2002W	(27,499)		2,400
$50 2003	416,032	2,050	
$50 2003W	(28,344)		2,400
$50 2004	417,019	2,050	
$50 2004W	(28,215)		2,400
$50 2005	356,555	2,050	
$50 2005W	(35,246)		2,400
$50 2006	237,510	2,050	
$50 2006W, Burnished	45,053	2,100	
$50 2006W	(47,092)		2,400
$50 2006W, Reverse Proof	(9,996)		2,500
$50 2007	140,016	2,050	
$50 2007W, Burnished	18,066	2,150	
$50 2007W	(51,810)		2,400
$50 2008	710,000	2,050	
$50 2008W, Burnished	11,908	2,200	
$50 2008W	(30,237)		2,400
$50 2009	1,493,000	2,050	
$50 2010	1,125,000	2,050	
$50 2010W	(59,480)		2,400
$50 2011	857,000	2,050	
$50 2011W, Burnished	8,729	2,050	
$50 2011W	(48,306)		2,400
$50 2012	675,000	2,050	
$50 2012W, Burnished	6,118	2,050	

	Mintage	Unc.	PF
$50 2012W	(23,630)		$2,400
$50 2013	758,500	$2,050	
$50 2013W, Burnished	7,293	2,050	
$50 2013W	(24,710)		2,400
$50 2014	425,000	2,050	
$50 2014W, Burnished	7,902	2,050	
$50 2014W	(28,703)		2,400
$50 2015	594,000	2,050	
$50 2015W, Burnished	6,533	2,050	
$50 2015W	(32,652)		2,400
$50 2016	817,500	2,050	
$50 2016W, Burnished	6,887	2,050	
$50 2016W	(41,621)		2,400
$50 2017	228,500	2,050	
$50 2017W, Burnished	5,800	2,050	
$50 2017W	(19,056)		2,400
$50 2018	191,000	2,050	
$50 2018W, Burnished	8,518	2,050	
$50 2018W	(15,564)		2,400
$50 2019	108,000	2,050	
$50 2019W, Burnished	6,365	2,050	
$50 2019W	(14,695)		2,400
$50 2020	747,500	2,050	
$50 2020W, Burnished	6,284	2,050	
$50 2020W	(17,358)		2,400
$50 2020W, 75th Anniversary of the End of WWII (with privy mark)	(1,939)		9,000
$50 2021, Fam. of Eagles	1,115,500	2,050	
$50 2021W, Fam. of Eagles	(15,774)		2,400
$50 2021, Head of Eagle		2,050	
$50 2021W, Head of Eagle, Burnished		2,050	
$50 2021W, Head of Eagle	(12,624)		2,400
$50 2022	850,000	2,050	
$50 2022W, Burnished		2,050	
$50 2022W	(15,819)		2,400
$50 2023		2,050	
$50 2023W, Burnished		2,050	
$50 2023W	(15,863)		2,400
$50 2024		2,050	
$50 2024W, Burnished		2,050	
$50 2024W			2,400

Gold Bullion Sets

	PF
1987 Gold Set. $50, $25	$3,600
1988 Gold Set. $50, $25, $10, $5	4,400
1989 Gold Set. $50, $25, $10, $5	4,400
1990 Gold Set. $50, $25, $10, $5	4,400
1991 Gold Set. $50, $25, $10, $5	4,400
1992 Gold Set. $50, $25, $10, $5	4,400
1993 Gold Set. $50, $25, $10, $5	4,400

	PF
1993 Bicentennial Gold Set. $25, $10, $5, $1 silver eagle, and medal	$2,150
1994 Gold Set. $50, $25, $10, $5	4,400
1995 Gold Set. $50, $25, $10, $5	4,400
1995 Anniversary Gold Set. $50, $25, $10, $5, and $1 silver eagle	6,800
1996 Gold Set. $50, $25, $10, $5	4,400

Chart continued on next page.

	PF
1997 Gold Set. $50, $25, $10, $5	$4,400
1997 Impressions of Liberty Set.	
$100 platinum, $50 gold, $1 silver	3,850
1998 Gold Set. $50, $25, $10, $5	4,400
1999 Gold Set. $50, $25, $10, $5	4,400
2000 Gold Set. $50, $25, $10, $5	4,400
2001 Gold Set. $50, $25, $10, $5	4,400
2002 Gold Set. $50, $25, $10, $5	4,400
2003 Gold Set. $50, $25, $10, $5	4,400
2004 Gold Set. $50, $25, $10, $5	4,400
2005 Gold Set. $50, $25, $10, $5	4,400
2006 Gold Set. $50, $25, $10, $5	4,400
2007 Gold Set. $50, $25, $10, $5	4,400
2008 Gold Set. $50, $25, $10, $5	4,400
2010 Gold Set. $50, $25, $10, $5 **(a)**	4,400
2011 Gold Set. $50, $25, $10, $5	4,400

a. The U.S. Mint did not issue a 2009 gold set.

	PF
2012 Gold Set. $50, $25, $10, $5	$4,400
2013 Gold Set. $50, $25, $10, $5	4,400
2014 Gold Set. $50, $25, $10, $5	4,400
2015 Gold Set. $50, $25, $10, $5	4,400
2016 Gold Set. $50, $25, $10, $5	4,400
2017 Gold Set. $50, $25, $10, $5	4,400
2018 Gold Set. $50, $25, $10, $5	4,400
2019 Gold Set. $50, $25, $10, $5	4,400
2020 Gold Set. $50, $25, $10, $5	4,400
2021 Gold Set, Fam. Eagles. $50, $25, $10, $5	4,500
2021 Gold Set, Head Eagle. $50, $25, $10, $5	4,500
2021 $5 Gold Proof Two-Coin Set,	
Family of Eagles and Head of Eagle	470
2022 Gold Set. $50, $25, $10, $5	4,000
2023 Gold Set. $50, $25, $10, $5	4,500
2024 Gold Set. $50, $25, $10, $5	4,500

2006 20th Anniversary Sets

2006W $50 Gold Set. Uncirculated, Proof, Reverse Proof	$6,500
2006W 1-oz. Gold and Silver Coin Set. Burnished	2,100

Gold Bullion Burnished Sets 2006–2008

	Unc.
2006W Burnished Gold Set. $50, $25, $10, $5	$3,900
2007W Burnished Gold Set. $50, $25, $10, $5	3,900
2008W Burnished Gold Set. $50, $25, $10, $5	4,200

AMERICAN BUFFALO .9999 FINE GOLD BULLION COINS

	Mintage	Unc.	PF
$5 2008W, Burnished	17,429	$400	
$5 2008W	(18,884)		$600
$10 2008W, Burnished	9,949	800	
$10 2008W	(13,125)		900
$25 2008W, Burnished	16,908	1,200	
$25 2008W	(12,169)		1,400
$50 2006	337,012	2,040	
$50 2006W	(246,267)		2,100
$50 2007	136,503	2,040	
$50 2007W	(58,998)		2,100
$50 2008 **(a)**	214,053 **(a)**	2,040	

	Mintage	Unc.	PF
$50 2008W, Burnished	9,074	$2,200	
$50 2008W	(18,863)		$2,600
$50 2009	200,000	2,040	
$50 2009W	(49,306)		2,100
$50 2010	209,000	2,040	
$50 2010W	(49,263)		2,100
$50 2011	250,000	2,040	
$50 2011W	(28,693)		2,100
$50 2012	100,000	2,040	
$50 2012W	(19,765)		2,100
$50 2013	198,500	2,040	

a. Includes 24,553 sold as Lunar New Year Celebration coins.

	Mintage	Unc.	PF
$50 2013W	(18,594)		$2,100
$50 2013W, Reverse Proof	(47,836)		2,200
$50 2014	180,500	$2,040	
$50 2014W	(20,557)		2,100
$50 2015	223,500	2,040	
$50 2015W	(16,591)		2,100
$50 2016	211,000	2,040	
$50 2016W	(21,878)		2,100
$50 2017	99,500	2,040	
$50 2017W	(15,810)		2,100
$50 2018	121,500	2,040	
$50 2018W	(15,756)		2,100

	Mintage	Unc.	PF
$50 2019	61,500	$2,040	
$50 2019W	(14,844)		$2,100
$50 2020	242,000	2,040	
$50 2020W	(11,887)		2,200
$50 2021	350,000	2,040	
$50 2021W	(16,958)		2,100
$50 2022		2,040	
$50 2022W	(15,493)		2,100
$50 2023		2,040	
$50 2023W	(13,731)		2,100
$50 2024		2,040	
$50 2024W			2,100

American Buffalo Gold Bullion Sets

	Unc.	PF
2008W Four-coin set. $50, $25, $10, $5.		$5,500
2008W Four-coin set, Burnished. $50, $25, $10, $5.	$4,500	
2008W Double Prosperity Set. Uncirculated $25 Buffalo and $25 American Gold Eagle coins ..	2,400	

FIRST SPOUSE $10 GOLD BULLION COINS
Half-Ounce 24-Karat Gold

Martha Washington   Abigail Adams   Jefferson's Liberty   Dolley Madison

	Mintage	Unc.	PF
$10 2007W, Martha Washington	(19,167) 17,661	$1,010	$1,020
$10 2007W, Abigail Adams	(17,149) 17,142	1,010	1,020
$10 2007W, Thomas Jefferson's Liberty	(19,815) 19,823	1,010	1,020
$10 2007W, Dolley Madison	(17,943) 12,340	1,010	1,020
$10 2008W, Elizabeth Monroe	(7,800) 4,462	1,010	1,020
$10 2008W, Louisa Adams	(6,581) 3,885	1,010	1,020
$10 2008W, Andrew Jackson's Liberty	(7,684) 4,609	1,010	1,020
$10 2008W, Martin Van Buren's Liberty	(6,807) 3,826	1,010	1,020
$10 2009W, Anna Harrison	(6,251) 3,645	1,010	1,020
$10 2009W, Letitia Tyler	(5,296) 3,240	1,010	1,020
$10 2009W, Julia Tyler	(4,844) 3,143	1,010	1,020
$10 2009W, Sarah Polk	(5,151) 3,489	1,010	1,020
$10 2009W, Margaret Taylor	(4,936) 3,627	1,010	1,020
$10 2010W, Abigail Fillmore	(6,130) 3,482	1,010	1,020
$10 2010W, Jane Pierce	(4,775) 3,338	1,010	1,020
$10 2010W, James Buchanan's Liberty	(7,110) 5,162	1,010	1,020
$10 2010W, Mary Lincoln	(6,861) 3,695	1,010	1,020

Chart continued on next page.

	Mintage	Unc.	PF
$10 2011W, Eliza Johnson	(3,887) 2,905	$1,010	$1,020
$10 2011W, Julia Grant	(3,943) 2,892	1,010	1,020
$10 2011W, Lucy Hayes	(3,868) 2,196	1,010	1,020
$10 2011W, Lucretia Garfield	(3,653) 2,168	1,010	1,020
$10 2012W, Alice Paul	(3,505) 2,798	1,010	1,020
$10 2012W, Frances Cleveland, Type 1	(3,158) 2,454	1,010	1,020
$10 2012W, Caroline Harrison	(3,046) 2,436	1,010	1,020
$10 2012W, Frances Cleveland, Type 2	(3,104) 2,425	1,010	1,020
$10 2013W, Ida McKinley	(2,724) 2,008	1,010	1,020
$10 2013W, Edith Roosevelt	(2,840) 2,027	1,020	1,030
$10 2013W, Helen Taft	(2,598) 1,993	1,020	1,030
$10 2013W, Ellen Wilson	(2,511) 1,980	1,020	1,030
$10 2013W, Edith Wilson	(2,464) 1,974	1,020	1,030
$10 2014W, Florence Harding	(2,372) 1,949	1,020	1,030
$10 2014W, Grace Coolidge	(2,315) 1,944	1,020	1,030
$10 2014W, Lou Hoover	(2,392) 1,936	1,020	1,030
$10 2014W, Eleanor Roosevelt	(2,377) 1,886	1,020	1,030
$10 2015W, Elizabeth Truman	(2,747) 1,946	1,020	1,030
$10 2015W, Mamie Eisenhower	(2,704) 2,102	1,020	1,030
$10 2015W, Jacqueline Kennedy	(11,222) 6,771	1,020	1,030
$10 2015W, Claudia Taylor "Lady Bird" Johnson	(2,653) 1,927	1,020	1,030
$10 2016W, Pat Nixon	(2,645) 1,839	1,020	1,030
$10 2016W, Betty Ford	(2,471) 1,824	1,020	1,030
$10 2016W, Nancy Reagan	(3,548) 2,009	1,020	1,030
$10 2020W, Barbara Bush	(2,896) 1,932	1,030	1,040

MMIX ULTRA HIGH RELIEF GOLD COIN (2009)

MMIX Ultra High Relief Gold Coin
*Photographed at an angle to
show the edge, lettered E PLURIBUS
UNUM, and the depth of relief.*

A modern version of the 1907 Ultra High Relief double eagle gold pattern was produced in 2009 at the Philadelphia Mint. It was made to demonstrate technical advances in minting techniques that make possible such a coin. The original design was never made for commercial use because it could not be made in sufficient quantities.

The design was by Augustus Saint-Gaudens. A version of it in much lower relief was used on double eagle coins minted from 1907 to 1933. To create the coin in ultra high relief, the 2009 version was made in a slightly smaller diameter, and composed of 24-karat gold, making it easier to strike and maintain the fidelity of the design. Through 21st-century technology the original Saint-Gaudens plasters were digitally mapped by the Mint and used in the die-making process. The date was changed to 2009, and four additional stars were added to represent the current 50 states. The inscription "In God We Trust" was not used on the 1907 version.

The MMIX Ultra High Relief gold coins are 4 mm thick and contain one ounce of .999 fine gold. All are Uncirculated (business strikes). All are made at the West Point Mint, and packaged by the Mint in a special mahogany box.

	Mintage	SP
(2009) MMIX Ultra High Relief $20 Gold Coin.	114,427	$2,200

400TH ANNIVERSARY OF THE MAYFLOWER GOLD COIN

In 2020 the United States Mint recognized the 400th anniversary of the Pilgrims' landing at Plymouth Rock aboard the *Mayflower*. Under authority granted by Congress to the secretary of the Treasury, the Mint issued two 1/4-ounce, ten-dollar gold coins from the West Point Mint, one in Proof and the other a Reverse Proof. Both have a reeded edge and a diameter of 22 mm, with a fineness of .9999. The Proof was sold individually, while the Reverse Proof was part of a two-coin set that also contained a gold £25 commemorative Proof coin from the British Royal Mint.

	Mintage	PF
2020W.	(4,743)	$480
2020W, Reverse Proof.	(4,881)	495
2020W, two-coin Proof set **(a)**.	(4,743)	960

a. Contains the 2020-W Proof coin and a £25 British commemorative Proof gold coin

75TH ANNIVERSARY OF THE END OF WORLD WAR II GOLD COIN

Under the Treasury secretary's authority to issue gold coins "from time to time" without specific commemorative legislation, in 2020 the Mint issued a .9999 fine gold twenty-five-dollar coin to mark the 75th anniversary of the end of World War II. Struck at the West Point Mint, the Proof coin weighs one-half ounce and measures 27 mm in diameter. Its edge is reeded. The Mint also issued a related one-ounce Proof silver medal, privy-marked West Point quarter dollars, and privy-marked gold and silver American Eagles in celebration of the anniversary.

	Mintage	PF
2020W.	(7,366)	$1,020

AMERICAN LIBERTY HIGH RELIEF GOLD COINS

The first American Liberty High Relief .9999-fine gold coin, with a weight of one ounce and a face value of $100, was minted at West Point in 2015. The coin was not congressionally mandated, instead being created under authority granted to the

Secretary of the Treasury by federal law. Its design was created in part to show "a 'modern' Liberty that reflects the nation's diversity."

The designs for the American Liberty High Relief gold coins are created to take full advantage of the same high-relief techniques used to create the MMIX Ultra High Relief gold coin. The Mint also issues each new design as a silver medal.

2015-W

1792–2017-W

2018-W, $10

2019-W

2021-W

2023-W

	Mintage	Unc.	PF
$100 2015W, 1 oz.	49,325	$2,050	
$100 1792–2017W, 1 oz.	(37,895)		$2,150
$10 2018W, 1/10 oz.	(52,403)		240
$100 2019W, 1 oz., Enhanced Finish	24,609	2,200	
$100 2021W, 1 oz.	(12,470)		3,200
$100 2023W, 1 oz.			

LIBERTY AND BRITANNIA GOLD COINS

In 2024, the Mint is releasing the first issue in a new series produced in collaboration with the United Kingdom's Royal Mint. The one-ounce coins, struck at West Point with a face value of $100, are composed of .9999 fine gold and measure 32.7 mm in diameter. The obverse depicts the allegorical figures of Liberty and Britannia, representing America and Britain, respectively; this is the first time the two figures are shown on a U.S. coin. Like the American Liberty High Relief gold coins and similar series, the Liberty and Britannia coins are produced under the authority of the Treasury secretary to issue gold coins "from time to time" without specific commemorative legislation.

	Mintage	Unc.
2024W		

AMERICAN PLATINUM EAGLE COINS

The one-ounce American Eagle platinum coin is designated $100 and contains one ounce of pure platinum. Fractional denominations containing 1/2 ounce, 1/4 ounce, or 1/10 ounce are called $50, $25, and $10, respectively.

Bullion values are based on spot platinum at $1,000 per ounce.

Obverse for Bullion and Proof, All Years

Reverse for Bullion, All Years; for Proof in 1997

$10 Tenth-Ounce Platinum

	Mintage	Unc.	PF		Mintage	Unc.	PF
$10 1997	70,250	$135		$10 2004	15,010	$135	
$10 1997W	(36,993)		$160	$10 2004W	(7,161)		$160
$10 1998	39,525	135		$10 2005	14,013	135	
$10 1998W	(19,847)		160	$10 2005W	(8,104)		160
$10 1999	55,955	135		$10 2006	11,001	135	
$10 1999W	(19,133)		160	$10 2006W, Burnished	3,544	300	
$10 2000	34,027	135		$10 2006W	(10,205)		160
$10 2000W	(15,651)		160	$10 2007	13,003	135	
$10 2001	52,017	135		$10 2007W, Burnished	5,556	250	
$10 2001W	(12,174)		160	$10 2007W	(8,176)		160
$10 2002	23,005	135		$10 2008	17,000	135	
$10 2002W	(12,365)		160	$10 2008W, Burnished	3,706	300	
$10 2003	22,007	135		$10 2008W	(5,138)		225
$10 2003W	(9,534)		160				

$25 Quarter-Ounce Platinum

	Mintage	Unc.	PF		Mintage	Unc.	PF
$25 1997	27,100	$270		$25 2004	18,010	$270	
$25 1997W	(18,628)		$350	$25 2004W	(5,193)		$350
$25 1998	38,887	270		$25 2005	12,013	270	
$25 1998W	(14,873)		350	$25 2005W	(6,592)		350
$25 1999	39,734	270		$25 2006	12,001	270	
$25 1999W	(13,507)		350	$25 2006W, Burnished	2,676	550	
$25 2000	20,054	270		$25 2006W	(7,813)		350
$25 2000W	(11,995)		350	$25 2007	8,402	270	
$25 2001	21,815	270		$25 2007W, Burnished	3,690	500	
$25 2001W	(8,847)		350	$25 2007W	(6,017)		350
$25 2002	27,405	270		$25 2007W, Frosted FREEDOM	(21)		—
$25 2002W	(9,282)		350	$25 2008	22,800	270	
$25 2003	25,207	270		$25 2008W, Burnished	2,481	700	
$25 2003W	(7,044)		350	$25 2008W	(4,153)		370

$50 Half-Ounce Platinum

	Mintage	Unc.	PF		Mintage	Unc.	PF
$50 1997	20,500	$525		$50 1998W	(13,836)		$700
$50 1997W	(15,431)		$700	$50 1999	32,309	$525	
$50 1998	32,415	525		$50 1999W	(11,103)		700

	Mintage	Unc.	PF
$50 2000	18,892	$525	
$50 2000W	(11,049)		$700
$50 2001	12,815	525	
$50 2001W	(8,254)		700
$50 2002	24,005	525	
$50 2002W	(8,772)		700
$50 2003	17,409	525	
$50 2003W	(7,131)		700
$50 2004	13,236	525	
$50 2004W	(5,063)		700
$50 2005	9,013	525	
$50 2005W	(5,942)		700

	Mintage	Unc.	PF
$50 2006	9,602	$525	
$50 2006W, Burnished	2,577	800	
$50 2006W	(7,649)		$700
$50 2007	7,001	525	
$50 2007W, Burnished	3,635	800	
$50 2007W	(25,519)		700
$50 2007W, RevPf	(19,583)		800
$50 2007W, Frosted FREEDOM	(21)		—
$50 2008	14,000	525	
$50 2008W, Burnished	2,253	1,000	
$50 2008W	(4,020)		700

$100 One-Ounce Platinum
Proof Platinum Reverse Designs

1998: Eagle Over
New England.
"Vistas of Liberty" series.

1999: Eagle Above
Southeastern Wetlands.
"Vistas of Liberty" series.

2000: Eagle Above
America's Heartland.
"Vistas of Liberty" series.

2001: Eagle Above
America's Southwest.
"Vistas of Liberty" series.

2002: Eagle Fishing
in America's Northwest.
"Vistas of Liberty" series.

2003.

2004.

2005.

2006: Legislative Branch.
"Foundations of
Democracy" series.

2007: Executive Branch.
"Foundations of
Democracy" series.

2008: Judicial Branch.
"Foundations of
Democracy" series.

2009: To Form a More Perfect
Union. "Preamble to the
Constitution" series.

2010: To Establish Justice.
"Preamble to the
Constitution" series.

2011: To Insure Domestic
Tranquility. "Preamble to
the Constitution" series.

2012: To Provide for the
Common Defence. "Preamble
to the Constitution" series.

2013: To Promote the
General Welfare. "Preamble
to the Constitution" series.

2014: To Secure the Blessings of
Liberty to Ourselves and Our Posterity.
"Preamble to the Constitution" series.

2015: Liberty Nurtures
Freedom. "Torches
of Liberty" series.

2016: Portrait
of Liberty. "Torches
of Liberty" series.

Common reverse:
2018–2020 and
2021–2025 series.

2018. Life.
"Preamble to the Declaration
of Independence" series.

2019. Liberty.
"Preamble to the Declaration of Independence" series.

2020: Pursuit of Happiness.
"Preamble to the Declaration of Independence" series.

2021: Freedom of Religion.
"First Amendment to the U.S. Constitution" series.

2022: Freedom of Speech.
"First Amendment to the U.S. Constitution" series.

2023: Freedom of the Press.
"First Amendment to the U.S. Constitution" series.

2024: Right to Assemble.
"First Amendment to the U.S. Constitution" series.

	Mintage	Unc.	PF		Mintage	Unc.	PF
$100 1997	56,000	$1,050		$100 2007W,			
$100 1997W	(20,851)		$1,400	Frosted FREEDOM	(12)		—
$100 1998	133,002	1,050		$100 2008	21,800	$1,050	
$100 1998W	(14,912)		1,400	$100 2008W, Burnished	2,876	1,850	
$100 1999	56,707	1,050		$100 2008W	(4,769)		$1,600
$100 1999W	(12,363)		1,400	$100 2009W	(7,945)		1,400
$100 2000	10,003	1,050		$100 2010W	(14,790)		1,400
$100 2000W	(12,453)		1,400	$100 2011W	(14,835)		1,400
$100 2001	14,070	1,050		$100 2012W	(9,081)		1,400
$100 2001W	(8,969)		1,400	$100 2013W	(5,763)		1,400
$100 2002	11,502	1,050		$100 2014	16,900	1,050	
$100 2002W	(9,834)		1,400	$100 2014W	(4,596)		1,400
$100 2003	8,007	1,050		$100 2015	20,000	1,050	
$100 2003W	(8,246)		1,400	$100 2015W	(3,881)		1,400
$100 2004	7,009	1,050		$100 2016	20,000	1,050	
$100 2004W	(6,007)		1,400	$100 2016W	(9,151)		1,400
$100 2005	6,310	1,050		$100 2017	20,000	1,050	
$100 2005W	(6,602)		1,400	$100 2017W	(8,890)		1,400
$100 2006	6,000	1,050		$100 2018	30,000	1,050	
$100 2006W, Burnished	3,068	1,750		$100 2018W	(16,904)		1,400
$100 2006W	(9,152)		1,400	$100 2019	40,000	1,050	
$100 2007	7,202	1,050		$100 2019W	(11,268)		1,400
$100 2007W, Burnished	4,177	1,700		$100 2020	56,500	1,050	
$100 2007W	(8,363)		1,400	$100 2020W	(9,825)		1,400

Chart continued on next page.

	Mintage	Unc.	PF
$100 2021	75,000	$1,050	
$100 2021W	(9,984)		$1,400
$100 2022	80,000	1,050	
$100 2022W	(9,940)		1,400

	Mintage	Unc.	PF
$100 2023		$1,050	
$100 2023W			$1,400
$100 2024		1,050	
$100 2024W			1,400

Platinum Bullion Sets

	Unc.	PF
1997 Plat. Set. $100, $50, $25, $10 ...		$2,500
1998 Plat. Set. $100, $50, $25, $10 ...		2,500
1999 Plat. Set. $100, $50, $25, $10 ...		2,500
2000 Plat. Set. $100, $50, $25, $10 ...		2,500
2001 Plat. Set. $100, $50, $25, $10 ...		2,500
2002 Plat. Set. $100, $50, $25, $10 ...		2,500
2003 Plat. Set. $100, $50, $25, $10 ...		2,500
2004W Plat. Set. $100, $50, $25, $10. .		2,500
2005W Plat. Set. $100, $50, $25, $10. .		2,500

	Unc.	PF
2006W Plat. Set. $100, $50, $25, $10. .		$2,500
2006W Plat. Burnished Set.		
$100, $50, $25, $10	$3,200	
2007W Plat. Set. $100, $50, $25, $10. .		2,500
2007W Plat. Burnished Set.		
$100, $50, $25, $10	3,000	
2008W Plat. Set. $100, $50, $25, $10. .		2,500
2008W Plat. Burnished Set.		
$100, $50, $25, $10	3,600	

Prices are for original Uncirculated or Proof pieces with box and papers.

American Eagle 10th Anniversary Platinum Set

	PF
Two-coin set containing one Proof platinum half-ounce and one Enhanced Reverse Proof half-ounce dated 2007W. Housed in hardwood box with mahogany finish	$1,700

AMERICAN PALLADIUM
EAGLE COINS (2017 TO DATE)

Designer Adolph A. Weinman; composition .9995 palladium; net weight 1 oz. pure palladium; diameter 32.7 mm; reeded edge; mints: Philadelphia, West Point.

The $25 American Palladium Eagle features a high-relief obverse design derived from artist Adolph Weinman's Winged Liberty dime of 1916 to 1945. The reverse is a high-relief version of Weinman's 1907 American Institute of Architects gold medal reverse, showing an eagle grasping a branch.

Bullion-strike coins are minted in Philadelphia and distributed through the Mint's authorized purchasers. Proof, Reverse Proof, and Uncirculated numismatic versions struck at the West Point Mint are sold by the Mint directly to collectors.

As of this printing, the spot price of palladium is about $1,200 per ounce.

	Mintage	Unc.	PF
$25 2017	15,000	$1,250	
$25 2018W	(14,986)		$1,500
$25 2019W, Reverse Proof	(18,775)		1,500
$25 2020W, Burnished	9,742	1,250	
$25 2021	8,700	1,250	
$25 2021W	(5,170)		1,600
$25 2022W, Reverse Proof	(7,366)		1,600
$25 2023W		1,300	
$25 2024W		1,300	

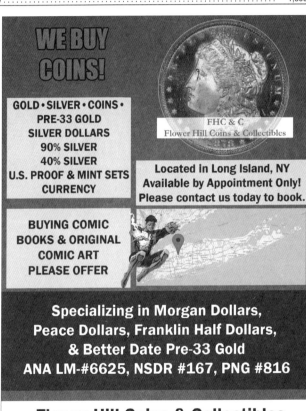

Private coins were circulated in most instances because of a shortage of regular coinage. Some numismatists use the general term *private gold* to refer to coins struck outside of the United States Mint. In the sense that no state or territory had authority to coin money, *private gold* simply refers to those interesting necessity pieces of various shapes, denominations, and degrees of intrinsic worth which were circulated in isolated areas of our country by individuals, assayers, bankers, etc. Some numismatists use the words *territorial* and *state* to cover certain issues because they were coined and circulated in a territory or state. While the state of California properly sanctioned the ingots stamped by F.D. Kohler as state assayer, in no instance were any of the gold pieces struck by authority of any of the territorial governments.

The stamped ingots put out by Augustus Humbert, the United States assayer of gold, were not recognized at the United States Mint as an official issue of coins, but simply as ingots, though Humbert placed the value and fineness on the pieces as an official agent of the federal government.

TEMPLETON REID
Georgia Gold 1830

The first private gold coinage in the 19th century was struck by Templeton Reid, a jeweler and gunsmith, in Milledgeville, Georgia, in July 1830. To be closer to the mines, he moved to Gainesville, where most of his coins were made. Although weights were accurate, Reid's assays were not, and his coins were slightly short of claimed value. Accordingly, he was severely attacked in the newspapers and soon lost the public's confidence. His mint closed before the end of that October.

	VG	VF
1830, $2.50	$75,000	$125,000
1830, $5	175,000	300,000
1830, TEN DOLLARS	350,000	750,000
(No Date) TEN DOLLARS	750,000	1,000,000

California Gold 1849

1849 TEN DOLLAR CALIFORNIA GOLD *(unique, in Smithsonian collection)*. . . . .

THE BECHTLERS
RUTHERFORD COUNTY, NC, 1831–1852

Two skilled German metallurgists, Christopher Bechtler and his son August, and later Christopher Bechtler, Junior, a nephew of Christopher the elder, operated a private mint at Rutherfordton, North Carolina. Rutherford County, in which Rutherfordton is located, was a principal source of the nation's gold supply from 1790 to 1848.

Christopher Bechtler

	VF	EF	AU	Unc.
ONE DOLLAR CAROLINA, 28.G, N Reversed	$1,500	$2,250	$3,250	$7,000
ONE GOLD DOLLAR N. CAROLINA, 28.G, No Star	2,750	3,750	5,500	12,500
ONE GOLD DOLLAR N. CAROLINA, 30.G.	1,750	2,500	3,750	10,000
2.50 CAROLINA, 67.G., 21 CARATS	3,750	5,750	7,500	13,500
2.50 CAROLINA, 70.G, 20 CARATS.	4,000	6,500	8,500	15,000
2.50 GEORGIA, 64.G, 22 CARATS.	4,500	7,500	10,000	16,500
2.50 NORTH CAROLINA, 75.G., 20 C., RUTHERFORD in a Circle. Border of Large Beads	12,500	16,500	27,500	55,000
2.50 NORTH CAROLINA, 20 C. Without 75.G.	12,500	16,500	27,500	55,000

Entry continued on next page.

Without 150.G.

	VF	EF	AU	Unc.
5 DOLLARS NORTH CAROLINA GOLD, 150.G., 20.CARATS.	$13,000	$22,500	$37,500	$75,000
Similar, Without 150.G.		—	—	
5 DOLLARS CAROLINA, RUTHERFORD, 140.G., 20 CARATS				
Plain Edge.	4,500	6,500	8,500	13,500
Reeded Edge.	12,500	20,000	25,000	40,000
5 DOLLARS CAROLINA GOLD, RUTHERF., 140.G., 20 CARATS,				
AUGUST 1, 1834	7,500	10,500	18,500	37,500
Similar, but "20" Distant From CARATS.	3,750	7,500	8,500	17,500
5 DOLLARS CAROLINA GOLD, 134.G., 21 CARATS, With Star.	3,750	5,500	6,500	12,500
5 DOLLARS GEORGIA GOLD, RUTHERFORD, 128.G., 22 CARATS	4,500	6,500	9,500	16,500
5 DOLLARS GEORGIA GOLD, RUTHERF, 128.G., 22 CARATS	4,500	6,500	9,500	16,500

August Bechtler

	VF	EF	AU	Unc.
1 DOL:, CAROLINA GOLD, 27.G., 21.C..	$1,200	$1,500	$1,850	$3,000
5 DOLLARS, CAROLINA GOLD, 134.G:, 21 CARATS	3,500	6,500	8,500	22,500

	VF	EF	AU	Unc.
5 DOLLARS, CAROLINA GOLD, 128.G., 22 CARATS	$7,500	$10,500	$16,500	$30,000
5 DOLLARS, CAROLINA GOLD, 141.G., 20 CARATS	7,500	10,500	16,500	30,000

NORRIS, GREGG & NORRIS
SAN FRANCISCO 1849

Numismatists consider these pieces the first of the California private gold coins. A newspaper account dated May 31, 1849, described a five-dollar gold coin struck at Benicia City, though with the imprint San Francisco, and the private stamp of Norris, Gregg & Norris.

	F	VF	EF	AU	Unc.
1849 Half Eagle, Plain Edge.	$4,500	$7,000	$8,500	$11,000	$22,500
1849 Half Eagle, Reeded Edge.	4,500	6,500	8,500	11,000	25,000
1850 Half Eagle, With STOCKTON Beneath Date *(unique, in Smithsonian collection)*					

MOFFAT & CO.
SAN FRANCISCO 1849–1853

The firm of Moffat & Co. was perhaps the most important of the California private coiners. The assay office they conducted was semi-official in character, and successors to this firm later sold its facilities to the Treasury Department, which used them to create the San Francisco Mint.

In June or July, 1849, Moffat & Co. began to issue small rectangular pieces of gold in values from $9.43 to $264. The $9.43, $14.25, and $16.00 varieties are the only known types. A similar ingot was made by the firm of Meyers & Company at this same time.

	EF
$9.43 Moffat Ingot *(unique, in Smithsonian collection)*.	—
$14.25 Moffat Ingot *(unique, in Smithsonian collection)*.	—
$16.00 Moffat Ingot.	$175,000
$18.00 Meyers Ingot *(unique)*.	—

Entry continued on next page.

The dies for the five-dollar and ten-dollar pieces were cut by Albrecht Küner. The words MOFFAT & CO. appear on Liberty's coronet instead of the word LIBERTY as in regular United States issues.

	F	VF	EF	AU	Unc.
1849 FIVE DOL. *(all varieties)*	$1,750	$4,000	$5,500	$6,500	$10,000
1850 FIVE DOL. *(all varieties)*	1,750	4,000	4,400	6,000	11,000
1849 TEN DOL.	2,500	4,500	5,000	10,000	25,000
1849 TEN D.	2,750	5,500	7,500	11,000	27,500

UNITED STATES ASSAY OFFICE
Augustus Humbert
United States Assayer of Gold, 1851

When Augustus Humbert was appointed United States assayer, he placed his name and the government imprint on the ingots of gold issued by Moffat & Co. The assay office, a provisional government mint, was a temporary expedient to accommodate the Californians until the establishment of a permanent branch mint. The fifty-dollar gold piece was accepted as legal tender on a par with standard U.S. gold coins.

Lettered Edge Varieties

	F	VF	EF	AU	Unc.
1851 50 D C 880 THOUS., No 50 on Reverse. Sunk in Edge:					
AUGUSTUS HUMBERT UNITED STATES ASSAYER OF GOLD					
CALIFORNIA 1851	$15,000	$25,000	$40,000	$65,000	$135,000

50 on Reverse

	F	VF	EF	AU	Unc.
1851 50 D C 880 THOUS, Similar to Last Variety, but 50 on Reverse	$16,500	$27,500	$42,500	$75,000	$145,000
1851 50 D C, 887 THOUS., With 50 on Reverse	15,000	25,000	40,000	65,000	125,000

Reeded Edge Varieties

	F	VF	EF	AU	Unc.
1851 FIFTY DOLLS, 880 THOUS., "Target" Reverse	$13,500	$16,500	$27,500	$32,500	$75,000
1851 FIFTY DOLLS, 887 THOUS., "Target" Reverse	13,500	16,500	27,500	32,500	75,000
1852 FIFTY DOLLS, 887 THOUS., "Target" Reverse	13,500	16,500	27,500	35,000	75,000

Moffat & Co. proceeded in January 1852 to issue a new ten-dollar piece bearing the stamp MOFFAT & CO.

	F	VF	EF	AU	Unc.
1852 TEN D. MOFFAT & CO.	$3,500	$5,000	$10,000	$25,000	$45,000

Entry continued on next page.   **269**

	F	VF	EF	AU	Unc.
1852 TEN DOLS. 1852, 2 Over 1	$2,500	$3,750	$5,500	$10,500	$18,500
1852 TEN DOLS.	2,500	2,750	5,000	9,500	16,500

	F	VF	EF	AU	Unc.
1852 TWENTY DOLS., 1852, 2 Over 1	$5,500	$8,500	$13,500	$27,500	$75,000

United States Assay Office of Gold – 1852

The firm of Moffat & Co. was reorganized by Curtis, Perry, and Ward, who assumed the government contract to conduct the United States Assay Office of Gold.

	F	VF	EF	AU	Unc.
1852 FIFTY DOLLS., 887 THOUS.	$13,500	$16,500	$22,500	$27,500	$55,000
1852 FIFTY DOLLS., 900 THOUS.	13,500	17,500	25,500	30,000	65,000

	F	VF	EF	AU	Unc.
1852 TEN DOLS., 884 THOUS........................	$1,750	$2,500	$3,500	$5,500	$12,500
1853 TEN D., 884 THOUS..........................	5,000	9,500	17,500	22,500	45,000
1853 TEN D., 900 THOUS..........................	2,750	4,000	5,500	8,500	15,000
1853 TWENTY D., 884 THOUS.	4,750	7,500	12,500	17,500	32,500
1853 TWENTY D., 900 THOUS.	1,750	2,250	3,500	5,500	10,000

Moffat & Company Gold

The last Moffat issue was an 1853 twenty-dollar piece that is very similar to the U.S. double eagle of that period. It was struck after the retirement of John L. Moffat from Moffat & Company.

	F	VF	EF	AU	Unc.
1853, TWENTY D.	$3,500	$5,500	$7,500	$12,500	$25,000

CINCINNATI MINING & TRADING CO. (1849)

The origin and location of this company are unknown. It might have been organized in Ohio, and conducted business in California.

	EF	Unc.
1849 FIVE DOLLARS	—	—
1849 TEN DOLLARS.	$750,000	—

MASSACHUSETTS AND CALIFORNIA COMPANY

This company was believed to have been organized in Northampton, Massachusetts, in May 1849. Pieces with 5D are not genuine.

	F	VF	EF
1849 FIVE D.	$85,000	$125,000	$200,000

MINERS' BANK
SAN FRANCISCO 1849

The institution of Wright & Co., exchange brokers located in Portsmouth Square, San Francisco, was known as the Miners' Bank.

A ten-dollar piece was issued in the autumn of 1849, but the coins were not readily accepted because they were worth less than face value.

	VF	EF	AU	Unc.
(1849) TEN D.	$12,500	$20,000	$30,000	$65,000

J.S. ORMSBY
SACRAMENTO 1849

The initials J.S.O., which appear on certain issues of California privately coined gold pieces, represent the firm of J.S. Ormsby & Co. The firm struck both five- and ten-dollar denominations, all undated.

	VF
(1849) 5 DOLLS *(unique)*	—
(1849) 10 DOLLS *(4 known)*	$350,000

PACIFIC COMPANY, SAN FRANCISCO 1849

The origin of the Pacific Company is uncertain. All data regarding the firm are based on conjecture.

Edgar H. Adams wrote that he believed that the coins bearing the stamp of the Pacific Company were produced by the coining firm of Broderick and Kohler. The coins were probably hand struck with the aid of a sledgehammer.

	EF
1849, 1 DOLLAR *(2 known)*	—
1849, 5 DOLLARS *(4 known)*	$350,000
1849, 10 DOLLARS *(4 known)*	500,000

F.D. KOHLER
CALIFORNIA STATE ASSAYER 1850

The State Assay Office was authorized on April 12, 1850. That year, Governor Peter Burnett appointed F.D. Kohler, who thereupon sold his assaying business to Baldwin & Co. Kohler served at both the San Francisco and Sacramento offices. The State Assay Offices were discontinued when the U.S. Assay Office was established, on February 1, 1851. Ingots ranged from $36.55 to $150.00.

	EF
$36.55 Sacramento	—
$37.31 San Francisco	—
$40.07 San Francisco	—
$45.34 San Francisco	—
$50.00 San Francisco	—
$54.09 San Francisco	—

DUBOSQ & COMPANY
SAN FRANCISCO 1850

Theodore Dubosq, a Philadelphia jeweler, took melting and coining machinery to San Francisco in 1849.

	VF
1850, FIVE D.	$200,000
1850, TEN D.	225,000

BALDWIN & CO.
SAN FRANCISCO 1850

George C. Baldwin and Thomas S. Holman were in the jewelry business in San Francisco and were known as Baldwin & Co. They were the successors to F.D. Kohler & Co., taking over its machinery and other equipment in May 1850.

	F	VF	EF	AU	Unc.
1850, FIVE DOL.	$5,500	$8,500	$15,500	$25,000	$45,000
1850, TEN DOLLARS, Horseman Type	30,000	65,000	85,000	115,000	175,000

	F	VF	EF	AU	Unc.
1851, TEN D.	$8,500	$20,000	$27,500	$45,000	$115,000

	VF	EF	AU	Unc.
1851 TWENTY D.	$175,000	$450,000	—	—

SHULTZ & COMPANY
SAN FRANCISCO 1851

The firm, located in back of Baldwin's establishment, operated a brass foundry beginning in 1851. Judge G.W. Shultz and William T. Garratt were partners in the enterprise.

	F	VF
1851, FIVE D.	$25,000	$45,000

DUNBAR & COMPANY
SAN FRANCISCO 1851

Edward E. Dunbar operated the California Bank in San Francisco. Dunbar later returned to New York City and organized the famous Continental Bank Note Co.

	VF	EF
1851, FIVE D.	$175,000	$350,000

WASS, MOLITOR & CO.
SAN FRANCISCO 1852–1855

The gold-smelting and assaying plant of Wass, Molitor & Co. was operated by two Hungarian patriots, Count S.C. Wass and A.P. Molitor. They maintained an excellent laboratory and complete apparatus for analysis and coinage of gold.

	F	VF	EF	AU	Unc.
1852, FIVE DOLLARS	$3,500	$5,500	$13,500	$22,500	$37,500

Large Head   Small Head

	F	VF	EF	AU	Unc.
1852, TEN D., Large Head	$2,000	$2,750	$3,750	$8,500	$20,000
1852, TEN D., Small Head	5,000	6,500	15,000	20,000	45,000
1855, TEN D.	7,500	8,500	12,500	15,000	30,000

Large Head   Small Head

	F	VF	EF	AU	Unc.
1855, TWENTY DOL., Large Head	—	—	$350,000	—	—
1855, TWENTY DOL., Small Head	$8,500	$20,000	25,000	$40,000	$85,000

	F	VF	EF	AU	Unc.
1855, 50 DOLLARS	$25,000	$45,000	$55,000	$75,000	$125,000

KELLOGG & CO.
SAN FRANCISCO 1854–1855

When the U.S. Assay Office ceased operations, a period ensued during which no private firm was striking gold. The new San Francisco branch mint did not produce coins for some months after Curtis & Perry took the government contract. The lack of coin was again keenly felt by businessmen, who petitioned Kellogg & Richter to "supply the vacuum" by issuing private coin. Their plea was soon answered, for on February 9, 1854, Kellogg & Co. placed their first twenty-dollar piece in circulation.

	F	VF	EF	AU	Unc.	PF
1854, TWENTY D.	$2,500	$3,250	$4,500	$7,500	$13,500	
1855, TWENTY D.	2,500	3,250	4,500	7,500	15,000	
1855, FIFTY DOLLS						$650,000

OREGON EXCHANGE COMPANY
OREGON CITY 1849
The Beaver Coins of Oregon

On February 16, 1849, the territorial legislature passed an act providing for a mint and specified five- and ten-dollar gold coins without alloy. Oregon City, the largest city in the territory with a population of about 1,000, was designated as the location for the mint. However, Oregon was then brought into the United States as a territory. When the new governor arrived on March 2, he declared the coinage act unconstitutional. Still, a local company coined these private pieces.

	F	VF	EF	AU	Unc.
1849 5 D.	$25,000	$35,000	$55,000	$100,000	—
1849 TEN.D.	55,000	100,000	165,000	300,000	—

MORMON GOLD PIECES
SALT LAKE CITY, UTAH, 1849–1860

Brigham Young was the instigator of the coinage system and personally supervised the mint, which was housed in a little adobe building in Salt Lake City. The mint was inaugurated late in 1848 as a public convenience.

	F	VF	EF	AU	Unc.
1849, TWO.AND.HALF.DO.	$8,500	$15,000	$25,000	$40,000	$65,000
1849, FIVE.DOLLARS	7,500	15,000	20,000	27,500	55,000

	F	VF	EF
1849, TEN.DOLLARS	$175,000	$300,000	$400,000
1849, TWENTY.DOLLARS	100,000	175,000	250,000

	F	VF	EF	AU	Unc.
1850, FIVE DOLLARS	$6,500	$13,500	$18,500	$30,000	$65,000
1860, 5.D.	12,500	20,000	35,000	45,000	75,000

COLORADO GOLD PIECES
Clark, Gruber & Co.
Denver 1860–1861

Clark, Gruber & Co. was a well-known private minting firm in Denver, Colorado, in the early 1860s.

	F	VF	EF	AU	Unc.
1860, 2 1/2 D	$1,500	$1,750	$2,500	$4,000	$10,000
1860, FIVE D	1,500	2,000	3,500	4,500	12,500

	F	VF	EF	AU	Unc.
1860, TEN D	$6,500	$10,000	$15,000	$22,500	$40,000
1860, TWENTY D	45,000	95,000	155,000	275,000	550,000

	F	VF	EF	AU	Unc.
1861, 2 1/2 D	$1,500	$2,150	$2,750	$5,500	$10,500
1861, FIVE D	1,650	2,500	3,500	6,500	22,500
1861, TEN D	2,750	3,500	4,500	6,500	22,500

	F	VF	EF	AU
1861, TWENTY D.	$35,000	$55,000	$85,000	$125,000

John Parsons & Company
Tarryall Mines – Colorado, 1861

Very little is known regarding the mint of John Parsons and Co., although it is reasonably certain that it operated in the South Park section of Park County, Colorado, near the original town of Tarryall, in the summer of 1861.

	VF
(1861) Undated 2 1/2 D.	$200,000
(1861) Undated FIVE D.	350,000

J.J. Conway & Co.
Georgia Gulch, Colorado, 1861

Records show that the Conway mint operated for a short while in 1861. As in all gold mining areas, the value of gold dust caused disagreement among the merchants and the miners. The firm of J.J. Conway & Co. solved this difficulty by bringing out its gold pieces in August 1861.

	VF
(1861) Undated 2 1/2 DOLL'S	$150,000
(1861) Undated FIVE DOLLARS	250,000
(1861) Undated TEN DOLLARS.	—

CALIFORNIA SMALL-DENOMINATION GOLD

There was a scarcity of small coins during the California Gold Rush and, starting in 1852, quarter, half, and dollar pieces were privately minted from native gold to alleviate the shortage. The need and acceptability of these pieces declined after 1856 and they then became popular as souvenirs. Authentic pieces all have CENTS, DOLLAR, or an abbreviation thereof on the reverse. The tokens are much less valuable. Modern restrikes and replicas (often having a bear in the design) have no numismatic value.

The values in the following charts are only for coins made before 1883 with the denomination on the reverse expressed as CENTS, DOL., DOLL., or DOLLAR.

Quarter Dollar – Octagonal

	EF-40	AU-50	MS-60
Liberty Head	$75	$100	$200
Indian Head	90	125	200
Washington Head	375	700	1,100

Quarter Dollar – Round

	EF-40	AU-50	MS-60
Liberty Head	$75	$100	$200
Indian Head	80	125	250
Washington Head	375	600	1,000

Half Dollar – Octagonal

	EF-40	AU-50	MS-60
Liberty Head	$75	$100	$200
Liberty Head / Eagle	500	800	1,250
Indian Head	100	125	300

Half Dollar – Round

	EF-40	AU-50	MS-60
Liberty Head	$85	$135	$250
Indian Head	75	110	200

Dollar – Octagonal

	EF-40	AU-50	MS-60
Liberty Head	$200	$300	$750
Liberty Head / Eagle	800	1,650	2,500
Indian Head	250	400	800

Dollar – Round

	EF-40	AU-50	MS-60
Liberty Head	$1,000	$1,450	$2,250
Indian Head	1,000	1,500	2,500

HARD TIMES TOKENS (1832–1844)

During the financial crises of 1832 to 1844 many government coins were hoarded, and privately made tokens were used out of necessity. The so-called Hard Times tokens of this period were slightly smaller and lighter than normal large cents. They were made of copper or brass and are of two general groups: political tokens whose theme centered on President Andrew Jackson's fight against the Bank of the United States, and tradesmen's cards, issued by merchants. Many different designs and varieties exist.

	VF	EF
Hard Times Tokens, 1832–1844, most common pieces	$20	$35

CIVIL WAR TOKENS (1860s)

Civil War tokens are generally divided into two groups: tradesmen's tokens, and anonymously issued pieces with political or patriotic themes. They came into existence only because of the scarcity of government coins and disappeared as soon as the bronze coins of 1864 met the public demand for small copper change.

These tokens vary greatly in composition and design. A number were more or less faithful imitations of the copper-nickel cent. A few of this type have the word NOT in very small letters above the words ONE CENT.

	F	VF	EF	Unc.
Copper or Brass Tokens	$5	$8	$12	$30
Nickel or German Silver Tokens	20	30	60	110
White-Metal Tokens	25	35	65	110
Copper-Nickel Tokens	30	50	80	125
Silver Tokens	80	150	225	400

Values shown are for the most common tokens in each composition.

In April 1899 control of the Philippine Islands was officially transferred from Spain to the United States, as a condition of the treaty ending the Spanish-American War. In July 1901 a civilian government (led by American judge William Howard Taft) replaced the islands' military administration; one of its first tasks was to sponsor a new territorial coinage that was compatible with the old Spanish issues, but also legally exchangeable for American money at the rate of two Philippine pesos to the U.S. dollar. The resulting coins—which bear the legend UNITED STATES OF AMERICA but are otherwise quite different in design from regular U.S. coins—today can be found in many collections, having been brought to the States as souvenirs by service members after World War II or otherwise saved.

The coins, introduced in 1903, also bear the Spanish names for the islands: FILIPINAS. Following Spanish custom, the dollar-sized peso was equivalent to 100 centavos. Silver fractions were minted in denominations of fifty, twenty, and ten centavos, and minor coins (in copper-nickel and bronze) included the five-cent piece, the centavo, and the half centavo.

Dies for the coins were made at the Philadelphia Mint. From 1903 to 1908 the coins were struck at the Philadelphia Mint (with no mintmark) and the San Francisco Mint (with an S mintmark). From 1909 through 1919, they were struck only at San Francisco. In the first part of 1920, one-centavo coins were struck in San Francisco; later in the year, a new mint facility was opened in Manila, and from that point into the early 1940s Philippine coins of one, five, ten, twenty, and fifty centavos were struck there. The coins produced at the Manila Mint in 1920, 1921, and 1922 bore no mintmark. No Philippine coins were struck in 1923 or 1924. The Manila Mint reopened in 1925; from then through 1941 its coinage featured an M mintmark.

Rising silver prices forced a reduction in the fineness and weight for each silver denomination beginning in 1907, and subsequent issues are smaller in diameter. The smaller size of the new silver issues led to confusion between the silver twenty-centavo piece and the copper-nickel five-centavo piece, resulting in a mismatching of dies for these two denominations in 1918 and again in 1928. A solution was found by reducing the diameter of the five-centavo piece beginning in 1930.

Japanese military forces advanced on the Philippines in 1942, prompting the civil government to remove much of the Philippine treasury's bullion to the United States. Nearly 16 million pesos' worth of silver remained, mostly in the form of one-peso pieces of 1907 through 1912. These coins were hastily crated and dumped into Manila's Caballo Bay to prevent their capture by Japan, then at war with the United States. The Japanese occupied the Philippines and did manage to recover some of the sunken coins (probably fewer than a half million). After the war, over the course of several years, more than 10 million of the submerged silver pesos were retrieved under the direction of the U.S. Treasury and, later, the Central Bank of the Philippines. Most of them show evidence of prolonged salt-water immersion, with dark corrosion that resists cleaning. This damage to so many coins has added to the scarcity of high-grade pre-war silver pesos.

Later during World War II, in 1944 and 1945, the U.S. Mint struck coins for the Philippines at its Philadelphia, Denver, and San Francisco mints.

The Philippines became an independent republic after the war, on July 4, 1946. Today the coins of 1903 to 1945, including a set of commemoratives issued in 1936, remain as interesting mementoes of a colorful chapter in U.S. history and numismatics.

The following are general descriptions of Philippine issues by type. For detailed date-by-date charts with mintages and retail values, see the *Guide Book of United States Coins, Deluxe Edition.*

BRONZE COINAGE UNDER U.S. SOVEREIGNTY (1903–1936)

Half Centavo   **One Centavo**

The bronze half centavo was struck from 1903 through 1908 (except for 1907), with some dates struck in Proof format only. Dealer buy prices for the most common pieces are $2.25 in EF to $40 in MS-63; for the most common Proofs, $125 to $150, depending on quality. The rarest Proof is the 1905, generally worth $125 to $400.

The bronze centavo was struck from 1903 through 1936. Dealers buy the most common pieces for $1.25 in VF to $35 in MS-63. The 1918-S, Large S, variety is the rarity of the series, valued from $125 (VF) to $1,500 (MS-63). Proofs were struck several years in the early 1900s; the most common Proofs bring buy prices of $60 to $95.

COPPER-NICKEL COINAGE UNDER U.S. SOVEREIGNTY
(1903–1935)

Large-Size Five Centavos   **Reduced-Size Five Centavos**
(1903–1928)   **(1930–1935)**

Copper-nickel five-centavo coins were struck by the millions in various years from 1903 through 1935. The most common dates are bought by dealers for $1.25 to $3.50 in VF, and for $30 to $150 in MS-63. The rare dates are the 1916-S ($75 to $1,200) and the 1918-S mule with the small-date reverse of the 20-centavo die ($300 to $6,000). Proofs were struck in some years of the early 1900s; the most common Proofs are bought by dealers for $65 to $140, depending on their state of preservation.

SILVER COINAGE UNDER U.S. SOVEREIGNTY (1903–1935)

Basic Design for Ten-, Twenty-, and
Fifty-Centavo and 1 Peso Pieces
(Large-size fifty centavos shown.)

Silver ten-centavo coins were struck by the millions in various years from 1903 through 1935. The most common dates are bought by dealers for their silver bullion value in VF, and for $25 to $50 in MS-63. The rarest dates are the 1903-S ($20 to $1,000) and the 1909-S ($20 to $800). Proofs were struck in some years of the early 1900s; the most common Proofs are bought by dealers for $75 to $100, depending on their state of preservation.

Silver twenty-centavo coins were struck in quantity in various years from 1903 through 1929. The most common dates are bought by dealers for their silver bullion value in VF, and for $85 to $250 in MS-63. There are several rarer dates in the series; the 1903-S, 1915-S, and the 1928-M mule (with a reverse of the 1903–1928 five centavos die) are bought for about $20 (VF) to $2,000 (MS-63). Proofs were struck in some years of the early 1900s; the most common Proofs are bought by dealers for $100 to $175, depending on their state of preservation.

Silver fifty-centavo coins were struck in quantity in various years from 1903 through 1921. The most common dates are bought by dealers for their silver bullion value in VF, and for $100 to $200 or more in MS-63. The rarest collectible date in the series, the 1905-S, is bought for $30 in VF but up to $1,500 in MS-63. Proofs were struck in some years of the early 1900s; the most common Proofs are bought by dealers for $120 to $250, depending on their state of preservation.

Silver pesos were struck in quantity in various years from 1903 through 1912. The most common dates are bought by dealers for $15 in VF, and for $325 to $350 in MS-63. There are several rarities in the series; the rarest, the 1906-S, is bought for $1,200 in VF and $35,000 or more in MS-63. Proofs were struck in some years of the early 1900s; the most common Proofs are bought by dealers for $300 to $600, depending on their state of preservation.

COINAGE UNDER THE COMMONWEALTH (1937–1945)

**Basic Reverse Design for
Commonwealth Coinage**
(1936 peso shown.)

By 1935 the momentum for Philippine independence justified the creation of a Philippine Commonwealth, with full independence planned by 1946. Circulating coins struck for the commonwealth (1937–1945) featured the same basic obverse designs as those struck under U.S. sovereignty (1903–1936), and shared a common reverse design of an eagle-surmounted shield. All are fairly common, with mintages ranging from the millions to tens of millions, and dealer buy prices ranging from $0.25 to $3 in EF for bronze coins, $0.25 to $1.00 in EF for copper-nickel coins, and $1.00 to $2.00 in EF for silver coins.

A set of three 1936-dated commemorative silver coins was issued to mark the beginning of the commonwealth. The fifty-centavo coin and one of the pesos feature busts of Philippine president Manuel L. Quezon and of outgoing U.S. governor-general Frank Murphy. The other peso has busts of Quezon and U.S. president Franklin D. Roosevelt. The fifty-centavo coin has a buy price of about $125 in MS-63, and the pesos of about $250 each.

These charts show the bullion values of silver and gold U.S. coins. These are intrinsic values and do not reflect any numismatic premium a coin might have. The weight listed under each denomination is its actual silver weight (ASW) or actual gold weight (AGW).

In recent years, the bullion price of silver has fluctuated considerably. You can use the following chart to determine the approximate bullion value of many 19th- and 20th-century silver coins at various price levels—or you can calculate the approximate value by multiplying the current spot price of silver by the ASW for each coin, as indicated. Dealers generally purchase common silver coins at around 15% below bullion value, and sell them at around 15% above bullion value.

Nearly all U.S. gold coins have an additional premium value beyond their bullion content, and thus are not subject to minor bullion-price variations. The premium amount is not necessarily tied to the bullion price of gold, but is usually determined by supply and demand levels in the numismatic marketplace. Because these factors can vary significantly, there is no reliable formula for calculating "percentage below and above bullion" prices that would remain accurate over time. The gold chart below lists bullion values based on AGW only; consult a coin dealer to ascertain current buy and sell prices.

Bullion Values of Silver Coins

Silver Price Per Ounce	Wartime Nickel .05626 oz.	Dime .07234 oz.	Quarter .18084 oz.	Half Dollar .36169 oz.	Silver Clad Half Dollar .14792 oz.	Silver Dollar .77344 oz.
$15.00	$0.84	$1.09	$2.71	$5.43	$2.22	$11.60
16.00	0.90	1.16	2.89	5.79	2.37	12.38
17.00	0.96	1.23	3.07	6.15	2.51	13.15
18.00	1.01	1.30	3.26	6.51	2.66	13.92
19.00	1.07	1.37	3.44	6.87	2.81	14.70
20.00	1.13	1.45	3.62	7.23	2.96	15.47
21.00	1.18	1.52	3.80	7.60	3.11	16.24
22.00	1.24	1.59	3.98	7.96	3.25	17.02
23.00	1.29	1.66	4.16	8.32	3.40	17.79
24.00	1.35	1.74	4.34	8.68	3.55	18.56
25.00	1.41	1.81	4.52	9.04	3.70	19.34
26.00	1.46	1.88	4.70	9.40	3.85	20.11
27.00	1.52	1.95	4.88	9.77	3.99	20.88
28.00	1.58	2.03	5.06	10.13	4.14	21.66
29.00	1.63	2.10	5.24	10.49	4.29	22.43
30.00	1.69	2.17	5.43	10.85	4.44	23.20
31.00	1.74	2.24	5.61	11.21	4.59	23.98
32.00	1.80	2.31	5.79	11.57	4.73	24.75
33.00	1.86	2.39	5.97	11.94	4.88	25.52
34.00	1.91	2.46	6.15	12.30	5.03	26.30
35.00	1.97	2.53	6.33	12.66	5.18	27.07
36.00	2.03	2.60	6.51	13.02	5.33	27.84
37.00	2.08	2.68	6.69	13.38	5.47	28.62
38.00	2.14	2.75	6.87	13.74	5.62	29.39
39.00	2.19	2.82	7.05	14.11	5.77	30.16
40.00	2.25	2.89	7.23	14.47	5.92	30.94
41.00	2.31	2.97	7.41	14.83	6.06	31.71
42.00	2.36	3.04	7.60	15.19	6.21	32.48
43.00	2.42	3.11	7.78	15.55	6.36	33.26
44.00	2.48	3.18	7.96	15.91	6.51	34.03

Note: The U.S. bullion coins first issued in 1986 are unlike the older regular issues. They contain the following amounts of pure metal: silver $1, 1 oz.; gold $50, 1 oz.; gold $25, 1/2 oz.; gold $10, 1/4 oz.; gold $5, 1/10 oz.

BULLION VALUES

Silver Price Per Ounce	Wartime Nickel .05626 oz.	Dime .07234 oz.	Quarter .18084 oz.	Half Dollar .36169 oz.	Silver Clad Half Dollar .14792 oz.	Silver Dollar .77344 oz.
$45.00	$2.53	$3.26	$8.14	$16.28	$6.66	$34.80
46.00	2.59	3.33	8.32	16.64	6.80	35.58
47.00	2.64	3.40	8.50	17.00	6.95	36.35
48.00	2.70	3.47	8.68	17.36	7.10	37.13
49.00	2.76	3.54	8.86	17.72	7.25	37.90
50.00	2.81	3.62	9.04	18.08	7.40	38.67

Note: The U.S. bullion coins first issued in 1986 are unlike the older regular issues. They contain the following amounts of pure metal: silver $1, 1 oz.; gold $50, 1 oz.; gold $25, 1/2 oz.; gold $10, 1/4 oz.; gold $5, 1/10 oz.

Bullion Values of Gold Coins

Gold Price Per Ounce	$5.00 Liberty Head 1839–1908 Indian Head 1908–1929 .24187 oz.	$10.00 Liberty Head 1838–1907 Indian Head 1907–1933 .48375 oz.	$20.00 1849–1933 .96750 oz.
$1,750.00	$423.27	$846.56	$1,693.13
1,775.00	429.32	858.66	1,717.31
1,800.00	435.37	870.75	1,741.50
1,825.00	441.41	882.84	1,765.69
1,850.00	447.46	894.94	1,789.88
1,875.00	453.51	907.03	1,814.06
1,900.00	459.55	919.13	1,838.25
1,925.00	465.60	931.22	1,862.44
1,950.00	471.65	943.31	1,886.63
1,975.00	477.69	955.41	1,910.81
2,000.00	483.74	967.50	1,935.00
2,025.00	489.79	979.59	1,959.19
2,050.00	495.83	991.69	1,983.38
2,075.00	501.88	1,003.78	2,007.56
2,100.00	507.93	1,015.88	2,031.75
2,125.00	513.97	1,027.97	2,055.94
2,150.00	520.02	1,040.06	2,080.13
2,175.00	526.07	1,052.16	2,104.31
2,200.00	532.11	1,064.25	2,128.50
2,225.00	538.16	1,076.34	2,152.69
2,250.00	544.21	1,088.44	2,176.88
2,275.00	550.25	1,100.53	2,201.06
2,300.00	556.30	1,112.63	2,225.25
2,325.00	562.35	1,124.72	2,249.44
2,350.00	568.39	1,136.81	2,273.63
2,375.00	574.44	1,148.91	2,297.81
2,400.00	580.49	1,161.00	2,322.00
2,425.00	586.53	1,173.09	2,346.19
2,450.00	592.58	1,185.19	2,370.38
2,475.00	598.63	1,197.28	2,394.56
2,500.00	604.68	1,209.38	2,418.75
2,525.00	610.72	1,221.47	2,442.94
2,550.00	616.77	1,233.56	2,467.13
2,575.00	622.82	1,245.66	2,491.31
2,600.00	628.86	1,257.75	2,515.50
2,625.00	634.91	1,269.84	2,539.69

Note: The U.S. bullion coins first issued in 1986 are unlike the older regular issues. They contain the following amounts of pure metal: silver $1, 1 oz.; gold $50, 1 oz.; gold $25, 1/2 oz.; gold $10, 1/4 oz.; gold $5, 1/10 oz.

The precursor to the best-selling *Guide Book of United States Coins* (the *Red Book*) was *The Handbook of United States Coins With Premium List,* popularly known as the *Blue Book* because of its cover color. The mastermind behind the *Blue Book* was R.S. Yeoman, who had been hired by Western Publishing Company as a commercial artist in 1932. He distributed Western's Whitman line of "penny boards" to coin collectors, promoting them through department stores, along with children's books and games. He eventually arranged for Whitman to expand the line of penny boards into other denominations, giving them the reputation of a more serious numismatic endeavor rather than a "game" of filling holes with missing coins. He also developed these flat boards into a line of popular folders.

Soon Yeoman realized that coin collectors needed other resources and supplies for their hobby, and he began to compile coin mintage data and market values. This research grew into the *Blue Book:* now collectors had a coin-by-coin, grade-by-grade guide to the prices dealers would pay, on average, for U.S. coins. The first and second editions were both published in 1942, indicating the strong demand for this kind of hobby-related information.

In the first edition of the *Red Book,* published four years later, Whitman Publishing would describe the *Blue Book* as "a low-priced standard reference book of United States coins and kindred issues" for which there had been "a long-felt need among American collectors."

The *Blue Book* has been published annually (except in 1944 and 1950) since its debut. Past editions offer valuable information about the hobby of yesteryear as well as developments in numismatic research and the marketplace. Old *Blue Books* are collectible, but they are not yet as avidly sought as the *Red Book,* and most editions after the 12th can be found for a few dollars in VF or better condition. Major variants were produced for the third, fourth, and ninth editions, including perhaps the only "overdate" books in American numismatic publishing. Either to conserve the previous years' covers or to correct an error in binding, the cloth on some third-edition covers was overstamped "Fourth Edition," and a number of eighth-edition covers were overstamped "Ninth Edition." The third edition was produced in several shades of blue ranging from light to dark. Some copies of the fourth edition were also produced in black cloth—the only time the *Blue Book* was bound in other than blue.

Valuation Guide for Select Past Editions of the Blue Book

Edition	Date*		VF	EF	Edition	Date*		VF	EF
	Title-Page	Copyright				Title-Page	Copyright		
1st (first000 printing) ..	1942	1942	$75	$200	6th	1948	1947	$10	$15
1st (second printing) ..	1942	1942	50	100	7th	1949	1948	10	15
					8th	1950	1949	7	12
2nd.	1943	1942	20	50	9th	1952	1951	4	7
3rd	1944	1943	20	35	10th	1953	1952	3	6
4th	*None*	1945	20	30	11th	1954	1953	2	4
5th	*None*	1946	12	15	12th	1955	1954	2	4

* During its early years of production, the *Blue Book*'s date presentation was not standardized. Full information is given here to aid in precise identification of early editions. For the first edition, there were two distinct printings. The most obvious difference between them is found at the bottom of page 70: in the first printing, the mintage figures for only the first nine months of the year are given for the 1941 half dollars; while in the second printing, the full annual mintage figures are given, followed by a two-paragraph notice regarding condition and mintages. Other differences also exist.

Combined with dealer's buying prices, auction data can help advanced collectors understand the modern market for high-end rarities.

It is important to understand that the following prices include a buyer's premium (a surcharge which the buyer pays the auction house over the final "hammer price," or winning bid; contemporary auction houses charge around 17.5%) and the seller's commission (a small percentage of the hammer price which the individual selling the coin pays to the auction house; this fee can sometimes be negotiated to less than 5%).

Rank	Price	Coin	Grade	Firm	Date
1	$18,872,250	$20, 1933 **(A)**	MS-65	Sotheby's	Jun-21
2	10,016,875	Silver $, 1794	PCGS SP-66 CAC	Stack's Bowers	Jan-13
3	9,360,000	Pre-Fed, 1787 Brasher EB on Wing	NGC MS-65★ CAC	Heritage	Jan-21
4	8,400,000	$5, 1822	PCGS AU-50	Stack's Bowers	Mar-21
5	7,680,000	Silver $, 1804 Class I **(B)**	PCGS PF-68	Stack's Bowers	Aug-21
6	7,590,020	$20, 1933 **(A)**	Gem BU	Soth/Stack's	Jul-02
7	7,200,000	$20, 1861 Paquet Reverse	PCGS MS-67 CAC	Heritage	Aug-21
8	6,600,000	Silver $, 1794 **(C)**	PCGS MS-66+ CAC	Heritage	Aug-21
9	5,520,000	$3, 1870-S	PCGS SP-50 893 Engraved	Heritage	Jan-23
10	5,280,000	$10, 1804 Plain 4 BD-2	PCGS 65+ DC CAC	Heritage	Jan-21
11	4,993,750	Silver $, 1794 **(C)**	PCGS MS-66+	SBG/Sotheby's	Sep-15
12	4,620,000	$5, 1821	PCGS PF65 Cam CAC	Heritage	Sep-22
13	4,582,500	Prefed, 1787 Brasher EB on Wing	NGC MS-63 CAC	Heritage	Jan-14
14	4,560,000	5¢, 1913 Liberty Head	PCGS PF-66 CAC	Stack's Bowers	Aug-18
15	4,440,000	$20, 1927-D	PCGS MS-66	Heritage	Aug-22
16	4,320,000	$20, MCMVII Ultra HR LE Inverted	PCGS PF-69	Heritage	Aug-23
17	4,140,000	Silver $, 1804 Class I **(B)**	PCGS PF-68	B&M	Aug-99
18	4,080,000	$5, 1825/4/1 BD-1	PCGS PF-67 Cam CAC	Stack's Bowers	Aug-22
19	3,960,000	Trade $, 1885	NGC PF-66	Heritage	Jan-19
20	3,877,500	Silver $, 1804 Class I **(D)**	PCGS PF-62	Heritage	Aug-13
21	3,840,000	$5, 1829 Small Date BD-2	PCGS PF-66+ CAC	Heritage	Aug-23
22	3,737,500	5¢, 1913 Liberty Head	NGC PF-64	Heritage	Jan-10
23	3,737,500	Silver $, 1804 Class I **(D)**	NGC PF-62	Heritage	Apr-08
24	3,600,000	10¢, 1873-CC No Arrows	PCGS MS-65	Heritage	Jan-23
25	3,600,000	$20, MCMVII Ultra HR LE	NGC PF-68	Heritage	Feb-21

KEY

Price: The sale price of the coin, including the appropriate buyer's fee.

Coin: The denomination/classification, date, and description of the coin, along with pertinent catalog or reference numbers. Abbreviations include: BD = Bass-Dannreuther; HR = High Relief; LE = Lettered Edge; Prefed = pre-federal issue. Letters in parentheses, **(A–D)**, denote instances in which multiple sales of the same coin rank within the Top 25.

Grade: The grade of the coin, plus the name of the grading firm (if independently graded). NGC = Numismatic Guaranty Company of America; PCGS = Professional Coin Grading Service.

Firm: The auction firm (or firms) that sold the coin. B&M = Bowers & Merena; Stack's Bowers = Stack's Bowers Galleries (the name under which Stack's and B&M merged in 2010; also encompasses the merger of Stack's and American Numismatic Rarities in 2006); Soth = Sotheby's.

Date: The month and year of the auction.

Auction records compiled and edited by P. Scott Rubin.

GLOSSARY

Over the years coin collectors and dealers have developed a special jargon to describe coins. Here are some terms frequently used within the hobby.

altered date—A false date on a coin; a date fraudulently changed to make a coin appear to be one of a rarer or more valuable issue.

bag mark—A surface mark, usually a small nick, acquired by a coin through contact with others in a mint bag.

blank—The formed piece of metal on which a coin design will be stamped.

bullion—Uncoined silver, gold, or platinum in the form of bars, ingots, or plate.

certified coin—A coin that has been graded, authenticated, and encapsulated in plastic by an independent third-party (neither buyer nor seller) grading service.

circulation strike—A coin intended for eventual use in commerce, as opposed to a Proof coin.

clad coinage—U.S. dimes, quarters, half dollars, and some dollars made since 1965. Each coin has a center core of pure copper and a layer of copper-nickel or silver on both sides.

die—A piece of metal engraved with a negative-image design and used for stamping coins.

die variety—Any minor alteration in the basic design of a coin type.

dipped coin—A coin that has been chemically cleaned to remove oxidation or foreign matter from its surfaces.

doubled die—A die that has been given two misaligned impressions from a hub (positive-image punch); also, a coin made from such a die.

encapsulated coin—A coin that has been authenticated, graded, and sealed in plastic by a professional third-party grading service.

error coin—A mismade coin not intended for circulation.

field—The background portion of a coin's surface not used for a design or legends.

fineness—The purity of gold, silver, or other precious metal, expressed in terms of one thousand parts. A coin of 90% pure silver is described as being .900 fine.

gem—A coin of exceptionally high quality, typically considered MS-65 or PF-65 or better.

intrinsic value—The bullion or "melt" value of the actual silver or gold in a precious-metal coin.

junk silver—Common-date silver coins in circulated grades, worth only their bullion value.

key coin—One of the scarcer or more valuable coins in a series.

legend—A principal inscription on a coin (e.g., E PLURIBUS UNUM).

luster—The brilliant or "frosty" surface quality of an Uncirculated coin.

mintmark—A small letter or other mark on a coin, indicating the mint at which it was made.

Mint set—A set of Uncirculated coins, packaged and sold by the U.S. Mint, containing one of each of the coins made for circulation at each of the mints in a particular year.

Mint State—The grade of a circulation-strike coin that has never been used in commerce, and has retained its original surface and luster; also called Uncirculated.

obverse—The front or face ("heads") side of a coin.

planchet—The blank piece of metal on which a coin design is stamped.

Proof—A coin struck for collectors by the Mint using specially polished dies and planchets.

Proof set—A set of each of the Proof coins made during a given year, packaged by the Mint and sold to collectors.

raw coin—A coin that has not been encapsulated by an independent third-party grading service.

reeded edge—The edge of a coin with grooved lines that run vertically around its perimeter, as seen on modern U.S. silver and clad coins.

reverse—The back or "tails" side of a coin.

rim—The raised outer portion of a coin that protects the design from wear.

slab—A hard plastic case containing a coin that has been graded and encapsulated by a professional grading service.

spot price—The daily quoted market value of a precious metal in bullion form.

third-party grading service—A professional firm that authenticates and grades a coin, encapsulating it in a protective hard plastic case; called *third-party* because it is neither the buyer nor the seller of the coin.

token—A privately issued piece, similar to a coin but not official legal tender, typically with an exchange value for goods or services.

type—A series of coins defined by a shared distinguishing design, composition, denomination, and other elements. For example, Barber dimes or Morgan dollars.

type set—A collection consisting of one representative coin of each type, of a particular series or period.

Uncirculated coin—A circulation-strike coin that has never been used in commerce, and has retained its original surface and luster; also called Mint State.

variety—A coin with a die characteristic that sets it apart from the normal issues of its type.

Colonial Issues

Bowers, Q. David. *Whitman Encyclopedia of Colonial and Early American Coins.* (2nd ed.). Pelham, AL, 2020.

Cents

Bowers, Q. David. *A Guide Book of Half Cents and Large Cents.* Atlanta, GA, 2015.

Bowers, Q. David. *A Guide Book of Lincoln Cents* (3rd ed.). Pelham, AL, 2018.

Snow, Richard. *A Guide Book of Flying Eagle and Indian Head Cents* (3rd ed.). Atlanta, GA, 2016.

Nickels and Dimes

Bowers, Q. David. *A Guide Book of Barber Silver Coins* (2nd ed.). Atlanta, GA, 2019.

Bowers, Q. David. *A Guide Book of Buffalo and Jefferson Nickels* (2nd ed.). Pelham, AL, 2017.

Bowers, Q. David. *A Guide Book of Mercury Dimes, Standing Liberty Quarters, and Liberty Walking Half Dollars.* Atlanta, GA, 2015.

Bowers, Q. David. *A Guide Book of Shield and Liberty Head Nickels.* Atlanta, GA, 2006.

Quarter Dollars and Half Dollars

Bowers, Q. David. *A Guide Book of Barber Silver Coins* (2nd ed.). Atlanta, GA, 2019.

Bowers, Q. David. *A Guide Book of Mercury Dimes, Standing Liberty Quarters, and Liberty Walking Half Dollars.* Atlanta, GA, 2015.

Bowers, Q. David. *A Guide Book of Washington Quarters* (2nd ed.). Pelham, AL, 2017.

Tomaska, Rick. *A Guide Book of Franklin and Kennedy Half Dollars* (3rd ed.). Pelham, AL, 2018.

Silver Dollars

Bowers, Q. David. *A Guide Book of Morgan Silver Dollars* (7th ed.). Pelham, AL, 2022.

Burdette, Roger W. *A Guide Book of Peace Dollars* (4th ed.). Pelham, AL, 2020.

Newman, Eric P., and Kenneth E. Bressett. *The Fantastic 1804 Dollar, Tribute Edition.* Atlanta, GA, 2009.

Standish, Michael "Miles," and John B. Love. *Morgan Dollar: America's Love Affair With a Legendary Coin.* Atlanta, GA, 2014.

Gold Coins

Bowers, Q. David. *A Guide Book of Double Eagle Gold Coins.* Atlanta, GA, 2004.

Bowers, Q. David. *A Guide Book of Gold Dollars* (2nd ed.). Atlanta, GA, 2011.

Fivaz, Bill. *United States Gold Counterfeit Detection Guide.* Atlanta, GA, 2005.

Garrett, Jeff, and Ron Guth. *Encyclopedia of U.S. Gold Coins, 1795–1933* (2nd ed.). Atlanta, GA, 2008.

Commemoratives

Bowers, Q. David. *A Guide Book of United States Commemorative Coins* (2nd ed.). Pelham, AL, 2016.

Proof and Mint Sets

Lange, David W. *A Guide Book of Modern United States Proof Coin Sets* (2nd ed.). Atlanta, GA, 2010.

Bullion Coins

Mercanti, John M., with Michael Standish. *American Silver Eagles: A Guide to the U.S. Bullion Coin Program* (3rd ed.). Pelham, AL, 2018.

Moy, Edmund C. *American Gold and Platinum Eagles: A Guide to the U.S. Bullion Coin Programs.* Atlanta, GA, 2013.

Tucker, Dennis. *American Gold and Silver: U.S. Mint Collector and Investor Coins and Medals, Bicentennial to Date.* Atlanta, GA, 2016.

Tokens and Medals

Bowers, Q. David. *A Guide Book of Civil War Tokens* (3rd ed.). Pelham, AL, 2018.

Bowers, Q. David. *A Guide Book of Hard Times Tokens.* Atlanta, GA, 2015.

Jaeger, Katherine, and Q. David Bowers. *100 Greatest American Medals and Tokens.* Atlanta, GA, 2007.

Jaeger, Katherine. *A Guide Book of United States Tokens and Medals.* Atlanta, GA, 2008.

Tucker, Dennis. *American Gold and Silver: U.S. Mint Collector and Investor Coins and Medals, Bicentennial to Date.* Atlanta, GA, 2016.

U.S./Philippine Coins

Allen, Lyman L. *U.S. Philippine Coins.* Oakland Park, FL, 1998.

Shafer, Neil. *United States Territorial Coinage for the Philippine Islands.* Racine, WI, 1961.

Type Coins

Bowers, Q. David. *A Guide Book of United States Type Coins* (3rd ed.). Pelham, AL, 2019.

Guth, Ron, and Jeff Garrett. *United States Coinage: A Study by Type.* Atlanta, GA, 2005.

Garrett, Jeff, with Ron Guth. *100 Greatest U.S. Coins* (5th ed.), Pelham, AL, 2019.

Schechter, Scott, and Jeff Garrett. *100 Greatest U.S. Modern Coins* (3rd ed.), Atlanta, GA, 2014.

Die Varieties

Fivaz, Bill, and J.T. Stanton. *The Cherrypickers' Guide to Rare Die Varieties (various editions and volumes).* Atlanta, GA, and Pelham, AL.

One of the most collectible denominations of U.S. coins is the one-cent piece, in particular the small cents minted for circulation since the late 1850s. Not only are these coins generally more affordable than larger silver and gold pieces, but they're equally rich in American history. This special section of the 82nd-edition *Blue Book* explores the entire range of the longest-running series in American coinage: the Lincoln cent.

THE LIFE OF ABRAHAM LINCOLN

Every year since 1909 the United States has minted one-cent coins honoring President Abraham Lincoln. That's more than a century of coins. *Billions* of Lincoln cents are made every year at the nation's mints in Philadelphia, Pennsylvania; Denver, Colorado; and San Francisco, California. Some have even been made at the West Point Mint in New York.

Many homes in America have a piggy bank or change-bowl full of Lincoln cents. Take a look through them, and you'll be surprised how many dates, mintmarks, and designs you find—enough to build your own coin collection. Among them are four different types minted in 2009 to celebrate the bicentennial of Abraham Lincoln's birth and tell the story of his life:

Lincoln's birth and early childhood in Kentucky—The first 2009 Lincoln Bicentennial cent shows a Kentucky cabin like the one where little Abe Lincoln was born on February 12, 1809. It was a very modest dwelling—"a hunter's hut, not fit to be called home," is how one neighbor remembered it.

Abe's parents, Tom and Nancy Lincoln, were both born in Virginia, "of undistinguished families," he later said. He would remark on the many Biblical names in his family: "Enoch, Levi, Mordecai, Solomon, Abraham, and the like." His father grew up without an education. While his parents may have been poor, they raised him to show generosity toward others and not to be selfish. They also taught him that anyone who worked hard could improve his own life.

2009, Birth and Early Childhood in Kentucky.

Replica of LINCOLN'S BOYHOOD HOME on Knob Creek 1811–18?? (Between Hodgenville & Bardstown Ky. on U.S. 31 E.)

2009, Formative Years in Indiana.

Lincoln's formative years in Indiana—The Lincoln family moved in 1816 from Kentucky to Indiana. "It was a wild region," Abraham would recall, "with many bears and other wild animals still in the woods." There were some schools, he said, but a teacher only had to be able to read, write, and do simple math. If a stranger happened to come along who knew Latin, "he was looked upon as a wizard."

One of his childhood friends remembered that Abe loved giving speeches and debating other children. He talked about the hardships of slaves and American Indians. His mother taught him at home, and he usually carried a book with him, studying Shakespeare, Byron, and even Euclid's geometry. "His chief delight during the day," a friend would later write, "was to lie down under the shade of some inviting tree to read and study." But he wasn't afraid of hard physical work. Lincoln was famous for chopping wood and splitting it into fence rails—400 rails in a typical day, for a wage of 25 cents.

In the second Bicentennial cent of 2009 we see both the studious side and the physical side of Abraham Lincoln. He is shown as a young man, sitting on a sawed tree trunk reading a book. He is not being lazy; it's obvious he's only taking a break from hard labor. He wears work boots, his sleeves are rolled up, and a handkerchief for wiping sweat from his brow is in his back pocket. Next to him is a sledgehammer used for pounding a spike into a log to split it apart.

Lincoln's professional life in Illinois—The third Lincoln Bicentennial cent of 2009 shows the Illinois state capitol in Springfield. This symbolizes Abraham Lincoln's pre-presidential career in law and politics. Lincoln is standing before the capitol building with a hand raised, as if speaking to an audience.

His political career started in the mid-1830s when he was elected to the Illinois State Legislature. Lincoln taught himself enough about law to become an attorney in 1837, and he was elected to the U.S. House of Representatives in 1846. By the 1850s he was one of the most respected lawyers in Illinois, working mostly in the state's Supreme Court. He argued more than 240 cases—and won most of them. Although he ran for the U.S. Senate twice and lost both times, Lincoln's 1858 debates with Stephen A. Douglas, another Senate candidate, made him famous. People saw him as ambitious, principled, fair-minded, honest, and intelligent—a believer in equal rights and united American democracy. This led him to the Republican nomination for president. He was elected on November 6, 1860.

2009, Professional Life in Illinois.

A 1994 sculpture of Lincoln,
"Prairie Lawyer," by artist Jim Nance.

Lincoln's presidency in Washington, D.C.—The fourth and final Lincoln Bicentennial cent of 2009 shows the partially completed U.S. Capitol dome, which was still under construction when Abraham Lincoln became president. The design is a symbol of the nation's unfinished business: the huge question of slavery still had to be answered, and the United States was falling apart as Southern states left to create their own nation.

2009, Presidency in Washington, D.C.

After he was elected, a crowd gathered in Springfield, Illinois, to watch as President-elect Lincoln left for his new position in Washington. He told them that he was about to struggle with a bigger challenge than George Washington had faced. He knew that if he didn't keep the Union together, then the noble experiment of American Democracy—which many brave patriots had believed in and died for—would go down in history as a failure.

Lincoln traveled east by train for twelve days to get to Washington, stopping in cities along the way to give speeches. He went to Indianapolis, Cincinnati, Columbus, Pittsburgh, Cleveland, Buffalo, Syracuse, Albany, New York City, and Trenton. On February 21 he arrived in Philadelphia. The police warned Lincoln that enemies were plotting against him and planned to kill him during his next stop, in the city of Baltimore. Instead of hiding, the next day in Philadelphia he dramatically raised the American flag over Independence Hall. It was George Washington's birthday. Lincoln went inside the Hall to speak to the state's legislators. "I would rather be assassinated," he told the men gathered there, than surrender the principles of liberty in the Declaration of Independence.

Lincoln had been warned about his enemies. He traveled through the state of Maryland to Washington, D.C., not stopping in Baltimore. At his inaugural ceremony he swore to preserve, protect, and defend the Constitution of the United States.

Throughout Abraham Lincoln's presidency, work continued on the U.S. Capitol dome even as he was working to preserve the Union. By the end of the Civil War, the dome was nearly finished and the United States was rebuilding. Sadly, Abraham Lincoln himself would not live much longer.

The incomplete U.S. Capitol dome is seen in this photograph from Lincoln's inauguration day, March 4, 1861. *Also:* an illustration of Lincoln's life journey "from farm to White House."

THE BEGINNING: WHEAT CENTS

Where did the Lincoln cent begin? It all started as a way to celebrate the 100th anniversary of Abraham Lincoln's birth. In 1907, sculptor Victor David Brenner had created a plaque with a profile portrait of Lincoln. He used a similar portrait in various other medals and plaques. In 1908 Brenner met President Theodore Roosevelt. The president was impressed with Brenner's talent and wanted him as the engraver for a new one-cent coin to honor Lincoln—one of his boyhood heroes. The U.S. Mint offered Brenner the job, and he used his earlier profile portrait for the obverse or front of the coin. The design would become famous in 1909 and would live on for more than a hundred years.

Victor David Brenner in his studio, working on a model for a Lincoln statue.

The Lincoln cent replaced the old Indian Head design,
which was minted from 1859 to 1909.

The first year of issue—The very first Lincoln cents were issued on August 2, 1909. These included the initials of the designer (V.D.B.) on the reverse or back of the coin. When the secretary of the Treasury saw this, he demanded that the initials be removed. There was a "feverish scramble," as the *New York Times* put it, for the new coins. Americans everywhere thought the cents would be stopped and become a valuable overnight rarity! However, the Philadelphia Mint made enough to meet the demand, and today this first-year issue remains a popular and affordable collectible. *Mintage: 27,995,000 (Philadelphia Mint); 484,000 (San Francisco Mint).*

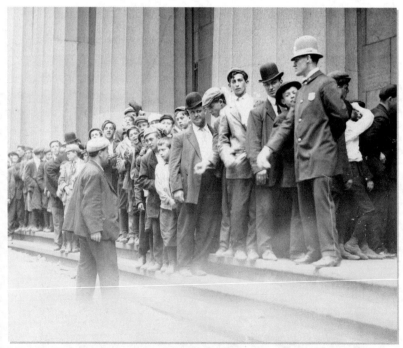

Americans were excited to buy the new Lincoln cent. Here, people are seen
lining up at the New York City Sub-Treasury building, August 2, 1909.

Brenner's new cent featuring Abraham Lincoln.

Brenner's initials on the new coin.

1909—Starting later in August 1909, the rest of the year's cents had no initials on the reverse. *Mintage: 72,702,618 (Philadelphia Mint); 1,825,000 (San Francisco Mint).*

Did you know? *The 1909 cents minted in San Francisco are much rarer than those from Philadelphia. The 1909-S, V.D.B., cent is the "key" to the series—the one that every collector searches for! Only 484,000 were minted, and today an Uncirculated example can cost thousands of dollars. 1909-S cents were minted* without *Brenner's initials, too. The 1909-S cent without initials is uncommon, with only 1,825,000 minted, and is worth hundreds of dollars if Uncirculated.*

Wheat cents, 1909 to 1958—The first design of the Lincoln cent was the "Wheat Ears Reverse." These coins were struck from 1909 to 1958. On the back of the coin are two ears of durum wheat, an important American crop. Durum wheat is high in protein and is used to make pasta, cereal, flour for bread, and feed for animals. Annual wheat production in the United States was rising when the Lincoln cent came out. Harvests more than tripled in the fifty years between 1871 and 1921.

After the coin's first year, did Victor David Brenner ever get to have his initials on the coin again? In fact, he did—they were finally restored in 1918, placed in very small letters on Lincoln's shoulder.

Brenner's initials, restored in 1918.

Billions of Wheat cents were minted over the years, making them one of the most popular American coins. Collectors have saved many of them, and today it is unusual to find one in your pocket change—but keep looking! You can also get rolls of cents from your local bank and search through them for older coins.

World War II steel cents, 1943—Copper was an important metal in the United States' war effort during World War II. To help save more of the metal for military use, the Treasury Department switched the Lincoln cent from bronze (made of 95 percent copper) to zinc-coated steel. This change was only for a single year—1943—but it helped save millions of pounds of copper for military use in cartridges and other ammunition. *Mintage: 84,628,670 (Philadelphia Mint); 217,660,000 (Denver Mint); 191,550,000 (San Francisco Mint).*

Today you'll almost never find steel cents in change. But you can easily buy one for your collection from a coin shop or from a coin dealer online or through the mail. These special coins are an important reminder of America's sacrifices and efforts during World War II.

Did you know? No bronze Lincoln cents were issued in 1943. . . at least, not officially. A few coins were accidentally struck on bronze planchets. If you find one today, it could be worth tens of thousands of dollars—but beware, many deceptive copper-plated steel cents exist. Here's an easy test: if it looks bronze but it sticks to a magnet, it's steel.

"Cartridge case" cents, 1944 to 1946—From 1944 to 1946, scrap ammunition cases were saved and mixed with copper to make into Lincoln cents. Technically, the new alloy was *brass* and not *bronze*, since it contained no tin (just copper and zinc). In Uncirculated grades, the Lincoln cents of these years have a slightly different color than earlier bronze examples.

Cartridges used in World War II German and American rifles.

THE NEXT FIFTY YEARS: LINCOLN MEMORIAL CENTS

In 1959, the 150th anniversary of Abraham Lincoln's birth, the U.S. Mint introduced a new reverse design for the one-cent coin. It featured a view of the Lincoln Memorial. The new design, by Frank Gasparro, was used through 2008.

Lincoln Memorial cents, 1959 to 2008—*Billions* of Wheat cents were minted from 1909 to 1958, making Abraham Lincoln's portrait the most often seen work of art in history. But as huge as that quantity is, even more Lincoln Memorial cents have been made since 1959: *hundreds of billions* of them!

Construction started on the Lincoln Memorial in 1914. By April 1917 most of the architectural elements were finished; then America entered the First World War. The memorial's work crews slowed down but continued to make progress on the landscaping around the site, the approach plaza, the granite terrace, and the interior decorations. The memorial was completed in 1922.

Did you know? *How many times does Abraham Lincoln appear on the Memorial cent? Not just once, but twice! If you look carefully, you can see the statue of Lincoln seated inside the Memorial, on the back of the coin.*

The massive statue of Lincoln inside the Memorial.

A Proof Lincoln Memorial cent, struck in 1982 at
the San Francisco Mint. (Notice the "S" mintmark.)

Did you know? *"Proof" Lincoln cents have been struck almost every year since 1909. Proofs are special coins made for collectors. They are struck using perfect, highly polished dies, which stamp the coin's design two times (or more) on polished coinage blanks, using extra pressure. The result is a high-quality, perfect coin. Proof Lincoln cents are affordable enough to include in your collection.*

The U.S. Mint used three different alloys (mixtures of metals) to make the Lincoln Memorial cent over the years. From 1959 to 1961, the coins were made of **bronze** (a mixture of copper, tin, and zinc). In 1962, some of the cents were made in bronze, and later in the year the alloy was changed to **brass** (copper and zinc, without tin). All of the cents from 1963 to 1981 were brass. Some 1982 cents were made of brass, but later that year they were changed to **copper-plated zinc**. All of the billions of Lincoln cents made for circulation from 1983 to today have been copper-plated zinc.

TODAY'S LINCOLN CENTS: THE UNION SHIELD

At the end of the Civil War, President Lincoln was widely praised as the savior of the United States. After the four Bicentennial cents of 2009, a new coin in 2010 celebrated his success in keeping the country together.

Union Shield cents, 2010 to date—The law that created the four 2009 Lincoln Bicentennial cents also created a new reverse design for 2010 and beyond: "an image emblematic of President Lincoln's preservation of the United States of America as a single and united country."

The coin has a federal shield with the legend E PLURIBUS UNUM, which means "Out of many, one." The United States is one country formed from many states, and Americans are many different people united in a single nation.

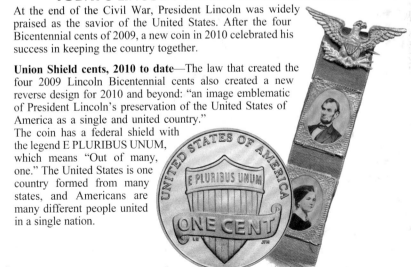

COLLECTING ABRAHAM LINCOLN CENTS

To make your own collection of Lincoln cents, you can start with *fifteen* coins of different years, alloys, formats, and designs:

First Year of Issue, 1909. You would have to be very lucky to find one of these in your pocket change! But you can search for a 1909 Lincoln cent at your local coin shop, or in a coin dealer's inventory online.

Wheat Cent, 1909–1958. You might find one in a roll of pennies from the bank, or in an old jar or piggy bank. Or you can buy one from a coin dealer; common dates are inexpensive.

World War II, 1943 Steel Cent. Minted only in 1943, these unusual wartime cents are affordable and interesting.

World War II, 1944–1946 "Cartridge Case" Cent. These coins have an interesting military story. They were actually made using ammunition cartridge cases from the war!

Lincoln Memorial, Bronze, 1959–1962. The Lincoln Memorial, one of the most famous monuments in Washington, D.C., is on all cents minted from 1959 to 2008. From 1959 to 1962, Lincoln cents were made of bronze (a mixture of copper, tin, and zinc). Look in your pocket change or piggy bank for a coin from these years.

Lincoln Memorial, Bronze, Proof. You can easily collect a shiny Proof version of the bronze Lincoln Memorial cent. They are affordable and many coin dealers have them.

Lincoln Memorial, Brass, 1962–1982. In 1962 the Lincoln Memorial cent was changed from bronze to brass (a mixture of 95 percent copper and 5 percent zinc). You can find these coins in circulation.

Lincoln Memorial, Brass, Proof. Like their bronze versions, Proofs of the brass Lincoln Memorial cents are easy to find, and inexpensive. Check with your favorite coin dealer.

Lincoln Memorial, Copper-Plated Zinc, 1982–2008. In 1982 the cent was changed from brass to copper-plated zinc—a total of 97.5 percent zinc and 2.5 percent copper. These coins are easy to find in circulation, so collect the nicest-looking one you can find.

Lincoln Memorial, Copper-Plated Zinc, Proof. You can find a Proof version of the copper-plated zinc cent from your favorite coin dealer.

Bicentennial Cents, 2009. There are four different cents celebrating the life of Abraham Lincoln, minted in 2009 for the bicentennial of his birth. Look in your pocket change for this coin!

Union Shield Cent, 2010 to Date. Since 2010, the Lincoln cent has featured a Union Shield design on the back. Search your pocket change and save the nicest example you find.

The Power Merger of CDN & Whitman

CDN Publishing and Whitman Publishing have united, creating Whitman Brands. Whitman's legendary brands, such as the revered *Red Book*, *Blue Book*, and an expansive line of folders, albums, and supplies, have long dominated the retail landscape. Meanwhile, CDN Publishing boasts esteemed wholesale brands like *Greysheet*, *Greensheet*, CPG, CDN Exchange, and the *Banknote Book*. CDN's data-driven wholesale expertise joins with Whitman's retail prowess, offering a comprehensive and intellectually rich coverage of collectibles.

Whitman Publishing
SINCE 1934

@ RARE COIN MARKET REVIEW

THE BANKNOTE BOOK

CDN EXCHANGE   GSID CATALOGING   GREYSHEET DIGITAL MEDIA

Collectibles Elevated by Intelligence

www.whitmanbrands.com